Praise for *Overhearing Film Music*

"This book offers an accessible survey of firsthand experiences from composers. It manages to engage in a journalistic and scholarly manner, with an appeal to a wide readership. It will be helpful to introductory students in filmmaking, film studies, and film music, but also offers much for advanced students, scholars, and practicing composers seeking specific lines of inquiry. These in-depth interviews regularly contain surprising information and go beyond the formulaic approach seen in so many collections. I am impressed by the extent to which the author has been inclusive by including interviews with Jermaine Stegall and Rachel Portman, along with a strong survey on Black composers. I would be excited to use this book in the undergraduate Film Sound course I teach. In this course for seniors, the book would open many avenues for approaches to composing and research."

— Matthew Sorrento, Department of Film Studies, Temple University

"The greatest strength of the manuscript is the inclusion of composers of recent films, specifically Jermaine Stegall and Rachel Portman, and the interludes, especially on Black composers for film and choral music for film. . . I would assign this in an undergraduate or graduate film music course."

— Reba Wissner, Schwob School of Music, Columbus State University

"Wow! What a wonderful chapter in what is clearly going to be a terrific and distinguished book . . . For anyone who wants an introduction to my film work, I can't think of a better source to recommend than your superb chapter about it."

— Composer David Shire ("All the President's Men," "Norma Rae," "Saturday Night Fever")

"Your encyclopedic knowledge of my oeuvre is almost embarrassing to me for two reasons. First, because some of the films you comment on I have almost completely forgotten and yet your awareness of their musical details is astounding. And second, your overall flattering evaluation of my music is based on true intelligence and musical/aesthetic sensitivity . . . far exceeding that of many commentators who profess to pass judgment on film music . . . I can't tell you how much it means to me and has for years."

— Composer Laurence Rosenthal ("Becket," "The Miracle Worker," "Raisin in the Sun")

"It is always very gratifying to be interviewed by someone of such obvious knowledge and background who has troubled himself to notice my work and I thank you for it very much!"

— Composer John Williams ("Star Wars," "Jaws," "Harry Potter")

Overhearing Film Music

THE SUNY SERIES

MURRAY POMERANCE | EDITOR

RECENT TITLES

Benedict Morrison, *Eccentric Laughter*

Hannah Holtzman, *Through a Nuclear Lens*

Matthew Cipa, *Is Harpo Free?*

Seth Barry Watter, *The Human Figure on Film*

Daniel Varndell, *Torturous Etiquettes*

Jonah Corne and Monika Vrečar, *Yiddish Cinema*

Jason Jacobs, *Reluctant Sleuths, True Detectives*

Lucy J. Miller, *Distancing Representations in Transgender Film*

Tomoyuki Sasaki, *Cinema of Discontent*

Mary Ann McDonald Carolan, *Orienting Italy*

Matthew Rukgaber, *Nietzsche in Hollywood*

David Venditto, *Whiteness at the End of the World*

Fareed Ben-Youssef, *No Jurisdiction*

Tony Tracy, *White Cottage, White House*

Tom Conley, *Action, Action, Action*

Lindsay Coleman and Roberto Schaefer, editors, *The Cinematographer's Voice*

Nolwenn Mingant, *Hollywood Films in North Africa and the Middle East*

Charles Warren, edited by William Rothman and Joshua Schulze, *Writ on Water*

Jason Sperb, *The Hard Sell of Paradise*

William Rothman, *The Holiday in His Eye*

A complete listing of books in this series can be found online at www.sunypress.edu.

Overhearing Film Music

Conversations with Screen Composers

John Caps

Cover Credit: David Shire conducting his score to *The Hindenburg* (1975). Photo courtesy of the composer.

Published by State University of New York Press, Albany

© 2025 State University of New York

All rights reserved

Printed in the United States of America

No part of this book may be used or reproduced in any manner whatsoever without written permission. No part of this book may be stored in a retrieval system or transmitted in any form or by any means including electronic, electrostatic, magnetic tape, mechanical, photocopying, recording, or otherwise without the prior permission in writing of the publisher.

Links to third-party websites are provided as a convenience and for informational purposes only. They do not constitute an endorsement or an approval of any of the products, services, or opinions of the organization, companies, or individuals. SUNY Press bears no responsibility for the accuracy, legality, or content of a URL, the external website, or for that of subsequent websites.

For information, contact State University of New York Press, Albany, NY
www.sunypress.edu

Library of Congress Cataloging-in-Publication Data

Name: Caps, John, author.
Title: Overhearing film music : conversations with screen composers / John Caps.
Description: Albany : State University of New York Press, [2025]. | Series: SUNY series, horizons of cinema | Includes bibliographical references and index
Identifiers: LCCN 2024019593 | ISBN 9798855800623 (hardcover : alk. paper) | ISBN 9798855800647 (ebook) | ISBN 9798855800630 (pbk. : alk. paper)
Subjects: LCSH: Motion picture music—History and criticism. | Film composers. | Film composers—Interviews.
Classification: LCC ML2075 .C3575 2025 | DDC 781.5/420922—dc23/eng/20240515
LC record available at https://lccn.loc.gov/2024019593

To Marilyn,
who gives and forgives without end.

Contents

List of Illustrations	ix
Acknowledgments	xi
Preface	xv
Introduction	1

Part I. A Veteran's Diary

1. Elmer Bernstein	23

Part II. From the Golden Age

2. Miklós Rózsa: Orthodoxy	51
3. David Raksin: The Provocateur	65
4. Jerome Moross: Americana to the Fore	87
5. Interlude: Black Composers for Film—A Mini-History	109
6. Interlude: Choral Music in Films—A Mini-History	123

Part III. New Ambassadors

7. Henry Mancini: The Populist Movement — 133

8. Laurence Rosenthal: More than Respect — 161

9. Richard Rodney Bennett: The Complete Musician — 191

10. Interlude: The Exasperating Michel Legrand — 215

11. Interlude: Women Composers for Film—A Mini-History — 221

12. Interlude: The Walk of Fame—Jerry Goldsmith — 239

Part IV. A Successor Generation

13. David Shire: Setting the Stage — 255

14. Rachel Portman: The Storyteller — 275

15. Jermaine Stegall: For a Digital Age — 285

16. Interlude: A Pair of Glasses—Philip Glass versus Paul Glass — 299

17. Interlude: The New Millennium—Enter Ex-Rockers — 309

Part V. A New Exemplar

18. John Williams: Another Birthday Toast — 319

Notes to the Future — 341

Notes — 343

Works Cited or Recommended — 361

Index — 367

Illustrations

1. Elmer Bernstein — 23
2. Miklós Rózsa — 51
3. David Raksin with Charlie Chaplin — 65
4. Jerome Moross — 87
5. Ulysses Kay — 110
6. Quincy Jones — 113
7. Henry Mancini — 133
8. Laurence Rosenthal — 161
9. Sir Richard Rodney Bennett — 191
10. Michel Legrand — 215
11. Elisabeth Lutyens — 221
12. Angela Morley — 226
13. Jocelyn Pook — 232
14. Kathryn Bostic — 233
15. Hildur Guðnadóttir — 234
16. Jerry Goldsmith's honorary sidewalk "star" on Hollywood's Walk of Fame — 239
17. David Shire — 255
18. Rachel Portman — 275
19. Jermaine Stegall — 285
20. John Williams — 319

Acknowledgments

Foremost thanks must go, of course, to the composers themselves, profiled here, who granted their time, their enthusiasm, sometimes their private music tapes and, once or twice, their coffee, to my interviewing project. Though all of my interview requests and correspondences were initially uninvited from their end and always unsponsored on my end, these busy musicians paused generously to talk about what they do, and listeners like me stayed for the sheer creativity of the music even though such scoring was only supposed to be background filler to the main event, the movie—and yet, here it is commanding our attention.

Especially at SUNY Press, I thank Murray Pomerance, editor of the press's Horizons of Cinema series who agreed to make a book of this, and who identified a few omissions and oversteps from my initial manuscript version. In deference, I believe I have repaired all but one of them—my own inherent prejudice. In the press's whole process of whether to approve or ditch a new manuscript, an anonymous quartet of so-called "peer reviewers" was convened by the publisher: a big thanks is owed to them for their fairness and forbearance wrestling with early drafts of this book. Finally, for both technical and moral support, a page like this provides at least a modest way to show personal appreciation to Jay Hilgartner; Laurie Matheson; Justin Kelly; Stanislav Viner; the faithful Deborah Unitus; the generous Elaine Kile and Marilee Bradford; and the next generation's highly creative, ambitious Shiloh Monaco and Garcia Jackson Jr.

Most thanks, however, on behalf of this whole book, must go to its patient editor, Senior Acquisitions Editor for music and education books Richard Carlin, ideal for that job since he succeeds in being a coach, a disciplinarian, an advocate, a well-wisher, and finally, a partner in wanting to put out the best book possible. His music of choice may be Eubie Blake but he knows his film music too, having worked on similar-themed books before and feeling comfortable with the whole twenty-first-century musical movement of pluralism—all kinds of music all at once. This is certainly the place, too, to acknowledge the intrepid work of our copyeditor, Dana Foote, who caught missteps and uncertainties throughout the manuscript, even suggesting wise ways to smooth things out—all of that final prep work being overseen with clarity and encouragement by Senior Production Editor Diane Ganeles, who then assumed the dual role, in my mind, of sherpa guide and project conscience.

Lastly, this may not be the best place to thank the country's leading movie music journalist, *Variety*'s and UCLA's Jon Burlingame for being a mentor and for doing some photo research, but it should be done somewhere; it is surely not the place to thank the webmaster Jim Paterson, whose music site originally posted a number of the so-called "Interludes" to follow in this book, for his contribution is elsewhere explained in the introduction. Suffice it to say that, just as any motion picture needs a whole team to produce it, so does a book. This is my thanks to the team.

Some of the interviews and essays in the present volume have appeared, much-excerpted and altered, in past periodicals and, where required, reprint permissions have been sought:

High Fidelity/Musical America 27, no. 6 (8–62), Richard Rodney Bennett interview, herein chapter 9

Film Comment (Lincoln Center Film Society, New York), on Bond films

The Cue Sheet (Society for the Preservation of Film Music) 5, nos. 3, 4, Moross interview excerpts

Soundtrack SCN (Belgium) 2, no. 6, Bernstein interview excerpts; 2, nos. 7, 8, Bennett interview; 2, no. 10, Mancini interview excerpts

Film Music Notebook 2, no. 1, Rózsa interview excerpts

Music website *mfiles.co.uk*. Early versions of the present volume's interlude essays on Williams, Mancini, Legrand, Portman, Goldsmith, choral music, ex-rock musicians, and African American composers in films have appeared on this site among other concert music and film music–related essays by the author.

CD booklet essays by the present author include disc releases of soundtracks for *The Big Country* and *The Proud Rebel* (label: Screen Archives Entertainment) and *Peter Gunn* (label: Harmonia Mundi)

Preface

By now, after more than a hundred years of cinema history, two marvels stand out when the subject of film music scoring comes up: (1) how soon after the very invention of motion pictures music in the form of a background accompaniment to the action onscreen seemed essential to the whole moviemaking, moviegoing experience, and (2) how that very music, originally and quite rightly criticized as crude and clichéd, seems to have greatly rehabilitated its reputation to the point where its composers have become the subject of admiring articles, symphony society concerts, and even college courses. Since film music is wholly dependent on the movie for which it was written, there remains a general consensus that it is never quite the pure art object that a piece of concert music aspires to be, where form and fluidity are paramount. Furthermore, the average film score, however seriously intended, proceeds only by starts and stops, one "cue" after another, separated by movie dialogue and action scenes, hardly ever able to establish its own momentum. Only the best, most practiced film composers can make such a stuttering sequence of music bits sound continuous, cumulative, or even musical. And yet, it has been done. Some few film composers have even succeeded in creating lasting music along the way. These are the masters of the craft and I have approached a few of them over the years and coaxed them into conversation about what they do and how and why.

Of course, not many film viewers, even now, notice the typical soundtrack score. They've come to watch a movie, not listen to it. As a result, even the best of those composers who begin to accumulate a history of interesting narrative music, typically remain anonymous, even their best scoring inconspicuous. And while they may truly value the esteem of their colleagues, what they say they would covet even more is some wider public attention to their music—some genuine listener appreciation, even excitement about what they have done. That would be an affirmation of film music itself, not just as soundtrack filler but as music with its own audience. And, of course, it would be a much-appreciated personal affirmation as well. Late in life, the veteran composer Laurence Rosenthal voiced this very frustration in a December 21, 2016, note to me: "Although the kind of impression my work has made over the years," he mused, "has been one that has earned respect, I have to confess that at certain moments, as a creative contributor, one longs for something beyond pallid admiration, a pat on the back, a kind of 'Job well done, old chap!' . . . [some reassurance] that someone has heard what I was trying to do all these years and that what I have tried to say in music has been really heard by receptive ears."

Rosenthal's lament for the relative invisibility of his profession actually coincided with a kind of renaissance for film composers—attention occasioned by the surprisingly successful adventure film scores of John Williams, first in the 1970s for films like *Jaws* and *Star Wars*, and extending into the New Millennium *Harry Potter* series. By now, the complaint that film music never gets its due may be something of a dated trope as multimedia broadcasting and streaming and film-sharing access to movies and soundtracks have broadened everyone's awareness. Still, there is a point to be pressed that a good deal of good music is still getting past us all as it performs its servile narrative function there in the background of mainstream cinema. The composers who write that music, at least the best of them, now and in the generation just past, make interesting spokespersons, each for the honor of the art and for music in general. What's interesting in this present discussion is how fully a few pioneering composers saw the potential of the movie soundtrack for musicmaking and went ahead with what was then a rather rash experiment. The inherent limits of the field would always be a factor: the extramusical origins of a film score, its secondary importance when compared to the visual focus of movies—but it also seemed to promise an opportunity for unlimited creativity in how it could be conceived and applied to the screen. A few impatient, ingenious composers were instantly intrigued.

A Medium with Potential

This was all sometime before Hollywood could boast its own cadre of studio composers who would develop the rules and traditions of the field. The very first important composers for the movies were not Hollywood characters at all but, rather, important international concert composers in their own right who, apart from their symphonic fame, had already been thinking about music for the movies of their day and had definite things to say about it. They had witnessed (and in one case, actually participated in) the sort of crazy improvised piano "scoring" associated with the early silent films such as will be described shortly here but, as moviegoers and music lovers alike, they felt a definite urge to take both arts in hand—sight and sound working together, screen story and music scoring. Storytelling music. In Europe, the boy prodigy Erich Korngold; in Russia, the politically embattled Dimitri Shostakovich; in America, the iconoclast Aaron Copland—all started dreaming of this new medium for music, perhaps a new way to reach a general audience with classical sounds. How did Korngold put it? "The cinema is a direct avenue to the ears and hearts of the great public.... Fine symphonic scores for motion pictures cannot help but influence mass acceptance for finer music" (Farach-Colton 32). Indeed, by 1934, he was intrigued enough to relocate to Hollywood. Of course, even his boyish optimism would be tested once he joined the commercial world of movies and faced that "great public." There were a few prejudices he hadn't counted on: he, as an outsider, being too classical for Hollywood and then too Hollywood to ever rejoin the classical concert ranks. Still, he charged into the make-believe movie world with gusto, especially effective in films with historical settings. Shostakovich had literally been involved with the movies since he was a teenager, accompanying silent movies in his local St. Petersburg theater with piano improvisations only very loosely related to the action he was seeing onscreen. But, like Korngold, he began to feel that a great opportunity was being missed to imagine finer and more specifically tailored music applied to each film. The casual, clumsy relationships between his extemporaneous piano playing at the theater keyboard and each scene up there onscreen was a nightly frustration to him. "It's time to take cinema music in hand," he cried in a widely quoted plea; "time to eliminate the bungling and the inartistic and to thoroughly clean the Augean stable. The only way to do this is to write special music" (Farach-Colton 32). He was twenty-three then, speaking in March 1929 at the premiere of his first formal film score for the silent picture *New Babylon*. By "special music," of course, he meant custom-tailored scoring, the earliest of true soundtrack composing.

Through the contributions of these outsider composers and their progeny, the considerable craft and strange art of film music was born and raised. It was Copland who, early on, addressed one main aspect of that strangeness: the fact that this was music for a mass audience that still went largely unacknowledged. Soundtrack music was a movie's chauffer, hired to guide the journey but expecting to be taken for granted. "Film music constitutes a new musical medium that exerts a fascination of its own. . . . Millions will be listening *but* one never knows how many will be really hearing," Copland concluded. Then, his friendly exhortation: "The next time you go to the movies, remember to be on the side of the composer" (Copland, *What* 210).

The purpose of this book, then, is to be on the composers' side; to hear from a variety of soundtrack contributors, in their own words, what they have "been trying to do all these years" and, through them, to experience some of the best of this music that still hides behind the movies we watch. Only some of it is really worth our attention—but the best of it we can certainly respect, and even be excited by it.

Introduction

MUSIC ACCOMPANIED MOTION pictures from the earliest days of the cinema, initially just to focus the audience's attention on "the show" happening up there on the screen, to envelop everyone in a common experience. Eventually, it was noticed that music could also help with the storytelling of a film itself, even influence the viewer's reactions to the movie by what kind of music was playing and, so, the role of the individual composer became important: to produce interesting soundtrack music and find effective ways to bring it out from behind the screen where any audience, if at all aware, could overhear what a composer was meaning to do.

It is in that spirit I sought these interviews with a handful of film composers whose work I had been overhearing and had come to know and respect—composers whose skill, sophistication, and versatility place them quite appropriately into the community of other modern concertizing musicians and place their music, even though written with ulterior motives, into the broader universe of musicmaking today.

What's a Film Score For?

At the most elementary level, what are the rules and tasks of a film score? What limitations and requirements are inherent in the genre of film music? For that matter, what can music do for a film? By what standards can it be judged? Traditionally, it can do a range of things: it can evoke the story's setting (music that sounds like a big city or a Welsh mining village or an Arab bazaar); it can empathize with a character (a blind girl, a brash gangster, a conscience-torn lover); it can underline a story's thesis (greed, guilt, heroism in the face of fear); it can even portend, through some dissonance or disturbance, some development in the plot that, so far, has only threatened to occur. Conversely, it can play against the screen (slow, sad music during a violent battle scene; bright, carefree music to deflect a scene of tension) so that the effect is one of dramatic irony.[1]

By its nature, music is indirect in its influence: it more often insinuates into our consciousness than declares itself. Of course, there are some major composers who deny any real emotional influence to film music: they say that any moods or messages you think you are getting from a film score are qualities that you, yourself, suppose and impose. But then, there are others who do sense the abstract power of a well-placed film score, even if it is a subtle secondary influence on a movie. Igor Stravinsky flirted with film music once in 1946 but was dismissive, writing, "My first premise is that good music must be heard by and for itself, and not with the crutch of any visual medium" (Cooke, *Reader* 278). At the same time, though, Copland was championing film music's subtle value, declaring, "In Hollywood I have looked at long stretches of film before the music has been added and I got the impression that music is like a small flame put under the screen to help warm it. . . . But background music is the most ungrateful kind of music for a composer to write. Since it's music behind or underneath screen dialogue, the audience is really not going to hear it; possibly won't even be aware of its existence." Yet, good or bad, "it undoubtedly works on the subconscious mind" (Copland, *Our* 260–75).

Even now, composers who admit to being heavily invested in the field still debate whether music created in support of some other medium can be a sovereign art, can be legitimate. One who frequently displayed discomfort being in Hollywood at all when he certainly had the aggressive gifts to be part of the concertizing avant-garde was Leonard Rosenman, whose nonetheless famous film scores include *Rebel without a Cause*. His assessment of film music was stoic and only barely tolerant: "(For a soundtrack) you really are not writing music," he declared. "Basically, you are using all the ingredients of music . . . but basically it doesn't function as music because the propulsion is not through the medium of musical ideas. The propulsion is by way of literary ideas . . . it's almost music but not quite. It smokes, but it's no cigar" (Rosenman in Bazelon 181, 186). This whole debate will come up again in the pages that follow.

Film Music: Wherefore and Why

But back to basics: it bears restating one last time how screen music is not self-inspired as is a piece of abstract music. It is composed on behalf of a given movie with an external scenario: the film comes first and suggests the story, the setting, and the moods to be evoked by music. Even the pace and the placement of each musical bit is dictated by the screen. What is more, that most important element of a concert piece—its developmental architecture—is mostly missing from a film score as there is seldom any opportunity in an ongoing movie for the background music to stretch out and pursue its own musical argument. It has only moments at a time to make itself heard. (Skillful, willful composers *can* create developmental scores with special attention to form, but more on that later.) Compositional complexity is another feature of serious concert music that usually needs to be tempered in the typical film score: a movie soundtrack with too much going on, too many multilayered musical ideas or busy orchestration, will tend to draw attention away from the story onscreen. And when filmmakers notice that happening to their movie, the composer is in trouble.

And yet, in the most facile hands, a fine film score can actually bypass all those deficits, satisfy all the needs of cinema while also being satisfying music. Copland knew how to honor both commitments—he could see where both music and the movies could blend honorably and, so, he was not ashamed to join the ranks of film composers at a certain time in his midcareer. Somewhere around 1940, he laid out very clearly what he said to be the ideals and characteristics of good film music. To him, the most important contribution of a film score to a movie, the primary "why" of having a music score there at all, was to "supply a kind of human warmth to the black-and-white two-dimensional figures . . . giving them a communicable sympathy that they otherwise would not have, bridging the gap between the screen and the audience." Then he listed five ways in which film music could aid any given film: by evoking the particular time and place of the film's story, by representing the thoughts and feelings of characters, by providing a neutral background to fill silent scenes or bridge transitional sequences, by supplying a sense of continuity across the film as a whole, and by heightening the drama itself. Three dangers he identified that were typical: the persistence of post-romantic-era music applied to films no matter what their settings or subjects, the overuse of the leitmotif approach in scoring so that every time a particular character appeared his particular motif was repeated and repeated, *and* the temptation to copy any physical action onscreen with illustrative music as if it were a pantomime or a cartoon, that is, music climbing up the scale when a character is climbing stairs or falling when he falls. Copland consciously avoided those flaws in the few scores he produced between 1939 and 1963 and he applied his scoring principles to films like *Of Mice and Men* and *The Heiress*, whose place in film music history would become important (Cooke, *Reader* 85–91).

Admittedly, as a general rule over the past century, the typical film score, in one trivial film after another, was more likely to be prosaic than praiseworthy. Did one even need to be a composer, it was being asked, to put together a soundtrack?[2] After all, almost any generic tonal or rhythmic accompaniment will blend with a moving image onscreen and seem intentional. Thus, in place of actual music-making in those early days you had haphazard improvisation—and by the late twentieth century you often had either bombastic orchestral music copied from past adventure movies or a cloak of synthesized drones and hypnotic beats that once were the voice of video games but now were marking time behind theatrical movies. Against all that, though, there were a few defiant figures, well schooled in composition and committed to real musicmaking, who valiantly kept the art of film music alive and encouraged it to evolve. Those are some of the composers this book presents.

It feels unfair, though—it smacks of elitism—just to say that recent movie music pales by comparison to some golden age. Mere scolding is the last refuge of the curmudgeon. After all, films now demand a different musical approach from days gone by; the whole field of films and film music, like the career of each film composer, is in a constant state of transition. The more naturalistic style of drama and performance onscreen today would not support the gushing kind of orchestral coaxing that a 1940s romance would want. Still, the wise film composer today will know how far to go and what to hold back; how much to support the drama directly and how much to merely suggest; what to underline with music and what subtly to imply. Music to excess can kill a dramatic moment, just as cute music can kill a comedy, but music wisely conceived and carefully placed can set the atmosphere for a whole film, can pace the drama, even narrate or portend the plot as I have said. What the composers interviewed here have aspired to is simultaneously cinematic effectiveness and compositional sincerity. We ask again, What do the best film scores try to do and what factors should be put forward to judge them? Three questions:

- Is there excellence, originality, or, at least, clarity in the composing itself?
- Does its tone and content complement the film?
- Is it "cinematic scoring"—does it interact with the film in some narrative or kinetic way?[3]

Once filmmakers and filmgoers are conscious of and begin to apply aesthetic and technical principles like those, film music becomes impressive again, no matter what the era. Indeed, it is a field that is always in transition. For any smart composer, it's a learning curve. And just to listen, through this book, to veteran composers describing what they've learned, what they have been through, what warnings they have, and then to take note of some of the genuinely expressive music that is still to be overheard on a few striking soundtracks—all of that is our purpose here.

A Quick History of Film Scoring

It is probably true that most people today are introduced to Western orchestral music of different styles and traditions, not directly through concerts or recitals, music schools or private lessons, but indirectly hearing the background music scores in mainstream films. Right from the 1930s when fanfares announced *The Adventures of Robin Hood* and calamitous chords sounded the alarm about *King Kong*, when brave marches in 1940s war films stirred the blood or delinquent jazz of the 1950s put society on notice, movie audiences absorbed, without meaning to, all sorts of very specific musical types and tropes from the background film scores.

Other books have traced the history of cinema music in great detail, so I will only summarize it here from silent film days through the era of the major studio music departments and on to the world of the freelance film composer in the New Millennium.[4] The origins of the film score are various, depending whose history you read (Buhler and Neumayer; Davis), but it was recognized very early on that the blunt stories enacted in those early silent film screenplays (*Intolerance*, 1918; *Hearts of the World*, 1919) needed some other sensory element beside the visual to hold an audience's attention. I have already hinted at two of the advantages of a "piano escort": (1) the sheer sound of music filled the room where the movie was being projected and focused the crowd on the screen; and (2) once those theater pianists or organists realized that they could tailor their improvisations to the moods implied by the screen story—that is, play fast and agitated for a chase scene, lovelorn for a romantic subplot, patriotic for a soldier, sentimental for the old folks back home—a gross kind of musical narration was achieved. Before long, film music came to be expected, even in small town halls across America where the movies were shown. Those scores were not composed in any real sense; they tended to be repetitions of familiar folk tunes, novelty tunes, and a whole lot of just connective tissue. By the same formula, some accompanists drew their thematic bits and quotes from the familiar classical repertoire—recognizable romance music quoted from Tchaikovsky, exciting gallops from von Suppé or Rossini, and anthemlike bits of Brahms. The ragged nature of this patchwork music being performed on a pitch-imperfect piano by rushed hands in the near-dark cannot have been an all-inspiring experience, but the general effect of lending emotion to the show was gradually creating a kind of mystique that would become a future American trend: a Saturday night at the movies.

As a corporate studio system was establishing itself on the West Coast of the United States, experiments with the new medium of cinema had long been underway in Europe—not only the multicamera/multiprojector epics of directors like Abel Gance and Serge Eisenstein,[5] but a few specific gala events matching live music and film visuals. Among the first of these were films from early French studios like Pathé and Gaumont: witness the 1908 production *L'assassinat du Duc de Guise* with its special silent-film score by Camille Saint-Saëns. Much was made of the innovation: music wedded precisely to what was seen onscreen. It is not surprising, though, that this gala version of live film music didn't catch on, the coordination of score and screen being a highly complex mathematical puzzle and the prospect of engaging an orchestra each time you wanted to run a movie being prohibitive. Saint-Saëns deflected his unexploited film score into a concert piece, his *Opus 128 for Strings, Piano, and Harmonium*, and the idea of live tailor-made film scoring was . . . well . . . reconsidered. The various entertainment emporiums where films tended to be shown, however, frequently had house organs built into the mezzanine or front and center at the head of the stage and, so, as films themselves grew more sophisticated, their scenarios more ambitious, tacky piano accompaniments seemed less and less satisfactory: organ improvisations took over the silent picture show.[6] And not so long after that, the Edison Motion Picture Company began issuing printed guides of suggested classical music quotes and medleys that could be played by theater organs as background for silent film programs: noncopyrighted bits of favorite music from Bach to Offenbach, available in a big thick chapbook of samples like swatches of cloth to make a quilt. American director D. W. Griffith had one such chapbook prepared for his 1915 *Birth of a Nation* (Darby 3–5; Cooke, *Reader* 15–16; Brown 51–53; Cooke, *History* 23–26).

The 1922 film by Abel Gance, *La Roue* (The Wheel), did have a very specific score composed for it by French-Swiss composer Arthur Honegger who appears to have used the exercise to develop his subsequent famous concert piece evocative of a train journey, *Pacific 231*. Gance's 1927 epic film *Napoleon* likewise had a carefully coordinated Honegger score premiered with the film at a gala evening at the Paris Opera. As with *La Roue*, the *Napoleon* score was made up of a certain amount of original composition (about twenty minutes' worth) blended with existing classical, popular, or folk bits of music to be played by a small ensemble of hired instruments; again, trying the live gala event to promote the new medium of the cinema. The resulting experience was a thrilling innovation for the inexperienced audience: music appeared to condone and complete the images onscreen into an art form more akin to opera or even a ballet scenario, a far cry from the flickering tent-show entertainment that was the earliest type of fairground cinema play or an Edison Vitascope projection in a back room somewhere. In Germany, composer Edmund Meisel was providing completely original scores for the important new films of Eisenstein, *Potemkin* (1925) and *Oktober* (1927) about the Russian revolution. Again, these were original music scores performed live as the film was being projected. But, also again, who could afford to sustain such costly indulgences? Still, the example had been made; the gauntlet had been laid down. Anything less was less prestigious; anything as modest as a house organist or a ragtime pianist was last year's movie show.

With such world-renowned films being produced in Europe now and classic silent comedies and melodramas coming out of American studios via Griffith and Chaplin, only the sound of something new would satisfy that burgeoning movie industry: new music behind every new film. And anyway, a whole new invention was coming to the movies in 1929: sound-on-film. Now you could actually hear the actors speak their lines; you could listen to the natural sounds around them and, if you thought about it, you could conceivably record any tailor-made music score right onto the soundtrack of the film so that it would play right along with every other sound effect, every time the film ran. Producers jumped at the chance to enhance the glamor and drama of their shows. And a few composers seized the opening—they immediately saw the movies as a new vehicle for narrative music. Where would these composers come from, though, at first? In Europe, some of the first were from France. There were seriously intended scores from men like Maurice Jaubert, Joseph Kosma, Georges Auric, or from Britain through established composers like Ralph Vaughan Williams, Sir Arthur Bliss, William Alwyn. Figures like William Walton and Benjamin Britten, while not heavily involved in movie scoring apart from their concert careers, did contribute on occasion to the movies if only, in the latter case, to documentaries. Some few of these scores, rearranged into concert works, served to bring their composers and therefore the whole idea of film music to a broader public. The Arthur Bliss score for *Things to Come* (1936) reached beyond its screen contexts to gain fame on its own as music. And through their mutual experience tailoring music to the film *Lieutenant Kije* (1933), both director Eisenstein and composer Sergei Prokofiev developed a collaborative working relationship in adapting score to screen and, in some instances, screen to scoring for 1938's epic film *Alexander Nevsky*, especially the battle on the ice sequence—a complex montage of quick visual edits and multilayered contrapuntal thematic scoring in which the Russian peasant theme, the Nevsky theme, and the oppressive German-invaders themes all contend in a scene of great fervor and virtuosity. Prokofiev had actually traveled to Hollywood to study the studio system in 1938 and to see how far they had come in the "art of montage"—blending music and moving images. He found the ambition of the American industry in producing and distributing films quite advanced but the film styles, genres, and aesthetics, not so much. He returned to Russia to revel in his own high degree of freedom, going all out on *Nevsky*. As with *Kije*, he fashioned a concert cantata version of the *Nevsky* film score that became his Opus 78.

But what was the tenor of film scoring in Hollywood now that sound recording had come to the cinema? Who were the composers supplying the new film music and from where had they come? What was their experience and training? Three figures can be said to have launched soundtrack music composing in early 1930s Hollywood: Max Steiner had come from Broadway and popular music theater (Thomas 56–78; Palmer 15–50; Wegele); Erich Korngold had come from operetta and the romantic/heroic traditions of Austria (Thomas 79–86; Palmer 51–67; Darby 157–86); and Franz Waxman had flirted with jazz, although first he had been schooled in all the modern German orchestral styles (Cooke, *Reader* 139–46; Cooke, *History* 98–107; Darby 116–56; Thomas 33–46; Palmer 94–117). Steiner especially could not resist the new linkage that was possible, thanks to recorded soundtracks, between action onscreen and directly illustrative music. In the early John Ford film *The Informer*, he did not hesitate to underline every action onscreen with some comment in the music score and to attach recognizable themes to each character and each event. The effect was not as sophisticated as a ballet score might be, matching gestures in the music to pirouettes in the dance—rather, the effect was like a Broadway musical where the pit orchestra chaperoned the actions on stage to be sure that no plot point went unsung. By today's standards, this kind of attention feels like overkill. In those early days, however, it was a conscious accomplishment suggesting that the movies could be a total entertainment vehicle—part literature telling a story, part performance being a play, and now part musical, even if the music was merely incidental. Steiner's brand of music was compositionally simple and obvious: for *The Informer* an obvious Irish tune, then customary tension music for the political plot. Film was not considered art to which serious music should aspire—it was a show and Steiner's Broadway background was in writing show music.

Still, the insistence of his scoring and how deliberately it was applied to the screen was creating, as it were, this new subgenre of music that was at least as descriptive as a tone poem, as functional as the orchestral portion of a concerto minus the soloist. The movie was the soloist. Steiner's job for the first five or six years of the sound era consisted of providing stylish opening and closing music for many of the films coming out of RKO Studios, only ten or twelve of which received any kind of internal narrative scoring. Among the latter, his hyperdescriptive, often dissonant music behind the 1933 thriller film *King Kong* was considered innovative in that it didn't try to please its audience with heroic themes or concertlike material, but laid a menacing ambient backdrop behind the monster Kong breaking the bonds of civilization and climbing the Empire State Building as easily as though it were a jungle tree. The sight of Willis O'Brien's innovative stop-motion animation of Kong was alarming enough for Great Depression audiences, but the film's closely attuned orchestral track exaggerated the experience to a degree that was wholly modern: the movies came of age and an interactive soundtrack was going to be very much a part of that.

No one ever called Max Steiner's music modern or progressive—his was a romantic nineteenth-century language—but its importance for films throughout the 1930s only grew. His scores for films like *The Charge of the Light Brigade* (1936), *A Star Is Born* and *Life of Emile Zola* (1937), then *Jezebel, Dark City, The Letter,* and *Now Voyager*, though theatrical in tone, became increasingly more noticeable and individual and brought him into the 1940s. His scores for *The Adventures of Mark Twain, Since You Went Away, Johnny Belinda,* and *The Fountainhead* represented the best of his narrative imitative accompaniment style and they were thematic enough to accomplish what we have been worried about so far in this examination: they were noticed by audiences. His 1949 prodding, obsessive score to *Beyond the Forest* seemed more modern and sophisticated than usual, choosing dramaturgy over musicmaking, using the crass tune "Chicago, Chicago" as a repetitive taunt, the very antithesis of a melodic entertainment score, to frame this Bette Davis murder mystery set in small-town America. Apparently, Steiner had a range after all. Before retiring in 1965 after thirty-six years, he had provided plainly noticeable musical framing to over three hundred films. His two most famous efforts were surely the theme and score for 1939's *Gone with the Wind* and his music for *Casablanca* (1942) with its variations on the Herman Hupfeld song "As Time Goes By." Interestingly, as he aged, Steiner's music for films came to sound ever simpler and more youthful until his main theme for *A Summer Place* became a teenager's jukebox hit in 1959 and his open-air trumpet theme for *Spencer's Mountain* (1963) seems to be the voice of a fresh newcomer.

A comparison between early film scores and the singing world of operetta was certainly one main component of the Hollywood success of Erich Wolfgang Korngold, late of the Vienna theater, whom we have already met, soon a well-anchored studio composer of 1935–1955 film scores starting with *Captain Blood* (1935) and soaring tonally through swashbuckling scores like *Anthony Adverse*, *The Prince and the Pauper*, and *The Sea Hawk* (1940). These were far more tonally complex than Steiner ever ventured, yet they trod the same romantic/adventure paths that Steiner knew. They embraced these costume dramas with an elegance that, unlike much of the Steiner catalogue, encouraged concert attention away from the films. For here was movie music solid enough to be considered for its own internal qualities . . . film scoring as real music that could be culled, edited, sequenced into a performable piece away from film. His former fame as a genuine child prodigy overseas, composer of the successful grand opera *Die Tote Stadt* and a popular cello concerto, ensured him a royal treatment on arrival in Hollywood and he never failed to impress the US studios. His score for *The Adventures of Robin Hood* was noticed beyond the music department offices; executives began to receive letters asking if the Korngold score to *King's Row* was available on a recording. With film music getting this much attention for its own sake, the logical next step for the evolution of film score history would be if the music itself began to mature—to incorporate not backward-looking operetta styles but a gradual awareness of modern idioms. Enter the eclectic German composer equally adept at the classics, contemporary dialects, and even jazz—enter Franz Waxman.

During studies at the Dresden and Berlin conservatories, Waxman supported himself as a light pop pianist in club-performing combos. The regional fame of those groups brought him into contact with both serious musicians like conductor Bruno Walter and figures in the growing commercial field of stage and film musicals like Frederick Hollander. But these were the early 1930s and national politics in Germany were crashing toward Naziism. Once, in 1934, Waxman was beaten by Nazi thugs on the streets of Berlin and so he moved with his new wife to Paris and thence, along with fellow Berliners like Hollander and young movie director Billy Wilder, immigrated to the United States and to Hollywood, maybe to catch hold of the new field opening all over, composing for the movies. Wilder certainly encouraged the idea. Experiments among the young generation of filmmakers convinced Waxman that he might indulge his own eclectic ear for modernisms by starting to write for film. In one sense, he was fortunate to begin his scoring career in the employ of Universal Studios, which just then was producing a series of flamboyant, even expressionistic, horror films based on the success of early productions like *Frankenstein* and *The Mummy*. His first job writing original movie music was for James Whale's *Bride of Frankenstein*, a darkening fable that embraced at once horror, blasphemy, the wonderment of Creation, and a sly sense of humor in the form of self-parody. His complex score gave the bizarre bride a kind of tropical glamor theme; gave a fugal development to the village violence that builds up around rumors of the monster's existence; and, for the creation of the creature herself, had the soundtrack sustain the steady pulse (as though the bride's new heartbeat) over a ten-minute passaglia[7] that climaxed in the introduction of the creature to the world: life created out of mankind's hubris—a creature with all the foibles, quirks, and doubts that everyone is heir to. Waxman's *Bride of Frankenstein* seemed to represent it all and "made music" even so.

Waxman's handling of various orchestral and dramatic devices found new applications as his days at Universal developed. Before long, one could spot other passages of fugal[8] writing, leitmotif[9] procedures, and sophisticated dissonances for dramatic effect in his scores. His use of passacaglia in some of the psychological tension scenes in *Sorry Wrong Number* or *The Invisible Ray* or *Devil Doll* was striking as was his adoption of some very effective Americanisms in *The Shining Hour* and *Captains Courageous* or, especially, *Lure of the Wilderness* or *The Philadelphia Story*. There were occasional experiments in dissonance and orchestral detail in *Dr. Jekyll and Mr. Hyde*, more fugal passages in *Objective Burma*, more modern jazzlike (or Stravinsky-like) metric patterns in the active music in *Night and the City*, a postwar lyricism in the pop sax theme for *A Place in the Sun*, but a postwar sardonicism in the cynical feeling behind *Sunset Boulevard*, a score and a film (by

Billy Wilder) that went to the very heart of the Hollywood system—a film about film fame, a score about scoring.

In the 1950s, Waxman supplemented his classically challenging scores with some early jazz flavor and a nod to the faddish popular music of the day, mixing it all with the recent rock 'n' roll craze to produce a score for the teen-delinquency film *Crime in the Streets* and some blatantly pop-driven scores to films like *Peyton Place*. One late score, just before his death in 1967, was the vivid orchestral showpiece, *Taras Bulba*, which encompassed some powerful action music for the Mongolian war lord, a lovely original ballad in the debt of a Ukrainian folk song, and a vigorously virtuoso saber dance that accompanies Taras's ride to Dubno, gathering his loyal forces along the way preparing for war. It was Waxman's spectacular climax to a brave career that, along with that of the American Bernard Herrmann, can be said to have brought American film scoring charging and braying out of the more formal golden age into a modern era, paving the way for ambitious conservatives like Hugo Friedhofer (*The Best Years of Our Lives*, *The Bishop's Wife*), provocateurs like David Raksin (*Laura*, *The Bad and the Beautiful*), pluralists like Alex North (*A Streetcar Named Desire*, *Death of a Salesman*), and by the mid-1950s, the first twelve-tone serial[10] scores by Leonard Rosenman (*Cobweb*, *Fantastic Voyage*). Neither Herrmann nor Waxman would ever go that far, but their daring flung open new doors.[11]

Immigrant figures still influenced the loosely associated Hollywood community of screen composers, even as the studio system began to break down. The 1950s saw Viennese composers like Bronislau Kaper who had begun in the 1940s and Russian/Ukrainians like Dimitri Tiomkin, whose early work for director Frank Capra had begun in the 1930s but who now was finding popular success scoring western films. Even the veteran Miklós Rózsa, so active writing exotica for films like *Thief of Bagdad* and *The Jungle Book*, and then noir crime music like *Double Indemnity* or *The Killers* in the 1940s, found himself renewed, if that is the right word, scoring a whole new genre of film: historical dramas like *Julius Caesar*, *Quo Vadis*, *Lust for Life*, *Ben-Hur*. In a sense, these were the last gasp (for a while) of old world European-influenced music scoring. For, even as the 1950s suggested new soundtrack styles, starting to use the dialects of jazz, pop music, and to a certain extent the modern avant-garde, a definite strain of

Americana was asserting itself too. Alfred Newman's use of Gershwin chords in *Street Scene*, of cowboy tunes and rhythms in *Drums Along the Mohawk* or *The Gunfighter*, or of simple hometown melody for *Two Brothers* or *My Friend Flicka* are examples of Americana-to-the-fore in film music. Bernard Herrmann's folk idioms used in *The Devil and Daniel Webster* (aka *All That Money Can Buy*) or *The Kentuckian*, not to mention scores of Herrmann colleague Jerome Moross (*The Big Country*, *The Proud Rebel*) and especially the mentor of that young composer group, Aaron Copland (*The Red Pony*), are all examples of how Americana music became a staple in film scoring, right through the 1950s. Even Herrmann's austere string music for Hitchcock's *Psycho* in 1960, driving and fierce at one moment, a long cold stare the next, represented a kind of holdover of between-the-wars American modernism, already taking its place with other identifiable modes.

There is no absolutely clear break from European golden age scores to these American examples, but a few jazzy newcomers really brought on the modern era in a big way and doused the melodramatic romantic past for good. Scores like Alex North's swaggering, bluesy score to *A Streetcar Named Desire*; Elmer Bernstein's biting brassy urban jazz in *Man with the Golden Arm*; or Henry Mancini in the late 1950s bringing cool jazz first to television scoring like *Peter Gunn* and then to the movies in productions like *Breakfast at Tiffany's* set the next new tone.[12]

Each of those guys also proved adept at exploiting a third element of modern film scoring after jazz awareness and classical contemporary know-how: the importance of a memorable title tune—having a pop song associated with your film either as a stand-alone opening gambit or as a repeating melody around which to build your orchestral score. Ever since David Raksin's popular melody for *Laura* in the 1940s and Tiomkin's country song "Do Not Forsake Me, Oh My Darling" from *High Noon* in the 1950s, composers and front-office moneymen had seen the advantage of having a hit song attached to their movie to serve as an audience ambassador of extra publicity. North/Bernstein/Mancini were not thinking in such crass commercial terms when they penned song-based scores—they were following a seemingly inevitable populist trend in media music at that time, which was gradually becoming more lyrical after the dry rock 'n' roll period. Melody was flourishing, and that was reflected by the way in which even dramatic film scores for epic films like *Exodus* or *Doctor Zhivago* relied on and exploited title tunes. In turn, those tunes that became hit records drew attention to all movie soundtracks and their composers to a degree not seen before. For a while, films invested special attention in the various ways soundtrack music might be exploited to promote the whole movie package. Thus began the period when a cadre of song and Big Band composers took over the scoring field: Mancini with his thematic approach to scoring (resulting in songs like "Moon River," "Days of Wine and Roses," and jazz standards like "The Pink Panther"); John Barry whose spy-movie tunes headed up a series of James Bond adventure films; Lalo Schifrin whose brand of hot rhythms and cool combos made catchy TV music for weekly series like *Mission: Impossible* with its 5/4 beat or *Mannix* with its jazz waltz meter. Quincy Jones and Dave Grusin likewise jockeyed between pop-theme scoring and experimental ensemble scores throughout the 1960s.[13]

Then came 1970s: the decade when a new assertive generation of young American directors made their stand, essentially taking the film industry away from the studios and into their own freelance hands—Spielberg, Lucas, Scorsese, Coppola.[14] (The studios still benefited, but it seemed more like the aging executives were looking to these young guys to reveal *their* next moves.) And those same 1960s composers I have just listed, at least the ones well trained in the essentials of real composition so that they could adapt to the new kind of films, found work with this new generation of filmmakers. Perhaps the two most vivid American composers arising out of this period were John Williams (whose scores for *Jaws* and *Star Wars* were the decade's most successful soundtracks) and David Shire (who had come from Broadway songwriting but had real Yale-credentialed composition skills to apply to innovative scores like Coppola's *The Conversation* [chromatic piano jazz variations] and *The Taking of Pelham 123* [an authentic twelve-tone score á la Arnold Schoenberg's serial style]). Shire, as his interview herein will show, produced an impeccable series of scores for all kinds of films starting in the seventies, all the while continuing to do Broadway. John Williams, accepting the huge *Star Wars* success (and sequels), joined forces with those same young directors, inadvertently resurrecting anew the large-scale symphonic scoring of the golden age through adventure films like *Indiana Jones* and *Jurassic Park*, but also giving intimate music to *Angela's Ashes*, country guitar music to *The Reivers* and *The River*, even third-stream jazz to *Catch Me If You Can*, and giving a patriotic slant to war films like *Saving Private Ryan* or presidential biographies like *JFK* or *Lincoln*. In short, Williams was drawing attention to film scoring itself, to a degree not seen since the forties, if ever.

But there was another stream, too, beginning in the 1980s and into the next decade—a sort of modified minimalism[15] taking over film scoring; clean, simple, repeating phrases and meters suggested by the concert works of Steve Reich or Philip Glass but less restrictive in the hands of 1990s composers like Thomas Newman (son of Alfred, having developed a major career of his own) and 2000s composers like Alexandre Desplat—somewhat linear music, not thematic but tonally bound; not entirely concentric in shape but circular in motion. Often these minimalist scores were given to synthesized instruments, causing critics to complain even more about their dehumanizing qualities. (Newman, for instance, has often recorded individual acoustic instruments one at a time then digitally combined them into layers of sound.) But since, as I have already said, it seems to be in the nature of the motion picture to accept almost any kind of tonal or metric background as natural, this sort of rolling nondetailed scoring has been used more and more against a wide range of movies, and since there were few, if any, match points to be met by the music in those films, these scores just unraveled in a line like a roll of wallpaper: screen music was being perceived as just the coloring on the walls, rather reminiscent of those very early silent film accompaniments. Gone were the days when the composer, intent on writing music that made its own sense, labored like a wordsmith to minutely shape the score to the drama onscreen while hopefully tying the characters and plot, theme and message of the film, to each scene. It seemed as though scoring was seldom narrative anymore; music was ambient and computer software made the sounds (Cooke, *History* 467–74; Doherty). And yet, true to history, this period, too, was already transitional in nature. In like manner, then, the career phases of each new soundtrack composer can be transitory, employing all kinds of music and every scoring style: descriptive, ambient, narrative, tuneful—a blend of influences and intuitions all at once—and, so long as they are well done, it is all welcome. After all, if soundtrack scoring can bring its own compositional variety and excitement while also effectively accompanying the story onscreen, then both media are well served; both the film and the viewer benefit.

Three generations of shrewd and sensitive composers, now, have worked in that cause. Thus, the craft of film scoring (only through the best practitioners, as I keep saying) has grown toward the character of an art. The cinema and, to a certain extent, the musical universe, has benefited from it, thanks to such composers of integrity as I've interviewed herein. Despite evolution, those three criteria for the best film scores, quoted before, have not changed over the years. A fourth characteristic would make a supreme film score: if that music were also, by virtue of the composer's originality and personal commitment to saying something sincere, self-expressive too. By then, film music would have come wonderfully close to what could be called a genuine genre all its own and the film composer honored as any other legit contemporary artist.

A Note about the Interviews

The composer conversations that follow were conducted over a span of decades—some in person, some via mail and email, some via long phone calls, most with combinations of all those contacts. Sometimes, for sake of clarity, I have run these various occasions together, when the topic was continuous—that is, for instance, combined without transition a composer's comments from an in-person session with comments made later in a follow-up letter. Only where it seemed important, then, have I identified the specific circumstance or occasion of a comment. Otherwise, I give precedence to the content of the conversation over its particular contexts. Additionally, as the Quick History section gives a general time line of the evolution of film music, I have divided the composer interviews of this book into three more specific historical periods: early, middle, and late, and summarized the musical styles there among classicism, modernism, and pluralism. Meanwhile, there are topic-specific essays interspersed throughout the interview sections that explore subjects such as choral music in films or the history of African American composers for the cinema, topics beyond the reach of the interview texts but worth suggesting as future subjects for study. Two veteran composers, exemplars of the field, whose careers span much of the given time line, receive separate opening and closing chapters.

By way of full disclosure, it is right to mention that some sections of these interviews have been published elsewhere in various magazines and small inside-the-industry journals, and some quotes from those pages may differ from what this book records—discrepancies due to new, more accurate transcriptions from the original audiotapes or editorial decisions made by past editors for their own journalistic reasons. This book represents the preferred versions. The generosity of these composers in granting permission for their original interviews, knowing they were to be quoted and wanting to promote film music in general, was and is greatly appreciated.

Finally, many of those topic-specific essays, called here "Interludes," I had written in response to special occasions—a composer anniversary or as acknowledgment of some award—so each is commemorative in that sense, rather than contemporary with this writing. For instance, what occasioned the career-summaries herein of composers Laurence Rosenthal or John Williams were birthday tributes, a ninetieth and an eighty-eighth, respectively. Those events are long gone, but the appreciative essays they inspired seem even more relevant, even overdue now, as chapters in a composer-centric book like this. A number of these interludes I wrote for the international music website *mfiles.co.uk*, a lively pub-like space for news and views about both film scoring and classical music. Site proprietor Jim Paterson is a composer and arranger who writes original music for games, television, and videos, and curates the *mfiles* site, which also provides music downloads for enthusiasts and for student/teacher use. Through a blog section of *mfiles* and the many essays and reviews on the site, Jim continues to give voice to all manner of composers, encouraging your average listener like myself to just generally "keep the music playing"—all kinds of music. Thanks to him for the generous permission to reprint my topical and once-timely, now salutary, interludes. Cuts and adaptations have been made.

One word about the composer dialogues themselves that follow: It's true they don't exactly "read" like the professional interviews of, say, a Hollywood newspaper reporter. Instead, as interviewer, I often prefaced my questions with a comment on the music or the film at hand, trying to suggest a context and, so, could seem to be leading the discussion when I should have just been posing a discreet question and waiting for the answer. But there is a reason I have called this book not "interviews with" but "conversations." I have wanted to reflect these composer encounters as they simply *were*: conversations not between equals but, let's say, between confederates—one the gifted professional composer, the other an eager amateur listener, mutual only in their shared enthusiasm for music.

Part One

A Veteran's Diary

1

Elmer Bernstein (1922–2004)

Figure 1. Elmer Bernstein. *Source*: Courtesy of the Estate of Elmer Bernstein.

A Hollywood history that runs from Cecil B. DeMille's stolid epic *The Ten Commandments* (1956) through the snarky comedy of *Ghostbusters* (1984), and even twenty years beyond that, would seem to be an ideal measure of both the evolution of film music and the versatility required of any musician entering the field of film composing. Elmer Bernstein is the man in question here, and even though he possessed such versatility as produced his successful fifty-year career, somehow he also maintained a consistent musical voice throughout many different film genres, never very far from his own personal refined version of Coplandesque Americana, whether he was scoring movie westerns like *The Magnificent Seven* (1960) and *The Comancheros* (1961), sultry southern morality plays like *Summer and Smoke* (1961) or *To Kill a Mockingbird* (1962), or odd chillers like *See No Evil* (1971) and *Saturn 3* (1980).

Even when he translated urban Americana into jazz-inflected scoring, writing alternately blaring and bluesy band charts, it still sounded like Bernstein. These were not just Copland reboots, then—there was always a Bernstein lyricism framing the jazz parts and, new to Hollywood scoring at the time, there was a distinctive emphasis on solo voicings—flute, piano, clarinet—that referenced chamber music: intimate elements in the midst of dramatic orchestral scoring.

He didn't start out as a composer, though; as a teen, he wanted to be noticed for his talent as a concert pianist studying under Henriette Michelson at the Juilliard School. So, he was sent to Israel Citkowitz for more than piano lessons: gradual grounding in musicology, theory, and harmony. Like so many others of that era, though, those seven years of fledgling classes and early recitals were interrupted by World War II. Among his duty for the Army Air Corps was service for the Media and Propaganda Division where he met the writer Millard Lampell and, together, they worked on promotional broadcasts for Armed Forces Radio. After hours, Lampell was active in a burgeoning underground movement touting American folk music—songs and singers of protest—and he brought the young Bernstein along to events. There, while Bernstein had his first experience arranging existing tunes for small, tight-harmony vocal groups, it was also his first contact with the politics of the late 1940s radical Left (see Wierzbicki 114–21).[1] That bunch never drifted as far downstream as the Communist Party of their day but was rather more interested in celebrating their repertoire of folk music, delighting in powerful protest songs and work songs. At the same time, Bernstein was finding a more general postwar political outlet of his own, writing radio music for various United Nations–sponsored programs—one of those, an audio documentary about the ongoing Arab-Israeli conflicts. Somehow, the program was overheard by film producer Sidney Buchman who contacted Bernstein, inviting him to come out to Hollywood to try his hand at dramatic screen scoring. Thus, Bernstein's first film score with distinctly American music was for Buchman's 1951 flick about college football, *Saturday's Hero*. A second featured definitely Coplandesque music for a horse race story, *Boots Malone*. A third—the first really distinctive Bernstein score—was the jittery, jazzy music to *Sudden Fear* in which star Joan Crawford discovered her husband trying to kill her. There, besides the broken nervous rhythms, we can hear those solo sounds of flute and cello making the suspense onscreen almost unbearably personal.

But just there, barely getting comfortable in Hollywood, with his career on the launch pad ready to be offered his first A-list film job, Bernstein suddenly found himself under congressional scrutiny and, therefore, unemployable. It was the era of political witch hunts in Washington: the vicious Commie-hunting crusaders of the radical Right in Congress, led by Senator Joe McCarthy (see Navasky 9–12; Ross 412–14).[2] It was their obvious ploy to accuse the most publicly recognizable figures first, bring in famous Hollywood names, and make them testify against any of their colleagues who might have ties to or sympathies for the Communist Party. News reports about the hearings, it was hoped by politicians, would then ruin a lot of Hollywood careers and, in the process of accusation, boost their own fortunes. Bernstein's association with the folk music crowd and his once having written music reviews for the Left-leaning *Daily Worker* newspaper made him suspect. Even though he was never a Communist follower nor was ever actually blacklisted for his associations, by the mid-1950s Bernstein did find himself graylisted so that, for the next couple of years, his resume of film scores was reduced to low-budget productions with laughable titles like *Cat Women of the Moon*, *Robot Monster*, *Miss Robinson Crusoe*, and *Never Wave at a WAC*. These were his penance for butting up against the political power-players of his day. Politically active folk singer Pete Seeger and associates suffered far more than he, being chased and surveilled by McCarthy and made to squirm. Yet, even they survived, especially into the 1960s resurgence of folk music in the recording industry.

Bernstein did not have to wait long, though. Fate nodded his way in the form of contact with two totally different Hollywood directors inquiring about his music services: the staid, conservative Cecil B. DeMille and the willfully progressive Otto Preminger, both cocksure and independent-minded executives, defiantly eager to step over the wall built around Bernstein and give him a chance. DeMille was already involved in producing the most expensive film anyone had seen, an officially reverent biblical epic on the life of Moses, *The Ten Commandments* with Charlton Heston and Yul Brynner. The veteran studio music man Victor Young was supposed to supply a dramatic score once the film was ready, but first they needed someone to compose and direct some quasi-Egyptian dance music for the royal court scenes. Bernstein was hired on a week-to-week basis to concoct those pieces. At the end of the allotted time, DeMille pronounced himself satisfied, both with this antique music and with his occasional side conferences with the articulate and enthusiastic young Elmer. When Victor Young proved to be too ill to start on the dramatic score (he would die within a few weeks), DeMille trusted his own instincts and offered the full score to Bernstein.

It was during those dicey weeks, with Bernstein still working on *The Ten Commandments*, that the other maverick director, Preminger, approached him asking about a totally different kind of scoring: dramatic jazz for a daring modern exposé about drug addiction, *Man with the Golden Arm* (1955). And he would have only twenty days to do the job. *Golden Arm* is not a jazz score per se, yet it perfectly blended dramatic orchestral writing with sharp sophisticated jazz elements: swaggering beats, blaring brass chords that shouted danger, countered by soulful sax or trumpet solos. Though not the cinema's first jazz-bound scoring behind a Hollywood film (see the "Quick History" section in the introduction to this volume), this was the first to grab public attention by virtue of its compelling motifs and personality. And what the public notices, Hollywood itself wants more of. Bernstein was off and running. From now on, he would enjoy a fairly steady career success, even for the next fifty years in the business, bothered only by occasional authoritarian or inarticulate directors, by a 1980s fad for replacing pieces of descriptive orchestral scoring with someone's rock song for publicity purposes, and by the constant threat, once you've had a certain success in one category, of typecasting. In Bernstein's case, as soon as his success with one jazz score was registered, the requests poured in for more jazz throughout the 1960s: *Walk on the Wild Side, The Sweet Smell of Success, The Rat Race*—likewise, when *The Magnificent Seven*'s theme became a popular horse-opera hit, Bernstein's Americana scoring was wanted everywhere: *Return of the Seven, Drango, The Hallelujah Trail*—and all those John Wayne westerns followed: *True Grit, The Sons of Katie Elder, Big Jake, Cahill U.S. Marshall, The Shootist*—all the way through the 1970s. And so, it would continue in the 1980s with a different genre, the sarcastic gag-comedy film. Though the composer for Moses would seem an unlikely choice to score a frat-boy farce like *Animal House*, Bernstein was given the assignment, being careful to underplay the laughs and comically overplay any tense scenes as though they were high drama. That was the joke.

Thus, for a time in the late seventies and early eighties, Bernstein became the court composer for lampooning slapstick comedy films, providing more exaggerated music to the satirical disaster film *Airplane*; a few sweet pop tunes for the summer camp farce *Meatballs*; melodic crescendos and mock-marches to the army farce *Stripes*; then some genuinely mystical sounds, catastrophic climaxes, and a playfully likeable main theme for the megahit comedy/mystery *Ghostbusters*, in which three flakey spook-hunters confront a ghost infestation in modern-day New York City. For Bernstein, though, the two positives he would associate with the *Ghostbusters* project were the chance to keep his name in the scoring forefront, and the introduction of a few electronic sounds in the orchestral palette. He was careful to keep his ear out for more sensitive, expressive, uncategorizable scoring jobs, though, too. In that regard, we have his gently amusing tribute to the innocence of girlhood, *The World of Henry Orient*; his swampy Deep South music for *God's Little Acre*; the historical British highwayman ballad in *Where's Jack?*; the steamy southern romanticism in *Summer and Smoke* about a fading southern belle scored with flamboyant violin solos, fluttering woodwind figures, and a large singing string section. The epic film *Hawaii* had a broadly symphonic seascape score, whereas *The Age of Innocence* featured a flowing Brahmsian sound and *The Grifters* had the dusky sound of film noir, all examples of Bernstein breaking away from any typecasting mold and yet remaining his own man. That early penchant for solo instruments and chamber ensembles is where many value him most: chamber scores with human insights like *To Kill a Mockingbird*, the ironic prison biography *Birdman of Alcatraz*, or the mood piece *Rambling Rose* and even smaller later scores like *My Left Foot* about the paraplegic writer Christy Brown, whose ensemble score included the ethereal electronic voice of the ondes martenot.[3]

The Bernstein catalogue of scores gathered a total of thirteen Academy Award nominations, though he won only once for an adaptation job in 1967, *Thoroughly Modern Millie*. His final nomination came the year before his death for the intentionally nostalgic music to a story set in the 1950s, *Far from Heaven*. Throughout, he was an articulate ambassador for the craft of the film composer: he even started a music society rerecording classic scores of the past—other people's music that had never been properly appreciated. Americana is certainly an unnecessarily limiting term for the overall Bernstein sound—for, although there are Copland ingredients to be heard in much of Bernstein's voice, I hear a definite Elmerness even more: lyrical, sympathetic music, aware of popular styles, but alert to classical grammar, with a strong sense of place but always personal and individualistic too. How to keep celebrating those qualities all the way from Moses's Mount Sinai to Atticus Finch's front porch; from the 1990s bleak film noir cityscape of *The Grifters* to the lonely 1920s women of a household in Georgia (*Rambling Rose*), is a lesson not only for any future film composers but any one of us listeners. In conversation, Bernstein proved to be as gregarious, articulate, and accessible as his music.

Interview with Elmer Bernstein

> ELMER BERNSTEIN: My career has been strange in one sense: on the one hand it has encompassed about every genre of film there is from old-fashioned melodramas to westerns, sophisticated comedies to sort of frat-boy farces, science fiction to childhood nostalgia—and yet I'm told, and I think it's true, that no matter what film genre I'm scoring or what style of music I'm using from standard symphonic to jazz to pop, that I have a consistent and recognizable sound.

JOHN CAPS: And I can imagine that consistency comes from your solid classical base of training—first as a hopeful concert pianist and then through at least four major teachers before you ever thought of doing films.

EB: And much of that training was before I had even considered composing at all.

JC: They were admittedly Americana influences, though, weren't they? Copland was one, and the orchestrator Roger Sessions . . .

EB: Well, technically I wasn't taught by Copland. My piano teacher at the time I was eleven or twelve just brought me to meet him and perform some little something for him and then said, Do you think he has any talent? And Copland, who was about thirty then, said something like, "Well, how should I know? Get him some more serious lessons"—meaning more specific lessons. And so, over the teenage years, I got training in harmony, counterpoint, and composition. You're right; that laid a solid musical base early on and gave me more strength and consistency later when I did decide to concentrate on composing instead of concertizing.

JC: And what would all those very formal composition teachers have thought if you'd said back then, I think I'll become a film composer?

EB: Ha, well, on the one hand, of course, my path wasn't so simple. I came by steps into screen music and, on the other hand, movie scoring per se had a different reputation in those days. Major composers like Prokofiev and Walton were doing quite substantial scores for the cinema, so it had a certain respectability then—not just a commercial or pop music stigma. Copland himself, of course, did a handful of very fine scores for films in the thirties and forties. So, I think those teachers that I had, while they might at first want to discourage the idea of my doing so-called background music for films, that they would at least respect the best scores I've been able to do in the medium and understand what the possibilities are.

JC: One negative difference between the average film score and, let's say, a major classical concert work is not necessarily the difference in complexity or originality, but the continuity that's possible in a symphony or sonata but not so likely in a film score that, let's face it, proceeds by starts and stops—short, isolated music cues spaced throughout a film. Talk about the musicology of a film score; whether it's possible for all those individual music cues to hang together and develop like a piece of concert music.

EB: Not like a piece of concert music, no. They're not supposed to. This is interesting. First, the composer has to decide among three things: what kind of music does this particular film story need: formal classical music or colloquial sounds or pop tunes; big full sound or intimate sound? Then, what instrumentation? Then, how is music to be strung throughout the film: are the individual cues to be placed evenly like page-turners through the narrative or is music going to underline the setting or the era of the story? Or is it just there in the background to provide a general atmosphere of tension or nostalgia or ethnicity? You see? One kind of score may participate in the storytelling by underlining the action; another kind of score may just be setting the scene. Most scores do both. Some scores are specific enough and interactive enough to actually comment on the characters within a story. But that's very rare—not only because it takes a dedicated and gifted composer, but because not many films will leave that much room for a music score to contribute.

JC: Yes; most films are just hoping to tell a clear story and don't want music to get in the way, anyhow, aren't most directors suspicious of any composer who might have ambitions of "taking over my film"?

EB: Oh, you're not kidding. Absolutely. Obviously, I prefer to have someone (and sometimes it's the director; sometimes the producer who takes the lead on this) . . . someone who leaves me alone completely or whose discussions are conceptual in nature rather than prescriptive or, as you say, coercive. What I actually prefer is to find a boss on each film who has definite, informed opinions about things and, mind you, the operative word is "informed." I prefer that to somebody who is vague and is involved on an uninformed basis: that's very difficult to deal with. But if a producer has thoughtful opinions, you can either agree or find a way to disagree, also in very definitive ways, and come to some conclusion. The bad times start when the boss thinks he or she knows a lot about music but can't articulate any of it; or when they've heard some score in someone else's film or a piece of classical music and they say they want "something like that, only different."

JC: Of course, the intention of a good score, even an assertive one, is not to "take over" such a film, but, in those rare cases if the film seems to warrant it, to lift the film up onto a special level where story and cinema and music are all streaming together.

EB: Absolutely. And I've had a few like that. But only when collaborating with those special directors—folks like Robert Mulligan[4] and Martin Scorsese and Martha Coolidge[5] and, strangely enough from way back, Cecil B. DeMille. I say "strange" because he was, y'know, a very old-fashioned and conservative fellow, but once he had understood what your plans were for the score and he could generally agree that your goals were in line with his own, he became very supportive and friendly and, in a couple of instances, actually taught me a thing or two about scoring.

JC: Well, before I ask about some of your scores, let me go back to your beginnings for a little context here; even before you worked for DeMille when, as a very young man, you were—or thought you were—preparing to be a concert pianist. This would have been circa the 1940s.

EB: Yes, as early as 1940 I was giving recitals at the Walden School in New York of Debussy and Chopin and by the late forties giving actual concerts—that whole period, then, being interrupted, of course, by World War II. During the war, I was working sometimes for Armed Forces Radio. And they knew I was a musician; so sometimes I did some little arrangements of special music for propaganda radio shows. That led to doing a little composing for them of, you know, descriptive music behind documentary programming. And anyway, through a combination of friends and strangers, I heard about this little low-budget movie to be made out in Hollywood—a football movie called *Saturday's Hero*—and someone said that I ought to try my hand at narrative music, so-called "movie music," after the war. And so, with no great plan or confidence but just a sort of "sounds like fun" mindset, I went out west to Hollywood. And that was my first experience putting music to a soundtrack. That was in the 1950–1951 period: still what you could call the movie studio period where, for instance at MGM studios or Warner Bros., you were working for that studio's music director and he, in a sense, guided you and, if necessary, protected you from any outside interference.

JC: And what's an example of interference for a film composer?

EB: Well, it's what happens so often today where you are no longer working with a musically knowledgeable music director on a film—you're at the mercy of a committee made up of finance men, sponsors, ad execs, the script writer's cousin, and of course, the producer. Everyone has a say. Half of them are only open to the kind of music they happen to like; the other half mainly want a music score that can be exploited along with the movie—a best-selling song, for instance, would be something they ask for.[6] I am sounding bitter here, but it does happen a lot and always did. Naturally, the thoughtful, organic, narrative orchestral music score is received very skeptically in that atmosphere. But attitudes change. When I was just starting out, the field was actually opening up to new sounds and styles. Even jazz was making itself known on soundtracks, which we can discuss. In the sixties, to some extent, pop songs in films became the fad, whereas in the seventies, because of the surprising success of the Williams scores—big symphonic scores for sci-fi pictures primarily—the pendulum swung back in favor of orchestral alternatives.

JC: The first score that I'd consider distinctively Bernsteinian was probably *Sudden Fear* (1952)—a score with all kinds of sharp agitated accents, dotted rhythms, solo and combo scoring, not quite avant-garde and not quite jazzy but drawing from each.

EB: Yes, that was kind of the first thing I did that got noticed, that got some mention in the press. But then, well, so-called McCarthyism hit and, oh, brother, look out!

JC: Yes, and you somehow got tangled up in . . . well, at least the latter stages of . . . that political witch hunt where certain US senators, puffing themselves up, decided that an easy road to fame was to start accusing public figures of being soft on Communism . . .

EB: And many careers all over the country, and in Hollywood particularly (perhaps because of the notoriety to be exploited there) were ruined just by the power of accusation—in fact, just by the power of insinuation: they didn't even have to have evidence; just insinuation of guilt was enough to ruin a person.

JC: You were not actually blacklisted like some.

EB: I was sort of graylisted, partly because my case came toward the end of that period and partly because they didn't consider me important enough to pursue.

JC: But why you, at all?

EB: Well, as you and I have discussed before, I had been involved in studying American folk music—folk songs and folk singers. Of course, after the war the subject of folk music became a well-known thing as people like Pete Seeger and Burl Ives and groups like the Weavers brought it into the general pop culture. But before that, it was a very exotic study for anyone to be doing. It was a province that was peopled by either eccentric hobbyists who liked collecting obscure Americana, or wanna-be Communists who liked folk music's political stance and anticapitalist messages.[7] And while I was certainly no Communist, there were aspects of both that I was sympathetic with. So, the upshot was that although legally or personally, I didn't suffer—I never, for instance, was called before the HUAC—my career did suffer. No studios would hire me. So that's the period when I was reduced to scoring anything that came along. And what came along were these sort of bargain-basement fantasy films—early sci-fi films made for next to nothing and headed for drive-in movie screens or matinee showings. Things with titles like *Cat Women of the Moon* and *Robot Monster*. What's interesting about those is that, because they were so obscure and ultimately so silly, I felt freer to experiment with their scoring, introducing elements like electronic instruments and semi-advanced . . . well, let's just say unusual . . . composition. And with exercises like those, I was able to survive and outlast the awful McCarthy period. But what bailed me out finally and let me back into the studios for a more legitimate career, it turned out, was one old veteran of that system who was so independent in spirit (though very conservative in politics and business) that he sort of operated above the system. That was Cecil B. DeMille.

JC: He first just needed a piece of believable Egyptian dance music for one scene in *The Ten Commandments*, didn't he?

EB: Yes, and in spite of his reputation for autocratic perfectionism and rages toward incompetence, he was perfectly polite with me initially. He said that, although nothing is known about true Egyptian court music of the biblical era, what he wanted was something that didn't offend our expectations: something like Puccini had done, he said, when writing Japanese leitmotifs for *Madame Butterfly*. I said I would try and I guess he liked the modesty of that and he accepted what I came up with and let me try other minor scenes as well. It wasn't all wonderful, though; I got yelled at for a certain chant I had written that he considered all wrong. But eventually, DeMille drew me aside and asked me to develop a number of character themes for the film—music that would represent Moses or Nefertiti or Rameses—and then, how each theme might change under different circumstances: Moses returning from Mount Sinai, for instance? Anyway, that exam-like session lasted two hours and with enough successful bits of scoring, I was eventually installed to do the whole dramatic score for *The Ten Commandments*. And he pronounced himself pleased. His shrewdness in being able to tell what works was something I learned from him, even though he wasn't very verbally communicative. Another lesson I learned came during that film's big exodus scene: the people of Israel heading out into the wilderness by the thousands. I had scored the sight of this mass exodus with a slow, dignified processional kind of music as befits the historical importance of the scene. Well, Mr. DeMille thought this was terrible. He hated it. And it was not until I went back and reimagined that scene as needing triumphant music, a joyous marching forth from bondage of the Hebrew people, that I saw how film music worked. Anyway, that was the film and the score that set me back in contention as a film scorer. And pretty much at the same time, I was being "shopped" by another doggedly independent producer-director from the exact opposite side of the political spectrum, the iconoclastic Otto Preminger. Now, *there* was a bold, brash character from Germany who didn't mind shaking things up. Don't forget he had already directed films like *Laura* about an obsession, *The Moon Is Blue* (1953) about seduction techniques, and *Carmen Jones* (1954) with an all-black cast. Now here comes *The Man with the Golden Arm,* not only set in a sleazy world of jazz clubs but a story about drug addiction.

JC: It's no surprise that you thought of a jazzy score for such a picture, but I wonder, first, if Preminger had fixed rules about the score he wanted, like the edicts DeMille had given you and, second, whether you had any experience with writing jazz before that time.

EB: I had practically no experience with jazz although my father had been a big jazz aficionado. So, I was aware of the jazz vocabulary and gestures and spirit but, in my writing, I had never scored something that left room for, and actually supported, any real jazz improvisation—improv being the real essence of jazz. Preminger, to his credit, just said whatever you think is best, just go do it.

JC: But, correct me if I'm wrong, in spite of its blaring jazz themes and reliance on hard beats, I don't think of this as a jazz score per se: it's a regular dramatic score that then resorts to jazz band climaxes.

EB: You're absolutely right; it's not technically a jazz score. I wrote in fairly standard dramatic orchestral terms for the story of this guy, played by Frank Sinatra who, fresh from jail, wants to make it as a jazz drummer but has this drug addiction getting the better of him. So, it was imperative to score those harrowing moments of his struggle with some screaming brass jazz chords in some complex minor keys and some soulful, bluesy trumpet improvs, some nervous drumming . . . and, elsewhere, to invoke the loneliness and frustration of the character through blues and some slow plodding rhythms (the walking bass) from the jazz ensemble that had been hired separate from the dramatic orchestra. As I said, I had no experience writing effectively for jazz players, but I did know the language of jazz, the vocabulary. And so, I wrote out all the jazz sequences and basically scored them as I heard them in my imagination, but then for more authenticity (as well as for interacting with the jazz musicians themselves) I brought in a real jazz arranger, Shorty Rogers.[8] And he was the perfect intermediary, because he had the respect of those jazzmen and yet he could speak very quietly and knowledgably with me in compositional terms about how to blend the classical parts of the score with the breakout jazz. So, it was a real breakout score for me and really gave me a reputation for having modern chops and for versatility. After all, if the same guy could score Moses and Sinatra, he should be good for anything!

JC: Then, of course, you experienced for the first time that other Hollywood cliché that follows success: typecasting. You started to get only jazz-oriented scoring assignments for a while.

EB: Yes, it happened a lot in my career. In this case, after *Golden Arm* came a whole line of films wanting the same sort of sleazy or corrupted kinds of jazzish scoring. *The Sweet Smell of Success* (1957) was about greed and graft and 1950s New York City nightlife and got a hard-edged jazz score, a little more controlled in its harmonics because it was about corrupt big business, not about back rooms in jazz clubs. *The Rat Race* (1960) had some much softer jazzy elements to it, similarly set in New York City but that was a kind of comedy drama. *Walk on the Wild Side*, however, had a widely swaggering kind of score because it was set way down south in New Orleans—deep southern jazz (1962). Even then, I was aware of the unfortunate cliché where jazz was always associated with crime and wrongdoing. But that's what the films were saying and so I had to score them appropriately, so most of my surviving jazz of the period is pretty scowling, pretty mordent.

JC: One of my favorite areas of typecasting for you is the unofficial series of films and film scores set in a sort of decadent southern milieu.

EB: How do you mean?

JC: All those steamy, sultry, southern summertime films and scores—the decadent Tennessee Williams world of fading dowagers and decaying plantations and tortured lovers and, in the music scores, either lush humid harmonies or shuffling rhythms with clarinet and banjo . . .

EB: Oh, I see, I see; well, of course, there were a slew of those films at one time . . .

JC: To my mind, you seemed to have an especial affinity for them. *God's Little Acre* (1958) was probably the first and the most blatantly "localized." The Erskine Caldwell story of a rowdy, lusty Georgia family—a story where the setting plays a role equal to the actors and where the score seems equal with them, too. Do you remember that one?

EB: Oh, yes, very well.

JC: Did you come in with that whole rural, southern sound in your head?

EB: Oh, absolutely, yes.

JC: It sounds authentic . . . makes me think very much of poor rural shacks and dirt roads and hardscrabble fields . . .

EB: I think, John, I would attribute that to that solid grounding I had in Americana folk music that we talked about. That experience carried over into what you're calling this southern style. *God's Little Acre* is certainly an entry in that family of scores. Very recently I finished a film called *The Great Santini* (1979)[9] about an ex-Marine living in the south who's kind of lost outside the military world he's used to and so he takes it out on his young son; and there's a little tune in that which is going to sound very folkish—very Americana—although actually there isn't a single folk instrument in the orchestra; it'll sound like an old banjo tune. And, oddly enough, analyzing it now after the fact, I didn't really realize I was doing it until you got me thinking in this way. Again . . . my folk music grounding.

JC: Your Americana sound is understandable just from the period in which you came of age, what with your brush with Copland and the American symphonists that were big at that time—Roy Harris and William Schuman[10]—your folk music concentration must have come out of that . . . but also maybe from your attraction to the left-wing politics associated with it?

EB: Yes, absolutely. I was still in school. I don't remember how it started. I think I heard by accident some record of the Library of Congress series of historical discs . . . or maybe it was through a friend . . . oh, I know what it was: yes, I had a friend who played banjo and it was the first time I had ever seen a five-string banjo. And he played extraordinary things on it. He used to play a tune about East Virginia called "Come All Ye Fair and Tender Maidens," which was a really ancient American folk tune, and I was fascinated by the culture so I started to really get into it.

JC: Are those lush chromatic tunes and waltzes that I hear in these southern scores part of that background too?

EB: Well, those chromatic waltzes, you'll find I use them . . . they're not really indigenous to the American scene . . . if anything, they feel sort of French to me . . . But they're a way to express that sort of "perfumed decadence" that you hinted at before in the Tennessee Williams version of the south.

JC: In *God's Little Acre*, the "Peach Tree Valley Waltz" is the perfect example of the swirling chromatic waltz that conjures up the south to me. And then, soon after that film, the whole score to *Summer and Smoke* is in this southern decadence "family"—story of a lonely spinster in a Mississippi town circa 1916.

EB: Yes, that's rather the perfect example of that kind of score.

JC: Both the southern milieu and the lush large string orchestra; the definitive Tennessee Williams sound. His plays though, we think of as Americana and yet what they really were is little European chamber pieces.

EB: You're quite right; absolutely right. And I think of *Summer and Smoke* as a rather unique score in my career.

JC: How so?

EB: I never wrote another quite like it. There's a lot more detail in that score than I ordinarily do. I usually use bolder strokes whereas that score is more tentative . . .

JC: You're talking about all the nervous details, the impulsive arpeggios, and the fluttering woodwinds up and down the scale to evoke the flighty dowager character of Alma . . .

EB: Exactly. And you find that even when that big tune is going, that big sort of passionate tune, inside of the tune, the figures are turning and turning with a restless quality. I don't think I've ever written so many notes in my life. But it was all keyed, as you say, to the character of Alma. Strangely enough, although southerners have continually told me that the score sounds southern to them, I must say that there is something under the conscious level that makes it that way. I certainly didn't try.

JC: There's a frustrated romantic quality to it all, somewhat reminiscent of that old Bernard Herrmann score for *The Ghost and Mrs. Muir* (1947), both of them expressing on the one hand a love affair that can't be fulfilled and, on the other hand, a strong sense of locale, of setting. And, of course, they both have all those swirling orchestral details—*Mrs. Muir* as a seascape and *Smoke* as a steamy summerscape.

EB: Well, now you're onto something there. They're not dissimilar in some ways. And it's interesting that you should mention *The Ghost and Mrs. Muir* because that's probably my favorite Herrmann score. I have a tremendous emotional reaction to that score but, I never realized, it's probably because I have some affinity to it through my own work.

JC: Before we leave discussion of that "southern family" of scores in your catalogue, whereas *Summer and Smoke* must be the most flamboyant of them, surely the most subtle, because it incorporates both attention to the southern setting and a focused attention on character, is *To Kill a Mockingbird*.

EB: Ah, yes, well, there, I guess you're right to relate that film and its music to the southern milieu. That's certainly in there, first with the choice of sort of shuffling rural rhythms and gestures in the score and certainly with a very real devotion to at least the tonal tradition of southern flavored gospel music. There, the solo piano and flute, for instance, provide the intimate beginnings of character delineation while strings and brass, as separate units, provide the dramatic setting—this small Alabama town whose recluse racist citizens oppose the black man accused of a local rape and threaten the white lawyer and his young children pledged to defend the black man. So, there's a score that has to perform on several different levels: the rural setting, the nostalgia (since the little girl in the film who's remembering how her lawyer father stood up for the defendant is supposedly narrating the tale from an adult perspective), then the threat of violence that is usually scored by having that same brass unit that's been helping to illustrate the small town suddenly violently breaking out in dissonant and threatening tutti with broken time signatures. But mainly, and this is the great distinction in that score and the element that was my one important contribution to that film, I figured out that what I wanted to illustrate with my music was the magic of a child's world.

After all, the whole story was being told through the eyes of the little girl, Scout, and so the music score particularly needed to get behind her, support her, and in a sense, be her. So, right from the beginning where, on the soundtrack, we hear a little girl at play, humming gently to herself, I started the score with a simple sort of lullaby, tender and nostalgic played by one hand on the piano, then filling in with sparse, rather tentative orchestration from solo winds, gradually swelling to the full orchestra on that same tune, giving it a broader emotion than just the little girl's POV, then returning to the intimacy of the piano. That was the Main Title sequence, setting you up for the whole narrative to come.

JC: And even though the children are aware of the local violence, they are actually more involved worrying about a mysterious spooky neighbor next door—and you score that with a little minor-key piano arpeggio that drifts into a sort of mystical waltz for the piano and a piccolo and sliding strings . . .

EB: Yes, that's that ongoing make-believe world of the child; a little spooky, shadowy fear that occupies their attentions, in spite of all the much more real political turmoil going on all around them.

JC: And in the end, when Scout realizes that the spooky neighbor next door was really the guy who saved her when the town villain was about to do her harm, the score uses a series of descending chords from the strings, almost a chamber sound, that have a real feeling of benediction there. Do you remember the moment at all?

EB: Yes, I know it well. [Plays the chords on a keyboard at hand.] Like that? Yes, that was very, very special to me. It was like a slow curtain coming down at the end of a play or an opera. It's very difficult to say much more about it because it was a very internal, personal reaction. It does have the feeling of benediction, yes. I love that part.

JC: And that sensitivity, particularly to a child's point of view, you've applied to a number of other films as well. You wouldn't think that a comedy film like *The World of Henry Orient* (1964), with Peter Sellers as a comically eccentric concert pianist who spends more time chasing married women than piano-practicing, is actually focused on two fourteen-year-old girls who have a crush on him.

EB: Yes, and I approached *Henry Orient* not as a comedy at all but as a really gentle, sweet story, a children/people story. Again, here, the main theme is quite innocent with thirds and fifths, easily played on a piano to give the feeling of a child's piano exercise but then also sort of broken up by alternating meters and little unexpected pauses. It is, as you say, another score sensitive to the child's world in a loving and sympathetic way. And yet, I also felt the need to somehow acknowledge the Sellers character as well, to make the score at least aware that there's a farcical element to the film—for instance, I speeded things up in one place and technically took things up an octave, just to try and admit Sellers's wackiness in the scoring a little bit; to acknowledge that it was a comedy, because everything else was so low key. But, yes, there's another child-centered score.

JC: Can you say a little about scoring comedy films. It has to be a tricky assignment. You can err so easily in the direction of overstatement—scoring like a cartoon score. As Henry Mancini has put it, music that mimics a gag onscreen absolutely squashes it (because it's redundant), unless they're going for exaggeration on purpose.

EB: Ah, yes, well, that's a very big question. I think if you interfere with the basic humor of a situation, you could hurt it and there are many different ways of interfering. One way is to simply write the wrong kind of music but, I mean, that would just be inept. But another way, as Henry has indicated to you, is to make musical jokes while the joke is already happening onscreen. And we were speaking before about the subject of the film composer becoming typecast for a certain type of score. Well, speaking of comedy films, it seems that lately that's the genre people have begun to associate with me—not the gentle humane comedies like *Henry Orient* but the out-and-out slapstick films that I happen to have scored. Because after the success of the sort of frat-boy comedies that I scored in the eighties like *Animal House, Meatballs, Airplane, Trading Places*, suddenly I've become the comedy composer. I'm being offered all these comedy films now. So, it runs in cycles. But even those films require different kinds of scoring from one another. For instance, John Landis was a school friend of my son Peter and that's how come I was brought in on *National Lampoon's Animal House* and what was wanted there, and on *Airplane*, was a really exaggerated kind of scoring—scoring that would prove humorous because it was written as a satire on seriousness: that is, I played all the big clichéd disaster-film crescendos, the builds and tremolos and orchestral explosions, as a way of making fun of them in this farcical world of these crude comedies. And it worked, I think; I think the films are funnier for the out-and-out exaggeration from the soundtracks. Overstatement, as long as it's obviously intentional, can be funny. Now in *Meatballs*, which was a slapstick summer camp comedy at a sort of junior high school level, you additionally had a sincere warm friendship developing between one counselor and one boy who's a camper, and that seemed to call for a more melodic approach in the scoring; in this case, a "friendship" song that's actually sung in the film and, in a later scene, is adapted to cover a tense foot race sequence, which the boy wins in the end. But it's gratifying to be part of something like that; to see people having a good time because of the comedy, but then feeling something like affection for the characters with your music coaxing them along. Or there's one scene in *Animal House* that I got such a kick out of having been a part of: when John Belushi makes that big speech, rousing everyone after being down. Anybody who knows anything about film scoring recognizes the role that music played in the success of that sequence. It's kind of fun to be part of that.

JC: Music contributed a whole lot to the success of the big-budget comedy *Ghostbusters*. There, you had a new generation of sly, hip comics and yet there's an element in the film that wants to be a little concerned about ghosts on the loose. I mean, they just might be real; just might be dangerous. So, you've got suspense elements to score and yet you have to sound cool as well; you have to prove that you get the joke. That's gotta be fun, too; but also tricky for a composer.

EB: Well, yes, on both counts. You had a real story there that needed some narrative attention from the score. But the first task was to set the tone, and you do that through choice of orchestration and construction of themes. I think we had a big orchestra of seventy players there, supplemented by the very old electronic instrument the ondes martenot and the relatively new Yamaha DX-7 for the spooky aspects of the film. But with those forces and a main theme that was both mysterious and playful, I could then have a field day of all kinds of scoring—big mock-crescendos when disaster looms, wafting chromatic passages when the ghostly spiritual realm floats into the room, a tin piano playing a sort of cakewalk tune, comic sneaking music . . . just about everything worked in that film because it was all carried along, even the differing comedy styles of the cast, by the compelling story line and the special effects. The only caveat for me was that I had intended that the film would rely more on the main tune I had written, but then the producers became enamored of the sort of rap song that they got from Ray Parker Jr. You know the rap lyric: "There's something strange in the neighborhood; who you gonna call? Ghostbusters!" And of course, that rap became a very successful ambassador for the film, for bringing people into the theaters and reminding them of the film afterward. And I have to admit, it's a perfect vehicle. I like it. Just a little disappointment that part of the score was jettisoned for a pop record. But that happens more and more these days. At least this type of a comedy/thriller film led me away from the more confining comedy typecasting and more different kinds of film became available to me.

JC: Before leaving typecasting, though, talk a bit about the genre you are even more associated with: the western film genre. *The Magnificent Seven*, one of the most famous scores of any kind, was the start of the Bernstein western scoring blitz!

EB: There was one before that, actually. The Henry Fonda film *The Tin Star* (1957). But, yes, *The Magnificent Seven* put me in people's minds when they had a western to score. It's a very rhythm-driven score and, when the picture lagged a bit, the music score was there to gallop for it. In a sense, it wasn't a traditional western score simply because it had all those Tex-Mex elements in it; it was a border-town western. But all those elements together, the strong confident theme, the constant rhythm, the ethnic interest that included both high energy accented chase music and a quiet sort of hacienda tune, made for a memorable score—one of those rare examples where people remember the film to this day at least as much for the music as for the story itself.

JC: And one of those people who noticed was John Wayne because he then hired you to do one western after another for him, or at least his people did.

EB: His people, probably; but, yes, there were a lot of them in the sixties and seventies: *Big Jake*, *Cahill U.S. Marshall*, *True Grit* . . . One of the best was *The Comancheros* where I probably said everything I had to say about the American west, mixed with a little Indian lore. But there were others starring the Duke, each with a slight twist: *The Sons of Katie Elder* (1965) with Martha Hyer as a frontier woman so that the score had some more lyrical moments, or John Wayne's final western, *The Shootist* (1976), appropriately enough about an aging gunfighter, where I tried to bring a more self-reflective tone to the thing, really only just referencing the typical western score milieu as if it were fading away along with this character's life. But, yes, doing that many scores of the same genre, not right in a row but right in a decade or so . . . that was certainly a kind of typecasting.

JC: Can you say what you try to feature most in a typical western score—where your attention goes?

EB: Well, interestingly enough, I've always found that western films, and therefore western film scores, usually end up being about the landscape. A western usually has stock characters you don't care about that much, but you do remember the landscape: the Old West.

JC: Finally, lest it seem like you've been a plug-in composer, just working in a few fixed genres over the years, there are a number of major stand-alone films you've scored quite uniquely, each with its own sound. The big budget three-hour epic *Hawaii* (1966) from a James Michener novel is one.

EB: That was certainly satisfying to score. One found, in the initial research, that Hawaii itself really had no indigenous music of its own that one could work from. It was a mixture, quite logically, of Chinese and Japanese influences with some tropical or island rhythms from who knows where. And, of course, a lot of it was produced by rhythm instruments—drums and gourds and logs—none of which were tonal. So, I found myself having to invent a pastiche of tonality that could sound historically proper and yet would avoid the sort of touristy Hawaiian sound—the hula sound—that would have been instantly fatal to the veracity of the whole film. The original novel, remember, covered the period from 1800 when the islands were first being colonized by Western civilization and preachers. It was a good score, I think, and way outside any of the typecasting we've been talking about.

JC: Even farther out is the sort of avant-garde score to the space adventure *Saturn 3*.

EB: A strange film there, about space travelers bothered by a sex-starved robot!

JC: Full circle back to *Cat Women of the Moon*.

EB: Ha, well; but this time wanting to be serious. But, come to think of it, like in *Cat Women*, I felt permission, because of the outlandishness of the plot, to experiment outside the box—in this case, I'm using very largely improvisational techniques through a number of different kinds of orchestras. One consists of four piccolos, four bass flutes, one soprano singer, four bass singers, four harps, organ, eight cellos, four basses. One of the other orchestras consists of nothing but various percussion instruments. So, I give this as an example to illustrate the fact that the situation in Hollywood scoring is somewhat looser now than it's been for some time. I mean, in spite of our talking about fixed genres of films and scores, I think soundtrack scoring is getting more attention than ever before and so filmmakers and audiences are interested to sample more kinds of things. I think we can thank careers like Henry Mancini in the 1960s and John Williams in the 1970s for making the public, and therefore the producers, more aware of film music and, in consequence, we as working composers can become more daring.

Part II

From the Golden Age

2

Miklós Rózsa (1907–1995)

Orthodoxy

Figure 2. Miklós Rózsa. *Source*: Courtesy of the Film Music Society.

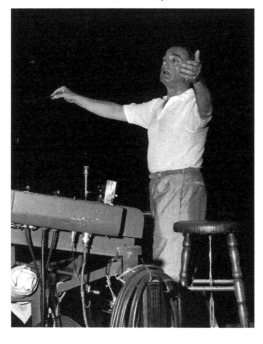

Dr. Rózsa tellingly titled his autobiography *Double Life*,[1] admitting that, although he had begun his career as a distinguished classical composer (a violin concerto for Heifetz; the *Theme, Variations and Finale, op. 13*, which figured importantly in Leonard Bernstein's premiere as a conductor), he would end it more famously as a distinguished film composer. The danger of a history like that was that he be judged too serious for commercial Hollywood, but not serious enough for the concert hall, a distinguished but incurable romantic in an ironic age. He studied in Budapest with Bartók and Kodály, then in Leipzig with Hermann Grabner, moved to Paris in 1932, then to London in 1935 in order to work on the successful ballet score *Hungaria* for the Markova-Dolin dance company. While in London, he met film director Jacques Feyder,[2] who had an idea, on hearing Rózsa's ballet: this guy should be composing for the movies.

Rózsa took eagerly to the new medium of screen drama, contributing colorful scores to two adventure movies from the late 1930s, *Knight without Armor* and *The Four Feathers*. It helped that the producer of those films was his compatriot Hungarian Alexander Korda.[3] And when, in 1939, Britain and all of Europe could feel the war coming on, Korda moved his whole production company to Hollywood USA, and Rózsa joined them there to begin work on their current film production, an exotic fantasy film, *Thief of Bagdad* (1940), which would be full of Oscar-winning special effects, an iconic villain played by the German émigré Conrad Veidt, an authentic Indian maharajah's boy servant turned child star, Sabu[4]—and a conspicuously colorful music score (that one critic called "a symphony accompanied by a movie") from Miklos Rózsa. Thus began a period of several exotica movie scores from the composer including *Sahara*, *Five Graves to Cairo* from 1943, and best of all, *The Jungle Book* (1942). There was passion in these scores, even though his typical tonality and orchestrations were somewhat thick and heavy and, when he scored a subsequent string of modern melodramas for Billy Wilder like *Double Indemnity* (1944) or *A Double Life* (1945), both about murder and subterfuge, or *The Lost Weekend* (1945) about alcoholism, he could sound very dark indeed.

His scoring proved especially expressive when tackling character studies in films like *Spellbound* (1945) for Hitchcock with its popular concerto theme, *Madame Bovary* (1949) with its detailed narrative score charting the emotional crisis of its nineteenth-century heroine, or *Lust for Life* (1956) charting the psychotic crisis of the painter Vincent van

Gogh. Rózsa's vivid settings for all these tortured souls and the way in which he framed them represented a kind of forthright musical portraiture—an old-fashioned melodramatic language that was natural to him but that would not have been appropriate (or respected) had he written his twentieth-century pure concert music in the same way. He realized that. And, indeed, his concert works of these same years were more stringent, sometimes sounding like early Bartók, sometimes neoclassical. But that did not, in any way, delegitimize all the romantic, exotic, melodic capital he also wanted to spend, so why not give it to the movies, even at the risk of leading a double life?

Throughout his fifties, Rózsa garnered a whole new kind of fame for the unofficial series of historical films he was hired to score: biblical tales like *Sodom and Gomorrah* (1962) or *King of Kings* (1961); storybook epics like *Knights of the Round Table* (1953), *Quo Vadis* (1951), *El Cid* (1961), and the Oscar-winning *Ben-Hur* (1959), although some critics squinted at him, noting that although he claimed to do extensive research into each historical period before beginning on these scores, they always ended up sounding a lot more like Magyar Hungarian music than like ancient Rome or El Cid's Spain. Still, this music was often the best part of these films and the conviction with which these scores were offered was compelling. Even into the 1970s, Rózsa was (a) willing to try new things such as his graceful French piano score to Alain Resnais's character study, *Providence* (1977), about a writer's last days, or (b) willing to reach backward toward the antique style of a parlor game to score the eccentric mystery fantasy film *Time After Time* (1979), which pitted H. G. Wells against Jack the Ripper.

It may be that Rózsa always felt a bit guilty about living in Hollywood, frequenting studios instead of conservatories, and a bit of that discontent in the form of crustiness comes out in my correspondence with him as he complains about the state of film composition in general in his latter days, a music trend that was being distracted by a preference for pop tunes in place of formal orchestral scoring and, as he would see it, movies with plots that were more frivolous than chivalrous.

None the less, almost all of his scores are solid and honest: his ecstatic dance music for the waltz scene in *Madame Bovary* or for Salome's orgy in *King of Kings* is thrilling stuff; his reprise of the main theme when Sabu rejoins his jungle home in *The Jungle Book*, or when Judah encounters the Christ in *Ben-Hur*, are genuinely moving soundtrack bits. Rózsa's legacy can be heard in the general influence he left on film scores like John Williams's *Star Wars* and in the specific lessons he taught through college classes attended by future masters like Jerry Goldsmith.

My contact with Rózsa was through a phone conversation and then a series of letters, usually written on that tissue-thin airmail paper from his Italian villa retreat—ever the cosmopolitan aesthete having come to terms, long ago, with whatever double life there was to be had.

Interview with Miklós Rózsa

JOHN CAPS: The title of your autobiography, *Double Life*, references both a famous melodramatic film for which you wrote the score *and* your own personal situation caught, as it were, between two musical worlds—equally famed for your concert works *and* your colorful film music starting in 1937 and encompassing famous films like *Thief of Bagdad*, *Asphalt Jungle*, *The Jungle Book*, *Spellbound*, and biography films of everyone from Julius Caesar to Vincent van Gogh to Jesus! How can one balance two such different, and sometimes deeply opposed, worlds?

MIKLÓS RÓZSA: By not seeing them as opposites. To me, it shouldn't matter for what or for whom I am writing music; it is my music in any case. If one disrespects movie scoring because it is a commercial field and because one is given the subject matter ahead of time and told to conform to the needs of the screen, then one is definitely in trouble and there will be a difference between what he turns out for a soundtrack and what he writes for the concert hall. But the sincere artist, the true composer, will do his best in response to any commission. Although my approach to widely different film subjects might have been different, I could never write (nor did I want to) any other music but my own. If one has a style, this is the only way to follow self-expression. Berlioz said that he changed his style for every new work—but I say that he only thought he changed.

Whether it is his *Roman Carnival Overture*, *Romeo and Juliet*, *The Trojans*, or his Hungarian march, it is always the purest Berlioz. His style, his self-expression was unchangeable and he remained true to himself, to his unique way of melody, harmony, and rhythm—and especially his unique way of orchestration. But, of course, today the so-called avant-garde doesn't need all this. There is no more melody or harmony or a unification of rhythm.

JC: That, of course, is a separate discussion . . .

MR: Whereas Berlioz and the other great orchestrators tried to use the best sound possibilities of each instrument, today one takes great pains to use the worst, just to be different! Four years ago, I heard a twenty-minute *Improvisation* from the BBC orchestra by Stockhausen[5] in which "not a single note has been predetermined," he declared profoundly. In other words, every musician played whatever he wanted . . . and he got a standing ovation for having "invented" this nonmusic.

JC: That is more theater than music, perhaps—something to illustrate an idea. You are saying that you write music, not for other musicians or to goad theorists, but for the listener.

MR: This should not be a revelation: of course, it's for the listener. In fact, to return to the subject of cinema scoring, this may be the one difference between concert music and music for the cinema: that whereas concert music is wholly for the listener, film music is for the film: you can't think of the listener first. I concentrate only on the drama. However, the purpose of the music is to bring this drama closer to the listener.

JC: So, to combine the two ideas, when you composed movie music for a number of different women characters—films like *Young Bess*, *Lydia*, *Diane*, *A Woman's Vengeance*, or my favorite, *Madame Bovary*[6]—you are writing psychological portraits of each woman with her specific characteristics but, taken all together, you are still expressing yourself, your own reaction to them, and perhaps to womanhood itself.

MR: Each theme I wrote for the women you are mentioning came out straight from their characters. Maybe not intentionally but by seeing the film often and then absorbing them.

JC: Such a sensitivity to drama must be gained along the way; it's not among the first lessons in music school. Can you summarize your musical background, from your origins in Budapest, on—before you ever considered this "double life"?

MR: My father was what would be called today a landowning industrialist and he was dead set against my seeking a career in music. At first it was the folk music I was hearing all around me that caught my attention. I even sometimes played violin along with the gypsies in our district. I certainly never studied or collected folk songs systematically like Bartók or Kodály, but it became an affectionate backdrop for me and when my father died during World War II and I came to the United States with my mother, that folk music took on even more personal resonance for me. I went through high school in Budapest, even became president of the Franz Liszt Society there and won a prize for a chamber trio I had written that I called *Hungarian Twilight*. But it was my *Piano Quintet, op. 2* that gained attention, caused me to move to Leipzig and finally enroll as a full-time music student. In other publications, I have traced the trail from those early works to my first success or from my move to Paris and then to the London music scene where I was arranging and orchestrating for a ballet company there. It was through that ballet music, then, that a fledgling film director, Jacques Feyder, heard what I was doing and hired me to actually write some original music for his new film.

JC: That was a score, together with *The Four Feathers* and, then, *The Thief of Bagdad*, that couldn't help but gain notice. You didn't pay much attention to historical detail in films like those. Instead, they carried a general heroic, adventure atmosphere full of color and swashbuckling energy.

MR: Again there, and always, my approach was the same: I write music that tries to bring the happenings and characters in each film close to the listener. No tricks, no gimmicks, thank you! I just try to write music, to create suitable atmosphere and to complete the psychological effect of scenes that need such treatment. It's no different if you are scoring the struggles of an unbalanced artist like Van Gogh, the conscience trials of Judah Ben-Hur, or the adventures of an innocent jungle boy like Mowgli in *The Jungle Book*: get into the story as a sympathetic observer and that will draw the viewer in too. The viewer doesn't have to realize that he is listening: he thinks he is just watching, but you, via the soundtrack, are able to influence in other ways.

JC: So, the film composer, almost as much a film director or writer, is actually communicating with the filmgoer in a very personal way—all the arts working together.

MR: In a subtle way, you're talking about the cinema as being like Wagner's opera aesthetic, the *Gesamtkunstwerk* expressed over a hundred years ago[7]—the cinema being like opera in that it can use all the arts at once: music, drama, poetry, dance or at least movement; everything. But does typical filmmaking today ever really rise to that level? I have just arrived back from the Thessalonian Film Festival where I have heard [director] Frank Capra's statement that film is the greatest of all arts because it uses all the arts. But does every commercial motion picture, because it uses writers, architects, actors, directors, cinematographers, and composers immediately become a work of art? Far from it. In Hollywood's dream factories, artists are in demand for their technical skill, but technique alone is not art. Capra's film *Lost Horizon* (1937) may contain great art individually and collectively but many of his moneymaking pictures (Hollywood's highest accolade) were merely entertaining technical clichés. Therefore, hardly to be considered as art. So, to answer your question, individual contributions, if they are the work of true artists, can be taken out of context (because a true artist always gives his best and is always himself as I've been saying) no matter what limitations were imposed on him. But that doesn't necessarily mean the whole production, whether a film or an opera, is automatically great art. And yet, to return to another point that's important here, there's nothing to say that an opera, because it's pure music, is greater or finer than a very well-done film score. Is the music for the film *Alexander Nevsky* by Prokofiev any less good than his *Peter and the Wolf*? As different as they are (not in personal style, of course), they are both masterpieces, even though the first was written for a motion picture. Salvador Dalí's[8] backdrops for the dream sequences in Hitchcock's film *Spellbound* are as good as many of his *l'art pour l'art* drawings, etchings, and paintings. By the same token, a really good motion picture script should read like a first-class play.

JC: Again, though, where several solo elements go to make up a film production, no single element should stand out and declare itself if that distracts from the production as a whole. Isn't that right? If Hollywood set design, for instance, overwhelms the story onscreen or if flamboyant dialogue distracts from the action or, to return to our theme, if a music score insists on claiming our attention so that the film's plot or characters are overwhelmed, that is a violation of The Whole. Teamwork is what's being violated there, although it's still important that each artist be able to contribute in an individual way.

MR: I believe in writers who can write a movie but also write a play or a book, and film composers who can also write "serious" music. So, although music is only one of the elements of the cinema topographic, it should be good enough to stand on its own feet. And yet if it takes the spectator's attention completely away from the drama, it defeats its own purpose. You understand the balance that's required of a cinema composer. Only a few succeed. Copland and Stravinsky, alike, have written about the peculiar demands of the field (Copland, *What* 205–6, *Our* 260–75; Stravinsky 35–36).

JC: And yet, composers for eons, ancient composers, have had to tailor their music to various prescribed forms: the sonata is a fairly fixed form; the Mass is another. There is always a danger that the music will be subordinate to the form.

MR: And those are all dramatic forms—forms of drama that are still practiced today. Not only ancient composers wrote Masses. Benjamin Britten's *War Requiem* is one of the outstanding contemporary works done in an extended form of the Mass. Brahms never wrote an opera but this doesn't make him a less dramatic composer than Wagner. His *German Requiem* is a perfect example for this. Composers who have a flair for the stage (Lully, Rameau, Monteverdi, Handel, Schubert, Bizet, et al.) wrote incidental music for plays and very often their music survived its original purpose. Think of *Rosamunde* (Schubert) or *Peer Gynt* (Grieg) or *L'Arlesienne* (Bizet) for instance. Therefore, composers today who have this flair for the stage or drama can find an outlet in motion pictures. Still, because of the limitations of the field, no film music will ever replace the spiritual demands or rewards of liturgical texts or the complexities of a symphony or a concerto. What's missing is the adherence to form and, as we've been saying, the fact that the inspiration for drama music comes from a given text or source, rather than from the composer personally (Rózsa, *Double Life*).

JC: Some quick questions, if I may, on five of my favorite Rózsa film scores. After many, many months of work on the score to the tale of ancient Rome, *Ben-Hur*—in fact, winning an Academy Award for the music—you then took the commission to score a film with a completely similar setting: *King of Kings*, an epic about the last years of Jesus of Nazareth. *Ben-Hur* had also briefly visited the passing story of Jesus. How did you manage to create such a melodically rich, emotionally centered score for *King of Kings* so soon—or at all? I note that your general compositional tone did not try to copy the rather drab authentic Roman tonality of that era but mixed a kind of antique modal sound with a more modern, emotional, hopeful feeling.

MR: It is true that both films, coming so quickly, caused a dilemma, being so closely related in one sense. My solution was twofold—first, to score what was similar in both films: hope is a good description of the general theme behind both stories although there was a lot of desperation and tragedy in each one, too. But the final theme of hope comes through in the end, in each. And the belief in a Redeemer. Second, each film had a different focus. *Ben-Hur*, though it was an epic, was following very closely the story of a single Jew pitting human values against the immovable Rome; whereas *King of Kings* personalized the various stories of the people affected by the Messiah, and I scored, with a variety of melodic approaches, the hope He represented for those people.

JC: There and in another historical epic, *El Cid*, about Spain's eleventh-century war hero, you scored both the historical setting and the locale very broadly while also providing a memorable, especially sensitive romantic theme for the Charlton Heston–Sophia Loren pairing.

MR: The love theme there was the element that personalized the score, whereas the bulk of the scoring was used to support the broad backdrop of the film—the era and the setting. The style of the music, which I researched carefully at the time, was made of three general sources: a general model medieval tonality, a Moorish/Far Eastern influence, and some flavor of the Iberian Peninsula.

JC: Different from those broadly scored epics is a literary classic like *Madame Bovary* in which your score more intimately follows and even sometimes joins the action onscreen. I'm thinking of one scene where Emma Bovary stands expectantly waiting for her lover's carriage to whisk her away to paradise, and, in the score, we hear her growing anxiety, the rhythm of the approaching horse's hooves, then the passing carriage, and the diminuendo in the music as the carriage rushes off and her disappointment sets in.

MR: There is an example of a more intimate story where a music score really could best tell the story by actually participating in it, mimicking some of the action.

JC: The grand waltz is another example.

MR: That is both a highlight of the music score and an important set piece in the film where Madame Bovary is first swept off her feet by the lover Rodolphe. It's a waltz that starts off politely enough at the ball but builds over fully five musical minutes to the edge of ecstasy. There was a case where music, if only for those minutes, takes over the film—a very dangerous prospect, as we've been saying, so as not to unbalance the film, but here used effectively. The alcohol-hysteria sequence in *The Lost Weekend* is another example where the music score was allowed to, indeed was asked to, intrude and take over the soundtrack.

JC: *The Jungle Book* is another favorite score, taking a cue from Saint-Saëns's concert fantasy from 1886, *Carnival of the Animals*, in assigning different themes and instruments of the orchestra to depict various jungle animals that the boy Mowgli alternately befriends and fears.

MR: Korda invited me to do a directly illustrative score for his film of Kipling's *Jungle Book*. The film was a great success and later I recorded the music again in New York with the boy from the film, Sabu, narrating the story. It became the first record album ever released of a motion picture score.[9]

JC: With all the colorful music I have been asking about and all the grand historical and biblical epics you've been asked to score, there are two kinds of anti-epic scores I will just mention in passing here: harsh film noir scoring for thriller films like *Double Indemnity* and *The Killers* (1946), and surprisingly gentle French-idiom scores for films like Alain Resnais's *Providence* about an aging author looking back over his life to the tune of a wistful minor key piano waltz.

MR: Compared with true progressive music of this century (twentieth), there is nothing shocking in the astringent scores to those crime dramas, although compared to much of Hollywood's Rachmaninoff-based melodious scoring, these were dissonant scores, dark and unforgiving. *Providence*, on the completely other hand, was, as you have said, a wistful score for a film full of reminiscence and regret—a story I didn't always understand, with its many shifts in perspective, but I gave what I thought it gave back: the sound of memories.

JC: Speaking of wistful, and following up on the disgruntlement you expressed in a past letter for the state of music and film music today, are you pessimistic about the future—of movies and of music in general?

MR: Artistic trends fluctuate, which is good; otherwise, they would become stagnant, but presently we have reached the nadir where sheer constructivity (electronic music?) and mathematic calculation (twelve-tone music?) have replaced inspiration, and the human spirit, without which there is no art, is missing completely. Light music with style and inspiration was always needed but, compared to today's animalistic, machine-made rock (the latest four-letter-word) music, a Johan Strauss or Offenbach or Lehar entertainment are as profound as J. S. Bach! Quo Vadis Domine? Is Stockhausen's electronic hysteria of sound, or Penderecki's orchestral imitation of sound effects, music? Where are we going? To a chaos in which anything goes. What can I say about it? But now I have to leave you. With best wishes, I am yours sincerely . . .

3

David Raksin (1912–2004)

The Provocateur

Figure 3. David Raksin (right) with Charlie Chaplin. *Source*: Photofest.

When the king of the early American cinema, Charlie Chaplin,[1] began working on his last silent film, *Modern Times* (1935), he insisted on controlling every aspect of the production as he had always done, this time including the film's composed music score—even though he had no musical training, could not play an instrument, nor read music. The studio's music director, Alfred Newman,[2] had the awkward task to accommodate the great Chaplin: the famous amateur needing professional guidance.

At the office of the publisher handling whatever music *Modern Times* would contain, orchestrator Edward Powell thought he knew a young man who could work productively with Chaplin, hear his ideas, suggest the film's musical needs, and translate them into a literate soundtrack score. That was David Raksin. So began a rocky working relationship between the brash young newcomer and the genius director. Chaplin would only put up with Raksin's revisions and scoldings for a week before the composer was fired. But the wise administrator Newman saw some of the sketches and orchestrations that Raksin had been submitting based on Chaplin's fragmentary themes and verbal descriptions of what he thought music should do for several scenes of his film: he went back to Chaplin and convinced him that Raksin really *was* going to be the musical answer to *Modern Times*. And so, Raksin was rehired. It is not that Raksin mellowed toward Chaplin or became more pliant; rather, the two men just managed to establish a working relationship that bypassed the personal. Raksin later wrote in the *Quarterly Journal of the Library of Congress* about that routine: how Chaplin would come to their sessions "and generally arrive with a couple of musical phrases . . . we would review that music . . . then go onto new ideas. . . . I would write them down, then we would run the footage (of today's sequence to be scored) . . . sometimes use his tune or alter it or we might invent another melody" (Cooke, *Reader* 76–77). It was Raksin's job, then, to fashion all this material, the general skeleton of the score, into a full-running composition, orchestrate it, and fit it into the film. Certainly, Raksin's natural twenty-three-year-old brashness and outspokenness were likely to offend the equally assured and insistent Chaplin during these sessions, but it certainly also took that same insistence and tenacity on Raksin's part to force the great director to take correction and to see that what was being recommended would, in the end, be best for his picture. *Modern Times* became David Raksin's first movie scoring accomplishment in Hollywood and he would stay for another seventy years.

Born in Philadelphia, Raksin had come from a musical family. His father had been a pit conductor leading live orchestras at the local movie house. He also owned a music store and, so, the teenaged David received an early education in the commercial uses of music before he gained an education in its aesthetics and its grammar. Cheeky and self-assured even then, he taught himself piano and organ, edited the high school literary magazine, and organized his own dance band at a very young age. He took music courses at the University of Pennsylvania, initially with jazz as his milieu. Moving to New York, he began writing dance band arrangements, catching the attention of the Benny Goodman organization, and eventually getting introductions into Harms, Inc. publishing house. It was there that he would be noticed by Alfred Newman and get a trip to Hollywood to face down Charlie Chaplin.

But this bald summary of arrivals and departures, jazz gigs and DIY lessons, misses Raksin's deep absorption into modern classical and even avant-garde composing, which began around this same period. He studied for nearly two years in California with the great serialist Arnold Schoenberg, not to learn the latter's twelve-tone serial technique of composing but to understand how essentially atonal music can be structured with an internal architecture that is as firm as any tonal piece. The semi-tonal style of the so-called Second Viennese School (music of Alban Berg, for instance[3]) was what Raksin began to adapt in his own writing. Thus, with that wildly varied (we can use the word "brash" again) packet of musical styles and abilities in hand—the early experience of tailoring music to drama onscreen, the fluent awareness of jazz gestures and language, and now the technical virtuosity of advanced classical grammar—a Raksin film score could be counted on to be cinematically astute, harmonically complex, and very self-aware. His first big-studio score to 1944's Otto Preminger film *Laura* not only had that intellectual sophistication but would produce perhaps the most renowned single songlike melody in any film of the era, the tune called "Laura," which later received a magical lyric by Johnny Mercer.[4]

Through the 1940s, Raksin scored films mostly at 20th Century Fox Studios, including two very different titles with contrasting scores, good examples of the composer's aforementioned range: the rich neoclassical score to *Forever Amber* (1947), set in the court of Charles II, which also flirts with folk ballad styles in some places and even with Handel in others . . . and *Force of Evil* (1948), set in the racketeering world of the modern big city with a music score à la Berg and the Second Viennese School.

Force of Evil was made during the period of the anticommunist crusades in the US Congress when so many artists and public figures were being investigated and condemned for alleged forbidden political activities: several of the script writers and the director of *Force of Evil* would be blacklisted and, in fact, David Raksin was threatened directly by the campaign unless he would name some names of people he knew to have communist sympathies. To his everlasting regret, he did supply a few answers to the committee, though it's unclear if there were ever any consequences, any follow-up, to his informing. To his credit, he chose only such names (in order to appear to be cooperating) of individuals who had ample defenses in place to spare themselves much suffering. Still, the whole disreputable incident knocked down his youthful confidence. Of course, the immediate result of appearing to cooperate with the witch hunt was that he was allowed to continue working in Hollywood. In fact, he was able to work regularly after that, scoring films throughout the 1950s—*Pat and Mike, Carrie, The Bad and the Beautiful, Separate Tables*—all scores that leaned more toward the edgy sophistication of narrative music than toward outright melodic scoring like *Laura*. And always, somewhere deep in the complexity of this music (you can see it in the dense, intense handwriting on his score pages) there is the reminder of the self-taught scholar, gifted and formidable, yet somewhat self-defensive on behalf of his homemade composing style.

By the 1960s and into the 1970s he scored less and less, yet lectured and essayed on film music more and more, and taught at UCLA. Frequently called upon throughout the 1970s and 1980s to speak among a renaissance of interest in film music history, Raksin brought his wry wit to the recounting of his own history, often adding caustic and biting comments when asked about working in Hollywood: about certain producers who had given him a hard time back in the day or certain actors who had groused about his music being too loud in relation to their dialogue onscreen. Whenever Raksin was the featured speaker, it was open season on such people. But all in good fun, at least the way he would spin it, sounding by turns like a noble crusader for the dignity of film music as an art form or like a good-natured worker teasing the boss. Certainly, there's a strain of cynicism and pessimism, even bitterness, to Raksin's interview as reproduced hereafter, which contrasts with Elmer Bernstein's spirit of optimism and forgiveness under similar circumstances. For Raksin it must come from his harsh experience in those difficult days of McCarthyism and such regret for his own decisions as none of us would want to carry.

Whatever the case, his defense of film music and its most serious composers, and his support of various projects to rerecord and preserve past film scores, was admirable. He continued to be much in demand as a banquet host or lecturer for his wit, most often disparaging modern industry practices and Hollywood windbags whom he couldn't tolerate, but also for his unparalleled experience across the whole accumulated history of the cinema, all the way back to the silents.

Interview with David Raksin

JOHN CAPS: I'm wondering if you feel that the climate surrounding film music and film composers has changed now that full-blown orchestral scores have been making a comeback through the success of works like *Star Wars*—symphonic scores, if you will, as opposed to pop scores.

DAVID RAKSIN: I don't notice any great change although I keep hearing all the time that it's happening. And I also anticipated that there would be some kind of a change because of the success of Johnny's [Williams] scores. The problem has been that there are an awful lot of people who are making pictures that they think are not responsive to that kind of opulent scoring. And they're probably right; if you do a picture like *An Unmarried Woman* (1978), theoretically the ideal way to score that would be with a bassoon and a serpent—but nobody did that!

JC: No, they didn't . . .

DR: No, Bill Conti scored it and so, you know, a story like that needs a colloquial score. And so many pictures these days seem to need that kind of approach. Now, in the old days there were different kinds of pictures and, therefore, different kinds of scores; not everybody did them the same way. One kind reflected a romantic approach that is today derided (but we should be so lucky as to have it back again)—and the other kind of films were things like *Force of Evil*, which I did and which had a completely different kind of score from what was done in those days.

JC: For which you provided a rather disturbing, highly chromatic score to underline the story of the numbers racket in New York City, a kind of allegory of corrupt capitalism. Certainly, anti-Hollywood scoring.

DR: That's right. And it's always kind of amused me to think that the fellas that are making films now seem to work on the opinion that those of us who scored films in the previous age didn't really know what we were doing, whereas *they* know best. And I find that to be kind of funny and a little crazy. But there it is, and we all live it.

JC: Are producers more open if you say this film needs some unusual kind of scoring, or the production of the music will take a little extra time?

DR: I deal very little with the current film-producing generation anymore. The most recent offers I've had, with the exception of two or three, have been television offers. I've turned them down, not because I'm snooty, but just because the time permitted to work on them was so totally insane and there were lies told about how much music there would be . . . Y'know, when somebody offers you an eight-hour TV miniseries—four two-hour shows—and you ask, "Alright, how much music is gonna be in it, do you estimate?" and they say 120 minutes, which means two hours or one quarter of the whole project's running time, you know that that is a lie. And you're gonna get squeezed between the time when the picture's ready and its release date. The fellow who finally wound up scoring that series wound up in the hospital. I've done that sort of thing for too many years and I think that it was wrong for us to go along with that sort of garbage. Some of us did it—put up with the torture—just out of sheer orneriness to prove that we could: like saying there's nothing they can throw at us that we can't do. But that was stupid, because we taught them to believe that they could get away with it at the expense of our bodies, our lives. They got used to saying, "Oh, those music guys complain a lot but they'll get it done." But the way we got it done was by killing ourselves, by drinking coffee, by taking Benzedrine or whatever it was in those days, and by sometimes farming out so much of the orchestration of a given score that the orchestrators were making more money than we were. It's a little stupid 'cause orchestration is really fun.

JC: And sometimes when you do write as much as they say they want, they end up throwing out pieces of it anyway.

DR: Oh, well, that will always be the case. I think, in order to be a producer, most of the time you have to take an ignorance test.

JC: Yes, well, I won't get involved there!

DR: Probably wise!

JC: I heard from Alex North[5] recently that the producers of his TV score to a film called *The Word* . . . that he wished they had used more of his dissonant, dramatic cues for the film—that, instead, they had just reused certain other music that they preferred. I mean, used music twice and just laid it in wherever they wanted.

DR: Yeah, well, people do that all the time. They do that in [theatrical] pictures too. You know, I did a film a few years ago called *Will Penny* (1968), and when I went to see it for the first time with the producer and Charlton Heston, who was the star and was also a coproducer, I found out that there was a sequence in which all of us had agreed there was no way there should be music there. It was totally wrong for music. But I came in to find out that they *had* put music there. And anyone who has any sensitivity to film scoring would have to say, "Has Raksin lost his mind?" as though I had scored it that way! They just took something from some sweet little scene somewhere else and put it over this scene where Heston is all trussed up like a Thanksgiving turkey (I wish to God, they'd cooked him), and he's trying to free his bonds. But they stuck music in there . . . it's sinful and stupid, but they do it all the time. Maybe my colleagues and I have harped a little too much on that kind of abuse when we do interviews like this, but it's nevertheless true.

JC: So, the time constraints you work under are often unfair and then, sometimes, how they use your music is unfair once you've turned it over to them.

DR: There's got to be some question about the validity of a profession in which the end result is determined by people who should never be permitted to judge anything more delicate than a nausea contest.

JC: . . . hope you haven't said that in print . . .

DR: Oh, yes, I've said it in print and on the radio as well! I find myself as I grow older able to say those things . . . though actually I said them before, in many ways. We were often in the hands of butchers. But when we were not, we did our best work.

JC: So, when you're doing your best work and you've got a new film to score, take for instance *Will Penny*. It's about a sort of over-the-hill cowboy, so it's a western but it's a character piece as well—are you thinking about individual scenes and themes right away or are you searching for a common denominator for the whole film out of which the individual scenes will come?

DR: I'm thinking about both. In a case like that where I knew they wanted some kind of theme that could be converted into a song, I would have been in trouble if I had differed with them. I felt that there was a way of writing a theme that could serve the purposes of the picture that could still be a song. Now, I'm not sure that's not a delusion, but actually the theme I came up with could fulfill that. It did turn out to be a song, a rather unusual song; so unusual that nobody ever sang it—which is rather an endorsement in some ways.

JC: Did someone put lyrics to it?

DR: Oh, yeah, Bob Wells, and he wrote a very good lyric. I was really delighted with what he wrote.

JC: On the theme of old cowboys?

DR: Well, in a way it is. It's called "The Lonely Rider," which is a title I suggested to him and I think he did an elegant job on it. I'm not always wild about lyrics that go with my things, but this one was really good. You know, in the very beginning of that picture there's this very long sequence . . . and when I went to see it for the one and only time, I found out that dear Mr. Heston had just suddenly taken out the music here and there; it would just disappear. And, as coproducer, it was up to him to decide this; it was not Tom Gries the director who was of a single mind with me. I mean, we really agreed on what was to be done; in fact, Gries was angry that they didn't make the music louder in certain sequences. But that was Heston's doing. There was one place where, if I remember correctly and I'm not sure I do, the music suddenly disappeared and I wondered what in the world did he do that for? It's embarrassing, it leaves a big hole. And I realized that somewhere along the line, Heston was going to be heard off camera mumble-singing something about "get along, little doggies." So, the music score was dialed way down in order to hear that. Yeah, it's brutal and stupid.

JC: They turn down eighty musicians so we can hear Will Penny humming.

DR: Well, they don't see why not. When you think on the scale of importance out here, who really has priority? The star or the music man? I think this is a very nifty exposition of where things are in this business. There is one aphorism to be drawn from experiences like this, and I think my friend [Hugo] Friedhofer would appreciate it: If you can't manage to be incompetent on your own, they'll always give you a little help.

JC: Ha, you should put out a book of these Hollywood sayings.

DR: Well, they're not Hollywood sayings; they're my own and they're mean! They're a way of, I guess, dealing with this kind of cruelty that happens to your work. I hate it and I'll never, never get used to it.

JC: Can you contrast all this to some of your work in the so-called Golden Age: your major score, for instance, to *Forever Amber*? How was music treated there?

DR: Yeah, that's one of my favorite picture scores. In a way, it's sort of wasted because if it had been written for a really first-rate big film that had succeeded the music might be better known. I like it a lot, though, and it was an opportunity to write a lot of music that was really fun to write. As I've said somewhere, elsewhere, it isn't easy to write at your best when you feel the motion picture at hand isn't really very good, but that's the time you look behind the actual film and write for the inherent interest in the setting or the subject; in this case, the historic melodrama set around the English court of Charles II, encompassing the Great Fire of London in 1666 and all that. It's a very complicated score, you know; it contains that thing that I called a "quasicaglia" because, as I quipped at the time, it had all the bad qualities of basso-ostinato and chaconnes and passacaglias without having any of the good ones. But it is, actually, kind of a passacaglia. And there's the sort of plainsong melody there for Amber with its fluid time signatures and there's the scherzo for the Great Fire, a royal trumpet piece for the King's mistress (one of them) . . . and it's a very, at once, narrative and pictorial score. And that G-minor scale at the heart of the score appears all over the place. You know, that kind of a picture needs the stimulation of music to elevate it above the humdrum. Preminger did a great job, I think, on that picture considering what he had. And so did the two writers who kidded the thing from beginning to end. The music, I think, is kind of exciting. It sort of tickles me to hear it; I'm proud of it. I always think of it as my Korngold score.

JC: Certainly, music makes the fire sequence more convincing.

DR: There is a thing in that sequence that is like a gigue in 9/8 and 6/8 meter, sometimes, or 12/8 or whatever, which is in that fast triplet rhythm and at the same time there's another rhythm that crosses it in the brass, who are playing a little chorale that lasts for just a few bars that actually is related to one of the main themes. All those things are interrelated. But in the beginning, there's an even stranger thing; there's a theme in the Main Title that is used quite a bit in the picture which is in 6/4, 8/4, 6/4, 9/4, 6/4, 12/4, and things like that.[6]

JC: The Amber theme . . .

DR: That's right. And that's done in order to have a flowing melody that moves with kind of equal notes, most of the time, and it's in order to give the effect of one of those tunes that grew out of plainchant.

JC: The folk song tradition.

DR: Well, it's a little too complicated for a folk song because it's a complicated theme. But it has a kind of a free flow that you're not gonna get any other way . . .

JC: . . . varying the time signature to resemble someone's natural breathing flow as they sing.

DR: That's right.

JC: Well, it's great that RCA has seen fit to rerecord *Forever Amber* so recently now and that you were able to conduct it, too. No one has ever recorded your music to *Force of Evil* but I came across, I think from the Library of Congress files, a transcription disc of a nocturne from that score and I wondered, after all these years, who owns the rights to all that music.

DR: I do, I'm very happy to say. As a matter of fact, I played it not long ago in a concert. It's been played a number of times. Eventually, I'll have to make a piece out of the whole thing: the nocturne and finale. It's an unusual piece, especially considering it was done in about 1948 (1947) the same year I did *Forever Amber*. And it's a completely different kind of score; but I like that score too; it's one of my best. I would dearly love to record a lot of those things; whether or not anybody will ever record them, I can't say. Things being what they are, it's so much more profitable for a recording company to do Elton John or Tomita or anybody like that, that they really can't be bothered with film scores. When that RCA album of mine came out (1976) there were a certain number of great hopes for it because of the way in which it was reviewed. And, as you probably know, that *Soundtrack Collector's Newsletter* picked it as the number 1 album of the year and all of that sort of jazz, and *High Fidelity Magazine* gave it a wonderful review and called it a jewel, etc., etc. And RCA didn't manage to lift a finger. No, the corporate branch out here took out one ad at the instigation of some of my students because they were doing a revival performance of *Laura* and they made a big gala evening out of it; so RCA and the theater owner took out an ad jointly but never did anything else with it and no ad appeared in a national publication that I ever saw. They did arrange for one very important interview with an AP writer who I thought did a fine article and I don't wish to appear ungrateful to them because I'm very pleased they put the record out at all, but they really messed up when it came to exploitation. In the current situation where there're so many albums coming out all the time, you can't just send an album out into the South China Sea and see if it makes it to shore! So, I had the original Boat People album.

JC: That's odd because the whole series of rerecorded classic film scores under the direction of George Korngold and Charles Gerhardt by folks like Herrmann and Rózsa and Waxman was reported to be fairly successful.

DR: Yes, it was successful; it did very well. But "very well" in terms of the film music we do is not to be compared with the sales of an album by one of the rock stars. And that's where they put their money. The people who are running the show have to be responsive to the bottom line. The need to expand and to make more profits all the time absolutely strangles everything of any consequence. And, consequently we're dealing with the lowest common denominator of public taste.

JC: And there are not enough discriminating people around to keep interesting music going?

DR: Well, how are they going to keep it going if they don't know about it?

JC: True.

DR: You see? And, as you know, film music, whatever we may say or think about it, lives below the salt. I mean, it's looked down upon by most people who make stupid generalizations about it and don't understand that what applies to one score cannot apply to another.[7]

JC: Because they only notice the loudest examples.

DR: Well, whatever it is that they notice . . . before the current pop generation, they had other reasons to despise film music. They'll never run out of reasons because there's a certain amount of envy and unwillingness to understand what it takes to be able to write even a bad film score. When Aaron Copland said to [orchestrator] Arthur Morton and me that time, "I go to concerts of new music in New York all the time and I say to myself, 'What's all the fuss about? The guys in Hollywood do this better every day of the week and think nothing of it.'" But those guys who disparage us are fellows who themselves are neglected and, so, they have to find somebody to feel better than. And with the university composers and the fellows who fill the avant-garde, the scapegoat is film music—which is a shame, but there it is. As I say, there's a lot about the whole business that I despise. The last film I've done is, I think, the last film I'll do.

JC: That's the semi-horror film *What's the Matter with Helen?* (1971). What was the story, there?

DR: Well, it's the story of two women who find themselves brought together by the fact that their sons have committed a murder. After the trial, these two women, one of whom is a dancer played by Debbie Reynolds, go out to Hollywood where they cash in on what's known as the Meglin Kiddie Syndrome in which every little girl and her mama aspires to be Shirley Temple and her mama. And so, they open a dance school. Now, the second woman is played by Shelley Winters who, it turns out about halfway through the film, is totally demented. So, it's really a horror film but the music doesn't really deal with that most of the time. My idea, and director Curtis Harrington's, was that it was important for music not to keep throwing "red herrings" on the screen but instead to make the plight of these two women seem as genuine as possible. In other words, you had to believe that they were two lonely women who were very much upset and trying to make a life for themselves. And the music is like that. The music of the Main Title, for instance, is very strange because it has an odd pounding rhythm on top of which floats this tune that I call a loser's tune . . . And the orchestra for that score, as I remember it, is totally without strings. It consists of three oboes, three English horns, three bassoons, and, I think, a group of four horns, I think baritone horn and tuba and then four trumpets, one of which is a high D trumpet, and two trombones—bass trombone and contrabass trombone—then a piano and some percussion. Oh, there are six cellos as well. But the thing is, it's fundamentally a double-reed score and there's this one soloist in the woodwinds section who plays alto sax, clarinet, and bass clarinet. That was John Neufeld. It's a kind of unusual score; I don't think there are very many like it.

JC: Switching topics, I was surprised that you have so much jazz in your background.

DR: Oh, sure. I mean, I played jazz as a young man all the time; I can still play it, or I think I can. I used to play jazz all the time and I had my own jazz combos. I had some really elegant little bands; eventually I arranged for all kinds of other people's jazz bands.

JC: There is, not often, but occasionally, a jazz influence in even your romantically inclined melody writing—the theme from *The Bad and the Beautiful* (1952) seems jazz saturated, the way it modulates.

DR: I don't think of that as a jazz-saturated melody—it's a melody that owes a lot to my feeling for jazz. Actually, it's just a great big, long tune.

JC: But not a jazz tune?

DR: No way. I can see where it has a jazz turn or two; that one Gb is rather jazzy. And nobody, I would think, would write a tune like that who wasn't partially saturated in jazz. But I don't think of it as a jazz tune; it's much too big.

JC: I guess it's the blues-tune feeling of it that makes me think of jazz. Anyway, it was the composer Richard Rodney Bennett who suggested to me once that, whereas, the greatest song ever to come from the movies was your song "Laura," the best stand-alone melody from a film was surely your "The Bad and the Beautiful"—as a melodic construction, he meant. And despite his classical credentials, he was likewise saturated in jazz, at least as a pianist.

DR: It's very funny that Bennett told you that because a very funny thing happened when I first met him. It was a party at the home of William Kraft who, as you probably know, is a marvelous composer and has actually done a couple of film scores, too. But he's a guy who's played a lot in concert halls. And Billy and his wife gave a party in honor of Richard Rodney Bennett. And I came there and I saw this guy walk in with Lenny and Lynn Rosenman.[8]

JC: He's always with Rosenman out here.

DR: That's right; he was staying at their house. He spoke to Barbara Kraft and she pointed me out and he came over and announced that he was Richard Rodney Bennett, and I said, "Of course, I know who you are!" And he said that he and Lenny Rosenman had been talking about film music and he'd asked Lenny what theme of all the themes ever written for a movie did he think was the most distinguished? And they both immediately said "The Bad and the Beautiful." Well, the next day, as it happened, I mentioned this story to one of those independent music journal publishers who soon, without asking me, prints it in his little magazine.

So, the next thing you know, I get a letter from Bennett saying, "I read that thing and I don't remember saying it but I agree with it absolutely." So, it's kind of weird that he now remembers and tells you, but I'm pleased with it.

JC: So, okay; I'll have to mention *Laura* here. Sorry, but everyone comes to it sooner or later.

DR: Oh, that's perfectly alright. Doesn't bother me one bit.

JC: What sequence do you use in your university demonstrations, your classroom lectures?

DR: Well, I use the apartment sequence and I break it down into several parts; the idea being to show them the way in which music, by understanding the contours of a scene, works to help it. Of course, it *is* of some use to be able to write a tune like that, I say with all undue modesty, but then you have to know where and how to use it. One old-fashioned way to use it would have been to simply play it for all it's worth behind that scene where Dana Andrews comes into that room and walks up in front of the portrait of Laura, contemplating her . . . and the theme would have soared there and climaxed and finished at the end of that scene like a traditional love song. Well, that's not what I did there; I just used fragments of the tune and fit them more precisely to the contours of that scene so that the music really works with and kind of narrates what you're seeing onscreen and what the Dana Andrews character must be feeling, being half in love with, but also disturbed by, this portrait. That's the difference between a clichéd method of the past and a more sophisticated tailoring of music to the screen, which we can only hope is characteristic of the future of film music.

JC: The concert version of *Laura* that you've arranged begins with a very atmospheric strings-only descending figure before any muted trombones start to suggest the main theme. But is that . . .

DR: The concert version actually comes from the picture; oh, yes; it's absolutely in the original score. It all comes where Clifton Webb is heard to say, "I shall never forget the weekend Laura died." Remember that thing? Where he's doing a sort of voiceover—which always fascinated me because the guy telling the story has been dead when the story begins to be told. But that music underplays that. And there are a lot of other places where the triads coming down are duplicated in another triadic position by three trombones who move up, you see. So that whole thing is very tightly integrated. But, yes, all that stuff is in the picture. There's nothing in that concert version that isn't actually in the picture.

JC: Before this current recording you've made, I knew only the old Werner Janssen disc of it on RCA Camden.

DR: Well, it's the same piece and that was the first record of *Laura* made, right after I finished the score. Werner came to the studio and I thought what he was looking for, since he was a concert recording artist, was long-hair serious music. So, I showed him some of the things I'd done I was very proud of but he didn't think any of them would fit his plans. Then I took him up to Leon Birnbaum's cutting room and arranged to play for him this marvelous piece of Benny Herrmann that had just been laid down for its film, which was the short piano concerto from *Hangover Square* (1945).

JC: Which is also on the Janssen record.

DR: That's right. Anyhow, he was vastly enthused about that music. But as he left, he said, "This is really weird; I came out to see you and to hear your music and what have you done? You've shown me music of some other guy. What am I going to record of yours?" So, anyhow, I put that Laura thing together from the score and played it to him and he recorded it. Then, some years later, when people began to ask for it, I made a new performing version that is the same thing except there is one place where I took the thing down half a tone or something.

JC: Again, thinking about your lectures on film music, I notice you use a scene from a 1950 UPA cartoon called *Giddyap*. I wondered what you use from that.

DR: Ah, yes. I use the one where the horse does his dance. If you know the cartoon, it's the story of this guy who has a horse-drawn milk wagon, but he's not doing too well because there's another guy with a truck who always beats them to the customers. Well, the horse is a former vaudevillian who once played the Palace in New York and his memory of all that is going to be crucial in solving the milk seller's problem. But I wrote this dance, which is the sequence I use in classes and have done in concert a number of times, this dance I called "Hoofloose and Fancy Free." It's a chamber piece. And when I do it, I do it with a click track and the audiences flip over watching how a click track works to match the details in a score to the action and the edits onscreen during the recording session.

JC: Another great theme of yours was in the 1960–1961 film *Too Late Blues*. But I've also heard it elsewhere, as though someone sneaked it into another unrelated film . . .

DR: Yes, that was *Sylvia* (1965). That was a film that was made by a guy named Martin Poll, directed by Gordon Douglas. Martin was a friend of John Cassavetes, the director of *Too Late Blues* (1962). Well, Marty heard my music for *Too Late Blues*, a film that had been, I'm sorry to say, a failure. Nothing ever happened to it. And he asked if I would use, as source music, a lot of the music from *Too Late Blues* in his new film *Sylvia*. And I was delighted. It was legal because the same studio owned both of those pictures. And Bill Stinson of the music department at Paramount—one of my very favorite people; he was my editor on *Carrie* (1952) in fact—thought it was a great idea, so we did it.

JC: Have you done any TV since *The Ghost of Flight 401* (1978)?

DR: No, I have not. Before *401*, I had been consistently refusing to do TV pictures because of the insane production schedules I talked about before. But when they came to me with this one, I said to myself, "Well, who are you to be turning them down all the time? I'll do this one. After all, it's at Paramount and they know me, I know them . . ." Well, by the time we got through with a rotten schedule (pressured to compose quickly; pressured to record quickly) and an absolutely ghastly recording engineer, one of the worst I've ever had, it was a mess. And that taught me: no more. Since then, I've turned down quite a number of things so that my agent despairs of me but, you know, why start out with something where you haven't got a chance? You can as easily do poorly when you have no constraints, so I'd rather have a chance.

JC: It's sad, then. But is TV different than it was in the days that you did *Ben Casey*, the medical series from the 1960s?[9]

DR: Well, *Ben Casey*, you know, was a kind of a joke. I did *Ben Casey* in between the prerecording and the postrecording of *Too Late Blues* while Johnny Cassavetes was shooting. And the guy who wrote *Ben Casey*, a really wonderful guy who also produced it, called me up and said, "Hey, listen, we're in trouble here. We need some dynamic music for this new medical drama series on TV." I went over and saw their picture, their pilot episode, and it already had a score in it. And I told them I liked their score; what was wrong with it? What do you need me for? So, they said the Main Title music is wrong. So, I said, "Okay, I'll write you a new one." And we shook on it and they started to walk out. And I said, "Wait a minute! What's this show about? What kind of a theme do you want for the Main Title?" They told me their weekly opening sequence would show somebody pushing one of those gurneys down a hospital hallway with a great sense of urgency and that would be the opening of each show. So, I said, "How about this?" and I sat down and played that rhythm in 5/4 that you're familiar with and they liked it right away. And so did I. When you've got that kind of momentum going for you—a musical idea that really works—it's a marvelous feeling. You just reach out and it's there. But I can' t count on that happening very often—or anymore at all—so I leave the future business to, well, the next guys.

4

Jerome Moross (1907–1983)

Americana to the Fore

Figure 4. Jerome Moross. *Source*: Courtesy of Susanna Moross Tarjan.

I ONCE VOLUNTEERED AN OBSERVATION over the phone to Jerome Moross: it has always seemed to me that although the western or cowboy film "ought" to have inspired a whole lot of exciting music scores throughout the years—westerns being basically heroic stories, set in wide-open spaces crossed by galloping horse herds and charmed by sentimental saddle songs—instead, the most famous western films always seem to have been scored by either anachronistic European music or pop country tunes. The one stand-out score for its assertive themes, athletic rhythms, and orchestral authority is the Jerome Moross music in 1958 to *The Big Country*, a William Wyler production starring Gregory Peck and Charlton Heston. While not a particularly striking example of the filmed western, its music set a standard. And that very rhythmic energy and thematic confidence can be surprising when you consider the parochial and refined theater music, songs, and recital works that the composer was known for, before that time. One could imagine a career for him developing a trajectory of art songs leaning toward those of Stephen Sondheim or sonatinas like Elliott Carter, both of which specialties he did tackle. But such alternately tough and freewheeling music as *The Big Country* is remarkable coming from Moross. It made me curious about his origins.

As a fledgling music student in Manhattan, even though he had commissions for early musical works already lined up around town in the 1930s, he was basically a camp follower—in this case, breaking bread with the so-called Young Composers Group (Pollack 185–88) mentored by the also young but far more confident and balanced Aaron Copland. Among this group of young firebrands that included such future composers as Lehman Engel, Henry Brant, and Vivian Fine, Moross had a special affinity for the sharp intellect and sharp sarcasm of fellow composer and film aficionado Bernard Herrmann. Together, they would attend all the current concerts, a few of the current films, and not be shy about announcing their opinions vocally, often in terms no more technical than "it stinks" or "I can do better than that." Around town, they were known as a pair: intellectual roustabouts, feisty and pugnacious. Herrmann would be on a Schoenberg kick, judging everything by that standard, while Moross seemed to vacilate between the neoclassicist influence of Stravinsky and some of the new experimental music of Charles Ives. At school, Moross complained that little of this new music was being discussed or studied. He excelled in the basic courses of harmony and theory and piano sight-reading, but he defied anyone to make him take formal lessons in composition, insisting that he didn't want to "learn how someone else composes." He wanted to compose for himself. I have always felt that whatever can be criticized in his limited tonal vocabulary thereafter (though he certainly did an awful lot to vary and exploit the grammar that he had mastered) was due to that early defiance—a deficit, not of technique, but of semantics that he might have bested had he stopped to study and learn from "how someone else composes."

Regardless, by 1935 he had a charming musical revue on stage called *Parade* (to be pronounced the French way) and several theater ballet scores for varying ensembles: the modest *Paul Bunyan* and, by the 1940s, the major *Frankie and Johnny Ballet* made of an introduction and seven dance sequences. Critics called its music and choreography "racy, humorous, flavorsome, and full of comment." The *New York Times* called it the best ballet of the season. Chief among its distinctions was Moross's use of American rags, blues, and stomps in the scoring, dialects he would also employ in his first symphony (1942), and in a two-hour stage show encompassing singers, orchestra, and dance called *Ballet Ballads* with its three staged tableaux: "Susannah," "Willie the Weeper," and "The Eccentricities of Davy Crockett"—Americana music all the way—a characteristic language that he would bring, likewise, to his first film score, a melodrama called *Close-Up* (1951), which, although its plot is about uncovering an escaped Nazi hiding in the United States, takes place entirely on the streets of New York City and so, consequently, is full of Gershwinesque Americanisms in its scoring.

Throughout the 1950s, Moross really hit his stride—in orchestral music (the twenty-minute ballet suite *The Last Judgment* in whose scenario Eve is vindicated completely of that "original sin"), in theater works (the major Broadway musical *The Golden Apple*, which seeks to adapt Homer's *Illiad* and *Odyssey* to a small town in Washington State circa 1910), and a whole ream of film scores, culminating in *The Big Country*, but including other Americana tales like *The Proud Rebel*, *Jayhawkers* (1958 and 1959, respectively), and a most picaresque, affectionate, and down-home score behind a rather dim film version of *The Adventures of Huckleberry Finn* (1960). In all this music, there is, quite beyond its general American sound, that same very loyal and limited Moross vocabulary. We can either consider this one of his frailties or, as I have already said, just appreciate how much he did within it and how consistently likable and workable he made it. It is only slightly expanded when he scored the medieval world of a film like *The War Lord* (1965) or of the modern Vatican in *The Cardinal* (1963), (much discussed in the interview that follows) but he made it all work for him.

A 1960s recording of his sonatinas for diverse instruments and a 1970s disc of some late string quartets (one with piano duo, one with flute) were free-flowing and friendly works, well built in the famous Moross voice. Each served to renew some attention to his career, even as he neared the end of his life. Following my posthumous study and CD booklet text of *The Big Country* score when a CD was reissued, I was contacted by his daugher, Susanna Moross Tarjan, who was beginning her own tireless crusade as steward of his music to have more of it performed anew and recorded for posterity by whatever orchestras around the world might be engaged. Thus, in 1993, she could announce the release of a glowing new London Symphony Orchestra performance of the Moross symphony and *The Last Judgment*. In 1995, she had the City of Prague Philharmonic recording a program of Moross film score excerpts featuring some of the Huck Finn music and an exciting overture to an action picture, *The Sharkfighters* (1956). The New Zealand Symphony Orchestra recorded *Frankie and Johnny* in 1996 and the City of Prague organization returned in 2000 with more Moross film excerpts on a two-disc set. Perhaps most unique of all was Susanna's 2001 disc, *Wildflowers*, a recital of Moross songs from the theater shows, both hits and misses, performed by a quintet of trained voices and a septet of instrumental backup.[1] Heard apart from their shows and in literate arrangements, these songs give one a whole new view of Jerome Moross, not so far removed from his orchestral and film work, but newly intimate writing, cozy with each song's text. Completely unknown songs like "It's Almost Time Now" and "I've Even Been in Love" from the failed musical about gangsters *Underworld*, and more famous songs (thanks to a Barbra Streisand recording) like "Lazy Afternoon," all do honor to Moross the melodist. Indeed, by 2015, Susanna had somehow managed to fund, produce, and record a full legitimate stage production of the Moross-Latouche musical *The Golden Apple*. Originally from 1954, so influential and charismatic was this score that it can be said to have been one source of inspiration to Leonard Bernstein's own musical a few months later, *Candide*.

But, in the end, it's right to remember that film music was at least as important to Moross as was any of those theater works or classical pieces. And *The Big Country* contains all the other film work—the symphonic aspect, the thematic, the rhythmic. Perhaps its most striking quality is that metric animation, and not just the muscular meters, the galloping patterns, the wagon wheel "moto's" that one would expect to hear in a western, but the use, in my phrase, of implied rhythms where a moto-perpetuo races alongside the flowing theme line, even though it is not stated aloud. We can hear it immediately at the beginning of the film with that revolving toccata-like motif in the strings that sets up the entrance of the noble Americana theme and then prepares the way for a series of dancelike meters and motifs all throughout the score to come. Like other Moross music we can sample from across his career, from the dance hall to the concert hall, so much of his music, but *The Big Country* most of all, comes close to ballet.

Interview with Jerome Moross

JEROME MOROSS: I haven't been out to Hollywood in a long while; I gave up film writing ten years ago.

JOHN CAPS: On purpose?

JM: Yes. I had so many things I wanted to write and I felt that the time had come to just stop all commercial work and write what I wanted to write. And I stopped it at a good time, I think, because as far as the composer goes, the film opportunities have become fewer and farther between.

JC: There are probably a lot of guys out there who wish they had done, or could do, as you have done.

JM: Well, they could.

JC: I suppose: just pull up stakes and move.

JM: Well, I never lived in California. I commuted when I had a film to do or went looking for work when I needed money. Then, I came back here [New York] to write concert music or theater music. One of those was *Ballet Ballads*, which is a series of one-act ballet operas that were done in New York. Another was *The Golden Apple*, which gets done all over the country now. And I also wrote *Gentlemen, Be Seated*, which the New York City Opera did. In addition, a symphony and some orchestral pieces and a ballet: in other words, I always mixed the media I was working in. And since I've quit Hollywood, I've written a lot of chamber music, which I never would have done before because that would have been put off in favor of bigger works. Do you know my *Sonatinas for Diverse Instruments*?

JC: Oh, very well.

JM: Oh, you do! Well, those are works of the postmovie period as well.

JC: Those were done, like, between 1969 and 1971? Do they get regular performances; I mean, at colleges and all over?

JM: I don't know. They're all published now and I keep getting royalties, so somebody's buying and playing them.

JC: Good. They're good to learn from as well; I mean, for students to study. Although they're a bit too hard for young players to tackle, they're valuable pieces for budding composers. Do you remember what sort of music, what sort of pieces, you first admired when you were young and just coming up?

JM: I was playing the piano by the time I was five and I was composing by the time I was eight, but I suppose at that time it was mainly European music. Then, I'll tell you, at the age of fifteen, I discovered Charles Ives!

JC: Uh-oh. To what effect?

JM: I became a devoted fan. Now, this is more than forty years ago.

JC: Which was before anyone had heard of him.

JM: Anyone at all! And I played him around wherever I could and I got to know him through composer Henry Cowell. He had wanted to meet me anyway because Benny [Bernard] Herrmann and I were the ones plugged into Ives's music when no one else was. And I remember arguing with Aaron Copland that he *must* program some of Ives's music when he was, when Copland was, going to run his Yaddo Festival. And I gave him a copy of Ives's *114 Songs* from 1922 and Aaron then did schedule seven of those songs at Yaddo and that started the Ives thing. And I met Copland around that time; I met Gershwin around that time, as well.

JC: Oh, wow.

JM: I was about eighteen or seventeen and Henry Cowell had published me in his *New Music Journal*, which I later learned was paid for by Ives. It was a magazine that gave a lot of unheralded American composers their first public exposure. And, in there, they published things like the scherzo movement of Ives's Symphony no. 4—and two pieces of mine.

JC: Do some of your early orchestral pieces like *Tall Story* or *Biguine* date from that time?

JM: Well, those are from somewhat later, 1935 and so on.

JC: And the famous *Frankie and Johnny* ballet?

JM: A little later: I wrote that in the winter of 1937–1938 and it got performed, then, in May—commissioned by Ruth Page of the Chicago Ballet. So, by that time, I was—what?—twenty-four. I'd been earning my living in music since I was seventeen.

JC: A whole living?

JM: Yes! The Theater Guild produced a show of mine, *Parade: A Musical Revue,* when I was twenty-one. The first concert piece I had performed was called *Paeans* that Benny Herrmann conducted.

JC: Where are those things now?

JM: God knows where *Parade* is. Two things have gotten lost that I'd really like to find. One was a suite for chamber orchestra that *New Music* was supposed to publish, but Henry [Cowell] sent it to be copied by Schoenberg's son or son-in-law, whoever it was, and then the Nazis moved into Vienna. It may still be there.

JC: Under the rubble.

JM: Under the rubble.

JC: What's the story of your formal musical training? How did you come up, as it were?

JM: Well, I had a degree from NYU and I had a year at the Juilliard on a fellowship and they both ended in 1932 when I was eighteen. I had my college degree and my year at conservatory, and I was through!

JC: Were you at Juilliard as a composer?

JM: No, I entered as a conducting fellow. And I never studied compositon per se. I had harmony, fugue, form; everything else. All the grammar you needed. But I always felt I didn't want to learn how somebody else writes. All he can do is show me how he writes. Besides, by the time I entered Juilliard, I was composing already and I felt that I was pretty good. I was vain. You know, an eighteen-year-old is generally very vain. But I did have a complete grounding in musical technique. And I had already been playing in pit orchestras so that I knew my orchestra inside out. So that was my training.

JC: It was around 1932 that Aaron Copland started up the so-called Young Composers Group, a confab aimed at promoting and encouraging performance of new music—a group that sometimes has been described as "feisty and pugnacious" (Pollack 186). Certainly, Herrmann had that reputation of being a contrarian and the two of you as being critical and dismissive, even disruptive, so that Copland had some concerns.

JM: Not dismissive, surely. But, sure, we were young and boisterous and wanting to make waves.

JC: Copland certainly saw your potential at that age and appreciated how loyal you remained to him.

JM: I think so, yes. He even got me involved assisting in the orchestration of his score to *Our Town*. It was partly his involvement in theater music and future opera writing that made me look into it more for myself. I wanted to join the experiment, maybe try some innovations of my own.

JC: So, have you given any thought lately to entering—reentering—the theater world . . . to activate some of the innovations you were starting back in the day—I mean, as far as pushing vocal theater more toward art songs and away from pop influences?

JM: Well, you know, for many years it was my idea to change the theater, to make vocal theater more operatic. The things I wrote in *Ballet Ballads* and *The Golden Apple* were at least along those lines. And I wrote a lot of theatrical pieces that didn't fit into any particular show. I spent a lot of years on the theater until, seeing that nothing was happening for me, I finally decided that the theater didn't want me. Now I'm moving into pure opera. The last thing I've done is a one-act opera based on Lucille Fletcher's play *Sorry, Wrong Number*.

JC: It would seem to be a good time to expand on vocal theater ideas since Broadway seems to be open to, at least, operetta forms these days, what with Stephen Sondheim's intricate musicals *A Little Night Music* and *Sweeney Todd*.

JM: Well, yes, of course, the last Sondheim piece is much more operatic. But then, *The Golden Apple* was a pure opera for Broadway circa 1954; the entire show sung—I mean, it wasn't a typical musical, which is usually a spoken play and then people suddenly break into song. This was a sung-through score. And it worked: it ran off-Broadway for five months, which is, you know, kind of unusual for a semi-opera.

JC: Who did the book on that, the lyrics?

JM: John Latouche, a brilliant lyric writer who died young, who wrote a couple of pieces with me and also wrote *Cabin in the Sky* with Vernon Duke and also wrote *The Ballad of Baby Doe* with Douglas Moore.

JC: It is the music that needs to carry a show, though; music that is not only fine in itself but that has a sense of drama and gives voice to characters. These would seem to be good traits for that other kind of theatrical composing you've done—music for the movies. And here I don't mean just pictorial music that mimicks what you're already seeing on the screen, but a soundtrack score that treats the overall tone of the film.

JM: I've always objected to the "Mickey Mousing" of film action—that is, making the music match the actions onscreen like a cartoon. Rather, I like to get the sense of a film scene that I'm going to compose for. But then you come up against that problem where a producer may say, "I want music through this whole thing," and you could even argue with him about it and he'll say he wants music everywhere in this film and you'll write it, and then he'll start tearing off chunks of it to fit his final film cut—which just detroys the musical form you've been trying to create for that scene.

JC: Let me pick a few films and ask your experience on them: that adventure/fantasy film *Valley of Gwangi* (1969). This was meant to be a matinee-type film, really a showcase for the impressive Ray Harryhausen special effects of, in this case, animated dinosaur monsters and the like. Were the producers clear about what they wanted from you? Did they hire you for your sound?

JM: No, they wanted exactly the opposite. They had done a whole series of fanatasy pictures with sort of mythical heros assailed by fantasy creatures and evil forces; pictures scored rather grandly and exotically by Bernard Herrmann like *Three Worlds of Gulliver* (1960) and *Mysterious Island* (1961). Benny had done marvelous things for them, but that's not my style. And I just wrote my style and the producers were startled. And I said, "Well, if you wanted that other, you shouldn't have hired me."

JC: Your style?

JM: Well, just Americana with an overlay of tension music on the one hand and sort of catastrophic exclamations and fanfares on the other hand. In the end, there was too much music in *Gwangi*—and they chopped it up in different places and reused certain cues and stuck them in where they wanted. You know how they do. It was an idiotic film anyway.

JC: But that's the charm of the scoring, that it realizes that. They were happy with it, weren't they?

JM: In the end, I think they were. You know, I developed a theory in Hollywood. I began to overscore films because the producers never really knew what they wanted and I figured they can always throw out what they don't like, but if they want something and there's nothing there, you're in trouble. So, you write music and they can use what they wish. In the end, you have no say, only they do.

JC: Well, sure. It's their picture.

JM: If a picture is weak, they'll want music every inch of the way. If the picture is strong, they'll usually start by saying they want music here and there, and then they'll begin throwing chunks of it out. If you want to be discreet, scoring very carefully and sparsely, they feel uneasy. So I started by overscoring, oftentimes.

JC: That Americana sound you spoke of: Did you do specific study on American or southern folk music as Copland and, for that matter, Elmer Bernstein did, before you came up with your personal voice?

JM: No, no. I was surrounded all my life by American tunes and folk music, things we sang when I was a child at camp and so forth.

JC: No more than most people?

JM: I don't think more than most people, except maybe, being musical, I reacted to it differently. I found myself writing themes that used the intervals and rhythms that were around me. So, now they're part of me, part of my style.

JC: . . . which is most famously on display in your score to *The Big Country*.

JM: That score does seem to have become something of a classic. I did a concert suite of some of the music for *The Big Country* about fifteen minutes in length and featuring the Main Title and scherzo, the waltz from the party scene at the ranch, and a ballad. It gets played around a bit. I also did another concert suite of excerpts taken from my film scores that I called "Music for the Flicks," which includes pieces from *The Cardinal*, *The Proud Rebel*, *Five Finger Exercise*, and things like that.

JC: Now *there's* an obscure production, *Five Finger Exercise* (1962).

JM: Ach, don't mention that film.

JC: Not the film; the music.

JM: Well, I'll tell you, I was working there with a director of great integrity, Daniel Mann, and we had both done what we thought was a marvelous film and what I thought was an excellent score. But then, when we left, the star Rosalind Russell's husband, who was producing, suddenly realized that the film made her character look like an unpleasant woman—and so he decided to recut the film. And, in the process, switched the music all around . . . cut and chopped it and placed it in the wrong scenes and so forth. This is a good example of what happens to your score after you've gone in and done the best you know how to, but then moved on. You have no control over what comes out the other end. The audience sees your name on the screen and thinks you've made all the artistic choices regarding the music. Well, you haven't. The situation may be changing now where composers are gaining more recognition out there, but back then, that's the way it was and that's among the reasons I left.[2]

JC: Well, something of integrity still comes through in the music, even if the film is not working.

JM: Does it? Well, I can't bear to watch it. Of course, sometimes you do meet producers that you love to work with. For instance, I loved working with Sam Goldwyn Jr.

He and I understood one another; we worked as a team; we discussed things. Nothing was ever messed up, you know? I did three pictures with him including *The Adventures of Huckleberry Finn* of which I'm thinking of preparing a concert suite—I like the sort of rolling motif for the river and some of its southern-flavored music—and *The Proud Rebel*, which I'm very proud of. You can do good work if the people around you on the production team will let you!

JC: So, speaking of production teams and bosses, what was your experience working for the infamous Otto Preminger on *The Cardinal*? He has both a dynamic and horrendous reputation.

JM: Well, it was horrendous, but I laughed through a lot of it.

JC: Did you? Could you?

JM: I just couldn't take Otto seriously. He knows nothing about music.

JC: And yet, so many of his films did innovative things with their music scores: Elmer Bernstein's jazz in *Man with the Golden Arm*, Duke Ellington's work on *Anatomy of a Murder* (1959), the avant-garde score by Paul Glass for *Bunny Lake Is Missing* (1965), Ernest Gold's popular score to *Exodus* (1960) . . . and he accepted your long, dignified score to *The Cardinal*. You'd think he was quite keen on music scoring.

JM: And this is the man who made musical films of *Porgy and Bess* (1959) and *Carmen Jones* (1954), and he literally hates music. No, working with Preminger is an experience I would never want to go through again. [Laughing] But I was glad I did it; it was fun at the time; it was interesting. He could be a great director.

JC: If what?

JM: Oh, I don't know. At the wrong moment, he gets impatient and sometimes he doesn't believe in himself. He did something that was so stunning in [*The Cardinal*]. Do you remember the scene where John Huston and Tom Tryon talk in Tom's room and Huston tells him to take a vacation? Well, that scene took more than nine minutes to play out. Otto rehearsed it quite thoroughly and then shot it in one long "take," which took a full reel of film as the camera moved in a complete circle around them, or at least all around the room following them. I thought it was sensational. But then he got into the cutting room back in London and Otto kept looking at it and saying, "Oh, I don't dare; I really don't dare." Reluctant to keep such a self-conscious long sequence like that, without a cut. And I kept saying, "Leave it, Otto, it's brilliant; don't touch it." Well, in the end, he rejected it—he intercut it with typical close-ups. But if he had run the whole nine-minute scene through, it would have been one of those things that people talk about in film classes, you know?

JC: Well, it's still interesting that his films would seem to go to so much trouble for distinctive music scores if Otto couldn't care less.

JM: Well, in the end, Preminger was interested in two things: artists of name recognition and artists who had quality—who had confidence. Add to all that the fact that his brother, Ingo Preminger, is a very cultured and musical man as well as a talent agent. In fact, he was the one who sold me to Otto.

JC: I see; that explains a lot. Anyway, you talk like you had a lot of time to do that film, being in on the shooting and the cutting . . .

JM: Well, Otto dragged me along. I was a moving music department. Even before we left for Europe, we recorded background vocals for music hall scenes in Boston and, once in Europe, every time we needed a background chorus for the Cardinal's church scenes, I was called in again. There have been other times when I was doing music for a film before the film was even shot. In the Danny Kaye musical film from the 1950s, *Hans Christian Andersen* (1952), they called me in—they wanted a ballet sequence using themes from Franz Liszt. It was going to be staged like a whole formal ballet within the film, where Hans supposedly becomes infatuated with a ballet dancer and imagines himself as part of the dance company. I like Liszt and I decided to really have fun with it, using excerpts from "Mephisto Waltz" and some things like "Gnomenreigen" that had never been orchestrated before because people said it couldn't be done. Well, there it is; I did it for sheer vanity.

JC: One piece of orchestration and original composition I'd like to ask about is the long, formal, multipart waltz you did in *The Cardinal*. Did you draw on any model in the writing of that?

JM: Well, I wrote it from scratch and, in fact, that's in *Music for the Flicks* as well. I love that piece. I had much joy writing it. In the end, I really enjoyed *The Cardinal*. The problems with Preminger were just that: Preminger problems and nothing more. They resolved themselves.

JC: There are a lot of what can be called characteristic Moross phrases and language in that score that, even though the story covers various settings from rural America to holy Rome, help tie the film together. But the similarities could also be questioned as a limitation.

JM: Well, I just don't know; I can't explain stylistic things. That's just the way I write. I sometimes find stylistic things repeating themselves. People say to me, "You know, you did this turn and this phrase in that other piece." Well, that's my style. I don't realize that. I mean, somebody once sat down and figured out that in almost every piece, Wagner utilized the turn (humming a phrase). It's in his Ring cycle, it's in *Tristan und Isolde*; it's in *Tannhäuser*; it's a basic theme of his and he varies it. And that's what style is about. In other words, style is actually something that's so deep in you that it exsists in what you write without your really thinking about it.

JC: There's a surprising fluke I've discovered in your catalogue that isn't about stylistic similarities but that appears to be a whole repeated or borrowed theme. It's in the western film *The Jayhawkers* when, in the middle of that film's score, anyone who grew up watching television in the 1950s and 1960s suddenly recognizes the familiar theme to TV's old series *Wagon Train* playing note for note—and there it is in *The Jayhawkers*!

JM: Ah, you found that!

JC: Why is that?

JM: Why? It's very simple. I wrote that theme, which is very unimportant in *The Jayhawkers*, and I forgot about it. And then they hired me to write a new theme for their new TV series *Wagon Train* over at Universal Studios through the NBC network[3] and, without questioning it, this theme was in my mind and I wrote it down as being appropriate for the TV series. Then Paramount Studios called Universal and said, "Do you know it's the same theme; the *Wagon Train* theme is already there in *The Jayhawkers*?" They brought the matter to me and I said, "No, it can't be." But, sure enough, it was. But, in the end, they just let it pass.

JC: They actually passed it?

JM: Yeah. It was unimporant in the film and, after all, I suppose Paramount felt they might have to ask a similar favor of Universal some day.

JC: OK. It comes up twice, I think, in the film.

JM: Yeah, twice, but very casually and I never extend it.

JC: It's still a surprise.

JM: Well, there it is and you've gotten the story out of me.

JC: Did you also score any of the weekly episodes of *Wagon Train*?

JM: I did six of them and then they wanted me to do the series but, oh God, that would be torture. I did a couple more TV themes besides that: *Lancer* was one of them. But I always hated doing the weekly stuff. Television is like sausages, anyway . . . assembly line work.

JC: So, in flight from television, you found yourself taking lesser film jobs, while you contemplated what kinds of theater projects or concert projects you might try—lesser films like *Hail Hero* (1969).

JM: Yes, that was the last film score I did out there and I think it was the one that finished me in Hollywood. If that was the way it was going to be, I didn't want to do pictures anymore.

JC: Because of behind-the-scenes intrigues, or what?

JM: Well, it was all just so idiodic, I didn't dare tell them. They thought *Hail Hero* was an antiwar film (clichéd story of a sixties hippie who confronts his conservative family over the Vietnam War) and instead they were actually making a prowar film.

JC: Did you take it upon yourself to tell them that?

JM: No, I told everyone else around me. Anyway, it was a terrible film and it died a terrible death.

JC: And yet, the music score seems rather airy and happy with itself.

JM: Really? I have nothing saved from that.

JC: There's a perky sort of baroque trumpet theme and, during a scene where they're painting a barn all sorts of bright colors as a politcal statement, there's a pleasing lyrical theme.

JM: I honestly don't remember. But I'll tell you, whether I like or dislike a film, once I'm in it, I try to do the best I can, you know?

JC: You don't have to enjoy it.

JM: I don't have to enjoy it. I have pride in my own work. If everyone else around a film has decided it's a turkey and tossed it away, if I happen to be on that film, I can't take that attitude. I wouldn't be able to write a note.

JC: Well, it is a very talkie film and very clichéd, but you have no reason to be ashamed of your role there. Some composers say they need to get inspiration from a film in order to, as you say, "write a note."

JM: Oh, but you can dig into yourself for inspiration. There's something in every film to hang on to, if you take that view. Also, it's drama—it's a kind of theater, even if it's bad theater: you're setting drama and you dig into your dramatic reserve and just write.

JC: Maybe the best film you did among those very last Hollywood projects you're talking about was the first directorial effort of Paul Newman directing his wife Joanne Woodward in that intimate, very personal film about the emotional life of an unattached schoolteacher, *Rachel, Rachel* (1968).

JM: A fabulous film, in many ways. We did all of that in New York, the scoring. That's one situation where people were saying, "This picture is so small and nothing special; toss it aside" . . . except me. And it turned out to be a big picture, with various award nominations; a real sleeper that even the people who made it didn't realize. Well, I suppose Paul Newman thought it was marvelous, but I mean the producers didn't know what they had till later, till glowing reviews started to come in. I remember I was working on a flat sum with only so much money alotted for music. And the production manager said to me something to the effect that if I wrote for just a few players, I could pocket the rest of the alottment for myself. And I said, absolutely not, and used an orchestra of about twenty players. He looked at me as if I was mad. So, I didn't make as much money as I should have, but I did use the right orchestra. I thought Joanne Woodward was just fabulous in that! And so was Estelle Parsons who is one of my favorite actresses.

JC: And of course, it's a beautifully cut film too, thanks to editor . . .

JM: Dede Allen, yes. Marvelous job. It's a lovely film, lovely film.

JC: That's another score you could do well to fashion into a brief concert piece or prelude.

JM: Well, but, you know, it's music that's not fashionable now with all the twelve-tone business. Even a concert of so-called Americana music wouldn't draw today.

JC: Are you worried about American music in general, today? Do you think it's on the right track?

JM: Well, it's on the right track inasmuch as composers have realized they've struck a dead end with atonality. So, you have a lot of people like George Rochberg[4] and others who are trying desperately to write again in classical musical grammar. But the only thing some of them can think to do is to stick in chunks of Mozart, Rossini, Mahler, anything.

JC: Ah, yes, the "collage" school.[5]

JM: But at least it's an admission that the way they had gone was wrong and they don't know how to write anymore.

JC: When did it go wrong?

JM: When did it go wrong? It went wrong when the academics got hold of it and started teaching everybody to write by theory, either Schoenberg's theories or somebody else's. You started getting all this music that exemplified theories and isn't music.

JC: But wasn't that because they were realizing traditional tonal music couldn't be stretched any farther beyond chromaticism and polytonalities and . . .

JM: Not at all, not at all. You say you love my sonatinas and I think you'll appreciate my new pieces. One can continue to write tonally. It just becomes a fashion not to write that way and then the critics and the academics take up the cause, and it can be murder. The same thing almost happened in painting except the painters were a little smarter; they're still teaching classic grammar in art. I think music has to make a big change now and I think it's on the verge of doing it because, first of all, audiences are bored with the new music; they won't listen.

JC: Because they think it's written for other composers, and not for . . .

JM: Not for them. It's gotten so that I'd give my shirt just to hear a live performance of *Scheherazade*, for crying out loud! There's a tremendous amount of music that isn't played anymore on the theory that it is only good for Pops concerts. And so, they've latched on to Mahler and Bruckner and . . . I don't know what all . . . but they're dull. Mahler symphonies: a little goes a long way, you know? So, what the audience has done is move on to chamber music.

JC: Really?

JM: It's a whole new world for them. For instance, when they do chamber music at the Mostly Mozart Festival or the Lincoln Center Chamber Society, it's just jam-packed; you can't get in. Or the chamber series at the 92nd Street Y concerts. It's a new repertoire for people. Last week the Beaux Arts Trio at the Mostly Mozart concert played the Bb Schubert trio and, you know, as I was walking out, I was listening to comments and one was saying to the other, "Wasn't that stunning!" as if it was a new piece! They'd never heard it before! They were orchestragoers and suddenly here was a new world—here was this absolutely gorgeous chamber masterpiece that people didn't know existed. You see? And I'm sure that if composers started giving them something that was interesting, it would be back like in the twenties and thirties when people used to run to concerts to hear new pieces of Ravel and Malipiero and . . . everybody . . . Stravinsky . . . It was exciting. The programs now are a bore, mostly, because there is no material of interest.

JC: Can orchestral writers do interesting things now, do you think?

JM: I think there's a new generation going to come up to do it. I really think so. I'm certainly trying. My latest works use classical grammar and make modern music with it without having to go into all the tortures. I write music that an audience will like, will listen to, not because I want to just cuddle the audience but because that's the way I feel I want to talk to them. I want them to know what I'm saying. And I think the audience, if they get a chance to hear it, will respond.

5

Interlude

Black Composers for Film—A Mini-History

Hollywood histories asking who was the first African American composer to write a narrative music score for a mainstream motion picture most often cite the jazz band master and songsmith Duke Ellington[1] as the answer, noting his fully orchestral soundtrack for Otto Preminger's 1959 courtroom drama *Anatomy of a Murder*. But, in fact, Ellington was a fairly late arrival in that history. Long before him, the film scoring business already boasted a fledgling cadre of black composers as far back as Will Vodery,[2] who had worked as an orchestrator with the Ziegfeld Follies, then came to Hollywood working at Fox Studios, and finally graduated (circa 1930) to general scoring duties around town. Once that example had been made, other black orchestral writers began to find occasional work serving the movie soundtracks of their day, like Sy Oliver who was an arranger at both the Fox and MGM studios, and pianists-turned-orchestrators Calvin John and Phil Moore.[3] (Not forgetting Ellington's frequent orchestrator/assistant Billy Strayhorn who also helped the Duke shape his more general musical ideas to the specific needs of the screen.)

Nor were these orchestrations necessarily jazzy as might have been expected of black musicians at the time; they were dramatic/orchestral when they needed to be and pop/melodic as each movie dictated. It is a fair question, though, whether Ellington's *Anatomy* score should be classified as "dramatic narrative" music in the first place and, therefore, any kind of "first" for a black composer at all. Because, as the score progresses through the film, it remains doggedly Big Band music most of the time as opposed to real descriptive or dramatic scoring. In the end, it does show itself to be at least nominally cognizant of the story onscreen when, for instance, a jazzy rhythmic driving cue slows and darkens in order to accommodate the mood of the next scene.

Still, for my money, there are other earlier candidates for first black dramatic soundtrack scorer—just that they are easily overlooked, having labored on much less visible productions, always on the fringes of Hollywood. But notice: predating Ellington by a full decade in film music was the pioneering classical composer Ulysses Kay,[4] who moved comfortably back and forth between successful concert commissions and movie scoring.

Figure 5. Ulysses Kay. *Source*: Courtesy of the E. Azalia Hackley Collection of African Americans in the Performing Arts/Detroit Public Library.

Witness Kay's tightly orchestrated ensemble score for 1948's half-documentary, half-dramatized film about a young black boy's experiences in the US child welfare system, titled *The Quiet One*. Produced by teacher Helen Levitt and directed by Sidney Meyers, the film's first half loosely chronicles ten-year-old Donald's brutal, lonely existence on the streets of Harlem; then, in the second half, it details his daily life once he's been committed to a reform school and how he tests the various counselors there. Ulysses Kay's music score for the film is built mostly on suspended chords, harmonies straining, posing unanswered questions, tensing, and jostling. It's a sound that draws on a previous era's New Deal composers[5] with elements of Copland and of Kay's own classical mentor Paul Hindemith, music that also reminds me of academic American composers of that day like Roy Harris, Marc Blitzstein, or Ingolf Dahl.

An ensemble of winds is joined by a string quartet, a solo trumpet, piano, and, when action is needed, a snare drum. There are some emotional, leaning harmonies when Donald's absentee mother visits him once, some agitated figures with spikey piano lines when Donald rebels against the unfairness of his whole predicament, and yet a happy cavorting energy for trumpet and bassoon when bright spots appear to give the boy some hope of fellowship with one of the counselors. Three horns and solo winds seem to suggest a more solid future for Donald late in the film, and yet the whole score, like the wary tale we're watching, can only manage a suspended harmonic at the end, still posing rather than resolving the same question of "Who speaks for the quiet ones?"

While postwar nightclubs booking cool jazz trios and a growing record industry backing hot jazz soloists flourished, the whole genre of jazz (as opposed to the wartime dance bands that only flirted with jazz) gained, evolved, and spread across the Western world. In the United States dueling coasts nurtured their own partisan brands of jazz music—West Coast cool, bebop, campus jazz á la Dave Brubeck, Dixieland á la Jelly Roll Morton—while meantime, far away but along parallel lines, a specialty line of jazz-savvy artists and audiences was materializing after dark in Paris nightclubs and bistros around the Montmartre district, the Latin Quarter, and the Left Bank. Why Paris? Why so receptive to black jazz? It was said that so many American soldiers—Harlem infantrymen—were still hanging around after the war that the thirst for American music was stronger around Paris than ever. At the same time, top jazz performers like Dexter Gordon or Nina Simone had fled to *Paree la nuit* seeking recognition that was not forthcoming in the United States, seeking also refuge from the prejudice and invisibility they had suffered there. And as for the loyal French patrons of those cabarets, something about the free insouciance of postwar jazz improvisation as they saw it, the otherness of the bold jazz vocabulary and syntax, and the secret wisdom it supposedly contained (which was really just the canniness of instinct)—and, of course, the shady charismatic biographies of the great jazz solo players/singers/writers of the day—was just irresistible.

As jazz on records became a more popular subgenre of the music industry, soundtrack jazz became a viable language for screen drama. Consequently, black composers were now more often consulted by filmmakers, not only for their assumed jazz familiarity, but for any broader descriptive orchestral music they could bring to a film. The most progressive moviemakers noticed that trend and moved to take advantage of it. Liberal theatrical director Martin Ritt, hoping to bring a dry realism to his films, hired Ellington for *Paris Blues* (1961), in which Paul Newman and Sidney Poitier portrayed jazz artists of Paris's Left Bank scene. Although there are more isolated set pieces of black jazz in this film than dramatic scoring, attention is definitely drawn to the presence of the black composer in film (the "Battle Royal" sequence is a standout piece of active narrative scoring). The soundtrack was nominated for that year's Oscar award.

By the 1960s, a whole new generation of jazz artists and writers, both black and white, was waiting in the wings to introduce dramatic jazz, movie jazz, to a whole new audience. In films, white composers were popularizing a rather domesticated kind of jazz—melodic with only traces of improvisation—composed by young Hollywood guys like Johnny Mandel, Henry Mancini, Elmer Bernstein, for the big studios. And yet, just outside those studio gates, unconventional filmmakers like John Cassavetes were hiring Afro-American jazzmen like Charles Mingus for his radical film *Shadows* (1960)—improvisatory music for an improvisatory cinema style. The French director and jazz aficionado Louis Malle hired horn great Miles Davis[6] to produce a soundtrack score for his new film *Ascenseur pour l'Echafaud* (aka *Frantic* and *Lift to the Gallows*, 1957), which was said to have been completely jazz-improvised. Davis commented on his compositional process: "Malle wanted me to write the score, but I had never written music for a film before. So, what I would do is look at the rushes of the film and get musical (modal) ideas to write down. Then I worked from there."

Also in Paris, the pianist/leader of the internationally famous Modern Jazz Quartet, John Lewis,[7] was beginning to score films like *Sait-On Jamais* (aka *No Sun in Venice*,1957) using some of his own strikingly original fugal techniques; scoring also Robert Wise's *Odds Against Tomorrow* (1959) with its famous "Skating in Central Park" music sequence—all of it with a chamber-music charm and clarity (piano, vibes, bass, drums). Each score reflected Lewis's distinctive musical voice, both in his penchant for neobaroque structures and references, and his most-identifiable harmonic lingo with its subtle jazz awareness—bent notes at the end of phrases and so forth. It was as if Bach or Purcell had known how to swing and were, perhaps, part black. Lewis's MJQ had always courted the black intellectual set, well versed in avant-garde jazz, but with his film scoring he found himself attracting an ever-wider variety of listeners and employing an ever-wider compositional language in service of each film, reaching well past jazz, certainly well past the traditional expectations of a black composer.

Figure 6. Quincy Jones. *Source*: Bridgeman Images.

Mainstream Hollywood would take a little longer to acknowledge the black composer for films, but a key figure in that acceptance was Quincy Jones,[8] composer/arranger for such disparate pop acts as Frank Sinatra and Michael Jackson and, almost from the start, a force for quality and variety in soundtrack scoring. Much of that resourcefulness must have come from his year of study under the tutelage of the Parisienne composer Olivier Messiaen. Through at least three distinct career periods, Messiaen had explored disparate compositional sources that can be said to have influenced Jones in his film scoring, at least in a broad conceptual way: (1) the concept of asymmetry (Messiaen studying and transcribing the precise rhythmic patterns of multiple ethnic cultures, and Jones scoring dramatic film sequences with free-flowing time signatures and broken, shifting rhythms); (2) the notion of incorporating "found sounds" into otherwise conventional composition (Messiaen's practice of traveling the world collecting bird calls, then notating them onto music paper and creating whole compositions around those note patterns, perhaps in some ways prefigures Jones's occasional practice of borrowing percussive sounds from the real world—rhythmic body slaps, tapped soda bottles, finger snaps, drum rims—to enliven and authenticate an otherwise conventional screen score/story that needed a funky touch). There was also (3) a strange lushly tonal period in Messiaen's career when he produced a series of uncharacteristically thick-harmonized and rather sensual orchestral pieces showing the wide range of his musical imagination. Jones apparently learned from that versatility, too, adopting a similar eclecticism to both his jazz band writing and his movie writing, able to score both sparse atonal ensembles and rich symphonic settings—both swinging big bands and the latest funk and rap charts, music of completely different musical grammars. Hollywood was initially skeptical of him, however: the persistent caveat in the industry as to whether a black composer could actually move beyond informal types of music, beyond jazz, toward a conventional score for a serious film. As late as the 1960s, Jones's future Hollywood colleague Henry Mancini once told me the story of receiving a phone call from some mogul at a big studio who was considering Jones for his first film scoring job. As Mancini described it, "I only gradually realized that I was being felt-out for an opinion about Quincy; and the question was, Did I think a black man could handle a dramatic picture??" (Mancini, *Mention* 151–52). This would have been for the

1965 Sidney Lumet[9] film, *The Pawnbroker*, starring Rod Steiger as a Holocaust survivor living a buried and bitter life in the slums of New York City. Could Jones handle the job?

Again, the film's Harlem setting may have been what first suggested a black composer to the producers of *The Pawnbroker*. Like so many of his classically trained predecessors and peers, Jones's prospects for film scoring jobs were habitually channeled into genres and grooves coded black. But the *Pawnbroker*'s director persisted and, in the end, Jones gave them a roiling, punchy, big band score, spiced with the neighborhood's Spanish lingo. But he also keyed the Steiger character's flashbacks of Nazi torture with jangling dissonant chords and orchestral effects, while supplying a milder, flowing melody to accompany memories of the prewar days when the pawnbroker still had a young, unmolested family and his own dreams were of the bright future rather than the dreaded past. The climax of Lumet's film and of Jones's score, though, comes as Steiger bends over the dead body of his young, naïve pawnshop clerk—a neighborhood kid gunned down in the lawless streets. Though we can see the pawnbroker's outrage, his mouth wide open screaming at the sky, we hear no voice: instead, there is just a shrieking solo trumpet from Jones's score and it is as if the whole world freezes there. (I take this to be Quincy Jones's tribute to a similar scene in a film from ten years earlier—maybe the most powerful film music moment in all of cinema—Ravi Shankar's scoring in the Satyajit Ray film *Pather Panchali* [1955] when, as a poor rural family kneels over the body of their teen daughter felled by a virus, the natural sounds of the soundtrack are erased and all we hear are the high, reedy, piercing notes of a tar shehnai pipe from the music score in place of the family's cries.)

An even more demonstrative score was penned by Jones in 1967 for Richard Brooks's chilling black-and-white film, *In Cold Blood*, about an ordinary midwestern family summarily murdered, for no apparent reason, by two aimless drifters. The score combines unsettling atonal lines, deep bass elements that even the film's sound engineers objected to as being unwieldy, some swagger-beats indicative of the misfit killers, and a whole cadre of tactile sounds as I have mentioned: the finger snaps, slapped body parts, empty soda bottles tapped rhythmically—all traditionally nonchalant sources of rhythm that seem to mock the intense violence we know is boiling under the surface of these characters.

Over the years, then, having been given the chance, Jones likewise excelled at a whole range of more conventional jazz-pop scoring, providing polished mainstream scores to romance films like *For Love of Ivy* (1968), caper films like *The Hot Rock* (1972), detective yarns like *Madigan* (1968), even a lushly scored western with a Spanish accent (working with singer José Feliciano), *MacKenna's Gold* (1969). By the 1970s, Hollywood was beginning to notice the money value of black music on the pop scene—not only through Jones's association with pop star Michael Jackson but through his own series of pop/jazz/funk albums like *Ai No Carrida*, *The Dude*, and *Stuff Like That*. He did a tribute album to the jazz of Mancini, too, in thanks for the leg up.

Hollywood was still wondering, though, how to get that very specific black energy and spirit onto movie soundtracks. One perfect vehicle would appear to be Isaac Hayes's Oscar-winning music to the black detective thriller *Shaft* (1971), a mix of funk beat, smooth sexy voices, and sharply written brass/sax punches. It won the award for Best Song but it really was a piece of exciting functional scoring and should have been nominated as such. The film's director, Gordon Parks, had brought Hayes on board and knew exactly what he was getting: a cutting-edge black-as-pitch soundtrack. For his part, Parks was something of a polymath—an expert at everything. He had started as an award-winning photographer for *Life* magazine, one of their few black employees, then had written an autobiographical novel, *The Learning Tree*, about his own growing up in rural Kansas, then had both written and directed the film version of that book. Surprisingly enough, he was also a schooled and resourceful composer in his own right. His orchestral score for the film version of *The Learning Tree* (1969) is full of nostalgic tuneful music, choral hymns, descriptive orchestral passages underscoring a tornado scene, even a playful buoyant vivace for a sequence at the old swimming hole. His main song, "Where Grows the Learning Tree?," is Disney-sweet, made of fourths and octaves, but then is varied endlessly throughout the film: heard first from a studio chorus, later as a baroque harpsichord piece, then as a mock-dirge during childhood games, still later as a Schumann-like piano concerto paean to young love and, at last, as a sober andante behind the life-advice soliloquy given by the wise old blind uncle of the main teenaged character.

Hollywood beyond the 1980s had its own cast of talent to add to the history of black composers for film. The multiple movie scores of Terence Blanchard,[10] carefully structured and classically aware within a jazz idiom, reflected his pluralistic background. He had been a student of the Thelonious Monk Institute of Jazz, eventually becoming its artistic director. His trumpet-playing experience in the Lionel Hampton orchestra is what had brought him to the attention of the recording industry, and his growing success there was quickly noted in Hollywood where, before long, he would become the favorite composer of director Spike Lee. A typical Blanchard soundtrack knows both how to swing and how to narrate storylines with tension-and-release motifs that frame the characters onscreen: nineties-era films like *Jungle Fever*, *Clockers*, the epic biopic *Malcolm X*, and the Oscar-nominated music in 2018's *BlacKkKlansman*. He has contributed to more than forty films for a variety of directors at this writing and, yet, also keeps up an active jazz recording career and a growing interest in the composition of extended orchestral, classically oriented, concert works. In 2021, he became the first black composer to have an original opera scheduled at the Metropolitan Opera in New York, the ambitious *Fire Shut Up in My Bones* with a libretto by Kasi Lemmons. It opened the 2021–2022 season following its premiere at the Opera Theater of St. Louis. A previous opera, *Champion*, on the life of boxer Emile Griffith, premiered successfully at the Opera Theater of St. Louis in 2013.

One younger musician, a generation behind Blanchard, graduate of the Johns Hopkins University Peabody Preparatory School with honors in classical and jazz piano and musicianship, is Camara Kambon.[11] At the age of fourteen, he was awarded a Eubie Blake scholarship, performed at Washington's Blues Alley with Dizzy Gillespie, and started meeting musicians who emphasized not only the compositional aspects of great jazz (as compared with improvisation) but also the applications of both jazz and traditional orchestral music in multimedia, in films. A scholarship in film scoring and music production/engineering to the Berklee College of Music in Boston followed, and not long thereafter came his first score for the Emmy-nominated film *Dancing: New Worlds, New Forms* from Orlando Bagwell. Flash forward to Kambon at age nineteen, scoring the Emmy-winning Bagwell documentary *Malcom X: Make It Plain* and then, at twenty-three, becoming the youngest composer ever to win the Emmy for his score to the HBO film *Sonny Liston: The Mysterious Life and Death of a Champion*. Subsequent films for HBO (*Questioning Faith*,

Confessions of a Seminarian, City on Fire, Story of the '68 Detroit Tigers), for PBS (*Citizen King, Matters of Race*), and for director Oliver Stone (*Any Given Sunday*) established his name as a dynamic and dependable collaborator, not only musically literate, thanks to classical training, but personally savvy and flexible thanks to his experience in jazz and doing studio arranging/composing/production work for rap and rock artists like Mary J. Blige, Dr. Dre, Eminem, and Sara Bareilles. Experience with all kinds of people, as with all kinds of music, can be the key to success and even survival in the music business, especially for the minority composer who is often slotted into clichéd kinds of projects. Says Kambon in correspondence from March 2023, "Diversity is a priority for the studios nowadays, which is good for underrepresented groups of the industry. There is a concerted effort to do this which has presented way more opportunities than even ten years ago." And still, these multimedia big screen/little screen projects can be a real challenge for the creative musician to also be a diplomat, even a counselor. "A lot of this has as much to do with overcoming obstacles as with creating music," he says. "It's important to understand that writing music for major motion pictures can be a psychological rollercoaster ride, dealing with different personalities and various personal interests. So, having the mental prowess to deal with the variables can be more important even than the music created. Without this, it's difficult to reach the finish line."

• In 2008, Kambon scored an Oscar-nominated short film, *La Corona*, whose soundtrack would become his first commercial release as a music artist. And all that training at the piano over the years has enabled him, oftentimes, to perform keyboards on his own film soundtracks, for instance on that Malcolm documentary, *Make It Plain*. There we get the unique Camara-blend of composer, performer, and dramatic scorer: a soundtrack for five players plus his own keys, using the score more for underlining than as narrative support—a sort of ongoing reflection on the legacy of Malcolm: quick background comments for tenor sax and piano and string bass that sound a bluesy, troubled note as Malcolm's story unfolds. Initially, there is rhythm and determination in the music that opens the documentary, but soon only a skeptical modal tonality is being offered and only in discreet passages that mark Malcolm's milestones: the death of his father, which may have been murder; Malcolm's prison years and the entrance of Islam into his young life; and the launching of his defiant spirit, first within and soon apart from the Nation of Islam Mosque. Malcolm's rage at the black/white impasse of his day, his frustration with the patient peaceful methods of the civil rights movement, his horror when white supremacists fire-bombed a church in Alabama where four little black girls were killed, are variously but ever-so-subtly rendered in this score by such compositional devices as trembling string bass figures and piano filigree, a high solo soprano sax, and then a flat-out passage of sax blues to a walking beat as Malcolm realizes all at once that he'll probably have to walk his path alone as white liberals, Black Muslims, African intellectuals, and so many of his own friends have begun to think him too radical for his own good and have begun to turn away. There are also Kambon's ringing, consoling chords on a Fender Rhodes keyboard behind tenor sax as actor Ossie Davis reminisces onscreen about "our Black prince, Malcolm." The modesty and steady sadness of most of this music score seems to be the only element left to sympathize with Malcolm's crusade. The end credits of *Make It Plain* return us to the opening blues rendered by Billy Pierce's sax and Camara's keys. It's a remarkably assured piece of scoring for one so young, whereas a more narrative form of scoring was drawn from him in the DreamWorks sport racing mystery film *Biker Boyz*. Scoring somewhat as Terence Blanchard might have done, Kambon shows a penchant for the jazz sound-world of his main characters but an awareness, too, of the dramatic functional grammar that a narrative score needs to have. It's all a matter of collaboration, he reminds us: "The direction of a score is a direct reflection of the central themes my director is trying to convey throughout his/her film. After getting a sense of the director's intention, I do two things: interpret that musically, which includes deciding about orchestration and tone, and establishing an overall concept for the music. So, it is extremely important to work with my director. . . . There was a time when music was considered to be just an afterthought to a film (and it still happens). But I've found it more common to work with directors who consider music a key element to their creative process, whether that means listening to it as they're writing or identifying specific music that works as key elements in the storyline. I think this is a generational change that technology has had a hand in, giving filmmakers nowadays the ability to work with varied media elements all at the same time. But regardless of whether the director is new- or old-school, I've never experienced being considered just a hired hand but rather a collaborator from the start. . . . That's the great thing about composing film music, the collaboration. And there isn't one size that fits all. Each film can offer an opportunity to tap into a different aspect of my creative palette. That's the joy of this process. And it's exhilarating when a synergy is established."

Carrying on the perspective of the black composer in films, if arriving from a different direction, is Texas native Chanda Dancy.[12] Dancy is a veteran of the indie rock music circuit, having played in and written for the performance group Modern Time Machines and gaining experience through exposure on YouTube, scoring Wong Fu Productions' ongoing melodrama series *Everything Before Us* (2015), which in half-hour episodes follows the young multicultural clients and counselors of a DEI agency as they officially work to integrate new citizens into the given society but unofficially integrate emotionally and romantically with one another. A scene where a new Russian émigré, Eskra, gives a piano lesson to her Asian counselor using the Chopin *Étude op. 10, no. 3* seems to give composer Dancy her basis for the ongoing score in future episodes—mostly a piano score as hesitant and laconic as the shy characters onscreen. Certain characters begin to take control of their new lives and relationships, and Dancy, as though on their behalf, spins a baroque allegro on the keyboard, introducing self-conscious scoring for the first time in the series. Piano motifs and arpeggios continue to spot the complicating relationships while, in late episodes, what sound like synthesized string chords, sometimes running backward, lay behind whole scenes.

This fragmentary approach characterizes Dancy's other soundtracks as well, along with an impressive vocabulary of sounds: *Thrasher Road* (2018) features country fiddling and vocals (Chanda is a violin player, pianist, and sometime vocalist); the horror film *Lift to Hell* (2013, in which there are five elevators to choose from and you don't want to pick the deadly one!) features spooky washes of orchestral coloring (synthesized again?) lushly harmonized like a John Williams score but never developed or cumulative in nature. Thus far in her career, Dancy's opportunities for scoring have often been for short films or limited-access small screen productions with titles like *Killer Cove*, *Pigeon Kings*, and *My Teacher, My Obsession*. As soundtracks, these scores don't read as "black" and they seem unaware of black cultural influences; they are unconcerned, too, with any sense of personal expression or the desire to make their own statement outside the immediate needs of the plot. In one sense, this sparseness and this modesty is laudable. But in the long term, it's an unnecessary modesty on Dancy's part for she seems to have a good deal to say and a strong atmospheric sense within which to muse.

I am thinking of her seven-minute concert work for orchestra and chorus, *Centrifuge: The Powers That Separate Us*. It opens with a searching line for solo flute; then other winds blend in increasingly speculative and restless ways. Sections within the orchestra begin to differentiate and bring animation to the work. Brass, used as a block, build a stronger foundation under the woodwinds and, before we realize it, the chorus has entered, first providing sustained harmony, occasionally breaking into shouts and picking up on the animation of the piece's development section. But soon, the mounting energy reverses course; the instrumental forces gradually rescind and we are left with just the solo piccolo repeating what it suggested in the beginning and, although the questions remain, there *is* the feeling that a discussion has been had. That very centrifugal shape and dramaturgy of Dancy's *Centrifuge* makes one wish that she may get some bigger future film commissions where she can feel free enough and driven enough to apply her orchestral skills to some more directly descriptive, interpretive movie music.

Certainly, the origins, the culture, the race, even the gender of a composer may each have an influence on what music comes out, but individuality is what's unique; that's what drives creativity. So-called black music these days encompasses all the genres and styles that are available to any composer. And in the same way that films by any black directors can range all over the spectrum of subject matter, all over the color lines, all over the map, so too have the contributions of black screen composers encompassed all kinds of music, many musical traditions, and a growing list of ambitious young composers intent on making not just black history but some history of their own.

6

Interlude

Choral Music in Films—A Mini-History

THE LAST THING MOST MODERN movie directors want to hear from their newly hired soundtrack composer is that she or he is planning to use a chorus in the new film's music score. What could be more intrusive to a movie's rolling narrative, to a viewer's concentration (or a director's authority), than the sudden dramatic presence of fifty voices—even wordless choral singing—forcing their way to the forefront? History holds a few examples of highly accomplished choral scoring that, nonetheless, were rejected from their films, precisely because of the vivid impression—the interruption—they would have produced had they been allowed to proceed. Film score advocates may think this yet another example of anticomposer prejudice on the part of nervous directors or selfish studio overlords, and yet there is a point to be made about the profligate power of music to exaggerate dramatic moments onscreen—and you can hardly sing out in bigger capital letters than with a forthright chorus, no matter if it's a tight-harmony madrigal group or a mighty studio choir. Filmmakers are wise to be wary. And yet . . .

. . . And yet, film composers continue to be tempted by the potentials of the choral alternative on the soundtrack. After all, when it works well—is well composed and well placed—the effect can be memorable, not only in the sense of musical interest but in a cinematic sense.

The most obvious screen vehicles where a bracing choral sound has often been heard are historical or religious-themed films, stories where noble choirs are already, as it were, in the air. Grand archaic choral music by Miklós Rózsa was applied generously to the soundtrack of *Quo Vadis* (1951) about ancient Rome in the time of Nero. It was appropriately blunt and thrusting choral music to support both the epic scale of the film and the antiquity of the setting, although it should be said that Rózsa's tonal approximation of ancient harmony, scored in parallel fourths and fifths, owes more to his own personal Hungarian Magyar heritage than to the Roman Empire. Still, the imperial point was made by the choral sound itself and it is that presence we remember most from that film. As much as fifty years later, that same vocal authority was still being exploited, whether in John Debney's resurrection music from *The Passion of the Christ* (2004), John Barry's royal court music for Britain's King Henry II in *The Lion in Winter* (1968), or Basil Poledouris's pagan chorus, "The Riders of Doom," in *Conan the Barbarian* (1982). These were each anthemlike choral declarations—that is, they tended to be complete pieces unto themselves for which a section of the film had been set aside to be vocalized. Other similar stand-alone choral pieces heard in certain films include John Barry's "A Christmas Song" in *The Last Valley* (1971), Rózsa's choral rendering of "The Lord's Prayer" in *King of Kings* (1961), Ennio Morricone's "On Earth as It Is in Heaven" from *The Mission* (1987), or the "Exultate Justi" in John Williams's *Empire of the Sun* (1987). When Patrick Doyle's stirring choral lament "Non nobis, Domine" caps the battlefield scene in *Henry V* (1989), both the grandeur of courage and the tragedy of war (as Henry carries a dead drummer boy across the slaughter fields at Agincourt) are sounded in choral terms. Perhaps the most moving choral battlefield hymn on film has been Serge Prokofiev's music for *Alexander Nevsky* from 1938, but we'll stay with more recent candidates for this survey, considering how John Williams's "Hymn to the Fallen" memorializes lost lives after the horrendous World War II battle scenes in *Saving Private Ryan* (1998).[1]

It needn't always be high drama that these choral inserts serve. Recall the half-satiric, half-prescient jazz/scat chorus that interrupted the odd/mod western film *Butch Cassidy and the Sundance Kid* (1969).

Burt Bacharach contributed complex contrapuntal choral writing in a bouncy jazz-waltz style and arranged a vocal blend that sounded more like a 1960s television commercial chorus than film scoring and yet harmonized and syncopated it in coordination with a silent montage of bank robbery scenes being pantomimed onscreen. How these wily characters, Butch and the Kid and their shared girlfriend, charmed their way into a series of bank vaults, cash offices, and money trains is all told with the help of that five-minute choir cue: multipart jazz singing alternating with a kind of quiet modern choral saraband. At the time, such a creative use of choral writing in the middle of an erstwhile western received both praise and blustery criticism. It took a few more adventurous critics to point out that what Bacharach's mod chorus did for the film was to suggest the idea that it wasn't just a posse chasing Butch and the Kid; it was the changing times.

More often the formal choral sound has appeared on film soundtracks not as a spotlighted interlude like the aforementioned but just as tonal coloring to, for instance, add an aura of mysticism to a sci-fi or fantasy plot. Occasionally, Howard Shore's heavy scores to the *Lord of the Rings* film trilogy (2001–2003) were laced with distant choral voicings hoping to imply a mystical aura. Although Shore composed a number of specific choral moments as in the "Great River" or "Eventide" sequences for unison voices, or the boy soprano and choir during the "Breakup of the Fellowship" sequence, more often he relegated his chorus to a backfield line. Its purpose seemed to be to add a gloss of prestige to the production, and many films have benefited atmospherically that way. Alan Silvestri's memorable choral crescendos for an undersea world in the nuclear sub rescue adventure film *The Abyss* (1989), James Horner's boy choir effects for the mad scientist story *Brainstorm* (1983), Alfred Newman's reverent choral décor for the miracle play *Song of Bernadette* (1943), Danny Elfman's "Ice Dance" scene from the fairy tale *Edward Scissorhands* (1980), even John Williams's eerie "glissing" choir reaching both ends of the scale as we first meet the possibly dangerous alien creatures in *Close Encounters of the Third Kind* (1977) are all good examples of such nonthematic choral sweetening.

And so, the many possible ways of incorporating choral music into films fill the archives: absolute thematic music (think of the choral folk song medley attributed to Alfred Newman and Ken Darby in *How the West Was Won* (1962), ambient coloring (think of Bernard

Herrmann's *Obsession* [1976]), Ralph Vaughan Williams's distant choir giving voice to the ethereal ice-world in *Scott of the Antarctic* (1948), Henry Mancini's little Greenwich Village chorus in *Me, Natalie* (1969), even eccentric appearances like the grunting, whooping choral sounds at the end of Ennio Morricone's *The Good, the Bad, and the Ugly* (1966). It all keeps the choral quarrel going into the next generation and the next.

Ethnic-oriented choruses have been another occasional focus of soundtrack composers from Elmer Bernstein's revivalist singers delivering their gospel message to an Old West Denver mining camp in *The Hallelujah Trail* (1965) to the vocal welcome at the beginning of *The Grand Budapest Hotel* (2014), wherein a Swiss *naturjodel* ensemble called Ose Schuppel sings a Balkan-flavored folk song, later subtly referenced in the sly instrumental score by Alexandre Desplat. If gothic/pagan choral music can, with a stretch, also be called ethnic, Jerry Goldsmith's chanting chorus in the devil-worship film *The Omen* (1976) certainly made a big impression in this category, though his diabolic choral incantations were borrowed from Carl Orff's 1937 "Carmina Burana," which, in turn, merely parroted Stravinsky. But for that gaudy horror film, it was most effective scoring.

The most interesting choral scores have been those whose functional narrative music used opening choral anthems to develop variations thereafter. It was one thing for John Barry to write his magisterial choral opening to *The Lion in Winter* (1968) along with two or three other a cappella choral songs for the medieval court setting, but his real accomplishment in that Oscar-winning score was to pace the film dramatically by placing choral interludes throughout the film that acted as scene markers. A choral presence, thereby, can be as effective doing that kind of prosaic page-turning duty as it can when singing out the main theme. Recalling Rózsa's *King of Kings*, its score was at its most emotional not at the height of its hymns but, for instance, when compassionate choral harmonies slid in behind the already-familiar Christ theme as Jesus quelled a demon-possessed peasant. There, chorus humanized the miracle.

In all such ways, the choral alternative continues to be intriguing and can tempt even the most defensive directors to consider the possibilities. As I have been warning, however, danger lurks. I am thinking of the French film *Clarembard* (1969) with its mock-baroque score by the Romanian-French composer Vladimir Cosma. The storyline plays like a fable and that very eccentricity is what permits, indeed welcomes, Cosma's choral surprises. Philippe Noiret plays a grumpy, failed aristocrat whose run-down estate has been turned into a textile factory and whose family is now employed there in futile drudge-work while he dallies, procrastinates, and complains. Then suddenly one day—is it a dream or a true miracle?—Noiret has a vision of St. Francis of Assisi who convinces him to divest himself of all his worldly burdens, reconsider his life, and thaw his stingy heart. Where St. Francis once famously "preached his Gospel to the birds," Noiret now has his own aviary encounter, wandering in the forest of his estate, an encounter with his own conscience. Composer Cosma uses the opportunity to encourage a most original chorus, indeed. His is a madrigal chorus performing a baroque theme we have already heard in the score but now he presents that theme through a series of bird calls—that is, the full choir mimicking birds: first, a counterpoint of twitters leading to a chirped version of that theme, then gentle commentary from a cuckoo, and so on. A lyrical legato passage for male voices returns us to the twitter of the opening and then the cuckoo brings *Clarembard* back down to earth for an ending. Only because Cosma's thematic material is strong, and his choral writing so clever, is this creative cue saved from seeming merely humorous or absurd. Instead, its boldness inspires admiration and could have drawn the filmgoer closer to the main character and deeper into the film, but here is where the choral quarrel manifests as we warned: for, presented with this rather brilliant bird chorus, director Yves Robert decided to cut the scene so that only a fragment of the original music now remains in the film, way in the background. Naturally, Cosma's bird calls, fully exposed, would have drawn attention to the composer and momentarily away from the film. There is one more choral moment, however, where the choir *is* allowed to preside when, in the end, Clarembard is inspired to head off in a horse cart to preach his newfound Franciscan message of generosity to the world. Cosma introduces a swinging, unaccompanied gospel choir, both jazzy and fervent, to see him off, and the film's director lets us hear it.

Michel Legrand experienced the same kind of music mutiny trying to complete his careful choral score for Jacques Deray's romantic murder mystery *La Piscine* (*The Swimming Pool*, 1968). The original Main Title music featured two voices (Legrand and his sister Christiane from the jazz group the Swingle Singers), then a serene chorus moving in around them, gradually adding dissonance to the harmony, hinting at the complications and betrayals in the story to come. Choral injections of new, more jazzy ideas were then meant to follow the intrigues of the plot. But as Legrand would discover, once he had demonstrated his plan to the director, "Deray's initial misgivings about any choral intrusion quickly turned to worries. Deray likely lost his footing during the recording sessions. What he heard frightened him; not the tunes themselves but rather their (choral) treatment. He asked over and over, Why the voices? Where do they come from (in the context of the screen story)? I tried to reason with him, to get him away from that kind of literal thinking . . . but I had been too radical."[2] And so, Legrand had to redress the orchestrations and curb the voices. Only twenty minutes of music remain in the film and it's the vocal bits that are best: one cue with two voices and solo violin; a single choral impromptu and only a few others. A similar fiasco occurred around Jerry Goldsmith's score for the fantasy film *Legend* (1985), where his playful use of chorus was, first, curtailed and then dismissed in favor of a less distinctive, less disruptive score by the pop band Tangerine Dream. With similar results, France's radical composer Antoine Duhamel created a whole eight-minute motet for church choir and timpani for use in Bernard Tavernier's sci-fi/social commentary film *Death Watch* (*La Mort en Direct*, 1980), yet only a fragment of it survives onscreen, buried behind Max von Sydow's monologue about a fictional composer who is supposed to have composed that music.

So, the lesson persists for any composer who thinks he or she wants to submit choral music to their latest soundtrack: take care. Unless the screen story includes Roman soldiers, ceremonial services, historical settings, or miracle/fantasy tales, there's likely to be a quarrel about it. And yet . . .

. . . And yet, when it works—when it is allowed to work and when it is especially designed to work—the choral presence in a film score can be tremendously rewarding. That proven friend of film music, Steven Spielberg, worked productively again in 1998 with John Williams to apply some effective choral scoring to his new film about the historic African slave revolt aboard an 1839 ship called *Amistad*. Here was vocal music being used in all three ways that we have seen in this brief survey: it is music with an ethnic slant, in this case African tribal affectations as filtered through Williams's style; it features an opening representative anthem, in this case "Dry

Your Tears, Afrika" for mezzo soloist, tribal choir, and hollow drum percussion, with its 3/4 meter broken by a repeating three-measure chant in 4/4; and it subsequently uses that choir and that anthem throughout the narrative functional parts of the score to help tell the story. With the film's given distance of history and ethnicity, such a bold choral score was not only accepted by the director and the audience for *Amistad*, but considered the film's finest single element, the heart and soul of the film.

Apropos of that, recalling how Howard Shore's ambitious scores for all those *Lord of the Rings* epics used choral powers more as ambient support than for comment or narrative help, chorus was there for padding and for the grandiosity it implied. But does anyone remember the 1978 animated version of the Tolkien *Lord of the Rings* stories directed by Ralph Bakshi with its piquant and detailed music score by Leonard Rosenman—his charming Hobbit march, the virtuoso orchestration throughout, and the most moving choral anthem for a mixed choir of children and adults in praise of Tolkien's wiseman and guide Gandalf, here known as Mithrandir the Gray Wanderer? They sing, "Mithrandir, though you're hidden, we're still guided by your light, you're walking beside us, a friend in the night." For that space of time, at least, chorus owned the movie and the audience.

As I have said, filmmakers are wisely wary of any such choral distraction from their precious visuals. But when it works well, there is certainly a thrill to be had. No quarrel there.

Part III

New Ambassadors

7

Henry Mancini (1924–1994)

The Populist Movement

Figure 7. Henry Mancini. *Source*: Courtesy of the Film Music Society.

Two innovations were already in progress in the entertainment industry when Henry Mancini came along in 1958 to make his own history with them: the introduction of jazz music into film scoring (which he domesticized into award-winning scores for the television series *Peter Gunn*), and the invention of high-fidelity stereo record albums for home listening (which he turned to his advantage by issuing soundtrack records of his screen scores—movie music without the movie). The fact that Mancini's music was inherently attractive, sophisticated, and memorable—at once "cool" by that era's definition and "warm" in a timeless sympathetic sense—was the main cause of his explosive success up through the 1960s and his endurance beyond.

Born near Pittsburgh, Mancini practiced piano and flute from a young age under the stern eye of his steelworker father and, as a teen, listened to the big bands over distant radio stations, soon writing out the arrangements he heard there and beginning to understand the orchestra. In the interviews that follow here, he talks of the local mentor who encouraged him in the direction of movie music and who arranged for him to enter the Juilliard School in New York, then how World War II interrupted those studies. Yet, even overseas he used the military orchestras to learn all he could about orchestration and composing.

The tough wartime atmosphere that informed his studies, together with that stern father figure leaning over his shoulder even miles from home, gave the music Mancini would eventually write an air of melancholy and a genuine sincerity so that his songs seemed more than pop tunes and his dramatic movie writing seemed to have an effective restraint of emotion, making them all the more compelling.

Three categories take the measure of Mancini's talent: as an arranger/orchestrator, as a screen dramatist through music, and as an original melodist. As arranger, we can hear him developing a personal style writing for the big dance bands just after the war, then creating a series of colorful pop-jazz orchestral record albums, starting with the tight, smart orchestrations of the *Peter Gunn* music, adding strings to a follow-up TV series, *Mr. Lucky* (1959), and carrying on with an album of standard tunes called *The Mancini Touch*, then experimenting with the lean sound of just twelve players on an album called *Combo*, and by the mid-1960s, adding electric guitar to a brassy band and calling the program *Uniquely Mancini*. Somewhere in there, he penned his own book on orchestration called *Sounds and Scores*,[1] and in a series of spectacular movie-score successes, he exploited unusual instruments—autoharps, calliope, stark solo French horn, out-of-tune pianos, electric violin—to make each soundtrack distinctive.

Mancini's dramatic ideas were often as noticeable as those unusual instruments: the sassy baritone sax accompanying a cartoon cat at the beginning of *The Pink Panther* (1964), the minor-key waltz (with a major-key midsection) that runs through the romantic mystery film *Charade* (1963), or the purposely off-tuned pianos at the heart of that creepy thriller film *Wait until Dark* (1967). Or notice the way that some Mexicali dance music filters up from the street of a sleazy border town and mixes with a murder taking place in an upstairs hotel room in Orson Welles's *Touch of Evil* (1958). These were dramatic ideas as well as musical ones. By the same token, if less demonstrably, his penchant for creating an expressive melody that somehow represented the main message or main character of a film was another way of being a screen dramatist: the naïvely yearning song "Moon River" that reveals the country-girl character at the heart of *Breakfast at Tiffany's* (1961); the sad, obsessive oboe piece with its uncertain meter that characterizes the disturbed final days of movie star Joan Crawford in *Mommie Dearest* (1981); or the long-lined piano piece that the composer-character George Webber is working on throughout the film called *10* (1979), which mirrors Webber's own evolution toward maturity—these are great lessons in simple, effective screen dramatization through orchestration and through memorable melody.

Mancini certainly had an original and personal way with melody, with song structure, whether or not those melodies were ever going to become singable songs. And those melodies came so fluidly and frequently to him that they stand, oftentimes unnoticed, in the background of many a film score and as ancillary tracks on many a Mancini record album. Some of the best of them are just instrumentals: charming and humorous like "The One-Eyed Cat" or "Without a Clue" or "What's Happening!"; some, as we've said, shaded with melancholy like "Lujon" or "Theme for Losers," which are merely album filler-tracks but quite moving in themselves, or "Cheryl's Theme" from *Sunset* (1988)—isolated music cues that I have elsewhere referred to as "stolen moments," composer-inspired grace notes in the midst of otherwise insensitive films.[2] Sometimes Mancini experimented writing longer forms: songs with multiple moving parts like "Le Jazz Hot" from *Victor/Victoria* the film version

(1982) or "Paris by Night" from *Victor/Victoria* the stage musical version (1995); or there are a few multipart concert works like his *Beaver Valley* suite or his *Piece for Jazz Bassoon*.[3] But it is all based in melody and it is interesting to hear how he could take even ethnic dialects (when films required them) and make totally personal melodies out of them: "Fumiko" in *The Hawaiians* or "Giovanna" in *Sunflower* or "Yasmin" in *Arabesque*.[4]

Some say that Mancini's jazzy *Pink Panther* music or the raucous *Peter Gunn* theme is his exemplar, or even the chilling waltz "Whistling Away the Dark." But if it isn't the song "Moon River," I would vote for the weary, nostalgic "Dreamsville," which comes from the days of *Peter Gunn*, with its empathetic sway between Cmaj9 and Gm7/C. Only later was it given lyrics and turned into a song, but it began life and survives to this day in Mancini's own recording as a simple kind of life-summary instrumental for brass choir, piano, and sad sax.

Through our numerous conversations and a bit of correspondence, Mancini was as easygoing as his Hollywood reputation, as welcoming as those songs, and yet as meticulous as his orchestrations.

Interview with Henry Mancini

> JOHN CAPS: People who know nothing about your work as a dramatic film scorer—your use of jazz as a dramatic form or your modernization of the old-fashioned composing styles—probably know your name mostly through the many popular songs that have come from the films you've scored. They think they know you as a songwriter and, in fact, one of the distinctive features of a Mancini score is that it *is* most often melody-based. And then, the other innovation that your career represents is that those themes, and the music from many of those scores, were issued as record albums so that people could get to know the music away from the films. As a result, you became familiar to the public in a way that no other film composer had ever experienced before. You really put film music on the map, both culturally and commercially.
>
> HENRY MANCINI: And there were both good and bad outcomes to all of that. Having some of those scores on

records helped my career and helped bring the whole craft of film scoring to public notice. But, on the other hand, it also took attention almost completely away from the less-melodic, more-orchestral dramatic music that I so enjoyed doing and think I have been good at. It was that kind of storytelling music—sometimes symphonic, sometimes jazzy—that I came out to Hollywood to do. It's what I always wanted to do, right from childhood, really. And just a word about the songwriting thing: don't think of me as a songwriter per se. Songwriting is a very specific art and classic guys like Gershwin and Arlen and Rodgers have been the real practitioners. I'm a film composer and I often do think in terms of melody. But only sometimes, only occasionally, do those melodies get lyrics added to them and are used as actual songs in a film. That's not my main purpose. It's true that, on occasion, a song is called for like the scene in *Breakfast at Tiffany's* where Audrey Hepburn, in the script, is supposed to sit casually on the fire escape of her Manhattan apartment and sing a wistful song in which she reveals her lonely country-girl background—and for that I had to come up with a nostalgic song for her to sing, which became "Moon River" and enjoyed a lot of popularity away from the film. But those are special cases. All of the so-called hits I've had have been outgrowths of dramatic situations in films before Johnny Mercer or Leslie [Bricusse][5] or the Bergmans[6] ever put lyrics to them. But as a songwriter, I don't know, I wince a little bit at that. I shouldn't. Of course, a lot of times, people don't even notice a background score when it's just doing its dramatic job . . . but they'll notice your name if there's a song in there. Anyway, my point is that songwriting is a very specific craft, and I don't consider myself up there with the classic guys of the so-called Great American Songbook. I'm a film scorer.

JC: I understand. And although there is a lot more to be said about the songwriting you have done and how your approach to the song format has evolved over the years, let me put that aside for now and concentrate on your contributions as a film scorer.

HM: Yes, the needs of a film score—the needs of a film—come first.

JC: What I'd like to do is choose a handful of films in which your music scores were not just a sequence of individual music cues but seemed to hang together, following what I call the central line of each film; where you, the composer, seek out the film's main message or point of view and the score tries to stress that central line. I can start way out in left field with a film that didn't have much success, but which drew a very insightful and subtle score from you, I thought: the rather scandalous life story of the 1940s actress Joan Crawford written by her real-life daughter and called *Mommie Dearest*. It's a very tentative kind of music, given Joan's unbalanced mental state, her doubts about her own career and relationships, her controlling behavior toward daughter Christina, and her out-of-control emotional condition most of the time. Your score right from the beginning, with an uneven piano figure and a lonely flute theme, has a lot of unsettled undercurrents to it.

HM: It's interesting that you picked that one because I had a vision of Hollywood, of the whole unsettling Hollywood mystique of yesteryear, that was funneled through this one character, Joan Crawford: old Hollywood with a touch of excess ego, a touch of nastiness, and a certain sense of isolation—that's all in the Main Title music. And I don't know if I ever convinced the producer and director of what I was trying to do there. I guess if the picture had been a smashing success, they'd have accepted my point of view, but it wasn't. Still, it's a unique kind of picture—a glimpse of the dark underbelly: that's the main music, the central line, as you call it. That's why the shifting rhythm is there: a three rhythm, going between three and two.

JC: It has an obsessive quality, too, which matches Joan.

HM: Yeah, but it's not steady, the pulse of it.

JC: And so sad.

HM: Well, it was a sad picture, wasn't it.

JC: To me, the music score was the only element of the film that caught, or even sought, any compassion or understanding for the character. If the film had understood what the score understood, they would have *had* a success. Instead, it was all just put up there like an exploitive soap opera.

HM: That's what I kept trying to tell them. Also, I have some reservations about the way it was treated because there were some scenes in there I had scored that I thought were psychologically helpful to expressing the main character. One especially when she's getting dressed in the bathroom and she puts one leg up like she's admiring it, the camera admiring it, and you hear her theme there and it's both tentative and sensual, which I thought was a perfect statement. Yet on the final dub of the film, they took it out. I guess it unsettled them, but that was the whole point: that theme with five repeated notes and then a little turn, all over that unsteady piano figure. Later on, there's the scene where she sort of loses control in her rose garden and starts whacking all the blooms to pieces, and the score goes dark and violent with some fragments of the main theme. Yes, you picked a good one there as far as trying to depict a central line, in this case a main character, through the music score alone.

JC: In shape and style, that rose garden hysteria is scored a lot like the similar scene in *Wait Until Dark*, which is my next central line film, where Susie the blind girl realizes she is under attack by drug thugs and rushes around her apartment smashing all the lightbulbs so that, in the dark, they'll be as blind as she. And the scoring uses that same shifting bassline and dark muddy coloring.

HM: I've always been a creature of texture and coloring in my orchestrations. Dark, close colorings are inherently dramatic in the way the chords are voiced; I am very aware of that, wearing my orchestrator's hat. Here again, you just sit down with a blank paper and you have an idea. When I mapped out that scene, the bulb smashing scene (I called it "Bulbous Terror") I felt it as an almost continuous gathering of tension with only a few synch points where the music should catch something in the action.

JC: Of course, the chief instrumental feature that is expressing the central line in *Wait until Dark* is the very unique sound, the gimmick if you will, of using two pianos and carefully detuning one of them a quarter-tone flat so that it sounds very, very disturbed. You're dealing with microtones.

HM: That was an instinctual thing. When I saw Roat, the really vicious villain, I said, That son of a bitch is really evil. How can I suggest his evil when he's onscreen and evoke the fear of him even when he's not around? So, they had twin Baldwin pianos at the studio and I decided to have one tuned a quarter-tone flat, all up and down the keyboard, so that when you played, say, a G on the one piano and then the same G on the second piano, it would sound twisted—sound a little sick. And if you played a whole phrase with one piano mirroring the other, the effect was diabolical. The two studio pianists were complaining of vertigo, recording that score! But that's exactly the disturbing effect I hoped for: it became synonymous with the villain who delighted in terrorizing people. The very sound became familiar to the viewer and, from then on, could be used like a conditioned reflex: when you hear these quarter-tones, beware.

JC: You also juxtapose that diabolical sound with the relatively benign sound of a guy whistling, though he's whistling a disturbing tune.

HM: Yes, doubled with a piccolo, I think. And the other strange sound in that score was the high piercing sound of a Japanese Shō, which is a kind of reed pipe. I used it in several places. Strange sounds like that gave you a little of the spooked feeling that this blind girl was going through.

That, plus those detuned pianos went a long way to do what you said: score a central line for the film.

JC: Many listeners would be surprised to find you scoring anything dark and sinister like that. You are known more, in a surface view, for scoring romantic or humorous films. And your way with comedy scoring is quite personal. Can you define it at all?

HM: The use of humor in music always seems a rich vein to tap, not musical jokes or gags that say "look at me; this is funny," like playing wrong notes or consecutive seconds on the piano, but lightly humorous references within the music where you wouldn't expect it. You see, comedy to me is a serious business. I like it to be warm and humorous but not funny. Often if you get a good melody going, it can enhance the humor onscreen. It depends on the film. An amusing clarinet theme for the main character in *W. C. Fields and Me* (1976) is kind of an obvious choice, just like the lighthearted melodies that opened those early comedies like *Mr. Hobbs Takes a Vacation* (1962) or *Bachelor in Paradise* (1961). It fits; it's expected. And you can do things with orchestration, too, that add to the humor: like the solo tuba that leads the score of *Who Is Killing the Great Chefs of Europe?* (1978) obviously satirizing the humongously fat Robert Morley character. It's a gentle tease, if you will, but it sets a humorous atmosphere.

JC: Way back before all of this, before your reputation for any kind of scoring, you apprenticed at Universal Studios in the early 1950s, which you've described as a kind of assembly line factory of cheap movies.

HM: We were a music staff of six guys and we must have worked on fifty pictures a year.

JC: Cheap comedy films and westerns and sci-fis, a whole range of B pictures in an era when formula films and certainly formula music scores were most common. But we can talk about those days, later. The first really famous film you had to score came toward the end of your Universal days and that was Orson Welles's *Touch of Evil* in 1958. You were still pretty much a junior at the studio then. How come they gave that one to you for scoring?

HM: I was next in line!

JC: Of course. I see. What was the central line there?

HM: Welles had written a whole memo, not to me but to my boss, about what he wanted for the music. It was about not having the traditional theme music and storytelling score but rather just hearing the ordinary Tijuana street music that you'd naturally hear in this little border town where the film is set and then occasionally letting that street music rise in relation to the action onscreen; in other words, that street music would occasionally join the action onscreen and start to mix with it. And I knew what he was talking about.[7] It wasn't Mexican music, really, more like an Afro-Cuban mix. And you notice, there are no strings in that score. Strings would have been the kiss of death in that kind of picture. The dramatic music had to be limited to the natural sounds of the setting, which in this case were the border-town bands—saxes and brass. That's what Welles was suggesting and, even though he never talked to me—I was just an employee, after all—it's what I had in mind all along. They call it "diegetic music"—music that's already coming from the story onscreen, but it rises subtly to become part of the narrative score.[8]

JC: You must have been impressed by the film's famous opening shot: that three-and-a-half-minute continuous tracking shot that sets up the car bomb incident and sets the whole film rolling.

HM: Yes! One of several brilliant touches in *Touch of Evil*. And, remember, Welles's original concept for that sequence was that it play alone, by itself, with just some ambient street music playing behind it. But the studio executives got nervous about starting their film with such a stark and "artsy" opening and so they covered it with two things: they used that sequence to run the movie credits over it, and they tracked my main theme music loud and clear under it like a traditional Main Title intro piece. It still works wonderfully well, starting from the single bongo on the close-up of the time bomb and then the band building, sinister and modal, as the sequence proceeds and the tension builds. But it wasn't quite what Welles had envisioned.

JC: Can you describe the movie scoring business at Universal just in that period, when you were just one of the music staff?

HM: Well, I was at Universal Studios from 1952 to 1957 . . . I had come up through the wartime big band kind of music but I had always really been interested in the movies. As a kid in Pennsylvania, I had frequented the movies a lot and I was fascinated by the big orchestral scores you could hear behind the movies, y'know. And it puzzled me as a little kid: I was wondering where the orchestra was—maybe behind the screen, or someplace! But the musical part always interested me. I started writing arrangements when I was fifteen. I did a great deal of listening; I was a fanatic about that. I really studied the orchestra until I felt at home with it. So, naturally I do all my own orchestrations now; a lot of the best guys out here do that: Jerry [Goldsmith] and Elmer [Bernstein] certainly. Johnny Williams and Alex North. You make a sketch that is so complete, you can give it to the copyist and all they have to do is the secretarial work on it. The composer's personal sound comes from how compete his or her sketch is. The more complete, the closer the finished product will be to your intentions. It's like a mechanics set of tools; I think I know it pretty well.

JC: Was there a part of the whole scoring and recording process that you enjoyed most?

HM: The thing that gives me the most pleasure is the first rehearsal with the picture, you know, where you're there with the orchestra all assembled and they project the scene on a screen in front of you and you get to try out your music right there along with the picture. You know, I've had a lot of experience across lots of years but it's all very detached until you say Rehearsal with Picture, and then you can tell in your gut how well you've done, creating the right kind of music . . . or not. It's that first rehearsal that gets me. Seeing how well that dramatic jazz was working with those early *Gunn* and *Lucky* shows was a blast.

JC: For us too! But finish up about your history . . .

HM: Let's see; I started studying piano and then the flute and I ended up getting a scholarship to the big New York conservatory, Juilliard. The war interrupted all that, but then I got a chance to play piano in a few army bands, then in the Tex Beneke band (which took up after the death of Glenn Miller).[9] And that's where I met my wife, Ginny, who was singing with the band. She was from California and knew people out here, and so that's where we moved after the war—and a job opened up at Universal Studios needing some young film music guys. At that time, they had a staff of scorers, all with their music supervised by Joe Gershenson, the department head. I learned a great deal from him.

JC: You also studied academically out there, too.

HM: Well, yes. After the war, I chose not to go back to Juilliard but I felt I wasn't qualified to do some of the more ambitious composing I wanted to get into, so I got accepted out here [California] into private studies. I went to these people's houses, not to a classroom. I studied music theory and harmony with Dr. Alfred Sendry who was a classmate of Bartók. I studied mainly orchestration with Mario Castelnuevo-Tedesco and, with Ernst Krenek, mainly counterpoint and fugue.

JC: Very different lessons than you had with Joe Gershenson.

HM: Well, sure. Joe gave me the practical side and the commercial side of music as it applied to media composing. He had conducted for films, way back when they were "live" in the orchestra pits of the theaters, and so he came to know a great deal about both the way music worked with moving images onscreen *and* how to deal with the people in the industry as it grew, artists and executives and exhibitors alike. He used to say, "Take partners," by which he meant if you are the composer assigned for the next film in line at the studio, find out who's really in charge on that particular film—sometimes it's the director, sometimes the producer or even the sponsor—and partner with him or her; be in close contact there. If there's a theme or a scheme that you think should be influential in your music score, make a demo for whoever is the boss on that particular project and it'll give them the idea you're wanting, give them a chance to experience for themselves. If you just go off and work on your own and then come back with a finished product, and say, "I'm finished; here it is!" what happens if they decide you've been on the wrong track all along, or you have a change of heart? No, "take partners" and be in touch all the way along. Be a little modest and realize that filmmaking is a collaboration and, if you're lucky (well, the point is, it wouldn't be luck, then) everyone will be in agreement, at least about what music is going to do for this film.

JC: So, you were the youngest guy of this six-man music department at Universal Studios.

HM: . . . and it was really an assembly line of films coming through the studio every week: black-and-white melodramas and Rory Calhoun westerns and *Ma and Pa Kettle* comedies or *Francis the Talking Mule* and thrillers including the famous horror films in the Frankenstein or Dracula series and then the middle 1950s craze for science fiction films—space stories and creatures from black lagoons and all that. And most of the time, no one staff member did a whole picture. Instead, say, Herman Stein or William Lava would do the Main Title for the picture and then score a few more scenes along the way, then I would come in and, using his theme, would score a handful of scenes in reel 4 of the picture, and someone else would fill in the climaxes. These were patchwork scores.[10] Or they'd tell me they were going to "stock this picture," and that meant you had to go into the Universal music library and pull out these huge books of orchestral cues, labeled as to what type of music it was—there was a book of sample chase music, of sample suspense music, sample romance; all part of their stock music library—and you could take thirty seconds of that existing music—these were conductor parts—and use it to cover a scene in the movie you're working on, then you compose a little bridge to get to the next fragment from the library or a theme of your own. And all those bits together, recopied and smoothed out, would make a patchwork score for this rather conventional finished product: another Universal matinee movie. So, on the one hand, you never really got an identifiable personal sound to any one of those Universal scores because it had so many different hands in it; and, on the other hand, all the sci-fi scores could be said to have sounded alike because they were done in such a formulaic way: mysterioso passages followed by huge crescendos followed by fanfares as the heroes arrive. The westerns had all their clichés, too. I repeat, it was a movie factory, producing films for matinee audiences to consume. Initially, though, I think the reason Joe started assigning me a few films all to myself there at Universal was that I was writing some in-your-face melodies for some of those patchwork comedies and so they sort of stood out: the family comedies starring little Tim Hovey (who they were hoping would be a new Little Rascal or Shirley Temple), films like *Everything but the Truth* or *Toy Tiger*. And I sort of became the pop guy there at the studio for a while. They even had me doing the first teen rock 'n' roll musicals there (*Rock Pretty Baby*, *Summer Love*). But Joe was generous about it: when he saw that I could handle a whole film, he started to give me some dramatic things to spread out on. *A Man Afraid* (1957) was the first of those where I was able to write a fairly complex opening tension cue, then follow it up with a lighter piece but then turn that light music into a minor-key as the plot thickened. I was doing real film scoring by then and with my name finally mentioned onscreen ('cause before, those patchwork scores had just been credited as "Music supervised by Joseph Gershenson"). And *Man Afraid* led to a couple more dramatic scoring assignments, then on to my final Universal film there, finally in the "big time," when I got to score Orson Welles's *Touch of Evil*, then on to television.

JC: All in all, a great school for learning the skills you'd need to master the craft, searching the central line in each film, and all that. Twenty years later, the skills are the same; the only difference is you're working on more sophisticated films than ever. I turn to the Tennessee Williams play *The Glass Menagerie*, which you scored in its 1980 film version directed by Paul Newman. What did you think was the central line there? It certainly starts out bleak.

HM: Well, there are two distinct directions in that score, maybe two central lines in parallel. One is the bleak main theme. The thing that you try to do there is sketch these three rather lost characters—the mother, the meek daughter, and the troubled son, and the unfulfilled dreams and passions of all of them. I mean, they all seem to be pieces of the same screwed-up pie. And it's only when the "gentleman caller" comes in to visit that we start to feel a little humanization in the family, a little opening up of the daughter. All that is the obvious soap opera onscreen. But for the composer on such a film, I think your job in the opening is to try to put a question mark in the minds of the viewer like, "What the hell is this guy . . . we're seeing the son walking around town talking to the camera about his wayward life and the persistence of memories. What is this guy about and what is this old building he's walking up to?" We don't know at that point that these are memory-places for him and he is about to let us into some of those memories. But what kind of memories: is it sinister; is it depraved? And the music is very chromatic and harmonized very closely for winds. It opens in D-minor but then the main motif is in A-minor falling to Bb. So, there is tension and uncertainty there.

JC: It's a kind of blues effect that just feels, I don't know, the epitome of hopelessness: the son's hopelessness, maybe; the whole hapless family.

HM: But the other focus of that score was the dance hall music. Just like *Touch of Evil*, here was diegetic music being used as a dramatic background to the family's conversation but actually emanating from the dance hall or club across the street and being heard only through the open windows of the apartment. Blues tunes and tangos and sentimental warblers like "Where Is Dear Old Dad?" or "The Rhumba You Saved for Me"—music that's being overheard from across the street but also from across the ages: obviously representing the fond lost memories of the mother. The daughter hangs on to the little figures of her glass menagerie and the mother hangs on to this music. Again, Paul [Newman] as director had this concept all along and it's something I got onboard with absolutely. We had many discussions on that. And he allowed me to do that very hesitant opening music that you call "bleak," which has several starts and stops in it—it took me so long in my career to learn to take a breath like that—to let silence play a little bit without having to fill the space all the time. I mean, *The Glass Menagerie* Main Title track is hardly a compelling, commercial piece: it's a question mark and more effective because of that. I enjoyed that picture very much. And after we finished the score, Paul came up to me and said, "Hank, I didn't know you could write that kind of music!" And I said, "What the hell did you hire me for?" But we worked together several times like that.

JC: Yes. The country music in Newman's *Sometimes a Great Notion* (1971), jazz for his film of *Harry and Son* (1984), and a quiet chamber score for his TV movie, *Shadow Box* (1980). A few more central line questions, if I may. One huge score from the middle 1980s, a sci-fi horror story about space vampire aliens (!) called *Lifeforce* (1985). For this you wrote for vast symphonic forces, used the London Symphony Orchestra, wrote in long-lined and thick impressionistic harmonies, and then, we can hardly believe it, had the whole thing, basically, taken away from you.[11] I know the circumstances have been chronicled elsewhere so we don't need to rehash that, but can you draw a central line of what you were trying to do before they smashed it all?

HM: Well, the reason I took the damn thing was that the whole beginning of the picture—the way it was originally set up—the first fifteen minutes were like a ballet, where they approach the spaceship and go in exploring and discover the vampire victims and all that. No dialogue; just the perfect place for descriptive orchestral music. And so, I wrote all this stuff with long developments and clusters of impressionistic color and, as I was saying, the freedom to have starts and stops. I even created a big thrusting rhythmic theme for when a little adventure-feeling was needed. It was all in there. And I thought, it will be good for everyone to see that I can do broad symphonic things like this as well as "panther themes." And guys like John Williams and Jerry Goldsmith and Alan Silvestri had done successful symphonic sci-fi pictures lately. So, here, I thought, was my chance.

JC: It's true, I'd never heard you do complex impressionistic scoring like that.

HM: No one ever gave me a shot.

JC: There's also an undercurrent of sadness and alienation to the whole score. It's not just space music; it's kind of soulful.

HM: But then, after previews of the film or maybe it was just executive meetings, someone determined that *Lifeforce* was running too long or it didn't spring into action fast enough or it didn't have the kind of horror film edge that a film like *Alien* (1979) had had. So, they started cutting the film; cut out the whole opening sequence; chopped up the most atmospheric scenes, because there was little action there. And that meant that they were cutting into or even cutting out my music for those sequences as well. That basically left my score in shreds. They made mincemeat of it and I was never given the chance to go in and do the needle-and-thread work it would have taken to put the remaining score-shreds into some new shape. So, I just had to walk away from it.[12] Although the first fifteen-minute ballet was gone, they did leave the last fifteen-minute sequence intact. And a record album was issued of the original score as I'd written it, so that's something. The central line? Not so much space or horror or fear, but the unknown. You face the unknown and this is what it sounds like, feels like, to me.

JC: One other orchestral score that you did outside of the usual romantic pop reputation that you had, but which also got altered and edited by the executives in charge, was *The White Dawn* (1974), an adventure story about a trio of nineteenth-century whalers shipwrecked in Eskimo territory. In one sense, it was a broad adventure score with a big symphonic ship-at-sea sequence and some pounding sealskin drum percussion; at other times, there were more personal themes for a young Eskimo woman, some humor for the awkwardness of white men trying to navigate the sophisticated Eskimo culture; there was even your arrangement of an authentic native chant that an old Eskimo woman sings. It's a favorite score of mine and yet, again here, there was a whole sequence that you scored at the beginning of the film that the filmmakers decided wasn't—I don't know—moving fast enough or something. And so, they cut it. What's that all about? Obviously, the central line should have been the landscape.

HM: That was one of the hardest things I've had to score—just to know what kind of music would satisfy the needs of the locale and the primitive quality of the people. There was a concern among the producers that, no pun intended, it could be a very cold and stark film that almost gave the appearance of being a documentary, which is not very well thought of at the major studios, of course. So, how to warm up this movie, as it were; how to humanize it? And I was floundering around there until I heard the old Inuit Eskimo lady's song. The director had recorded her up in Baffin Bay and when I heard that, it triggered not only that theme but it sent me in a direction for the rest of the score, too, the migration across the ice and the seal hunt and the coming of winter. All that.[13] But, if you remember the film, it opens with the black-and-white footage of the whalers' shipwreck, which is scored with a full brass allegro as they chase and harpoon the whale; then the wreck comes and we switch to the aftermath: three sailors stranded in the arctic, trekking across the ice to they-know-not-where. And I had scored that desolation with, first, a high lone piccolo suspended over nothing . . .

JC: . . . which gives me the feeling of the thin frigid air and just the whiteness . . .

HM: . . . then juxtaposed with deep brass . . .

JC: . . . which could suggest the vast depths of ice underfoot. To me, when I heard the studio tapes of that music, I thought it was perfect. And if it had been allowed to stand, together with the whale hunt music, that would have constituted another practically fifteen-minute opening of a film with nothing but visuals and music. But, instead . . .

HM: . . . yes, instead, the producer and director didn't feel that ambient music captured the plight of the sailors in this dangerous land, the risks. Now, I had been scoring the alienation of this freezing no-man's-land and the strangeness.

JC: A question mark again?

HM: Well, just a suspended sense of strangeness. But they weren't buying it.

JC: So blind and shallow of them.[14]

HM: Well, what are you going to do? For me, the question was, we're sitting there in the dubbing studio and the filmmakers are throwing out my arrival-on-the-ice music and I have to come up with some alternate suggestion, there on the spot.

JC: Even though it's unfair?

HM: Well, so it occurred to me, if I brought in Emil Richards, the ethnic percussion expert from right there in Hollywood, right then and there while we're hashing this out, we could audition some strange percussive sounds: we ended up using a rubber ball scraping against a large gong, which produced an otherworldly sound; actually, you could say it sounded like an underwater whale song, a whale's call. And as soon as they heard that, everyone said, that's it. And so, that's what you hear in that scene: just nontonal percussive sounds, which leaves the characters unsupported in a strange land.

JC: Well, I still wish they had let your original sequence stand or, at the very least, put that eerie percussive effect over the music you had written. That would've pleased both angles.

HM: I wish so too, but in the end it's their film and you are hired help.

JC: One last score with a need for a central line to tie a lot of disparate scenes together, scenes that jump around in locale and in time is the Audrey Hepburn romantic tale, *Two for the Road* (1967). In one sense, it's a smart-aleck script (by Frederic Raphael) about a modern couple observed from their young honeymoon days traveling around Europe on the Grand Tour, to the almost-dissolution of their marriage. It jumps all over the place, but somehow there's one thing that's constant and the music score has the task of confirming that central line, right?

HM: I read the script and I couldn't understand what was happening. The story worked on, I think, four or five different levels—periods in the life of this couple—and it would go back and forth. And I just felt that you were going to need some sort of a guide to help you through all of that. So, this is a case where a theme . . . I mean, let's make a case for the theme now . . .

JC: Okay!

HM: . . . a case where the theme was the thread that tied the film together: no matter what part of their life they were in, traveling all around Europe and seeing them at different ages and stages, the theme was the one constant, you know. The theme represented their ongoing love; even though they bickered a lot and fought, their theme kept coming back. I don't know if I mentioned it in my book but, at first, I had submitted a different theme for that film.

JC: Which the director, Stanley Donen, hadn't wanted?[15]

HM: It was a little more "down," let's put it that way. It had long notes and was kind of reflective. And Stanley said that he wanted something that moves a little more because the opening animation behind the credits is going to have a car moving—it's "two for the road," after all. It's a traveling saga so its main theme ought to have a sense of motion—not only more notes in it but a constantly shifting harmony underneath. And so that's the direction I went in for the second try at a main theme. In fact, the bassline is constantly going contrary to the melody, but both have a solid harmonic structure.

JC: And the fact that the main tune, the final version, starts interestingly on the dominant before it modulates to the tonic chord; but it goes back and forth like that. And always in the background there's a running figure in the piano, the idea of constant motion.

HM: And remember, it was never used as a song in the film; it was strictly an instrumental theme. A while went by before Leslie [Bricusse] applied a lyric to it. I mean, we all agreed that there was no real place for the thing to be sung in the movie itself—it would have been intrusive to suddenly have someone singing about "two for the road, we'll travel down the years"—redundant to the story you're already telling onscreen. There could only be a cheap commercial reason for shoe-horning a song into that film and so Stanley and I agreed not to do it. As an instrumental melody, though, it's that film's central line, especially as played by the great French jazz violinist Stéphane Grappelli, whom I had asked for specially.[16] His sound is so French and sensuous, he was perfect for that film. And speaking of that, I often hear particular players in my mind when I'm writing a score, especially if they're very distinctive players. I compose with their sound in mind. Like Grappelli's sensuous jazz violin for *Two for the Road* or Plas Johnson's tenor sax for *The Pink Panther* or Vince DeRosa's French horn in *Days of Wine and Roses*. Or there was a young guy [David Wilson] who played this electronically altered violin that I'd heard at a cocktail party as he wandered around among the guests and I used his sound in the score to the witchcraft film called *Switch*. I heard those guys while I was writing; I wrote for them. Certainly, that theme in *Two for the Road* would have been different if I hadn't been thinking of that Grappelli sound.

JC: Rumor has it that, for you and your wife Ginny, it's the favorite of all your stand-alone songs.

HM: It is, yes. It kind of summarizes our "travel down the years."

JC: And it's not so much a love song as a road song, which is what Donen had been lobbying for, all along. Perhaps this is the time to ask about your melody writing history; I mean the evolution of your melody writing from some of your early, early songs for films like "Foxfire" or "Six Bridges to Cross," which was a hit for Sammy Davis Jr., circa 1956 or so. You did a few simple rock 'n' roll songs for those 1950s Universal teen musicals, but the first real undeniable Mancini song must be "Dreamsville" from TV's *Peter Gunn* show.

HM: Yes, a sultry sort of blues ballad for the Lola Albright character to sing in her most speakeasy voice.

JC: Like other songs of yours, I think it's essentially a piano song more naturally than it is a vocal: its midsection release goes all over the place harmonically and is hard to sing, but . . .

HM: Well, it *was* a piano construction but a lot of people sang it too.

JC: Movie songs meant to be sung are the next stage in this evolution, chief among which is "Moon River" from *Breakfast at Tiffany's*, which we've mentioned before. It had more separate recordings than almost any movie song in history. That was in the 1960s. By the cynical 1990s, people started to call it "maudlin," possibly because they remembered all the hundreds of sloppy, soppy records that were made of it: bad arrangements by second-rate bands and D-grade singers. But actually, "Moon River" has a very sparse and rather sophisticated harmonic to it: although it's supposed to be a country girl's ballad in C-major, it passes through some tasty seventh chords and some major/minor shifts that reveal just enough of an edge to keep it interesting. The lyric by Johnny Mercer also lifts the song from its movie origins to something universal: "We're after the same rainbow's end, waiting 'round the bend . . ." And it's a waltz: something Mercer never believed could be a hit in the stoic Baby Boomer generation!

HM: It was a surprise in that sense. I cast around for a whole month trying to come up with a concept. I knew Audrey Hepburn had to sing this thing in the film. And I didn't want to give her something she couldn't sing; she certainly wasn't known as a singer, at all. So, I found a copy of her previous film, *Funny Face*, with Fred Astaire in which she had to sing a Gershwin tune. And I discovered that, there, she was singing within a range of an octave and one . . . something like that. So, I knew I would be safe within that. And "Moon River" was constructed from there quite quickly—and from wherever these things come, inside the composer. As I said in my book, "Moon River" took a month and an hour to write.

JC: Fast on the heels of that success came two other Mancini-Mercer movie songs, the main themes of "Charade"—a minor key waltz with a major key bridge—and "Days of Wine and Roses," which is unusual in that it's not the typical A-B-A song form: it's two long musical sentences.

HM: Yes, I guess a little unusual in form. It just seemed to come out that way, starting with the title itself, "Wine and Roses," and the long five-count on the word "days." And the falling, kind of sighing, harmonic to help express this love story with a lot of tragedy in it—the trials of an alcoholic couple. Again here, as in *Two for the Road*, having a memorable song helped bind the film together. The one constant in their turbulent addictive relationship was their ongoing devotion to each other. The song underlined that. And you remember the end of that picture? Where you're not sure how these characters are going to fare from now on with their mutual alcoholism and all that? . . . he's looking out the window as his wife walks off and the wine-and-roses theme comes up and you're expecting it to rise into a big emotional climax where it says "The End," but instead the solo French horn plays out the last phrase of the song, but leaves the last note up in the air and ends it there.

JC: You talk about putting question marks at the beginnings of film scores to draw the listener in: here is big question mark at the end.

HM: That's the idea.

JC: There are some more carefree waltz tunes in your next films: "Dear Heart" and "The Sweetheart Tree" but I note, after the sophistication of "Two for the Road," you evolve to a real experimental song with long extended lines, pauses, inserts, add-ons, and recapitulations: the main song in the Patty Duke film *Me, Natalie* (1969). It sounds perfectly natural and legitimate as a song but it really goes all over the place, structurally.

HM: I know exactly what you're saying. It doesn't go where you think it's going. It's in three-quarter time but it adds on extended measures, almost impulsive, conversational, and yet firmly constructed. The film was kind of like that—one of those free-form New York plays you could see in a little theater somewhere, a gentle romantic comedy about this homely working-class girl looking for love. And the song for Natalie was meant to be gentle and impulsive too, with those two-bar extensions at the end of lines. A thoughtful, introverted song. In E-minor. Sometimes a deeper harmonic structure like that just feels right. I guess those minor ninths I was brought up with still get to me at times! You know, the big band era when all the ballads were being influenced by Ravel and Debussy and were kind of nice like that. It sticks with you.

JC: One more wandering song like that, a piano song with extensions and, like "Days of Wine and Roses," constructed in two long lines—but more complex than ever—is the main song in the movie *10*, called "It's Easy to Say."

HM: Yes, we needed a song for the Dudley Moore character, who's a composer, to be working on at the piano all through the film. He's trying to put together this song just as he's trying to keep together his life and his marriage. And it's a C-major-seventh piece, almost a piano impromptu, but a singable song about middle age: "You walk away and for a while you try the summer of a younger smile," says the lyric. That sort of thing. And the song has a complexity of form that the composer-character supposedly hammers away at throughout the film. I guess, in a way, the very complexity of the song and its sincerity, being honest with yourself, was what the film was about.

JC: And there are two other songs in that movie: the sort of Hoagy Carmichael blues, "Don't Call It Love," and the more mod "He Pleases Me" for Julie Andrews to sing.

HM: Yes. Those are basically four-square songs, though. Not wanderers. The song "Crazy World" that Julie sings in *Victor/Victoria*, that's another one that goes wandering a little bit or has extensions beyond the simple waltz it might have been. But it's all about having a strong theme, whether it's simple or sophisticated: the power of a theme. But there's a danger there, too. If all you have is a commercial tune in a movie and you keep repeating it all the way through, that's what gives us pop guys a bad name. I've tried never to do that. Even in *Tiffany's* where "Moon River" becomes, if you will, the conscience of the film—the theme that everyone remembers—I really only used it there a few times: as the harmonica opening of the film, as Audrey sings it to herself in the middle of the film, as a kind of cheap cha-cha in a party scene, and then as the big denouement with the chorus and all that at the end. In other words, it wasn't abused; it had a dramatic job to do and it worked very well. And that, I think, is a legitimate use of melody in film scoring, whether there are words attached to it or not. And I'm telling you, if you have a modern story up there onscreen with contemporary characters, you'd better not have an old-fashioned melodramatic Vienna-based music score underlining every line of dialogue and exaggerating the emotions. Something sparse, something with a little discretion, a little irony perhaps, goes a long way these days. That's what I tried to bring to *Peter Gunn*, to all those Audrey Hepburn films, to the *Pink Panther* series, to *The Glass Menagerie*, even *The White Dawn*. Plus, a little humor at times, the idea that, hey, we're all in this together. Then when you *do* have to come up with more of a heartfelt, truth-speaking melody like "Life in a Looking Glass" or "Two for the Road," it's real, it's sincere, and the listener receives it that way.

JC: Another like that is your "Soldier in the Rain." Or that memorable chromatic song ("Little Boys") in *The Man Who Loved Women* (1983). And let's not forget the chilling waltz that Julie Andrews has to sing in *Darling Lili* (1970), "Whistling Away the Dark."

HM: Yes. That's another sort of French waltz like "Charade" but a little more involved harmonically with turns that were almost approaching operatic. And I thought Johnny Mercer wrote a very moving lyric for that one. ("Often I think this sad old world is whistling in the dark . . . Sometimes I think my poor old heart has given up for good, but then . . .") The lyric is really *about* something. And the film was actually meant to be a musical, so, as a song, it really had a place in the film.

JC: And as I've been noticing, the naturalness of your melody writing comes out, not just in planned songs, but in instrumental melodies too, like "Lonely Princess" or "Sound of Silver"—tunes that are first meant as orchestral showpieces: I'm thinking of your Latin flavored "Blue Mantilla" with its French horn lead or that sultry piece with the thick strings harmonies called "Lujon." That's so songlike, it actually got a lyric years after the fact ("Slow Hot Wind"). But it is, first, a lesson in orchestration.

HM: Well, first of all, the Latin instrument called a lujon is a simple box fixed with metal plates that, when struck, make a five-note scale. So, the piece I wrote there had to be limited to those five notes—or, rather, I constructed a counterline from those five notes that would be the bassline behind the melody. And then I gave the melody to the strings section harmonized, as you say, very lushly . . . strictly a Ravel takeoff . . . the blocks of four in the harmony: it's just eight parts starting four parts in the violins and then four parts doubled an octave lower in the violas and the cellos. It's a very sensuous sound that Ravel made famous. So, he was my influence there, going for the almost tropical, Latin feeling. Again, that's the arranger/orchestrator in me, working in conjunction with the composer. That's the way it should be: if you're actually composing music, rather than just coming up with a tune, you should be working it out on multi-stave scoring paper, thinking in terms of structure and instrumentation and tonality. It's instinct as much as experience: to feel a scene and to feel when you should be in and to feel when you should make the weight of the strings heavier and to feel when you need the oboe doubling the flute or the bass clarinet and the clarinet together or just the bassoon. These little varying adjustments that you talk to yourself about when you're looking at the music timing notes. I think it's a sensitivity that's been missing for a long time and I think it's coming back.

JC: All these examples of the evolution of your songwriting from fairly simple to these more extended and more subtly harmonized pieces, though still hoping to write clearly and plainly. That's a full career circle, I guess. But, overall, I sense an evolution, too, as I've been saying.

HM: Of course, the films have evolved too. Each film gives you the platform: whether to write ethnic stuff or simple Americana or sophisticated jazz or classical or avant-garde, a song score or a jazz combo or a symphonic thing. It's interesting. It keeps your legs alive. And hopefully in the midst of all that variety of genres, it still somehow has the essence of you in it, self-expressive.

8

Laurence Rosenthal (b. 1926)

More than Respect

Figure 8. Laurence Rosenthal. *Source*: Photo by Richard Whittaker. Used with permission.

Toast on the Occasion of a Ninetieth Birthday

November 2016, which was the ninetieth birthday of the indispensable composer Laurence Rosenthal, furnished a welcome chance to celebrate his fifty-plus-year career in film, television, theater, and concert music, and to say why he has been of such value to those varied fields.

Passersby will recognize the most famous of his film scores—his intimate musical description of the deaf-blind world of Helen Keller in *The Miracle Worker* (1962); his medieval and Gregorian sounds that hang like an austere wall tapestry behind the twelfth-century screen story of *Becket* (1964); the open-air anthem and robust rhythms that bring scope and fervor to the western film *Return of a Man Called Horse* (1976); and the diverse ethnic idioms that spark the scoring of that 2000s George Lucas TVs series about the world travels of Indiana Jones.

Scores like those are fairly well known by now. And yet, long-term appreciation of Rosenthal's lifework reveals a rich history beyond those hits and award winners. It also discloses a fully self-expressive composer who just happens to write mostly in service to multimedia vehicles.

From his studies at the Eastman School of Music and from two years in Paris with the twentieth century's greatest music teacher, Nadia Boulanger,[1] Rosenthal brings a high level of literacy (he once orchestrated Bach's solo *Chaconne* "for amusement") and a scholar's array of compositional techniques to any assignment. In films, hear his cunning evocation of nineteenth-century Paris café music for fifteen instruments in the score to *Hotel Paradiso* (1966) but then how he applies a modern dialect to it—that is, makes a conventionally A-minor phrase descend by half steps headed for a major key, then unexpectedly reasserts the minor. Catch the dissonant gestures of urban jazz mixed with Stravinsky mixed in his brief cues for *Requiem for a Heavyweight* (1962) or in certain scenes of TV's *Night Chase* (1980). There are surprising key resolutions throughout the sci-fi score to *Meteor* (1979) and dark, daring harmonies in *Who'll Stop the Rain* (1978), and even more complex, almost pointillist writing in a stage score of incidental music for *Rashomon* (1959). Extending this notion of scholarship and craftsmanship from specific compositional details to the broader vision of a whole score concept, there is his politically darkening, slowly deepening score to Graham Greene's story *The Power and the Glory* (1961, TV). He called it "mordent Mexican music" and the progress of the score conceptually mirrors (and sometimes seems to lead) the progress of that drama.

Those were each flash points of advanced musical literacy that made professional musicians—and the curious rest of us—sit up and take notice. It's true, though, that none of that music was as publicly conspicuous as other blockbuster soundtracks of those days with their simple themes and memorable mottos. This is the Rosenthal modesty of method, which I will mention again shortly.

That powerful music for *The Power and the Glory* brings up another aspect of Rosenthal: his facility with dazzling full-scale orchestral writing—symphonic showpieces. In recent film music, perhaps only Sir Richard Rodney Bennett and John Williams have matched him in this. Some examples are the colorful fantasy score to *Clash of the Titans* (1981), the alarming and alluring orchestral mayhem to be heard in *Island of Dr. Moreau* (1979), certainly the Great Plains tonal landscapes and complex orchestral abstractions of Lakota Sioux chants in the aforementioned *Return of a Man Called Horse*, but also the more circumspect and nuanced exotic ensemble assembled for the biography of Asian mystic Gurdjieff in the film *Meetings with Remarkable Men* (1979). When theatrical film jobs began to thin out, his bravura scores for historical TV films like *Mussolini* (1983, where music mixes reminders of Rome's ancient glories with brutal warnings of contemporary Fascism), and 1985's *Anastasia* or 1986's *Peter the Great* (with their gloriously Russian voicings) were composed without apparent concern for the limits of the TV medium—each retained the necessary epic-and-ethnic feel for the subject matter.

One other sign of a shrewd symphonist is the ability to make reduced orchestral forces sound substantial. Note how in the 1987 TV film *Downpayment on Murder*, the modest instrumental elements (with some synthesized voices) are made to sound gutsy and aggressive by emphasizing individual sections of the ensemble as power blocks, rendering even the melancholy main theme forceful. Likewise, in 1977's *The Amazing Howard Hughes*, Rosenthal acknowledges the narrower TV focus and resources, yet doesn't compromise when the score needs enlargement: his main sax theme perfectly portrays the sleazy (and troubled) glamour of Hughes the shameless entrepreneur, yet by opening up the same smallish forces, that theme becomes a stirring fanfare that gives lift to the scenes of Hughes's early test flights as a fledgling aviator. And again, in energetic Americana scores for TV films like *Gore Vidal's Billy the Kid* or episodes of *The Young Indiana Jones Chronicles* (1992–1993), the orchestras were fairly small but the orchestrations were so shrewd as to seem fully cast and fitting.

Although Rosenthal includes among his concert works numerous formal song cycles, variously vocalizing the poetry of Rilke, Shakespeare, Langston Hughes, Brecht, and Rumi, his melody writing elsewhere has the feel of piano composition rather than of the singable song. Again, there he differs from other film composers whose melodies seem openly waiting to be crooned. Instead, the harmonic luxuriousness, the sophistication of modulations in Rosenthal's lyrical themes is warm and sensual but more classical in nature than what could be called a tune. I am thinking here of the lovely lullaby with its tenderly rocking lines for the young orphan girl J. P. in the historical TV drama *Orphan Train* (1979) or the "family theme" for *A Raisin in the Sun* (1961) empathizing with the burdensome life of an urban black household in midcentury Chicago. As in any great gospel hymn, the blue notes in this melody and the emotion-disguised-as-stoicism in its harmonies evoke both suffering and endurance. Familial love and conflict are also at the heart of his melodies in *Echo of Thunder* (1998), this time flavored with the story's Australian setting. And just as charismatic were the love theme in *Brass Target* (1978) and the concerto-like Main Title theme for TV's *The Patricia Neal Story* (1981).

Perhaps because he began his career in the theater, writing ballet music for Agnes de Mille and incidental music for *Ah, Wilderness* and *The Music Man*, Rosenthal's instinct for music that illustrates movement was developed early. Cinematic music, of course, not only needs to represent and interpret the story onscreen, it needs to physically set the pace of the film, sometimes shape certain scenes, sometimes even mimic the action. And it may be that because of his ability to form-fit his scores so precisely to his films, his name is not so well known as those others we have mentioned whose music declares its independence blatantly. Rosenthal's music performs a mighty service but often in the modest capacity of a Counselor rather than a Host. Consider again *The Miracle Worker*—how that score guides the characters along, matching scene by scene: two lone clarinets that are Helen and Annie at the beginning of the score, later playful pizzicato strings as they wrestle for dominance, ultimately a tense suspended unison line for strings just before the moment of Helen's revelation. Audiences (and the Academy Awards that year) failed to notice music that was so tied to its film scenes, so cinematic, yet its effect was absolute.

The same can be said for the sparse scoring in the 1971 experimental film *A Gunfight*. With only a handful of music cues (scored for two trumpets, one electrified, playing against thick string clusters and a cold hard backdrop of winds and chimes/bells), Rosenthal aurally captures and holds the film's key suspense scenes, building at length to the shoot-out and to the depiction of two separate (this is the experimental part) alternate endings. Again, it's a score concept so enmeshed with its film that few viewers were aware of its clout. One other example of sparse but influential scoring is the 1999 version of *Inherit the Wind*. Rosenthal's trick there is to stay out of the way of the extensive Scope's Trial courtroom dialogue, yet manage to match the music cues to the protagonists of the play—a brittle motif-and-variations for the truculent prosecutor, a solo horn for the beleaguered defense attorney, and a naïve tune for the accused that then begins to go sour as his case turns ugly. Some guys in the production company front office said that a famous stage play like this would never need a music score. But now the verdict is in.

As I've said, Laurence Rosenthal's modest methodology all along has been the belief that film scoring should support but remain subordinate to cinema, even at the risk of obscurity. Yet in so many instances his mastery of the medium has assured at least a cloaked influence. And in the end, it's no matter that his first film score (*This Is Russia*, 1952) and another fifty-six years later (*Stealing America: Vote by Vote*, 2008) were nonfiction documentaries—his music has always been dramatic and personal—the scholar-craftsman, the symphonist, the melodist, the cinephile—always serving the medium but quietly having his own musical say. His modesty of method belies his mastery of means.

With respect, let me add to Larry Rosenthal's Lifetime Achievement prize at the World Soundtrack Awards of the 2023 Gent Film Festival, his ASCAP Life in Music Award, his two Oscar nominations, Golden Globe nods, and all those Emmy wins this modest ninetieth birthday toast.

Interview with Laurence Rosenthal

JOHN CAPS: You started out composing for incidental music for theater. But what about in films: what would you say were the films that launched you, that you hold as your standard-bearers to this day?

LAURENCE ROSENTHAL: Well, earliest, not a famous film but one made in 1961 for both broadcast and theatrical release that you've mentioned before, was *The Power and the Glory* about the Communist Revolution in Mexico in the 1930s with Laurence Olivier as a troubled priest, George C. Scott as a police investigator hounding him. I had worked for producer David Susskind before, once on a stage producton of the samurai fable *Rashomon* and again later on film versions of the plays *A Raisin in the Sun* and *Requiem for a Heavyweight*. Those were both ethnically flavored scores of course; the first bluesy in character, the second more spikey with urban jazz. And although there is a sentimental tune at the heart of *The Power and the Glory*, I think of the score overall as mordent Mexican music. Tragic yet noble for Olivier's priest character (though his music symbolically never reaches a resolution), pulsing and intractable for the relentless police pursuit in the story, a rather subdued tune for Julie Harris as the peasant woman, a shaky five-note figure for the "Judas" character played by Roddy McDowell and, all the way through, a shifting harmonic foundation that speaks of the moral dilemma that ultimately sends Olivier's priest to his doom.

JC: And because of the quality of the script and the performances, you've said that this score is quite personal in nature and, therefore, a particular favorite.

LR: That sounds suspect as though any other scores weren't representative of my best, but all I mean is that this one hangs together as a single composition, even though it has the parts I mentioned; it seems to have a singular voice and is as close to what I meant to say as I could hope.

JC: And the other launch-score: was it also from that same period?

LR: Right after that, yes; it was the 1962 Arthur Penn film, again from a play, about the education of the deaf-blind girl Helen Keller by the pioneering teacher Annie Sullivan, *The Miracle Worker*.[2] Again, I felt inspired by the performances and the direction of the film to write some of my most personal music ever—and it's a score that's all of a piece: it seems to hang together as a single statement on those characters and the breakthrough they had as teacher and student, getting this unapproachable, chaotic adolescent deaf and blind girl to understand that words represent concepts and objects out in the real world, and then to understand the very idea of communication. I used an orchestra of strings and winds, often in long straining lines, other times in almost dancelike meters of excitement as Helen and Annie sparred and tested each other.

JC: The two lone clarinets that open the score and the film, I think of as representing Helen and Annie.

LR: Then sort of swirling figures fill in behind them as we see Helen, pre-enlightenment, stumbling forward through her yard, becoming tangled in a line of washing hung out to dry. We see initially how vulnerable she is and how untrained.

JC: The sympathetic nature of the scoring sets up a good deal of empathy for the characters but there is a whole internal variety to the score as well . . .

LR: . . . the tentative music phrases that accompany the first meeting between student and teacher, the double-time mischievous music as they test one another for dominance, the long lonely passages trying to evoke Helen's deaf-blind isolation and Annie's sense of failure at various stages, and then, of course, the suspended, striving lines in the strings as they start to achieve their breakthrough: Helen understands that the word for water "means" this wet substance coming from the pump. Annie has succeeded with the concept of communication.

JC: And it's a tribute to the strength of the score that hearing it apart from the film is just as moving an experience as experiencing the film.

LR: Well, that is the hope: to evoke, in music, the strengths of the film as the two play together. Anyway, those were what you could call two launch-projects that stand at the head of my career, there in the early sixties: *The Power and the Glory* and *The Miracle Worker*. Important to me, still.

JC: One of my initial interests in your career was the realization that your history includes studying under the greatest music coach of the twentieth century, Nadia Boulanger. Could we talk about that . . .

LR: Ah, with pleasure. I was with her for just over two years living in Paris. And, well, to put it succinctly, I would say she was the major musical influence in my life. She was a monumental teacher. It's been said a thousand times by her thousand pupils but it doesn't diminish the fact that every one of them has indelible memories of not only her great genius of teaching, but of her deep humanity, her totally inspiring quality as a teacher. She absolutely made you walk out of her lessons feeling like Beethoven; you felt you could do anything, because she really affirmed all of her pupils, made them believe in their own possibilties. She was very tough, not overly flattering—you had to write something pretty damn good to get a really complimentary phrase from her, but when it did come you knew it really meant something. Meanwhile, it was just a total daily inspiration just being awash with her great love of music and her profound understanding of how music is made and what music is all about to the point where she could really crawl into your mind, as it were, and realize why every note you wrote was written and why, perhaps, it could have been done better another way. For herself, as you know, she eschewed composition after her sister died but she nevertheless maintained contact with the whole subject of modern composition. I've never known anyone who was more deeply aware of precisely the function of the composer's mind, the whole process of the evolution of a piece of music. So, in short, it was just a total thrill, two years of nonstop ecstatic experience with a teacher. I know it sounds exaggerated but it was in fact that way, the two greatest years of my life. I kept contact with her more recently and saw her just shortly before her death. And even though she was physically by then really in a bad state, very weak, nearly blind, she was still full of fire and warmth and enthusiasm about some little harmonic progression in a motet or the whole inspirational development of the *C-Major Fantasy* of Schumann. Her enthusiasm was so rich and so full; I'm sure she had it right up until she drew her last breath. So that's Boulanger; you can see I'm rather warm on that subject. Right to the end of her life, she was open to many kinds of music. I don't think she was ever stuck in one musical point of view, even though her attitude was essentially classical toward music. She admired lucidity of thought and absolute logic brought to its sublime level by genius. Clarity of musical speech was what she admired most in composition and, as well, in musical performance.

JC: Yes, all of her former pupils whose music I know have a transparency in the things that they've written.

LR: That's what she encouraged. And we all worked toward that as, I suppose, every pupil tries to please his teacher. Now, I did have some fights with her, rather early on. Some songs that I'd written to texts of Rainer Maria Rilke had certain central European echoes in them, perhaps mirroring some of my own central European background by way of my family and a certain atavistic connection I feel with that part of the world. And she absolutely excoriated me for that and couldn't understand it and made various derrogatory comments about Mahler and what the hell was I, as a young American, doing dipping into this kind of neurotic late nineteenth-century European tradition? The songs didn't really sound like that, but they did have those cultural echoes and she protested. But I just stood up for what I felt: I said I didn't want to be characterized as just one of the American boys. I am myself, I said, and these are my influences. But she wasn't really upset; she liked a good fight . . . we argued about that sort of thing quite freely. She had a way . . . she would love to argue about music . . . not really argue but just get into very lively controversial discussions. In other matters such as literature, painting, religion, and so on, she was much more rigid, but not wanting to debate about them because she realized she wasn't an authority there. She said one great thing and this has always remained with me. She said, "You know, in order to have real humilty, you have to learn how to do one thing really well. I really know music," she said. "I know music from top to bottom; I'm sure of it and I accept it. And because of that, I can realize how profoundly ignorant I am about everything else." And that was a wonderful way of being realistic about oneself and it gave her a kind of essential humiltiy that was never phony.

JC: Who else was with you there at that time?

LR: There were a few composers who I thought were extremely gifted; two Americans, one named Paul Des Marais and one named Douglas Allanbrook.[3] Allanbrook I thought was just a brilliant young composer; wrote music that I admired to distraction. Of course, visiting frequently were people like Copland who would come by, but they weren't my contemporaries. I guess the one contemporary, my classmate, who everybody has heard of was Michel Legrand.

JC: Ah, yes, that would have been his era as a student . . .

LR: And he was, a bit, the clown of the class; he was very entertaining. In fact I still remember one morning before class we were all waiting around the room at Conservatoire waiting for Nadia to show up and he suddenly sat down at the piano and began playing in a very rhapsodic manner something that sounded like some extravagant Hollywood movie score with great fluidity and great lucidity and then he turned around and said to us Americans who were in the class, "Voilà! Votre Max Steiner!"

JC: Ha. As though he were mocking it?

LR: But yet there was something about the way he played it and about the enthusiasm with which he played that suggested to me that this was what he really liked the best, as it turned out, of course. He certainly had tremendous vitality; he was certainly good in the class. He could do all the things that conservatoire pupils are supposed to do: read scores, transpose on sight, do figured bass, and all of that. He was very fluent at all that. I never heard any of his compositions in those days actually because, you see, the class we were in together was not a composition class—it was this dreaded class called Piano Accompaniment, which is an innocuous name for the toughest class in the conservatoire. It had to do with all kinds of harmonic analysis, sight reading, score reading in all the clefs, being given the first violin part of a Mozart quartet and having to improvise the other three voices. All that kind of stuff. And he was pretty fluent in all of that. The only thing I remember Nadia Boulanger saying about him was after she had brought to class the Bartók *Sonata for Two Pianos and Percussion* just for us to study. And it just happened that he and I were selected to read the two piano parts. And there in the classroom, we got through the piece and when it was all over, there was a pretty impressive silence. You have to remember, this Bartók music was still rather new; I mean new to the world: this was 1948. And she asked Michel, "Well, what did you think of that?!" And he sort of looked at her and kind of shrugged his shoulders and said, "*Pal mal*. Not bad." Well, she was infuriated and told him off and called him a conceited ass and how did he dare to speak of such a masterwork in such a flippant manner? But I think that she got angry with him because she essentially liked him very much and did recognize his talent. In fact, come to think of it, I have heard her speak of him more recently, saying that he evolved absolutely as he should have evolved; that he ended up writing exactly the kind of music he loved most and was best suited for. Yeah, I remember hearing that; it's come back to me now. I'm not suggesting that she would consider this movie music the highest callling, although she was very unsnobbish about such matters. I remember, in that regard, that she was very kind to me one time when I went to see her many years later. I met her in New York after she had conducted the Philharmonic in a performance of the Fauré *Requiem* and she asked me what I was doing these days and I said, with a shade of embarrassment, that I was principally occupied writing film music, and she was furious for my disparagement of such work.

JC: Generous.

LR: And she went on to say that, first of all, she respected me enough to think that anything I did would be of high quality, then went on in a very interesting way to talk about the fascinating possibilities of the relation of music to images. She was always very open and unglued to traditional ways of thinking.

JC: It is understandable, though: the skepticism about film music.

LR: Well, sure, and as far as dispargement or let's say skepticism about film music is concerned, it *is* perfectly true that a great deal of film music is junk; we all know that. I mean, a lot of not-very-talented people do a lot of dreary stuff. But there's a lot of music that gets played in Carnegie Hall at the ICM concerts that's just as junky. So, I just feel that there are only two kinds of music: good and bad—or as Nadia used to say, "Better a beautiful song-for-two-pennies than a boring symphony."

JC: There you go!

LR: And of course, the natural disparagement can also come from folks who have heard the old cliché that people who work in films and theater make a lot of money—something which is partially true but pretty exaggerated.

JC: The other aspect of that kind of envy is that film composers get to have their music performed and recorded immediately, something that the majority of mere concert composers wait a lifetime for. Anyway, let's get back to *your* composing, which, fortunately, has been pretty broadly respected right across the board, from those film and theater people to the concert purists as well. What I noticed from fairly early on is that the grammar of your composition—well, I guess I mean the language—seems pianistic to me with, then, the orchestration in service of that. There's a way of singing that can seem pianistic; modulations that would fit comfortably within one hand or arpeggiations within the orchestra that, written out, would seem to have been piano moves . . . I'm not being very clear, but do you know what I mean? I'm wondering, with the most elementary kind of question, whether you compose at the piano or strictly on paper, or . . .

LR: That's pretty perceptive of you to notice that . . . I mean, well, if it comes through that much, there must still be some truth . . . Well, I do compose at the piano, I always have. It's always been my way of working; I somehow feel that while I'm composing I want to be constantly in contact with the sound itself. I really want to hear it out loud. Certainly, at times that could be a hazard in that I might tend, at least in the early days of my composing, to be writing piano music for the orchestra, without realizing it—and only then do my best to orchestrate it. But I find it much less so recently; I mean even though there are certain arpeggiations that are pianistic, I do really feel that when composing for the orchestra, I am thinking almost from the beginning in terms of the orchestra. However, other times, you're quite right, a musical idea will just be found by my fingers and will have a certain pianistic quality about it.

JC: Maybe I'm just imagining the bones behind some orchestral passage and noticing that it would make a very logical and satifsying piano piece, by default. Which is not a bad quality at all.

LR: What orchestral pieces have you been investigating in that way?

JC: Well, it's certainly there in your smaller scores that rely on ensemble writing. I guess the first score I heard of yours that turned my head was for the film *Hotel Paradiso*. That very deft ensemble writing—a chamber score, really—that's understandably pianistic, since the group is actually led by or grounded by piano.

LR: Well, that's a special case: there are several "only's" about that score. First of all, I think it's the only comedy score that I've ever done—the only kind of comedy I'm much good at: sort of high comedy, very stylized satirical comedy. [There would be other comedy films later in Rosenthal's career, films like *Easy Money*.]

JC: Speaking of orchestration, though, it has a distinctive accoustic to it, as far as the balance among the ensemble is concerned.

LR: The thing is, I used just one instrument of each—well, there was a string quartet—but then there was one flute, one clarinet, one oboe, bassoon, trumpet, trombone, horn, etc. So, it was a very small orchestra of fifteen or sixteen players.

JC: But to balance those is quite remarkable, don't you think?

LR: Ha, well, I worked very hard to make it a balanced sound, which a chamber group would inevitably have, but not make a point of the chamber quality. To have it sound right for the film, I felt that the great use of soloistic instruments would point up the comedy whereas a richer orchestral texture would tend to wash over it. So, yes, a balanced ensemble was important there. And of course, the piano is used in a very kind of Frenchy manner, interlaced through all the woodwinds and strings.

JC: And the muted trumpet seems to evoke more of the comic French music hall tradition.

LR: A little bit, yes: the whole thing trying to evoke turn-of-the-cenury French farce, which is what the film was about, with all its mock sentimentality and inside jokes. I enjoyed doing that score; there's a lot of private jokes in it—a lot of sort of subtle references that people don't get but it doesn't matter. Yes, that one certainly is pianistic in its chamber feeling. Another one that has certain qualities of chamber music is *The Miracle Worker*.

JC: How so? I think of that as fully orchestral.

LR: Yes, but the string orchestra there is used in a very delicate fashion. And there are several parts of the score that are carried by very, sort of, lonely woodwinds.

JC: Of course, in a sense it's a chamber-styled film with just two characters playing off of each other.

LR: Exactly.

JC: Now, there's a film that really needed music, right from the opening scene where Helen is flailing around the back yard, blindly. Music is needed there for the audience to know how to take that scene and the whole emotional story to come. Music sort of provides the audience with permission to get emotionally involved. And I have a personal connection to this story, too, since I spent two years teaching deaf-blind kids at Helen Keller's old school, the Perkins School for the Blind near Boston, one of our students being the sort of modern-day version of Helen: Sharon, a deaf and blind girl the same age and temperment as Helen is portrayed in the film.

LR: That's remarkable. I was tremendously affected as well, working with the film—I don't know if I've ever done a film in which my own emotions, being a father of small girls myself [and later a son] . . . somehow the distressing, yearning childhood of Helen Keller was tremendously affecting. So, the score was more emotionally motivated than anything I've ever done for the screen. That's my whole feeling about writing for film, almost without exception, that no scene in a movie should have musical accompaniment unless, emotionally or pictorially, it can't do without it. If it absolutely doesn't work without music, then I step in. When you have really superb actors and excellent direction, perhaps music is not so urgently needed but that's a dangerous assumption. Anyway, in the old days of Hollywood they used to pour music over their films like syrup. But I love the idea of sparsensss in a film score unless it's a film that requires a kind of sumptuous musical framework like *Becket*, which has a lot of music in it because it needed it, even though there were two strong performances at its heart. I was prejudiced toward a lot of music there, anyway, because I happen to love the music of that period, sort of late medieval/early Renaissance composition with those characteristic cadences of which the *Becket* score is full. And the influence of Gregorian chant and the heraldry of some of the French hunting horn calls. There's a lot of richness in that picture from musical sources that I'm sort of addicted to. Not so much the characters, and not so much the physical setting of that film, but the historical setting needed scoring there.

JC: Speaking of setting, how much attention did you give to the creepy setting of the film *The Island of Dr. Moreau*, that H. G. Wells story about the doctor's blasphemous medical experiments to link Mankind genetically and surgically with animals? There was a whole nightmare look to the setting of that film.

LR: Yes, the whole look of the film: I just was listening to parts of it the other day because somebody asked me to give them some excerpts of it for some purpose, so I really had a chance to haul out the tapes. And I had sort of forgotten how elaborate and intense and how grittily dissonant a lot of it is . . . sort of full of arcane-sounding, almost primordial-sounding woodwinds for some really desolate kind of horror scenes about these nightmare creatures that were called, I believe, Humanimals.

JC: It's a very nasty score: that frightening pursuit motif with its stamping rhythm and that weird solo trumpet call that sometimes sounds like a warning and sometimes like a hunting horn call-to-the-hounds . . .

LR: It is a nasty score, although it also has a practically Wagnerian love theme.

JC: Yes.

LR: But most of it is quite nasty. That's another score that I really feel has so much good material in it that I have sometimes thought of creating a symphonic piece out of it. It's that rich. The thing about that film is that it had a lot of scenes that needed rather long stretches of music in the sense that made it possible for me to develop ideas in an almost orchestral/concert way such as you would expect in a concert hall. So many films never give you the chance to get that far.

JC: Most films.

LR: Well, yes. With most films, you have only a few brief moments to score or maybe a scene that lasts two minutes but you rarely get five or six minutes to get an idea going and to really chew on it and to develop it and expose it in diferent ways and make it really go somewhere. And with *Dr. Moreau*, that chance existed right from the trumpet solo that opens the piece against the clustered basses and cellos. I really was trying in that score to somehow match the horror and the ugliness that was happening within that setting, that dark jungle setting. It's curious, I don't think the picture had much success in America, although in Europe it did extremly well.

JC: And it's a vigorously orchestral score—it doesn't sound pianistic at all!

LR: No, that one really is pure orchestra all the way through.

JC: There are echoes in, at least, the atmosphere of *Dr. Moreau*, and even in the sultry love theme, of another jungle-set film score of yours for *The Comedians*, that Graham Greene story of political corruption in Duvalier's Haiti.[4]

LR: Yes, that's another film I was very keen to do. And I really did a considerable amount of research—the material of that film was so fascinating—listened to a lot of Haitian music and then, which is usually the way I work, put it all away and stopped listening to it after jotting down one or two folk themes that I thought might be useful. But generally got it out of my head and started working on the score and sort of letting come out what had been absorbed. So there are a lot of characteristic kinds of Haitian drumming and those rather infectious and very gay, wonderful tunes that are characteristic of Haitian music. And what was interesting about the eventual score is that, against this native sound, so much of the score is made of rather out-of-place European music—neurotic waltzes and throwbacks of elite aristocracy—all to suggest this really unhappy bunch of visiting European characters played by Richard Burton and Elizabeth Taylor in the film.

JC: The score opens with that native chant while, underneath it, there's a disturbing current of classical mysterioso.

LR: Well, that is really intended as unvarnished irony: these children's voices chanting, having been totally brainwashed to sing this paean of praise to their ruler, Duvalier, also known as Papa Doc. And the orchestral backdrop to that is supposed to represent the whole turbulence of the country while, officially, there is harmony and obedience across the nation. I tried to set the whole tone of the film right at the beginning in all its aspects; almost really a kind of overture in which the rather sick love theme for Burton and Taylor . . .

JC: . . . maybe call it sinuous . . .

LR: Yes, well, serpentine in its chromatic configuration . . . is introduced fairly early on; then comes a kind of jolly Haitian song (the tourist's view of the island?) and then on to this political comment, which is at least suggested in the music at that early point in the film. We did that one in France, which I somehow felt was the right place to record it. I rather liked the film, too; I thought it got less than it deserved. For example, I thought Peter Ustinov gave one of his most distinguished performances—not at all a comic turn, but extremely touching: the cuckolded ambassador.

JC: Let us switch to a very different film that certainly had as strong a need for music to embody its setting: the vast and varied Asian continent including Afghanistan and the Caucasus—*Meetings with Remarkable Men*, a story of the teacher and mystic Gurdjieff and his journeys, his wanderings, searching for, as it were, the meaning of existence. And for the score, we are presented with the music of one of Gurdjieff's disciples, the composer Thomas de Hartmann[5]—but transcribed and reshaped, rearranged and richly orchestrated by Laurence Rosenthal. And I am curious what exactly you had to work with there. How much was there of de Hartmann's material? Actual score sheets or just tunes or piano sketches . . . ? I count more Rosenthal in there than these supposed outside materials.

LR: Oh, I had more than sketches to work with; there's a whole body of printed published music—some privately published, but de Hartmann was a perfectly respected (not terribly well known or very major) composer of that school. I think he was a contemporary of Scriabin and Rachmaninoff of that period. He composed ballets for the Marinsky theater in St. Petersburg and all of that. In any case, the music that I used was all written while he was under the influence of George Gurdjieff as his spiritual master.

JC: Is it orchestrated, though?

LR: No. None of it is orchestrated; I orchestrated it all and then it was all sort of put together, so that very often what you're hearing is not one piece but a kind of conglomeration of various pieces that I linked together and sewed together in order to fit the dramatic situation onscreen.

JC: I guess it's in the orchestration that I'm hearing familiar Rosenthalisms.

LR: Yes, well, it's interesting, when you hear that music on the piano it has a certain quality of its own whereas when you orchestrate it with conventional Western symphonic combinations, it tends to take on the color of Rimsky-Korsakov, of Liadov, of Glazunov; you know, that ilk of late nineteenth-century Russian composers that was unavoidable. And yet, we all who were working on it felt that de Hartmann's music was totally appropriate for the film, although it did have to be considerably reorganized. But only reorganized; I didn't essentially recompose anything; I didn't change harmonies; I just orchestrated in a perfectly faithful way. Only, before orchestrating, what I did have to do was make cuts, repeats, extensions, and also the combining of different pieces, because you could hardly hope to find an entire composition that would perfectly fit an existing film scene.

JC: Having done all that, it does perform like a normal interactive film score: there are orchestral upsweeps in the canary market scenes and there are scherzos during Gurdjieff's boyhood scenes . . .

LR: And even those upsweeps are in the original music, but I just put them exactly in the right place. It just required a considerable amount of cutting and pasting, but my hope was that it would sound perfectly spontaneous as though it had been composed for the movie.

JC: And it absolutely does sound . . . well, intentional.

LR: Well, I can only take that as a compliment. It's a certain skill, I suppose. But, I mean, it's not unknown—I mean, for example, I'm a tremendous admirer of—though not all the time and only of certain aspects—of Ken Russell's film work. In a film like *The Music Lovers* (1971), a biography of Tchaikovsky, I thought his use of Tchaikovsky's music was so brilliantly employed in the film that it really sounded like Tchaikovsky had composed the music as a film score for that movie. Now, of course, Tchaikovsky's music is very theatrical and already lends itself to that sort of melodrama very much, but it turned out that de Hartmann's did too. It is true that, sometimes in sewing pieces of de Hartmann together, I did have to compose transitions of my own or even whole sections of film cues, which were my own to make the scoring fit.

JC: Like the journey to the monastery that ends at that long footbridge?

LR: That's right.

JC: . . . which has modernisms in it but also sounds like sort of Pythagorian intervals.

LR: Well, yes, you're very good; that's exactly what I was trying . . . trying to make my own bridge between de Hartmann and myself because there was literally no point in trying to ape him. If that had been possible, we could have just found something in his rather large body of work that would work for those scenes. But a scene of that particular intensity and drama really required something tailor-made. Of course, when you get that deeply involved in someone else's music, it's strange the kind of things that begin happening; you begin to half-walk into his shoes in a certain way. You become so involved that what you compose yourself begins to take on some of that tone as though it's all coming out of the same pot; his flavoring gets into everything. It's unavoidable and probably a good thing because it gave the score a certain quality of unity. The press was, almost universally, very flattering to the music; even reviewers who didn't particularly like the film. It won one award at the Oxford Film Festival. Quite gratifying, although I feel only partially responsible for its quality; a lot of de Hartmann's melodies are quite moving.

JC: A similar situation happened when you were invited to take someone else's music and rearrange it and orchestrate it for the famous Broadway show and then film version, *Man of LaMancha* (1972), including its popular song, "The Impossible Dream," and all that stuff. But the same question I have there: What were you working from? Song sheets or sketches?

LR: What I worked from was the same elementary piano/vocal score of the show that anyone can buy at Schirmer's. I listened to the recording of the original show but, of course, that was designed for a very small theater orchestra, like a little band. I don't know what [the show's composer] Mitch Leigh thought about what I did opening up the scoring so much for the screen version; I've never spoken with him about it. The film was, regrettably, not successful, but I remember he said something about "holding back on the strings." Well, you just couldn't do that; no way. But we did try to maintain an identifiable Spanish sound . . . we used three terrific guitarists that we found in Rome. The whole film, *Man of LaMancha*, was shot in the Dino De Laurentis studios there.

JC: It seemed to be conducted more violently than I've heard you do before, maybe with the exception of *Dr. Moreau.*

LR: Ha, well it seemed to require it, or maybe because I was working with someone else's material I just suddenly changed hats or reacted differently. There was also a considerable amount of orignal music in that, by the way; I mean, I had to compose a lot of background scoring for which there was nothing in the song score. For instance, Don Quixote's famous tilting at the windmills required a whole sequence of dramatic orchestral scoring. It took a whole year to do that film; the only time I've ever taken a job like that—the kind of thing that John Williams had done with *Fiddler on the Roof* (1971)—that is, starting right from the beginning: recording the playbacks with the voices that will eventually appear on the screen once the filming begins—and having therefore to rehearse with the singers and somewhat with the actors who would be lip-synching to the previously recorded tracks—since the stars were not reliable singers, Peter O'Toole and Sophia Loren.

JC: With whom you worked as well?

LR: Oh, of course, we all worked together intensively for months before we began shooting. Anyway, it was lovely to be in Rome and we all had a terrific time working on it although that particular kind of music supervision is not my favorite thing. I'd obviously prefer to work on something original.

JC: Any Sophia Loren anecdotes for a fan?

LR: Oh, well, I can tell you that she's an absolutely lethal poker player and she hates to lose. I remember one night at our house she came by with Peter O'Toole and Jimmy Coco, who was playing Sancho Panza, and my wife and I took her for about $160 that night and Sophia was absolutely outraged because my wife had done some very unorthodox bidding and Sophia said, "You have no right to win when you bid like that!" So, she was determined on revenge and there was a return engagement at her villa in Marino the following day—she couldn't wait to get back at us—and she absolutely cleaned us all out.

JC: Was it rigged?

LR. I don't believe so, she's just a good player—with husband Carlo in the background rubbing his hands with glee as he saw her pile of Gucci chips rising in front of us.

JC: What a picture.

LR: Yeah, she is really a terrific person. I liked her very much and she's wonderful to work with—a very hard worker, totally devoted to what she's doing. She loved to rehearse; a real professional and I just liked her, not too difficult to spend a lot of time with her, for obvious reasons.

JC: Absolutely. Well, I still want to somehow get at a specific characteristic of your music that I associate with more than one film score of yours, maybe starting with the chromatic side-stepping in *The Comedians* but also with the way *Hotel Paradiso* sets up certain keys and then resolves by resorting to a completely different key. That's a gesture done most blatantly in the score to *Meteor* (1979), *where* we're looking up into the stars and the mysteries of space and even the mystical implications there are evoked by chords that lift and then back down and lift again and then, as though miraculously, resolve in some distant key. I could play you the particular bars I'm thinking of if I had the recording at hand. But whenever it appears, I think of it as the same sort of Rosenthalian modulating.

LR: Ha, well, I guess it's essentially a bitonal or polytonal structure there; you do feel the root movement: it's old Boulanger coming through, I guess. But, yeah, I think that's rather characteristic of me, whether Rosenthalian is the term or not. Again, I'm flattered that you noticed that particular place; it's early on in the film when the camera is just exploring the heavens, which seem rather gossimer. Yeah, I suppose that every composer, maybe some more than others, has his or her fingerprints that are just recognizable. You can't listen very long to a piece by Ravel without knowing that it's got to be him or someone who's shamelessly imitating him.

JC: Yes, or Poulenc . . .

LR: Or Poulenc in his Ravel hat. So, I suppose it's true that most composers, if they're real composers, have a personal way that they make music move from one moment to the next . . . a manner . . . like the way somebody walks that is characteristic.[6]

JC: Well, those same Rosenthalian modulations, together with that warmth we speak of, come out in a little score I know for a TV film called *Orphan Train*.

LR: Oh, yes!

JC: A score that seems to be composed with a sort of basic "journey motif" that has a chugging meter for the train, and then another one for the urban setting circa 1854 . . .

LR: Well, I'll tell you how that came out: that score had to be written very quickly, and I was up here, in fact, on this [Maine] island and I had the film on video cassette, and the most amazing thing happened—I think it's unique in my history. I knew that there were several basic themes that had to be part of the film: the train and the young girl who is masquerading as a boy, a theme for the young woman that would sound like a Salvation Army hymn . . .

JC: Reworked as a lullaby.

LR: That's right. And what happened was that I simply sat down and in one morning composed all of those themes. I think they all came up within about an hour and a half—bang, bang. They just came; I didn't find any reason to fiddle with or change them; I was quite pleased with them and so the rest of writing the score was really a question of going on adventures with these themes, watching them interact and follow their normal bents and developments. Again, like *The Miracle Worker*, it was a film about children . . . and children continue to be among the most touching members of the race! Something about their being unspoiled is very moving. So, that score was again one that . . . even though I was intentionally staying with an absolutely plain tone—what Virgil Thomson used to call "the beauty of the commonplace"—the themes, except for one, which was rather romantic and yearning, were all very plain, square-cut tonic and dominant in nature. But the minute I played any one of those themes on the piano against the video tape I sensed immediately that it was right.

JC: And there are modulations, even in that plain Americana music, that are Rosenthalian enough to remind me of other scores . . . a repeat and a modulation at the end of each phrase. Phrases or gestures in common . . .

LR: Well, I hadn't . . . I hadn't noticed that. You're going to make me go back and burrow in all these old scores and see what I was doing.

JC: And yet, it is the challenge and, I guess, the pleasure of any film composer to always be composing outside of one's natural sound, outside of one's comfort zone because you are given all sorts of story specifics—ethnic cultures to score and foreign settings and past periods. Even within the Amercan setting, there are specific voices you have to catch. I'm thinking of the very different needs of a film like *Orphan Train* from a story of the Plains Indians like *Return of a Man Called Horse*: a huge symphonic score full of orchestral detail in the classic sense, but haunted, if you will, by a Native American sense. Did you, for instance, find there was any authentic Northern Indian music to draw on for that score?

LR: Oh, yes, it's full of Northern Indian music, the Plains Indians. I was given all kinds of tapes that I used and created an entire instrumental symphonic superstructure around these very authentic Indian chants, which are usually just a few Indians and a drum. They are wonderful, those chants; they are very characteristic and once you get to know them, they really can get to you. They certainly got to me.[7]

JC: Do they have pentatonic elements to them?

LR: Yes, they do! The pentatonic scale appears everywhere: Japan, China, Scotland, American Indians, all kinds of places. But, anyway, the notion of familiar gestures in one's own composing: I guess it suggests that I have my own language. And I guess, in some ways, I'm less concerned about expanding the language than I am about trying to perhaps go deeper into what I have to say with the language I'm comfortable with. Certainly that was the case, if I can find myself in good company, with a composer like Chopin, who by the time he was twenty really had established his style and really had very little to add from the point of view of musical language till his death. And yet his music gained and gained in profundity and in poignancy, and just general depth of feeling. And so I suppose that I still find myself doing certain characteristic things that I was doing in songs that I wrote when I was twenty-one.

JC: I wondered if you ever looked back at things like that.

LR: Yeah, I have done, and in fact just the other day I happened to come across some songs that I wrote in the fifties, and just out of curiosity to see how I would respond to them, I put them up on the piano and played through them. And, I must say that even though perhaps I wouldn't say things quite in that way today, I found it . . . I thought,

Gee that was a pretty nice song. They were so-called "art songs."

JC: Unpublished.

LR: They are, regrettably, still unpublished, but I could hope that somebody's going to figure that they're worth publishing. I don't mean that my songs or my little modulations are so great, but I do feel that any of my best, careful music—yes, even film music—can add to the universality of musical language so that it can be a more communicative kind of speech. And the fact that you spot it in my music is very gratifying to me. It means that you're really trying to follow what I'm trying to say.

JC: And all thanks to Nadia!

LR: Thanks to Nadia!

A Rosenthal Addendum: Shadowing

Whereas Laurence Rosenthal was able to prepare himself so well as a composer through his years at the Paris Conservatoire and later learning the nuts and bolts of scoring through television, so also one student at the Eastman School of Music attributes his own apprenticeship in similar fields to time spent with LR. This is Steve Bramson, Emmy-winning scorer for hit American TV shows like *JAG* and *The Young Indiana Jones Chronicles*, and films like *Last Call*, *In Enemy Hands*, and *Dominion* on the life of poet Dylan Thomas. As soon as I mention the name of Rosenthal, Bramson's memories are specific: a quick view now of just how these film composers meet their project deadlines while remaining true to their own quality standards as well. Steve Bramson:

> I met Larry in my final year of graduate studies at Eastman. My time with him at school was very brief. I think he had one master class and then each of us had fifteen to thirty minutes, maybe an hour, showing him our own

work . . . interspersed with anecdotes about the experience and some scattered talk about technical and artistic points. So, I would not characterize my time with him as being "taught" in any formal way. The same was true when I flew out to LA about a year later to "shadow" him as he worked on his project, a TV historical mini-series, *George Washington*. The first things I observed were the logistics of the relationship of composer to director: attending the spotting session (where it's decided what scenes want music), understanding the work flow (planning in order to meet the deadlines), receiving notes from the music editor (timings of each music cue), sketching themes and ideas, then orchestrating, copying, and recording. My initial two-week shadowing experience unexpectedly extended to a couple of months when Larry asked me to assist him with the orchestrations. So, I did learn an immense amount from him during my entire time, but it was all informal and really all the result of watching and doing. For example, I would stand beside Larry at the piano as he ran through a sketch of a scene he had completed and was handing off to me to orchestrate. As we worked, I would obesrve how he notated his timings at the top of the score . . . he used colored sharpies . . . and when I began doing my own composing, I adapted this same system and have used it now for years. Watching and listening as he played through each scene was an education in the construction of vivid themes. He was, as you well know, a master at this. These mini-series were well suited for the use of leitmotifs and they were a composer's tool he often relied on for these biographical TV projects that came along in a row to him, like *Washington, Peter the Great, Anastasia*, etc. Those sessions with him at the piano reviewing the sketches and then transcribing them to the score page on my own at home were the real kind of lessons I experienced. His sketches, though reduced to eleven lines, were extremely detailed. I did make suggestions at the piano with him, some of which he'd occasionally accept, but every note was there. In fact, there was rarely anything extra for me to do other than to transfer his work carefully to the score page and, in doing so, keep an eye out for mistakes. I would often call him at night to clarify because he did use shorthand frequently. For example in a tutti section, he might notate the brass and then ask me to add the woodwinds. This did give me the opportunity to use some of my own skills in a limited way. But I would describe Larry as both precise/fastidious and conceptual/intuitional. I think he relied heavily on his emotional reaction to the story and characters of a film, but then he was fastidious in crafting those reactions. It was not unusual for me to get a phone call in the middle of the night for me to come by and pick up a cue to be orchestrated for the next day's recording session. But having now found myself behind the eight ball many times on my own scoring jobs, I understand the demands of schedules and have found nothing really unusual about this. And again, I stress that not once in all the years and projects I worked on with him did he ask me or anyone else to ghostwrite a cue for him, as so many of us have resorted to from time to time. Every note is his and his alone . . . Not till the end of my time working with him did an opportunity finally come along when he was asked to write one of the first scores for Steven Spielberg's TV show *Tiny Toon Adventures*. For whatever reason, Larry asked me if I'd like to write a short cue there. He probably knew of my enthusiasm for Carl Stalling's classic cartoon style for old Warner Bros. cartoons . . . so I got my chance. The producer Bruce Broughton heard my music and liked it and, over time, I was worked into the rotation of composers who worked on that series and eventually won an Emmy for one of my scores! I don't think Larry ever heard my dramatic scoring work. But there is no doubt that my time with him and his music was a huge influence on me.

9

Richard Rodney Bennett (1936–2014)

The Complete Musician

Figure 9. Sir Richard Rodney Bennett. *Source*: Bridgeman Images.

PROBABLY BECAUSE HE WAS such a big movie fan as a youth, Sir Richard Rodney Bennett ignored all the warnings about classical composers doing film music—how any association with the movies would compromise one's reputation as a serious artist for the rest of one's career.[1] Instead, Bennett dove into writing soundtrack music as early as 1956 with one documentary film for the British Insurance Association and one feature film, *Interpol*, when he was just twenty years old. Seventy-six films, documentaries, and TV plays later, he was accepted as a considerable Hollywood force while also maintaining his place in the hierarchy of major postwar British composers—if not at the rank of William Walton or Ralph Vaughan Williams, certainly with enough prestige to insure permanence and an eventual knighthood.

Early film scores blended his own atonal education (he was the first pupil ever accepted by Pierre Boulez,[2] in Paris) with the standard conventions of whichever movie genre he was working on: pop harmonies for Cary Grant in *Indiscreet* (1958), horror film clichés for *The Man Who Could Cheat Death* (1959). Soon enough, the creative freedom granted him by director John Schlesinger starting with films like *Billy Liar* (1963) or *Far from the Madding Crowd* (1967) brought more thoughtful and original scoring out of him with films like *Figures in a Landscape* (1970) or *Return of the Soldier* (1982). Public attention solidified his posture as a major film composer through scoring hit films like *Murder on the Orient Express* (1974) or *Four Weddings and a Funeral* (1994).

At the same time, and all along, Bennett was also indulging his lifelong fascination with the so-called Great American Songbook—actually appearing in Manhattan cafés and piano bars, playing and crooning the better songs of Gershwin and Arlen and Rodgers and a whole host of unknown pop gems in his craggy tenor, making record albums of this repertoire, either from a solo perch at the keyboard or in tandem with a select list of cabaret-styled songstresses from Cleo Laine to Claire Martin. And all the while, beyond the piano bars, beside the film jobs, he continued to pursue his pure music agenda, first as a loyal serialist, later as a wandering modernist, lately as a repentant tonalist, seemingly regretting some of his stringent serial youth, lamenting all the lyrical things he *could* have been composing all those years when his schooling, his pride, and his audacity made him produce orchestral, vocal, and piano works of increasing atonality, brilliance, and aggression (*Guardian* [26 December 2012]; Robert Barr, *AP Wire* [28 December 2012]).³ People praised their solid architecture and the fluidity of their ideas but, perhaps, questioned a certain impersonal tendency about them.⁴ With the New Millennium (and just his own natural aging and mellowing) Bennett started to explore more tonal melody in his concert composing, plainly tuneful orchestral works like "Partita" or "Reflections on a Scottish Folk Tune," sentimental vocal cycles like "Songs before Sleep," and a highly lyrical, confessional Symphony no. 3. Critics were still skeptical: "Bennett's fluency, like his versatility, has often been held against him, but in these post-avant-garde days, it can perhaps be appreciated without qualms for the Mendelssohnian gift that it is" (Paul Driver, *Guardian* [16 April 2006]). As is frequently the case, extreme versatility in a musician often registers publicly as criticism, at least as critical wariness. Still, some critics and ever more fellow composers ignore the labels, the limits, and just appreciate solid music wherever they may find it. Said composer Mark-Anthony Turnage, "[Bennett's music] has always meant a lot to me. Indeed, when I was a boy, I nicked a score of his second symphony from the local library! . . . But I also love the more recent stuff. Some of it is really gorgeous. Richard has an incredible technique—a technique to die for!—possibly the greatest of any living composer" (*Opera Magazine*, March 2006).

It must have been that sort of openness to all kinds of music and all kinds of people that led him to invite me, as a young no-account journalist, to interview him in New York (this was before he moved there permanently from London; certainly before his knighthood) to talk film music and to stray into other aspects of twentieth-century music—adjourning from the parlor to the kitchen, making what was supposed to be a two-hour interview into a whole evening of conversation, so enthusiastic on behalf of music was the tone he set. It was a tone that carried forward through subsequent correspondence and, when the New York City Opera restaged his famous opera, *The Mines of Sulphur*, a final telephone interview before his death. Together with Laurence Rosenthal, Richard Bennett always seemed to me to be the most advanced and erudite film composer writing in my lifetime—by virtue of his literate concert work, his emotional singspiels, his café crooning, and his masterly soundtracks, a model of the complete musician. Bennett died on Christmas Eve 2012.

Interview with Richard Rodney Bennett

RICHARD RODNEY BENNETT: I'm a serial composer and even if I'm doing films, I still think in that way—using intervals and building something out of nothing. If you think of Pierre Boulez and the way he used the pure kind of serial technique but then integrated tonal harmonies back into it if necessary, then it seems to be an endlessly fruitful thing.

JOHN CAPS: There are elements in your symphonies, of course, that are neo-tonal.

RRB: I don't take the academic line, "Here's the serial technique but let's not even admit any other influences." That's too much technique. Rather, it's the flexibility I spoke of—relaxed sorts of sounds and harmonies that are so free that they can open up to anything. It just comes naturally to me.

JC: How did that develop?

RRB: Well, my mother was a sometime composer and she was a pupil of Gustav Holst, so that contributed to it and—well, just the times. At school back then, things were slipshod. My school (Royal Academy of Music, mid-1950s) was geared to producing either virtuoso instrumentalists or teachers, and I wasn't either. I was very much involved in contemporary music, which at that time just wasn't the thing. But I spent a lot of growing-time there when I really had a chance to look around and practice. So, I'm glad for it. For example, I know a boy in England whose first performance of a symphony he had written when he was still a teenager was at Festival Hall and the second performance was at Carnegie Hall! And then what do you do from there? Now, he's perhaps in his early twenties and he goes around like a grand old man. He's really become shaggy and tweedy and very patronizing. It turns out he's a very good composer, but that's a horrendous way to start.

JC: The first large-scale success you had for your concert music, at least in the United States, was your opera *The Mines of Sulphur*. When was that?

RRB: It was written in 1963 and premiered in the States in 1968 at the Juilliard. I've just attended another production of it in Toronto by students and it was done very well. It still works. That's what I noticed most. It really startled me. That sounds naïve—all the effort that went into that piece seems long ago. Now I think of it as my warhorse. I'm very proud of that opera. There's a dark atmosphere to the whole thing, and even the performers are affected by the ghostliness of it.

JC: And, interestingly, your first symphony, premiered by the London Symphony and very much a virtuoso show-piece—almost a concerto for orchestra—has a certain vocal feeling to it as well.

RRB: Well, of course, opera is my favorite medium of the moment and I wouldn't be surprised if much of what I do has a singing quality.

JC: Yet, your piano music is seldom lyrical in that sense; it tends to explore juxtapositions.

RRB: Now, that's a different thing, you see. I play a great deal but I have to be careful what I play because I don't have a conventional technique. I don't want to do the classical repertoire because there are millions of people who can do it better than I. I'll play Boulez and all kinds of wild music that doesn't demand a conventional technique. Say you go to Juilliard, that wonderful machine for turning out virtuoso pianists: there, you are not geared to play contemporary music at all, unless you're lucky with a particular teacher. In fact, a conventional finger technique can often get in the way because the demands of contemporary music are not the same. Still, I love to play old Tin Pan Alley tunes on the piano: I have a collection of old sheet music of Gershwin, Porter, Arlen. And all those are the epitome of the lyrical approach. So, you see, I'm as well versed in the lyrical tradition as the next guy—and, in fact, you'll find all sorts of lyrical allusions in even my serial music, as I've been saying: it shouldn't be restrictive or academic for its own sake.

JC: The conventional debate, wearing thin by now but still around, is that twentieth-century tonal music couldn't go any farther in harmony than Wagner or in form than Mahler and, so, on the one hand, Schoenberg came along and redefined the grammar of scale-and-harmony, and Stravinsky came along and redirected the old grammar by introducing bitonality and broken rhythms and folk elements. And the debate goes that Stravinsky was just a trickster bypassing the real twentieth-century dilemma, whereas Schoenberg, perhaps unpopularly, at least cleared the game-board completely and invented something new (Ross 104, 215, 389; L. Bernstein 263–324).

RRB: I can't imagine a world without Stravinsky but I don't know exactly what he led to except a lot of talented people imitating him. In a sense, he devoured himself as he went along. You know, he was a composer of the most dazzling genius, but he fed off what was around him and when he died what did he leave? Yet the Schoenbergian tradition goes on and on. I could never understand Stravinsky's later music at all. Some pieces like *Threni* or *Canticum Sacrum* and the rhythms in *The Rite of Spring*—his instrumentation—it's just the music of a knockout composer. But his later stuff, his serial music, no . . . He did some things that were terrifyingly new, but I just don't know where it got anybody. He was like a comet that lit up everything and then was gone. At one time, all I wanted to do was take music apart and Stravinsky looks endlessly interesting when you do that with him. But again, what have you got? A lot of little elements all laid out in front of you but nothing has been advanced.

JC: One relatively trivial but obvious influence from Stravinsky has been on film scoring: all the many films that utilize his rhythmic schemes or, at least, his rhythmic freedoms and tonal universe.

RRB: Absolutely. Absolutely. They even asked him to score a film once but he turned them down not, as it turned out, because he had wanted more money or anything like that, but because he had wanted more time. I'll have to tell you, I'm simply not a film-music buff though I love the cinema. There are two things that repel me about the worship of film music. First, the moment it approaches the sort of French *Cahiers du Cinéma* attitude, I just shrivel up. I lived with that for so long because I was a movie nut in Paris, reading all the film magazines and I really can't stand that auteur business now. Second, I think a lot of that film-music worship is a throwback to the Bette Davis/Barbara Stanwyck/George Raft mystique. It's fun, but either it's very trivial or it's inflated. Working in films is important for me—but the music, considered apart, is not very important. That's why I won't take my movie music out of context. When I was in Toronto, somebody came up to me saying, "Please, can I get permission to have the 'Elegy' that you wrote for the record album of your film score to *Lady Caroline Lamb* (1972) done as a ballet by some of the national ballet here?" And I said, "Absolutely not!" It works well in the context of its film and I'm very pleased with it, but I don't want it done as a ballet! It's really only a kind of high-class schmaltz!

JC: Well, quite high class, yes. What was your edict on that film? It was directed and written by the *A Man for All Seasons* playwright, Robert Bolt, not a known director . . .

RRB: . . . who was directing his then-wife Sarah Miles in the lead, yes. I didn't set out to do a wildly romantic score for that film. In fact, the orchestra was chosen for a rather cool sound: woodwind, notably oboe and English horn (my favorite instruments, as in *Madding Crowd*), harpsichord, solo viola, etc., it was intended to be a very lyrical and lucid score. But the music was about Caroline Lamb who was a very passionate lady and I suppose that's why it turned out as it did. Robert Bolt wanted a "classical" feeling for the husband character and a "romantic" thing for her, but I found this too theoretical and, anyway, there was practically no music over the husband.

JC: What sort of treatment does a legit world composer receive in Hollywood?

RRB: I'm very well received by composers out there. But I guess they're rather surprised that I've actually wanted to come—and that I'm not Robert Russell Bennett [Broadway orchestrator], whom I often get mistaken for. I was out there recently. The picture I did (*Sherlock Holmes in New York*, 1976) was a TV movie, which doesn't pay all that much but I wanted to work there just to establish the fact that I'm available. Otherwise, there's always somebody nearer at hand; there's always somebody who's hustling harder. Why, I was about to do a very big picture recently for which they had to use an English composer and I couldn't get to Hollywood two days earlier . . . and so I lost it. But there are a few magnetic reasons for going out there now and then, if only to be among some of the guys who've done such wonderful screen work over the years: Alex North, who did the first real jazz film scores; Elmer Bernstein, who kept the spark alive—I mean, I love those fifties neurotic jazz scores like he did, *The Man with the Golden Arm*, and all that.

JC: When, rarely, you do stay out in Hollywood, you can often be found in the company of another accomplished serial composer, Mr. Leonard Rosenman.

RRB: Yes, he's a good friend and a marvelous composer. He is, after all, the first composer to have done a fully serial score for a motion picture way back in the mid-1950s (*Cobweb*). And one can only admire the more mainstream films he has turned his hand to: *Rebel without a Cause* and *East of Eden* (both 1955).

JC: He has done a good deal of television, too.

RRB: . . . whose cramped schedules and conservative attitudes I know he resents. I know he resents, too, the very notion that a serious composer can suffer a genuine and permanent artistic censure just because he agrees to do some media music.

JC: Do they worry in Hollywood that you might be too lofty for the movies or, worse yet, too pure to really take film music seriously?

RRB: Well, that's why it's good I started early; I have a track record by now and they can see what I have done and what it might be like if they chose me. I'm aware that film is an entertainment medium; I get that, and they can tell I'm on their side in wanting to grip the audience, wanting to help their project.

JC: Do they worry that you don't conduct at all, that you're just the composer?

RRB: Not really. I was at the Royal Academy and if I had stayed on for a fourth year I could have learned to conduct. But by the third year, I was scoring feature films already and I wasn't about to handle all of it at one time and learn to conduct as well. It's rather strange: it's like I don't drive a car anymore and now I'm scared of taking it up again. You know, I'm sure if I had learned to conduct when I was nineteen, there'd be no problem now. It's just a psychological thing.

JC: Back in your Academy days, did your classmates know you were occasionally scoring films on the side? Would they have approved or even envied?

RRB: We had a new music society and we used to give concerts every week of all the current avant-garde stuff; so that's where their attentions were. Films would have seemed trivial to them, had they known. About fifteen or twenty people would turn up to these recitals . . . That's the way you learn; you make your mistakes in front of twenty people.

JC: And do you know of any of those avant-garde composers who were active in film music?

RRB: No, they were too pure—though, there's something to be said for purity and focus. Of course, a good many major composers have done films: Prokofiev, Milhaud, Shostakovich, Poulenc, Ireland, Britten, Walton, Hindemith.

JC: Honegger, Vaughan Williams, Copland . . .

RRB: When film music first developed away from the pit band, it was those composers who did it. The Hollywood composers were much later, in the forties: you know, the big overblown symphonic thing. But film scoring began before Max Steiner and the others.

JC: Was it visual music, though? Cinematic music?

RRB: I'm sure it was and I think the composers in those days—particularly in France—had a closer relationship with the filmmakers, too. I think there's a really good generation working in Hollywood at the moment: people like John Williams and Jerry Goldsmith, David Shire, and Billy Goldenberg. You could talk to any of these composers about contemporary music and they'd know what was going on.

JC: You've commented in the past that your experience on any motion picture job—your experience with the director—can change the way the music comes out.

RRB: You can go through traumatic times on films. A director I worked for a while back, for instance, was one who couldn't make up his mind about anything. I've heard that even Henry Mancini had a frustrating time trying to accommodate this director with a score. I could never be sure that my music wasn't going to be all messed about. Another famous director just barely held the lid on chaos during his own filming processes and then, later, during his working with me on the music score, it was just as chaotic. I just can't be dealing with that anymore so I won't work with him. On the other hand, there was a little horror film starring Bette Davis that I did, called *The Nanny* (1965), which was just a happy experience that worked very well.[5] One cannot help being influenced by these things.

JC: I heard you actually visited the location of filming while working on the score for *Far from the Madding Crowd*.

RRB: That was a different kind of experience. John Schlesinger, the director, loves everyone to be involved from the word go. I had done *Billy Liar* with him in 1963 and I knew him socially before that too. He was terribly anxious, in a very endearing way, that one should be part of his "gang" and really involved in it all. That's fine in principle, except in actual fact I don't like to do it. There's nothing I can do there on the set in the South Devon countryside while they were filming this Thomas Hardy novel. I was, in fact, brought up in South Devon within a hundred miles of where *Madding Crowd* was shot; but I'm not a country person and can't account for whatever success I had in composing "landscape" music for that film. It is not, at all, an evocative experience being out there on the set: you have to do dumb things like supervising people singing in crowd scenes when they were shooting this sort of harvest supper sequence. That day I just sat in the field feeling terribly out of place and getting appalling hay fever. It was only later that I started working on my music. I can't do anything, you see, until I have that finished film. Music is supposed to respond to the finished film, not to the shoot, not even to the script.

JC: Let me ask about your experiences on a few specific films you've taken for scoring. One big Sam Spiegel epic about the last of the Russian czars was *Nicholas and Alexandra* (1971). There you wrote a sweeping, part-noble, part-tragic main theme for a dark, formal orchestra, but also a fragile naïve barcarole for the Czarina, a continental waltz for the royal daughters, a sober nationalistic theme for Lenin and his cohorts, and then a scherzo version of that theme as the people take up arms in Lenin's name; then a strutting march for the Russian troops, and some frantic horror music for the death of the mad monk, Rasputin. That was scored, I believe, in London but what was your experience dealing with the Americans who were directing and coproducing?

RRB: Well, I know that Jerry Goldsmith was supposed to get that picture, in that he had a tight working relationship with the director Franklin Schaffner. But the producer, Sam Spiegel, was casting around for some classical celebrity to do the music and he had the thought of trying to get Leonard Bernstein to score it—Lennie, who had only done one film score in his life! So, that was the level of royalty Spiegel was dreaming about. But Lennie wouldn't do it and yet he recommended me, which was very sweet of him. Well, Spiegel had probably never heard of me but he went with the suggestion and I'm sure Jerry was puzzled by all of that, because he knew Schaffner had wanted him. Anyway, we finally met, Jerry and I, and we got along well. But he's a little guarded, always. I never know whether Jerry is very happy in the company of other composers. Also, I think he's a little bitter at having done such marvelous and daring work all these years and yet, for some reason, hardly ever being recognized at awards season for all of that. But he's a nice man and I get on well with him; I admire him a lot: his progressive scores for *Planet of the Apes* or *A Patch of Blue*. Still, Leonard Rosenman is the one I know best, there. In fact, he has conducted for me that TV movie I mentioned, *Sherlock Holmes in New York*.

JC: Maybe your most successful score here in the States, and certainly in Britain where you won the British Film Institute award, is for Sidney Lumet's version of *Murder on the Orient Express*, that famous Agatha Christie mystery. But rather than scoring it like a classic dark mystery story, it feels that you scored it like a theater piece—a grand entertainment.

RRB: Very much; I saw it like that. Sidney got me out to the studio to see some of the rushes, the early bits of unedited film, because he had originally wanted it to have a score based on 1930s tunes to go along with the period of the story. But I wouldn't do it that way, because I'm not an arranger and I don't know how to do that kind of specialist orchestration, nor do I believe in that kind of score. But I had been recommended by Steve Sondheim, who thought I could contribute something here, so Sidney brought me to the rushes and said, "Here, take a look and see what you think." And it was a sort of make-or-break situation for me there; I could have said two skeptical words and blown the job opportunity. But I said, "Well, it ought to begin with a kind of theater music because this doesn't have a thriller opening. It's more like Curtain Going Up. That's where it starts from." But I was talking about this with David Shire the other day: What did I wish for this film score? I felt it had to have a certain period flavor like the thirties that had been suggested, but then the rest of the score couldn't just be period tunes; it had to be an integrated score so that when you hear tension music or development music, it is all in the same stylistic pattern: a solid narrative score. In fact, the TV movie I talked about already, *Sherlock Holmes in New York*, actually opens with a theater curtain, a red velvet curtain and the film credits come up on the curtain, and I wrote a rather shameless nineteenth-century light opera overture as though the curtain were going up and you were about to see . . . what?

JC: A well-mannered farce-mystery, only a little less serious than *Murder on the Orient Express*?

RRB: Well, yes; or, anyway, a period entertainment—not a shocking crime/horror story but a whodunit that tests your cleverness, not your courage. And so, the opening theme for *Orient Express* is a kind of florid Eddie Duchin type of piano decoration to set the extravagant tone.

JC: And that's the ultimate clue that, like doing the grand tour of Europe on the Orient Express, this film is mainly meant to be a rousing entertainment. So, what you do on the soundtrack is to send the train off on its way with a glorious and gradually accelerating waltz.

RRB: Well, even that has a shaky history. As you remember, the early parts of the film show the Orient Express in all its glory steaming there by the siding, ready to ride. So, it's "all aboard" and the locomotive gets up its head of steam and very slowly grinds forward, a lot more steam, a little more speed, gradually gaining traction and forward motion, heading up toward climbing speed, then cruising speed, and so forth. And for that sequence I could just hear, as the Express is overcoming inertia, a comparably accelerating waltz: the slow one-two-three, then a faster one, then gaining speed down the tracks—the circular motion of the crankshaft mimicking the circular motion of the waltz, until both the music and the Orient Express are full steam ahead. I thought it would work wonderfully well and it certainly was within my concept of the grand entertainment. But there was a snag. The film company had brought in, at some expense, a "steam train sounds expert" who had carefully calibrated the exact audio track that should go with this sequence of the train moving off and gaining speed—absolutely precise train sounds, ready to lay in on the film soundtrack, either over or in place of my waltz. There we were, at the recording session, with the orchestra sitting around ready to play and a conference is going on across the studio, out of my hearing, between this train specialist, the director, and the film's producer. What will be better for the film; for the storytelling: music or sound effect? Authentic train sounds or, if I can put it this way, adventure-setting music? Well, it's a tribute to Sidney that they chose on the side of this film as an entertainment and, so, that accelerating waltz is what most people remember about the film now . . . and about the score, though there's a lot more to it.

JC: *Far from the Madding Crowd* was the first Bennett score I noticed—I suppose initially for the English pastorale qualities it has, but then for how you manipulated fragments of those folk songs or folklike themes to join the story and characters. One of those comes in the dream sequence where Bathsheba fantasizes being romanced out in the fields by the grenadier soldier: the manipulations of the main piccolo tune into different meters as he makes sport of her by flashing his sword, or into swaying crescendos as he charges around her, out on the heath . . .

RRB: And there again it's a matter of establishing the right thematic material, in this case the opening piccolo theme—which seems to speak of both the land and time and tradition—and then arranging it in different ways, breaking it up, creating extensions, reconstituting it in fragments, all the while expressing the immediate needs of the scene, in this case Bathsheba's fantasy about Sergeant Troy indulging her. There's a wild storm sequence in there, too, with a couple of pianos tearing around. The folk music of that area is especially lovely and we borrowed a couple of those, as well as using the original pastorale theme I had created.

JC: One sort of anti-pastorale score of yours, even though the story is set entirely out of doors, would be the atonal music in *Figures in a Landscape*, music more in your personal tone-of-voice, would you say?

RRB: Well, at least not a popularized melodic tone. That film is very heavy going, very humorless—a rather obvious allegory about two fugitives fleeing across some unnamed country pursued by some unnamed antagonist in a helicopter. I had a very large string orchestra there and I think I had six French horns and percussion. And it's all atmospheric music; I mean, there's not one shred of melody in the whole score. It's all sort of buzzing noises, a scary picture. And one of the main characters is this helicopter and it's hovering and swooping around and suddenly appearing out of nowhere. And the music is part of that landscape; it's not involved with the people at all. But there are some nice bits, which is exactly what I'm talking about when I say "trying to compose something that isn't on the screen." I remember one bit where they were trying to get away from this helicopter and the music score goes absolutely motionless like a cloud with just strings suspended above them, creating a whole different kind of tension. That's an interesting juxtaposition of music and movie. So, I like it for what I did dramatically in that film and for the fact that the compositional language was allowed to be, was appropriately, atonal. Still, only about three people ever got to see the film. I'm glad you did.

JC: One more obscure and practically undefinable film, Joseph Losey's *Secret Ceremony* (1968): another allegory, this time with Mia Farrow as a young woman who thinks Elizabeth Taylor is a dead ringer for her mother who, in turn, thinks Mia is her daughter. I often try to assign a "central line" or main purpose to the music score for a film. Can you say what you were scoring here in this abstraction?

RRB: That's a very sick film.

JC: What, you mean in construction or content . . . ?

RRB: It's just sick. The whole situation and the male character who comes in is very distasteful. I mean, I'm not shockable but there was something revolting in all that, to me.

JC: So, then, what aspect of it were you scoring? How do you get a handle on what music should do?

RRB: I tend to go much more for a color thing, an instrumental color thing.

JC: Are you scoring sensory elements, then?

RRB: There isn't always a principle. I mean, sometimes I go all out for one part that the music follows, but not every film conveys that, yet every film conveys some sort of coloristic theme. In *Lady Caroline Lamb* I was focusing almost entirely on her but in *Secret Ceremony* I don't remember that there was actually a principle behind the music. I used to be more self-consciously "artistic" about what I was doing—I mean, more formal about having a philosophic underpinning for my film scores: some carefully attached reasons and shapes behind my music so that, if there were a flashback sequence of some kind, you'd hear the music associated with that area of the person's life and so forth. And I would get those associations from reading the scripts and start planning accordingly. Well, that proved very often to be wrong because (a) you can't get ideas from a script, you have to score the finished film; and (b) you're just restricting yourself when you impose all sorts of interpretations on what you're doing. So, I don't do that anymore; it's much better to have an open mind. And in the case of *Secret Ceremony*, I just set up the atmospheres, the ingredients, among some rather crystalline sounds: piano, celeste, harp, small percussive objects, organ—almost a nursery-like atmosphere. That's the commentary I contributed to that film.

JC: So, that's a kind of central line you're scoring.

RRB: Well, you can be a better judge of that than I. I just go in there and react spontaneously to what's up there onscreen. It's why I hate to theorize and why I don't like to read scripts ahead of time or talk in very specific terms with a director about what I'd like to do. The more people say to me about what music "should do" for their film, the less spontaneous my reaction is and, very often, the more phony the music gets. It gets contrived. You start to compromise your original ideas in deference to what others seem to be wanting or think they want.

JC: Are there compromises to be made, both in film scoring and in concert commissions, because you are working at the behest of others, not to mention whatever concessions a composer makes wanting to please an audience?

RRB: As a person and as a composer I do try to please a little bit, but I try not to compromise my ideas. Of course, some people would say that it's a compromise already for me to be working in films, but I don't think it is at all. It's just like wearing different hats. Music is music. Some is meant to explore the possibilities of the art, and some is meant just to illustrate the love affair of Caroline Lamb and Lord Byron on the screen. Why despair about it?

JC: Let's talk a little bit about the despair, though—the times when director and composer can't agree.

RRB: Ah, well, I've had very few of those, but a few. Most of the time it's just a matter of rewriting a scene or two. In *Nicholas and Alexandra*, for instance, there's a scene where the Czar and his family under arrest are being taken off the train by the Red Guard through a very hostile and perhaps dangerous crowd. And I scored the threat of it with a very volatile, angry kind of music and Spiegel or the director or someone was saying, "What's all this? This is the sad end of the monarchy," as though they expected there should be tragedy in the music there instead of violence. And so, I went back in and did a strings-only lament there, just the saddest version possible of the main Russian theme. But that was not an unreasonable request; that's just a matter of interpretation and the scene works very well, either way. There have been other times, though, when either I couldn't come back to do the fixes the filmmakers had in mind or I refused to.

JC: *The Go-Between* is a particularly public example—Joe Losey, again.

RRB: Yes, and I was particularly sad about that because I had known the novel since I was a teenager and, so, I had a definite slant on it. Occasionally in films I dare to do something in the music score that goes violently against what you're seeing on the screen. What I did on *The Go-Between*—what I did that was so disastrous that they finally threw my score away—was that I tried to convey the corruption and the black magic element from the original novel and say something about the ways in which this child, twelve-year-old Leo, was being used. Remember, he was just visiting his schoolmate in this lovely country estate for the summer and he ends up being used by two clandestine lovers as their message-bearer, their go-between, and then is further pressured by his rich hosts to tattle on the young lovers, in essence to spy on them. Now, I've known the novel since about the age of fifteen and, to me, it's a thoroughly frightening fable about the corruption of a child, and so I wrote my music score against the sunny estate and the polite manners of the landed gentry. And Joe was quite shocked. But, you see, he had recently been out to America and had got to know a young trumpet jazzman called Don Cherry there. And then he had me out to the location where they were filming *The Go-Between* in that extraordinary estate house. And I was standing in one of those elegant Edwardian rooms with him, and he said, "I want avant-garde jazz and electronic music in this film!" And I just looked at him as though he had gone insane. And it went downhill from there.

JC: Did you actually record your score for it?

RRB: Oh, yes. But I would have redone it because I realized it wasn't what he wanted, but there was no way I could salvage it, unfortunately. That was back when I was teaching at the Peabody Conservatory in Baltimore and I just couldn't make it back and forth. Otherwise, I would have done another score for him. It would have been so easy to do a more obvious illustrative score for that film.

JC: Instead, it got . . .

RRB: He got Michel Legrand who used two pianos and an orchestra modeled on, of all things, the Bach Orchestral

Suites. After that he asked me to score his film version of Ibsen's *A Doll's House* and I refused to do it, partly because of the first debacle and partly because I just didn't see a place for any music in the Ibsen play.

JC: And he got Legrand again, there, providing a suite of brass interludes. Legrand seems to have dogged your tracks over the years. And didn't someone once complain that your theme for Caroline Lamb mimicked the four-note phrase Legrand used in his song "The Windmills of Your Mind"?

RRB: Yes, and there's more! The year that my *Nicholas and Alexandra* score was nominated for an Oscar, who should win that year but Michel Legrand for his admittedly lovely but much simpler, smaller score for *Summer of '42* (1971). But, listen, I do think he's a kind of genius—it's just that he works far too much and so he lets a lot of cheap things out. He used to be one of the few composers whose films I would automatically go out to see. One thing I *did* copy from him was the swirling-pianos-effect with which he began his score to a French film called *Bay of Angels* (1963) about gambling addiction and I used the same sort of device, the jangling sound of multiple pianos, at the beginning of the film *Billion Dollar Brain* (1967), which was about computers and global intrigues. Furthermore, when I occasionally teach film scoring, one example I use is Legrand's chess game sequence from *The Thomas Crown Affair* (1968). The scoring is absolutely dazzling, even if you explain to an audience what it is and they haven't seen the film. You can tell them this is a very erotic chess match, Steve McQueen and Faye Dunaway matching wits, his move and her move, and the camera keeps cutting back and forth between them as they make their plays, while the score offers one leading phrase, then answers it, lifts the next one, then answers that. Everything happens in the orchestra that's implied on the screen. I mean, it's brilliant. Listen, when he was at the Paris Conservatoire and under the tutelage of Nadia Boulanger, I know for a fact that at one time he was her most talented pupil; she always said that. But he just works too much; I can't say I've sought out a film of his in a long while.

JC: Have you ever been asked to be like Legrand and come up with a hit song for one of your films?

RRB: Well, the worst part is, they don't ask: they just go ahead trying to make it happen on their own. Someone at the studio put words to the Czarina's theme from *Nicholas and Alexandra* and sent it to me and I wrote back saying, "This is the worst lyric I've ever seen." Happily, I never heard from it again. Someone put a lyric to the opening theme in *Murder on the Orient Express*, calling it "Silky." It went something like, "Silky, there is something in your eyes . . . !"

JC: You're kidding. You have no power over that?

RRB: No power. Legrand may have control, but I have none. The music rights for future performances or adaptations are owned by the respective studios or publishing wings [see Cooke, *Reader* 341–47].

JC: Has your attitude toward the ideal film score or your method of film composing evolved over the years?

RRB: I do tend to use less and less music in my films. Also, I won't do it at all unless there's something I can contribute. In *Lady Caroline Lamb*, for example, which has only twenty minutes of music, people noticed the score and I got more mentions in the press for it than ever before. I think to a certain extent it was because each piece of music was so specific. One thing I've learned after all these years of working in films is that it's much better in the long run to tailor your music as specifically as possible to each scene you're involved with and that includes subordinating your music to any dialogue that's happening up there on the screen. There's no point in thinking you're going to be able to play through dialogue with your music or, for that matter, overwhelm the dialogue—dialogue will win. And so, I work out my cue sheets very carefully so that I know exactly where I am at all times and what else is going to be there, sound-wise. I mean it sounds utterly basic but it takes a long time to learn those things and realize that's what you've got to do. Those instances in Leonard Bernstein's one film score, *On the Waterfront* (1954), where he let his musical phrases extend to their logical conclusion in several scenes without regard for the fact that dialogue needed to be heard there—the result was that they had to abruptly turn down the music tracks there so that the dialogue could be heard. That's a fatal flaw on the part of the score composer; that's Lennie Bernstein behaving like a concert composer, indulging the music's needs rather than the film's and you just can't do that. One recent example I had of a film that needed a good deal of music but—and here's the difference—the filmmakers had created good places for it: it's the BBC television drama *Gormenghast* (2000) set in a very medieval castle with all sorts of mythlike characters and my score was very dark and unforgiving but the producers, I'm very pleased to say, left it exactly as I had intended—not a single thing was cut or messed around. The whole experience and the people I was working with were marvelous—ideal. But, still, let it be said: film music has rules of its own that must be respected and no composer should just waltz in and expect to be accommodated. It's a collaborative craft. Film music can be said to be an independent art in its own right but it's a secondary one, a supportive one, because its form is not generated by the composer. The spark comes from up there on the screen, not from down here within the music itself. So much is dictated by the preexisting film: the length, the dramatic structure of the sequence, the places where music is subordinate to, say, dialogue—to a certain extent the style, and so on. This is not a quality judgment and "secondary" does not mean inferior, but film music is only part of a whole whereas concert music is its own whole thing. I'm a concert composer first and foremost, but my only musical ideals in any medium are to keep on working and improve. I just want to feel that my music is liked and needed.

10

Interlude

The Exasperating Michel Legrand

Figure 10. Michel Legrand. *Source*: Photofest.

On the Occasion of His Eighty-Fifth Birthday

THE WORD FOR MICHEL LEGRAND, as every interviewer knows who has ever tried to sit him down for a chat, is restless. His musical backpack is jammed with baroque influences, classical affectations, pop songs both exquisite and banal, jazz both melodic club-piano and free-range styles, and of course, film music that can follow action onscreen as impetuously as a hyper child. And in further evidence of such impatience, Legrand has said that once a film score or a new record album is finished, he never wants to hear it again. Move on, move on, is his motto. There is no such thing as the past. To this day,[1] he remains in motion—composer, conductor, pianist, vocalist, erstwhile film director, licensed pilot, boatman, horseman, and now, octogenarian-plus-five. He says his goal for 2017 (he was born February 24, 1932) is to give eighty-five live concerts in his eighty-fifth year and his website lists them all, along with sixty-four years of film scores and sixty-two years of music recordings.

Such capriciousness would be merely amusing if he were just a facile tunesmith, but the fact is that Michel Legrand has been, for at least sixty years, one of the most melodically fluent and orchestrally colorful souls on the planet. The best of his chansons (indebted to Franck and Bach and Pigalle) are among the most singable songs around—the best of his film scores are striking indeed. Compositionally, they don't declare any progressive agenda, they're not harmonically daring. They're most often, when they're not being jazzy, on the fence between romanticism and renaissance. A Legrand melody often has a circular shape—one memorable phrase stated, then repeated in steps up or down a scale, rotating toward a resolution—"What Are You Doing the Rest of Your Life?" or "Pieces of Dreams" or "Windmills of Your Mind" all have that revolving music-box quality. It's a formula that can result in cliché, yet just a fine adjustment of the same ingredients and some self-discipline can result in such charismatic songs as "The Summer Knows" or "China Doll" or "Dis-Moi." Other pop writers pause in envy. So, he has admirers in the highest places even when they have reservations, any disapproval aimed usually at the flash-dance aspect of his career. But, of course, out of eclecticism comes impulse, comes creativity, comes discovery.

From where does this Legrand-restlessness come? His parents (half Parisian, half Armenian) were both musical, his father Raymond a popular band leader. But the latter's four marriages and general absences from home left Michel alone for most of his early childhood toying with the family piano alongside his sister Christiane (later a celebrated soprano soloist in her own right with the Swingle Singers). Still, before very long, Michel's piano games started to manifest as real talent and, by age ten, he was enrolled at the prestigious Paris Conservatoire where he would study for the next eleven years. There, he would master classes in composition, piano performance, counterpoint, fugue, solfege. And, ever impatient, when he could not find a class for orchestration, he would spend his extra time auditing tutored classes for trumpet, trombone, violin, cello, harp—lessons that would later aid him as a master orchestrator, knowing the most comfortable range in which to score each instrument and the best blends to use.

After five or six years of the conservatory's toughest curriculum, Legrand would merit the most famous music teacher of his time, Nadia Boulanger, and yet there were times when his insouciance, born of that restlessness, exasperated her to the breaking point.[2] But underneath, she must have recognized that his rudeness was part of his improvisatory character; music was fun for him and to take anything too seriously, too reverently, made a chore out of it, a lonely chore like those childhood days practicing solo.

Boulanger's exasperation at the brash sixteen-year-old can only be imagined. But Legrand did graduate from her class and from the conservatory with honors, if also with a playful sense of impudence. Thereafter, no moribund classical career was going to satisfy him. So much was happening on the 1950s musical scene. Almost immediately, Legrand got himself hired to score his first films, *Beau Fixe* (1953) and *Les amants du Tage* (1954), helped to ghostwrite a rock 'n' roll hit, "Tell Me That You Love Me, Rock," and arranged/conducted the best-selling easy-listening album *I Love Paris*.

Someone else can trace in proper detail Legrand's intermediate rise as a film composer from that point on—except to say that he rose on the surfboard of the French New Wave filmmakers[3] from 1959; splashed into international fame by 1963 by composing the first film musical whose script (by Jacques Demy) was entirely sung, *The Umbrellas of Cherbourg*; and then, through recommendations from Henry Mancini and Quincy Jones, landed in Hollywood to win Oscars for songs and scoring—*The Thomas Crown Affair*, *Summer of '42*, and *Yentl*—and to create albums for a whole host of pop singers and jazz folks with programs of his endlessly lyrical, adaptable, and memorable songs. His broad reputation, then, was for pretty love ballads most prized during that retro-romantic pop era, but his professional reputation was high for the fluency of his best songs and the zest of his best orchestral writing.

One who I found watching his rise with both envy and something like Boulanger's exasperation was Richard Rodney Bennett, who used some of Legrand's music for demonstration purposes in his own syllabus teaching film scoring technique and who, at one time, had attended certain films just to hear what Legrand was up to next. Inevitably, Bennett began to lose interest, though, as Legrand took on more and more work on lesser and lesser films. But I have told that whole story already elsewhere.

Not unaware of criticism, Legrand sometimes seemed to be courting it—again, the bored child, defiant at the piano at home—now taking too many jobs on purpose, either tossing off a cheap tune or, conversely, writing in ways that were sure to challenge his boss's expectations, telling ASCAP's Jem Aswad, "I never approach a score in a safe way, I try to find an oblique way to bring something different and to put myself in danger . . . yes, I'm an adventurer" ("Playback: ASCAP Henry Mancini Award Honoring Michel Legrand," ASCAP. com).

To me, Legrand's best music is that which combines that explorer's sense with a genuine love and loyalty toward the Boulanger legacy of music-from-the-heart. You can see him clowning around onscreen in Agnes Varda's 1961 film *Cléo from 5 to 7* (sitting on the floor, playing a keyboard over his head, obviously enjoying fame and freedom), but to experience Legrand the responsible musician, I seek out film scores like *Cherbourg* or *Dingo* (1991, far-out jazz with Miles Davis), *The Thomas Crown Affair*, *Ice Station Zebra* (1968, blatant Hollywood thriller music), *La Piscine* (1969, scat and fugal vocal jazz, though largely rejected by the director), *Summer of '42* (composed in five days, developing a fragment from *La Piscine*), *Parking* (juxtaposing rock music with a lush strings-only orchestra), *A Time for Loving* (1971, charismatic pop), *Adventures of Don Quixote* (1973, soulful gypsy violin versus Spanish guitar), *The Three Musketeers* (1974, frenetic opera buffa music plus one of the loveliest string adagios), *Polly Magoo* (1966), *Yentl* (1983, an even more complicated vocal score than *Cherbourg*), *L'Amérique Insolite* (1959), the happy storybook scoring of *Madeline* (1998), the intense balladry in *L'Evénement le plus important* (1973), the rejected score for *Robin and Marian* (1976), or single tracks like Barbra Streisand singing his tune "Martina," Jack Jones singing "Years of My Youth," Stan Getz playing "Moods of a Wanderer," or opera soprano Kiri Te Kanawa singing "The Picasso Summer," all with Legrand's fastidious orchestrations . . . or Legrand himself at the piano jamming with drummer Shelly Manne and bassist Ray Brown on one great Verve album (Verve Records V6-8760, *Michel Legrand at Shelly's Manne-Hole*).

There is much to admire in all of that music and it makes you forgive any exasperation that his perhaps too-eclectic, still-restless, and even at the age of eighty-five, still on-rushing career may deserve.

❧

Not so long as two years after Michel Legrand's bold plan to tour and concertize across Europe in his eighty-fifth year, in spite of aging into what most would consider retirement time, the ebullient maestro's passing was announced by his friends, agent, and reps. He had kept going to the end—just did not want to slow down if there was still music to be made and played. I duly reported the news and summarized his career on the same website where, seemingly so recently, I had celebrated his birthday:

On the Occasion of Michel Legrand's Passing

Only a few weeks before his eighty-seventh birthday, Michel Legrand died, January 26, 2019. With apparently endless energy and, as I have described in an earlier tribute, restlessness, Legrand had vowed to fulfill eight-five concert dates during his eighty-fifth year—and did so. Along the way, he produced sixty-five years' worth of film scores; composed, arranged, and conducted elegant pop albums for the likes of Maurice Chevalier, Stéphane Grappelli, Sarah Vaughan, Aretha Franklin, Jack Jones, Stan Getz, and his own pop albums beginning at the age of twenty-two with the best-selling *I Love Paris*; then alternated classical and stage-musical works and, of course, a whole lot of movie soundtracks.

If his eclecticism and the impulsive nature of his creative choices seemed not just restless but reckless, his motives were honorable, his credentials were impeccable: eleven years at the Paris Conservatoire and seven years under the care of Nadia Boulanger. His own career trajectory, then, happened to coincide with the rise of the so-called French New Wave in cinema so that his first scores for directors like Jean-Luc Goddard and Jacques Demy were quickly noticed. They were fragmentary scores at first (*Une Femme est une Femme*, 1961), but he broke into the mainstream circa 1964 with the first all-singing French film, *Umbrellas of Cherbourg*, giving him an international audience. America rewarded him with Oscars for his screen scores and there were many individual pop song hits in the United States to follow.

Throughout the 1990s, Legrand produced a number of his own stage musicals, including *Dickens's A Christmas Carol*, *Le Passe Muraille* (aka *Amour*), and *Marguerite* about the French resistance in World War II. The 2000s saw him composing classical works including well-received concertos for cello and piano; he even received from the French government the Légion d'honneur for services to the general culture.

One of his final scores was for the posthumous reconstruction/release of an unfinished Orson Welles film, *The Other Side of the Wind*. Legrand had scored Welles's quasi-essay film *F for Fake* (1974) forty-four years earlier and Welles had him in mind again here, but Welles could never get the completion funding to finish *The Other Side* . . . nor decide how to structure the thing (it remains a relic of a film rather than a true Welles product). The completion/release deal was finally put together by Netflix and Legrand's score completed in 2018. We note that one excerpt from a past score, *L'Amérique Insolite*, is part of the soundtrack to *The Other Side*. For the rest of his film, Welles had planned on a jazz score but, in the end, the restless Legrand described his finished score this way: "somewhere between a fugue, a swing-jazz trio, the influence of the Second Viennese School (Schoenberg, Berg, etc.), and a piano duo where one pianist does jazz and the other classical" (Michel Legrand to Stéphane Lerouge, LaLaLand Records 1474). Sounds like a summary of Michel Legrand's whole life and career. Who is left to equal him?

11

Interlude

Women Composers for Film—A Mini-History

Figure 11. Elisabeth Lutyens. *Source*: Bridgeman Images.

THE STORY IS TOLD OF THE eleven-year-old Richard Rodney Bennett, brilliant but sheltered music student circa 1947 waiting between trains at London's Victoria Station to return to school, picking up a music magazine and discovering there an article all about an up-and-coming composer who had written a piece based on some decadent poetry by Rimbaud and cast in the progressive musical language of twelve-tone, or serial, technique. The aggressive nature of the piece, *Ō Saisons, Ō Chateaux, op. 13*, composed with an equally eccentric instrumental ensemble behind the vocalist—harp, guitar, mandolin, strings—caught the boy's attention. This was a new experience for him, his first real close-hand and personal brush with modernism. And there was one additional astonishment about the whole discovery: the composer was a woman, Elisabeth Lutyens, trailblazer, forerunner—and also rebellious, cantankerous, entertainingly foul-mouthed.

Born in 1906, Lutyens was forty years old when young Richard Bennett heard of her and not yet famed or even much respected for her careful avant-garde composing; thus, she hardly knew how to respond to recognition such as that article represented or flattery such as this naïve student was about to confer on her. Which self would "crazy Liz" present to a young fan like him: the driven sage (she eventually composed nearly two thousand works) or the impish rebel (she once showed up to a formal cocktail party dressed as Peter Pan); half crusader (dispenser of insults and curses when she felt things were unfair) or half victim (burdened by her own habits, chain-smoking dozens of cigarettes and downing a bottle of brandy per day)?

But the boy Richard knew none of that. He just envied her daring and her skill with the difficult grammar of serialism. He fired off a fan letter to her, bought and studied some of her piano scores, and was abashed when she answered him by return post. "It was as if a door had opened," he said later (Meredith 143). Up until then, at school, he'd been writing music more like Vaughan Williams or Delius; British pastorale stuff or pseudo-Debussy. But this woman—a woman, mind you—was writing with far more vision and bravery. "This, I knew, was the kind of music I wanted to know about." After the fan letter, he tracked her down by phone and she actually picked up the line and spoke with him, showing great and simple respect. "She was very nice—thrilled that such a young person wanted to know her." And Bennett did indeed launch a similarly aggressive composing career, writing serial music much influenced by the Lutyens example. If a woman could dare these self-assertive compositions and make the rest of the world listen (well, they would hear her eventually), why couldn't a kid? At fourteen, Bennett sent her some of his own compositions and she invited him to visit. And although all of this coincided with a difficult period in her own life—separating from her husband, still substance abusing—she graciously allowed the boy to come by her flat for casual lessons and for chat. "She was wonderful . . . Liz had that wonderful glamor; a kind of magic . . . she was kind, patient, and oddly (for such a bohemian) very motherly . . . Her influence was immense." And that influence included telling him about the way she was currently earning a precarious living: writing music for films.

Lutyens probably saw the film composing as just another bohemian indulgence, not worthy of full honors—and yet, while she worked at it, she absolutely devoted her full energies there, so that much of the movie scoring she *did* do is at least the equal of (if not in form and formality) her concert works, just in a different dialect. It is anti-serial music. In fact, in character and grammar, Elisabeth Lutyens's film work tried to be as far from serialism as possible. She knowingly surrendered her personal language to score her very first movie and it sounds rather like a society party piano rhapsody. Some few purists, she knew, would hold it against her and consider her willingness to do film work (which apparently was okay for male composers like William Walton or Arthur Bliss) just another example of her much-maligned "unladylike behavior," but she didn't care—she had enough other pressures to worry about and her family had learned to put up with her "antics." Anyway, while she was growing up, her father had been distracted with his successful architecture business; her mother was swept up in the abstract world of ancient theosophy mysticism. All five of the Lutyens children made their own way; Lizzie into music through the Paris Conservatoire and then the Royal Academy. She fell in and out of one marriage, then settled in with the struggling conductor Edward Clarke, who was eighteen years her senior and who would prove as vulnerable to substance abuse as she was becoming. Her reputation in progressive music circles, though, did begin to grow, but one thing was still clear: movie scoring jobs would have to pay the bills, at least for a while. The fact that she found the movie work somehow to her liking, interesting and challenging, felt like a gift.

That first film score was a shock, though, to her friends and colleagues who found the idea of writing movie music so unlike her and yet, in another way, they could see how it was also a Lizzie-move, as shrewd as ever. The film, *Penny and the Pownall Case* (1948), told a pulp fiction story of a young British fashion model who assumes the role of amateur detective to track down a smuggling ring securing passage for former Nazis out of Europe. Lutyens conceived her *Pownall* score as a kind of tonal and tuneful piano concertino, often resorting to conventional suspense cliches with the scoring; familiar gestures like tremolo strings for political intrigue, brass announcements for official declarations, a quasi-tango as Penny's search takes her to Spain, even a carefree waltz to somewhat remind us of the fact that women characters are running the show this time. It is conventional music all the way, then; a far cry from the composer's personal serial style, undertaken partly out of desperation, needing to become the breadwinner for her growing family and disastrous marriage, but also partly (as I have already observed) finding that the storytelling/scene-setting aspects of this strange side-craft of film composing were actually quite fun.

Being involved with the movies brought her out of the severe enclave of academia—also out of bankruptcy. She wanted more of it and she also enjoyed the rebellious aspect of being the only woman so engaged. It is a measure of her inexperience with soundtrack scoring, however, that in this first film so many of her music cues just keep playing in the background of scenes behind dialogue, making their musical statement in competition with, even to the detriment of, hearing what the characters are saying. Thus, while the director is trying to tell his story onscreen, Lutyens the composer often seems oblivious, making music in her own world. She would learn fast, though, and end up being a valuable collaborator with many films to come. By the 1950s and 1960s, the very dissonance and atonality of her so-called art music, her personal sound, was being viewed as a great asset to the new genre of campy horror films coming out of studios like Hammer and Amicus. *The Skull* was one example in 1965, introduced by atonal unison brass declarations followed by a stalking meter and blurry chords for winds and strings suggesting a mood of menace, then ear-splitting cries from high brass as the skull itself shrieks. She saw those soundtracks not as musical atmosphere but as blatant illustration.

A better example of Lutyens's talent for supporting such lowbrow entertainments while making them seem like genuine thrillers is the 1964 sci-fi matinee classic *Earth Dies Screaming* about invaders from another planet. The experienced British studio music director Philip Martel conducted and perhaps guided Lutyens through this very specific score. It begins with nervous lurking strings rising by chromatic steps through a growing sense of urgency—each step a question mark, exploiting the special Lutyens way with atonality not tied to any serial row but taking great advantage of the unanchored, unresolved tones of thriller scoring. Unpredictable music, certainly, but wedded to the action onscreen and, musically, all of a piece. And this is only the Main Title introduction.

Elsewhere, brass are used for the official military response to the alien invaders while familiar orchestral gestures create suspense. But here in the relatively new sci-fi genre, the soundtrack begins to experiment, to mix in the sound of electronic instruments: signals supposedly emanating from radio antennae aimed at detecting the invading spacemen who (awkwardly) stalk the village, threatening to take over the streets. Like a counterpoint, synthesized sounds and radar beeps become part of the narrative orchestral music to create a particularly creepy soundtrack appropriate to that era's space paranoia. What is clear is that Lutyens is taking this whole film music thing seriously and her commitment is what is engaging. Women who had already been working within the film industry as arrangers and conducting assistants began to wonder from now on: What about taking on a whole original score next time? If Lutyens could do it, what about women composing? Before long, subsequent Lutyens scores for those cheap thriller films like *Theater of Death* or *Dr. Terror's House of Horrors* brought her the unofficial title of Queen of Horror and she took pride in that eccentric accolade ever after—hers was no more "unladylike" a reputation, she would say, than that of Lady Macbeth or Mary Shelley!

What she may not have noticed in her final years (she died in 1983) was that even as her example of being an avant-garde composer willing to tame her own personal voice to the mainstream media—to come as an outsider into the movies—was inspiring the young Richard Rodney Bennett to indulge a similar career and not feel bad about it, so also she was inspiring other women—outsiders in a man's world—to open the studio doors and make their voices known in the cinema—gender be damned.

For some other female composers like British composer Doreen Carwithen, born 1922, the path into film scoring was more direct than it had been for Lutyens. Carwithen's marriage to established screen composer William Alwyn (*Odd Man Out, The Fallen Idol*) was her obvious introduction into the field. And yet it was mainly the working catalogue of Elisabeth Lutyens that truly gave her the confidence to enter the fray. Her reputation today is more for her being the first full-time female composer in British movies than for any kind of musical or cinematic innovation such as Lutyens could boast—there is not much progressive or distinctive orchestration in the Carwithen file: most of the thirty films she accompanied during her limited career were conventionally scored. She had begun as a copyist and graduated to writing transitional passages in other people's scores at the Dunham Studios before launching her own career transition into original scoring—titles like *Mantrap* and *Boys in Brown*. Her list spans from 1948 to 1963, winning not only steady commissions but lasting respect within the industry and succeeding in making colleagues out of male rivals.

Figure 12. Angela Morley. *Source*: Courtesy of the composer.

Given that growing acceptance of gender equality, her contemporary Angela Morley would prove both more prolific and more compositionally ambitious as she moved from arranging and orchestrating soundtracks for other people to composing her own. Interestingly, Morley's professional path as a female composer for films would prove to be a lot easier than her personal evolution as a woman. For what history records is that Angela Morley, six-time Emmy-nominated, three-time Emmy-winning composer, born in 1924, once upon a time was known as the British orchestrator and conductor Wally Stott. He was once a successful light music arranger in the 1950s and did a certain amount of orchestration for films and, like Carwithen, provided transitional scoring passages for others. Twice happily married with two children, suddenly at about the age of fifty, he seemed to disappear from both the music scene and from film credits, only to reappear after several months as Angela Morley, transgendered. And a more successful metamorphosis could not be imagined for she whose whole family supported the sex change and the several stages required for the transformation. Happily, there seemed to be very little trauma to mark the end of Wally Stott and very little career disruption before establishing the career of Angela Morley in his place, as it were.

This personal saga coincided with the gradual acceptance of women into film composing we have been summarizing here, so Morley's timing was fortunate. Right away, two important film jobs came along for her, musical films that wanted not only arranging and orchestrating other people's songs for each film (a Cinderella story, *The Slipper and the Rose*, 1976; and the French fable *The Little Prince*, 1974). Morley was to create the orchestral settings for these songs as well as create a semi-narrative dramatic score to tie each whole film together. It was multileveled projects like these that put Hollywood on notice that here was a formidable and dependable soundtrack scorer who now could be given some composing responsibilities of her own. That would come circa 1978 in the form of the major full-length animated feature *Watership Down*, the story of a rabbit family threatened by the encroaching human civilization and rapidly degrading natural environment around them, searching for safety (with no subtle symbolism) across a landscape of increasing peril. As a scoring assignment, along with the delight of finally being able to compose completely original material, Morley's task would include the extra burden that scoring cartoons requires: hyperactive music that needs to capture every action onscreen with an exaggerated attentiveness—a technical challenge, a physical marathon. Elder composer Malcolm Williamson had originally been signed to do the score but ill health had forced him to step down, and here came Angela Morley to take over, incorporating Williamson's opening music into her own scoring and establishing her own authority over the drama—this rather dark fable that can't seem to make up its mind whether to be a cultural bellwether with environmental warnings or a heroic adventure in praise of the little people (or rabbits) who flee oppression. Onscreen, the animal characters are simply, clearly, and effectively drawn while the backdrops—the woods and fields and blackening skies—are rendered as complex atmospheric paintings. Similarly contrasted, the big active music score from Angela Morley is by turns playful and atmospheric, ominous, and warm while also plainly, even methodically, illustrative of nearly every action onscreen. It seems perfectly suited to its film.

Soon, though, the new medium for cartoon and animation art would be computer generated and in the case of the Disney studio's first computer-created entertainment, *Tron* (1982), even the story being told onscreen was going to be set in cyberspace: the tale of a young computer whiz kid who finds himself literally sucked into a video game and forced to survive in competition with all the other virtual characters and forces at play there: humankind versus AI. With no apparent comparison so soon after Angela Morley's *Watership Down* cartoon music, another woman was chosen to do the complex music score for this new generation animation and, with no irony intended, she who was chosen was another case of transgender. In 1968, electronics expert and keyboard virtuoso Walter Carlos had produced a best-selling record album performing the multipart fugues and preludes of J. S. Bach reprogrammed for the new Moog synthesizer. Carlos called it *Switched-On Bach* and it seemed to promise two things to that present era: the popularization of electronic modes of musicmaking (of which the Moog was only one promising brand) and the resurgence of Bach himself to a new generation, if only through this artificial resuscitation. Suddenly, though, like Wally Stott before him, Walter Carlos seemed to disappear from the music scene for a number of months even as *Switched-On Bach* was still on the charts—only to reappear as an even more sophisticated, experienced, and aggressive advocate for electronic music, now venturing into the field of composing and the specialty of film composing, only now transformed into the woman Wendy Carlos.

Initially, the filmmakers of *Tron* who had requested her collaboration based on that "switched-on" fame were suggesting a music score made of familiar classical excerpts, wanting Carlos to extract, to "download," and adapt them to match the action onscreen. For two films by director Stanley Kubrick in the 1970s and 1980s she had done just that. Kubrick was already known for courting controversy in this way: laying-in classical concert pieces as the whole soundtrack of his 1969 film *2001: A Space Odyssey*. In 1971, he chose Wendy Carlos for his new film, *A Clockwork Orange*, to stitch together a soundtrack full of classical quotes but to utilize them there as absurdities—half satiric, half satanic, including some crazy synthesized manipulations of pieces like Rossini's *William Tell Overture* and *Thieving Magpie*, all to be heard in the context of the film's depiction of a society where anarchy rules and acts of extreme violence are tolerated and enjoyed. Technically assisted by Rachel Elkind, Wendy Carlos understood Kubrick's intentions, creating a detached and stoic tone right from the opening use of Purcell's "Funeral March for Queen Mary" and then returning to the piece elsewhere in the harrowing story-to-come. Its quality as a funereal lament perhaps also privately endorses a message from Carlos herself about the sheer sadness of this nihilist movie, but we can't be sure to what degree Carlos separated from Kubrick's POV and wanted her own say. Along the way, the main character Alex also professes an admiration for the music of Beethoven and so that encourages one more uncomfortable (blasphemous?) link between noble art and the ignoble human behavior of rape and greed that our hero Alex seems to celebrate. Rimsky-Korsakov and Elgar are other composers adapted by Carlos to color this clockwork world of the future. "Violence," Kubrick is supposed to have said somewhere to guide his chosen music director, "is turned into a dance."

The year 1980 saw the other Carlos and Kubrick collaboration, *The Shining*, about the horrible happenings to an apparently ordinary family staying at an isolated (and haunted?) hotel. Again, Kubrick said he wanted a soundtrack made up of classical quotes, extracts, and adaptations, this time from the progressive likes of Bartók, Penderecki, and Ligeti.

Certainly, anyone with Carlos's sophistication in so many eras of music should also be a formidable composer capable of original film scoring, and Wendy Carlos's magnum opus in that regard must be her hybrid orchestral and synthesized music for Disney's *Tron*. Happily, an early plan for scoring this film with classical excerpts had been dropped and Carlos set to work creating an original dramatic/narrative score. This would be her first experience mixing the synthetic and the acoustic sound-worlds, here to represent the crisis of human-against-machine. And the *Tron* music is not just atmospheric or suspense scoring: it is scoring-on-a-mission, every bit as narrative and illustrative as the soundtrack that hugged so close to that hand-drawn animation of *Watership Down*, only here electronically enhanced. It is not thematic scoring except for a five-note motif that recurs and sometimes a 7/8 meter pumps in behind, but its main feature is the constant interaction between a traditional studio orchestra and a whole array of computer-generated instruments and atonal sounds: at once a blend and a battleground of the two worldviews. This, of course, is Carlos's rendering of the central plot point: man versus microchip, the soul in cyberspace. *Tron*'s score builds into an aggressive villain all its own with threatening brass and the introduction of electric bass guitar and a high shrieking rock guitar effectively driving us into a virtual frenzy. A clever cadre of unidentifiable computer sounds, taps, and tones, gets mixed in with the musical score, reminding us of the virtual amusement park in which we're trapped. Without recognizable themes and conventional voicings, the *Tron* score was not much noticed in its day, but as a sample of Wendy Carlos's dramatic instincts and orchestrating skills, including her vast knowledge of computer-based instrumentations and equipment, it contains screen scoring that became seriously influential.

And all the while a new generation of women composers born after the war years was more freely entering the business of film scoring, often ghostwriting for male composers but then being offered the chance to produce their own original scores. More and more unique and effective storytelling music was what was wanted; less and less did a composing candidate's gender matter.

Shirley Walker, born in 1945, first became the guiding orchestrator and musical mentor for young 1980s film composers like Danny Elfman (*Edward Scissorhands, Batman*) and Hans Zimmer (*Rain Main, Day of the Dog*), then went on to score in her own right (*Memoirs of an Invisible Man, Batman: The Animated Series*). Said journalist Jon

Burlingame, "Her memorable military motifs (for TV's *Space: Above and Beyond*), powerful brass writing, and undeniable ability to musically convey the horror and tragedy of war made her the first choice (for many future TV projects)." It was also part of Shirley Walker's record that she had so successfully "saved" the soundtrack crisis surrounding the otherwise lyrical and inspiring adventure movie *The Black Stallion* (1979), whose awkward, ill-conceived scoring by a number of ill-prepared composers had threatened to hobble the whole production. Walker's guiding, smoothing hand brought the music track in line with the gracefulness and strength that the director, Carroll Ballard, had wanted all along. At the same time and with a similar authority, Walker's scoring for the kids TV series *The Flash* used an adult-sized orchestra of forty-two players and achieved a bigger, more compelling sound than the producers had ever hoped for. Where were the age-old doubts about the clout of women composers now? Walker was also unique for not only saving other people's films and composing powerfully on her own but for orchestrating and conducting all her own music tracks. In 2014, ASCAP (the most powerful composer-rights organization) established the Shirley Walker Award in her name.

In that same spirit, women began entering film music from all directions—classical and colloquial alike. Witness British-born Anne Dudley, classically trained, synth-savvy, and a virtuoso member of the high-tech rock band The Art of Noise. Her score for the comic romp *The Full Monty* won 1997's Academy Award for Best Score, using pop and mock-reggae to tease the strip club subculture comically depicted there. And yet she seemed at ease with all types of films, bringing dark black clouds over the sober story of skinhead gang warfare in *American History X*, then humanizing it through a few emotional piano lines—and using solo trumpet calls and suspense string lines to frame the saga of the Irish Republican Army war years in *The Crying Game*. Here was a composer who could not be labeled.

It was in 2014 that Emmy/Grammy-winning composer Laura Karpman took up the cause of increasing visibility for women in film composing to the next level by cofounding the Alliance for Women Film Composers. By this time, she had scored a host of major films of her own from *Paris Can Wait* to *The Cotton Club Encore* and *Black Nativity*. In 2024, she found herself nominated for the Best Score Academy Award for her jazzy scoring to the film *American Fiction*.

Figure 13. Jocelyn Pook. *Source*: Courtesy of the composer.

One other émigré from a rock-band fellowship has been Jocelyn Pook whose range of creativity extends from pop and minimalism to the most formal classical and even liturgical musings. Her score for the film *King Charles III* is profiled elsewhere in this book. Her experience working to decipher the purposes and preferences of the aforementioned director, Stanley Kubrick, this time for a 1999 psychological poser-film, *Eyes Wide Shut*, was comparable to that of Shirley Walker: serving the filmmaker's muse before making musical sense. As with those previous Kubrick soundtracks, outsourced music cues were imported here that are not by Pook: an old waltz tune by Shostakovich, a two-note piano bit distilled from Ligeti, and so forth. Pook's ability to perform in the frankly oppressive universe of a Kubrick production is another example of her versatility while also able to flourish with so much more freedom in later film jobs like Björn Runge's *The Wife* (2018), Sarah Gavron's 2007 *Brick Lane*, or the 2009 documentary *The People v. Leo Frank*.

Perhaps the most famous female film composer as of this writing is Rachel Portman, the first female to win the American Academy Award for Best Score in 1997 for her wise and attractive score to the film version of Jane Austin's novel *Emma*. A full interview with Portman occupies its own chapter in this volume.

Along with all female composers, by now women of color are likewise increasingly well represented in the annals of film composing, often first as arrangers or through documentary work, then moving into scoring major feature films. Kathryn Bostic's literate work underscores several civil rights documentaries and biographies. As a classical pianist with a jazz sensibility, Bostic became known for her free hand in scoring both documentaries and television, often drawing from both musical styles at the same time as in the film *Dear White People*, where electric keyboard plays a classical theme while a raucous jazz motif plays against scenes of a race riot, or where a high bluesy

Figure 14. Kathryn Bostic. *Source*: Everett Collection, Inc./Alamy Stock Photo.

sax with a piano vamp and strings behind it helps narrate the biopic *Toni Morrison: The Pieces I Am*. Some of her most intimate music was written for another biopic, *Amy Tan: Unintended Memoir* (2019): opening with a piano prelude based on jazz chords but developing into a more classical allegro drawing in electric guitar and a few strings as Tan's own career as a writer would focus and mature. The Bostic score was nominated for an Emmy. From 2016 to 2018 she was vice president of the aforementioned Alliance for Women Film Composers.

And what all these collaborations and personal accomplishments led to by the 2020s was, to a great extent, an open studio door for women, even multicultural women, being considered for each new film project whether it came out of a traditional movie studio, a web-based production entity, or some streaming-serviced indie filmmaker. Thus did Germaine Franco become the first Latina woman to be honored with an Oscar award for her music to *Encanto* (2021) and Turkish-American Pinar Toprak become one of the first women to score a comic book–based superhero movie, *Captain Marvel* (2019).

Figure 15. Hildur Guðnadóttir. *Source*: Photo by Maxime Ballesteros. Used with permission.

More striking yet was the debut season of Icelandic composer, singer, cellist Hildur Guðnadóttir in which she won an Emmy, two Golden Globes (from the Hollywood Foreign Press), a British BAFTA award, and a Best Score Oscar, for what some called an unorthodox cello concerto to 2019's film *Joker*. Adapted from a graphic novel, the *Joker* plot followed a down-and-out actor, Arthur Fleck, who descends into his own hellish role as a sad, broken, and ultimately crazed and murderous clown crushed by a cold and hostile (Manhattan-based) Gotham City. As Guðnadóttir's instrument of choice, cello features almost exclusively in scoring of the bleak urban setting—a night setting, mostly, and right in the middle of a citywide garbage strike so that the gutters and alleys and even the parks are overflowing with refuse. Such urban pollution seems to stand in for modern corruption; it certainly contributes to the Joker's depression, desperation, and growing madness. The sound-world of this music score appears to come from a whole ensemble of celli and string basses—not soloing but establishing a kind of dead drone of low unison tones as if to say of the Joker, This is how he feels. Any harmony is limited to elementary minor thirds and any variation from the drone sounds almost human, like a groan. "Is it just me or is it crazy out there," says the ailing, deteriorating Joker, and the cello score (still unison lines) takes up a mocking waltz while the drone under it never ends. Arthur is on seven different medications and has a demeaning job as a street busker, but there is no emotional relief and the cello lines offer no anesthetic. The film's art director has created a cityscape of garish glamor, flashy without warmth, and the soundtrack continues without themes, apparently without sympathy. The film does reveal a more poignant side of the Joker's character as we see him with his invalid mother but the music doesn't soften there; it tenses into one of its rare flurries of reaction, the strings glissing between octaves and a throbbing meter begins over the bass drone, then quickening and rising, reaching a shriek as the Joker begins his stabbing killing rampage on a subway train and spilling into the streets. And much like Wendy Carlos's use of indeterminate computer sounds, part of the careful sound design of Guðnadóttir's *Joker* score involves sirens in the distance—police, ambulance—distant and disembodied emergencies that are part of the soundtrack of any great fearsome city and that become so important to this hellish and mournful soundtrack. The only tonal memory we are likely to have of the *Joker* score is its two-note motif, backward, forward, a one-third span, eventually subsumed completely into the basal drone even as the joker is ultimately absorbed into Gotham.

It is certainly unusual for a themeless, monochrome score like this to generate such attention from multiple directions—international awards and a breakout season of fame that its composer had not achieved even with her previous history as a performing/recording artist. Something about the single-mindedness of her approach to the film (another composer's score could easily and justifiably have been flamboyant, even operatic) gave it an inverted power of its own and, thus, let us know how the Joker felt from the inside. By the end, we do hear only a single cello as the rest of the low-strings have fled or, like sympathy in the city, have simply worn out.

The driver of all this urban commentary, born in 1982 and based in Berlin, Hildur Guðnadóttir debuted first as a singer and a cellist with a most eclectic repertoire but, like Pook and Portman, used the movies to expand her compositional skills and ambitions and has sought ever more challenging opportunities there. Not long after *Joker*, she was called into a Todd Field film about a troubled symphony conductor named Lydia Tár. Her contributions to the film called *Tár* would be limited, though, to a quasi–hip hop song that covers the end credits and a simple piano tune that Lydia is writing for the one steady person in her life, the child Petra (a tune that seems to be mimicking the old 1930s DeRose–Mitchell pop song "Deep Purple").

On her career and on being a female composer, Guðnadóttir is quoted in *Billboard* magazine as saying, "In the past, I definitely came across a kind of reluctance to trust me for projects. I always wondered if it's because I'm a woman, and then I started talking to other female composers experiencing the same thing. In the last few years there has been so much awareness of this—people are starting to take the so-called risk of trusting women for these jobs and finding out that there's no reason we can't do it" (November 2019, 16). Naturally.

And maybe if Hildur G. had known more of the history we have been surveying here of women composers on active duty all these years, she'd be encouraged even more about the progress of her own career and the prospects of the female colleagues who may come after, mentored by her example.

So far have these daughters of Lutyens come from those early works by female film composers that it no longer seems relevant, if it ever was, to consider them in some separate category, except perhaps as part of some sociological study. There is nothing gender-specific about their music or the way they perceive the dramas onscreen to be scored. The best of their music is full of individual personality, which is unique to any artist, gender be damned.

Somewhere in the genetics of any serious composition it is possible to locate qualities that both genders, even transgenders, share. By now, it matters not at all that you are a woman composer scoring films. Elisabeth Lutyens succeeded by sheer talent and defiance; Angela Morley by applying a solid orchestral technique to, for instance, an animated epic; Rachel Portman by gaining acceptance for her very British-but-universal dramaturgy.

There are still occasional articles and panel discussions, lectures, and chapters in books that rehearse with some concern the limited history of women composers struggling to find work, but with each new credential, the subject becomes less a category than a curiosity. And as the young Richard Rodney Bennett would finally say of the female composer he had first read about in that train station, headed for school, "Elisabeth Lutyens was the first professional composer of any sort that I ever knew. She's certainly the English composer who influenced me the most." It was her quirky way with twelve-tone music that made Sir Richard sit up and take notice. But it was her strength and originality, orneriness, and persistence, entering a supposedly masculine enclave—the movie studio scoring stage—that convinced now two generations of women composers that it was high time to even up the score.

12

Interlude

The Walk of Fame—Jerry Goldsmith

Figure 16. Jerry Goldsmith's honorary sidewalk "star" on Hollywood's Walk of Fame. *Source*: Courtesy of Marilee Bradford.

THE VERY IDEA THAT SOMEONE nominated eighteen times for, let's say, twenty of the best film scores ever should have been rewarded with an Academy Award just one begrudging time seems manifestly unfair. But then Goldsmith's equally accomplished colleague, Elmer Bernstein, also won only a single Oscar award after an exemplary career and for the most trivial of his efforts. So probably there was no real prejudice at work in Goldsmith's case. Still, it must have been frustrating to him, and, to many people, Goldsmith did seem a guarded figure, reluctant to mingle—not grumpy like Bernard Herrmann, but edgy; something of an outsider. Meanwhile, though, close associates like conductor Lionel Newman and orchestrator Arthur Morton protected and promoted him.

The status of an outsider does seem odd because we learn from his biography that Mr. Jerrold Goldsmith was actually the ultimate Hollywood insider—one of the few screen scorers born in Los Angeles and then rising through the ranks from studio staff typist to assisting with, and then composing for, some very early 1950s "live" TV shows like *Climax!* and *Studio One*. Those were minor scores because the budgets wouldn't support more than a few instruments and the shows were being broadcast Now. But right away in Goldsmith's earliest music there's an efficiency and empathy—and more musical ideas in the scoring than those dramas required, more than they deserved. Insiders did take notice.

Technically, his music studies had not been all that great: he came at scoring almost exclusively from the commercial world—some piano lessons from a Hollywood tutor Jakob Gimpel; some drama-scoring classes from Miklós Rózsa; and then, of course, everyone dropped in on Mario Castelnuevo-Tedesco for a few coaching sessions. Maybe it was his lack of official musical credentials that fed his supposed inferiority complex at cocktail parties, shy before conservatory composers. But we have news for him: by the time he graduated from television to big screen scoring, most of those elite composers were already beginning to envy him. Back in the day, when I wrote a piece surveying what we knew of Goldsmith at that time, I reported how, in Irwin Bazelon's book, *Knowing the Score*, when a wide range of film composers were asked which colleagues they most admired, fully seven out of nine mentioned Goldsmith.

So it is, to a certain degree, a shame that Goldsmith's career has never been properly rewarded in concrete terms and, more importantly, that his overall accomplishment has still to this day not been adequately cited or permanently appreciated. Sure, sci-fi fans collect his space scores and comic book enthusiasts tout his superhero music. But that's just a hobbyist mentality—those folks praise anything that soars. And noting how copycat film composers were inspired by Mr. Goldsmith is hardly encouraging. If he were still working, he'd feel more edgy than ever.

In May 2017, someone saw fit to award him, thirteen years after his death, a tribute star on the Hollywood Walk of Fame. That's a rare compliment for a composer even if it wouldn't really earn points before that academic crowd he coveted. But it is a public gesture that, at least, puts the Goldsmith name out there, literally, on the street. The point here is that Jerry Goldsmith, for all his history, is in danger of being lumped in with other B-genre and opportunist composers, hijacked by genre-hobbyists who care little for the subtleties of composition and, thus, muffle and blur what we should all hold as special about him: his compositional excellence and heart. It is true that he scored too many films and, so, there are a number of rather noisy and/or bland soundtracks he churned out for stories he couldn't care about—maybe he felt edgy and oppressed in private life too and so never dared to stop working and relax. Chronic workaholic. In the second half of his career, he also took on concert gigs, conducting suites of his hit films with symphonies around the world—maybe (I always wondered) to overcome his early awkwardness as a conductor (when he started out, he had a hard time at the podium keeping up with the complex time signatures and orchestral balances he had written into his own scores). At length, he mastered the baton, of course, and earned the respect of experts like Alex North and orchestras like the Royal Scottish National Orchestra, the Pittsburgh Symphony, the Hungarian State Symphony with whom he recorded . . . So why would he ever feel uncomfortable in the company of other composers?

I don't write here to solve that question but, rather, to ask what all his best scores have in common, although they're written for many different genres and use radically different musical styles. It turns out that, as a composer, Goldsmith actually seemed to rely on three specific techniques or traits when approaching any particular film commission. Of course, his own instincts colored his output and made it "Goldsmithian," but underlying that personal voice was a procedural routine to which he regularly resorted. Rather than survey the long list of films he scored over fifty years, and since I never got to (or dared to) interview him, let me trace the evidence of those three compositional traits in just a few of his best scores here and thus suggest that he deserves more than a transient groupie fan base; that posterity should also give him his due, more than just a slab on the Walk of Fame. Some history first.

From the start, Goldsmith was writing music that was very conscious of its own voice. To this day, you can hear, for instance, in a 1950s TV episode of *Perry Mason*, how carefully shaped each music cue is behind even such a pedestrian courtroom tale. Likewise, the early days of TV's *Gunsmoke* received a few elementary Goldsmith scores, eschewing the usual cowboy clichés, treating each show like it was a serious drama instead of the horse opera that it was. His first big screen theatrical film score actually came out of having scored radio drama circa 1956. That was the generic western *Black Patch*. And even there, he did not seem lured by the bigger-than-TV budget or the luxury of a wider rectangular screen into composing macho music. His tone was terse and stringent and modal, almost resembling Native American chant—and with a preference for solo writing including bass clef piano, harp, marimba; only modestly adding more rhythmic and expressive lines for horns along the way. This was scoring that commented, not through themes, but by maintaining a steady grim air. His second feature score, 1959's *City of Fear*, pushed that same monothematic tonal language to a darker place: a drab cityscape crossed by two escaped convicts. How bold of Goldsmith at such an early stage in his career to be writing what is essentially atonal music for a Hollywood entertainment film. At times, one suspects this music could be an adapted form of serial composing, but in a score like *City of Fear* any formal tone row is impossible to peg, so let's just call it a brave atonal score and say that it served its dire plot well. Its moodiness was further spiked with harsh, pointed sounds like xylophone, barking brass, and again, piano details in the bass clef.

Goldsmith continued to compose for TV during those same apprentice years. Particularly notable were his seven scores for the classic 1959 fantasy series *The Twilight Zone*, making sure each episode had its own musical identity: "The Big, Tall Wish" about a black child hero-worshipping a boxer featured a blues-oriented harmonica and ensemble, while the famous segment "The Invaders"—a wordless parable showing an old hermit woman terrorized by (apparently) space aliens—was colored by a unique atonal sound-design made of solo violin, piano, Vox organ, harp and strings that were hesitant at first, then made increasingly violent interjections, chord patterns, and rhythms, building to a devil's dance as the woman fought for her life. Network producers would rent or steal those particular music cues for years thereafter to track-in behind other programs without, of course, crediting Goldsmith, so effective were they in setting a scene and embodying terror. For Goldsmith, such anonymity continued to limit his reputation: he was still not seen as an industry insider. What his *Twilight Zone* success did lead to was an invitation to score another TV anthology series by 1960, *Boris Karloff's Thriller*. These were more conventional stories, gothic instead of cosmic and occult and, so, inspiring more thematic scores: a richly colored Gaelic peasant dance for the episode "Hay Fork and Bill Hook"; a fiendishly chromatic piano waltz that wafted through "What Beckoning Ghost"; a sleazy sax theme for "Yours Truly, Jack the Ripper"; and some of his loveliest flute/strings/celesta ensemble writing for the episode "Mr. George" about a lonely girl with a guardian angel. For their times, and certainly beyond anything written for television now, these sensitive, skillful scores stood out from all established norms. From them would come Goldsmith's mature career in scoring theatrical films: almost immediately six jobs from Universal Studios. Two were broad and bland scores, though busy with good intentions (*The Spiral Road*, 1962, and *A Gathering of Eagles*, 1963); two drew on offside sources (*Lonely Are the Brave*, 1962, recalled Copland Americana music as filtered through Elmer Bernstein, and *Freud*, 1962, more subtly invoked the modal tonality of someone like Béla Bartók for a biopic on the early life of the great psychoanalyst). Again, we should say that music as sophisticated and daring as the latter or as direct and descriptive as the former was audacious from such a young composer. Goldsmith was behaving like someone who would set his own place at the table and maybe even order for everyone else.

An earlier drama in that Universal group, *Studs Lonigan* (1960), inspired probably the first Goldsmith score to openly draw attention to itself. This was a film about a young rogue and his aimless pals prowling and pranking through the streets of 1920s Chicago and Goldsmith attempted to depict him three ways: through a lonely cheerless harmonica theme; through sly ironic references to another idle drifter from music history, Stravinsky's *L'Histoire du Soldat*; and through a dynamic ten-minute multimovement ragtime suite that accompanied a montage sequence of Studs's mischief-making around town. There, Goldsmith had become the film's main character. Still, no critics at the time would mention any music from this film nor knew the name of its composer. The final Universal film of the period was the mystery/romp *The List of Adrian Messenger* (1963), noticeable (except that no one did) for its rousing fox hunt music (Did this coax Bernard Herrmann's similar fox hunt music in the next year's *Marnie*?) and its dour sax theme, obviously derived from the aforementioned Ripper episode of *Thriller*.

From now on, for a variety of studios, Goldsmith freelanced his way into the front ranks of film composers, still without really establishing his own name as a "brand" via hit movie melodies like Henry Mancini was doing, or hit films like Bernstein served, or ongoing director relationships like Hitch had with Herrmann. Goldsmith had only the content and quality of his music working for him, an introverted advocate at best. But in the second half of the 1960s, it was enough: it seemed that he would at last come into his own—not through public attention but by producing three of the best, most germane film scores ever. We only skim them here:

First, consider *A Patch of Blue*, the quiet story of a blind girl abused by her own family but soon championed by one decent stranger who periodically stops by the park bench where she loiters each day, just to chat and ask after her. The 1965 civil rights–era irony of this plot was that the kindly stranger was a black man and the girl's family was going to have a problem with that if they ever found out. She, of course, was literally "blind to all that." This delicate, hesitant, tactile world of the sightless girl is voiced in Goldsmith's chamber score by solo piano, repeating a triplet motif in three-quarter time, often calmed and comforted by warm major-key string harmonies, sympathetic solo winds, even homey harmonica chords—all of which have their own individual reflective passages to offer during the score and convey great compassion. (For some of us, they also recall the Goldsmith music for that other angel-unawares story, TV's *Mr. George*.) Only once does the scoring cloud over with blurred cluster chords and agitated pizzicatos as the girl remembers the violent incident that blinded her; and there is also one utterly joyous musical sequence that stands out for its gentle pastoral scoring, but we'll describe that later.

A second masterwork of this Goldsmith launching season was the soaring, heroic, fully symphonic tone poem for a film about a squad of

WWI flying aces, *The Blue Max* (1966). As one of his most cogent and concentrated traditional works, redolent of Richard Strauss or Mahler, this was a score with rich and detailed orchestration (in those days aided by orchestrator Arthur Morton). Thick woodwind groupings and brass blends against light and transparent string writing, all gave the very feel of biplane flight, of dodging and diving dogfights in the air. Then a dogged passacaglia represented the awful struggle and drudge of the trench war on the ground. If such a score had been coupled with either of the great screen versions of that classic WWI saga *All Quiet on the Western Front* (1930 and 1979) instead of being tied to this puffy melodrama, Goldsmith might have had an award-winner here. (When the Pittsburgh Symphony concertized this music in the 1970s, it stood up well alongside pieces by Copland, Prokofiev, and Korngold.) As it was, a tiny record label, Mainstream, bought up the tapes of both *Max* and *Patch* and put out a soundtrack disc of each: the cult of Goldsmith collecting had begun.

Most striking of all, though, of this breakout trilogy would be Goldsmith's aurally startling, conceptually complex, quasi-serial score to the sci-fi allegory *Planet of the Apes* (1968). Its main theme is only quasi-serial because it was made of more than the twelve tones allowed in strict serial composing. Still, the order of the tones is constant and all the subsequent musical material is reliant on that series. A generally atonal score would not have suggested the same deliberate sinister design that a serial row conveys here, even abstractly. And this well-known story of *Apes*—in which a space crew crash-land on a hostile planet where apes have evolved past primitive humans—needed that special undercurrent of systematic evil. Conventional action scoring would have sufficed, but Goldsmith saw an opportunity to exaggerate the nightmare by two gimmicks: exploiting the foreign sound and implications of serial music, and assembling a weird conglomeration of instruments to represent the apocalyptic plot. His orchestra consisted of aggressive brass, shrill woodwinds, active string sections, one bass slide whistle, and a lot of jabbing syncopated solo piano work—all of that constantly punctuated by a cohort of strange percussion instruments: tropical drums, clapper sticks, bamboo rods, conch shells used as bugles, even stainless-steel mixing bowls swiped by wire brushes and made to reverberate like a gong. Much praise is due to this score's unique sound-design but we are focusing here on the compositional content of these three scores. In this present case, whereas this music appears to "ape" a serial row and, in its broken primitive rhythms and vivace piano details, seems to invoke Stravinsky, what it really draws on for inspiration (again, remembering the music to *Freud* six years earlier) is Bartók again, specifically that composer's 1936 *Music for Strings, Piano and Celeste*. Its piano parts have just a passing similarity to the *Apes* music but for more absolute likenesses, compare the "Clothes Snatching" sequence in the film score with the staccato figures four minutes into Bartók's third movement or that same movement's main theme, which is at least a close cousin (though not serial) to the apes' main theme, complete with xylophone and piano accents and all. The high, mysterious unison strings in Bartók's first movement are referenced all through the film music by Goldsmith and solo piano commenting over a churning orchestra is a feature of both scores. The composer Varese seems also to lurk in the background. As bold music in its own right, this was the soundtrack that brought *Planet of the Apes* much of the public and critical attention it enjoyed that year. Even so, it lost its nominated Academy Award to a conventional period score. Thus, in spite of those three masterworks just described, it was still true that few people knew Goldsmith's name or wrote seriously about his work. In one brief article from the *National Observer*, Goldsmith complained about neglect outright: "I resent being looked down on by the so-called musical purists who are still more likely to start a review of a serious piece of mine with something like 'motion picture composer Jerry Goldsmith'" (7 November 1966). One could say that Goldsmith was just young and pouting there—that film composers are specialists and that until there are concert works to outnumber your film scores, you're not likely to be thought of outside your specialty, so why grouse? Critics were just acknowledging the limits of the profession he chose. At any rate, Goldsmith has always composed along his own strict guidelines and certainly deserves acknowledgment of that. By the late 1960s, at least he was known inside the Hollywood studios for those three milestone scores—and all that impeccable TV work. And he continued that same self-conscious work ethic for the next thirty-five years.

In examining that, we were about to identify three recurring compositional traits that Goldsmith seems to have applied to each of his most serious and personal scores no matter whether he was scoring a dark horror film, a comedy, an adventure film, or a sensitive character study. Certainly, technical experience and personal qualities are ultimately what any composer's music has in common but I have been curious to analyze Goldsmith's means and methods more closely. So, I have noted three traits—well, two procedures and one stylistic result. The *Planet of the Apes* score is a good demonstration of the first characteristic: his scores were most often monothematic—one representative theme standing for each film, either expressive of the setting or of some subtext in the film story. Out of that theme, then, he would typically extract a three- or four-note cell to be used as a seedling replanted throughout the score and developed into the rest of his narrative and descriptive music. In *Apes*, there is one main theme, a quasi-tone row from which he then derives a distinctive three-note motif (C-A-Bb), sometimes followed by an answering phrase. That motif becomes iconic, posed as a question or a warning or just a reminder throughout the scoring, buried, varied, manipulated into action sequences or scenes of meditation, usually harmonized in unresolved ways—not just baldly repeated but unraveled slowly as part of a chord or tossed into a piano run, even rendered by the tonal percussion instruments. That practice of isolating small cells of notes and using them to build your developmental material (which is a tenet of the formal serial system) was already in Goldsmith's composing repertoire and for him it became a habit. The triplet piano figure in *A Patch of Blue* (G-G#-G-C as sixteenth notes) became a similar motto or repeating cell for that film score. Goldsmith used it as a stand-alone melodic figure, as a harmony to his sympathetic legato theme for the blind girl, and as a kind of tonal totem around which the other instruments could modulate in some of the functional, transitional music cues in the score. One especially joyous use of the triplet motto we have hinted at already—where the repeated variation of that single cell actually seems to drive and inspire the action onscreen, not just follow it—comes during the scene where the blind girl shares some unexpected cheer with her new friend, Gordon. On his way to work, he has paused to watch her at her menial handiwork in the park—stringing beads to make cheap necklaces—then briefly joins in helping her, to their mutual delight. The scoring, so far for this scene, has been a lingering backdrop of woodwinds; now as the two new friends interact, Goldsmith introduces a gathering sense of excitement by stirring the triplet figure into more rhythmic patterns, bringing in woodwinds with contrapuntal lines, and soon even inserting a castanet click to mimic each bead that drops into place on the necklace string. Through the music score, the girl's rote work has become a happy game. It is still a monothematic score but it has become both functionally cinematic and satisfyingly musical.

Though not always comfortable coming up with wholly natural or believable melodic themes, Goldsmith's bluesy world-weary trumpet theme that becomes the voice of a cynical detective in *Chinatown* (1974) proved instantly charismatic and expressive—a monothematic score if there ever was one. Its first three notes are his motto here and provide a speculative introduction to almost every cue thereafter, whether or not the rest of that trumpet torch song is carried to its climax. In a similar vein, motto-based composing derived from monothematic scores has been Goldsmith's habit since the early days of *Lonely Are the Brave*, noting his nine-note phrase there which became a motto (this time on cowboy trumpet), or the propulsive brass opening of *100 Rifles* (1969) developing into a recurring motif, both tremendously exciting and somehow joyful! Or consider the jittery accented two-note trope, confined within a strict 6/8 meter, that kept tensions high around the fictionalized US space program in *Capricorn One* (1978).

None of this is to say that Goldsmith always stuck with monothematic scoring. The intrepid fanfare of open fifths that stands as the main motto in the Moroccan adventure score *The Wind and the Lion* (1975) is actually challenged and equaled by a compelling love theme (reminiscent of Alex North's *Spartacus* [1960]). In the Moroccan story, both themes sweep in and out of some of Goldsmith's most vigorous and virtuosic orchestral scoring for the film's desert battle scenes. So, too, is the main theme of the first theatrical version *Star Trek* (1979) equal to, but kept separate from, that film's strong exotic love theme. But even ethnically specific scores, like *Under Fire* (1983) with its Peruvian flute-motto or *Russia House* (1990) with its dark Soviet era ambiance and voicing, did break off a single motto for use as score-starter. Even the heavily panting sexy thriller *Basic Instinct* (1992) got a harmonically ambiguous main theme (reminding us of the composer's chromatic piano waltz from thirty years earlier in TV's *What Beckoning Ghost?*) from which a descending chromatic five-chord motto was extracted to spawn that whole score. So that is the first composing habit we attribute to Goldsmith, monothematic scoring from which a brief motto is broken off and used in variations.

A second characteristic of the Goldsmith method of composing that seemed to distinguish him was his penchant for somehow hearing in his head and then recreating in fact a unique sound-world for each film—that is, custom tailoring unusual combinations of instruments that, in theory, would become part of the film's distinctive memory, at least part of its atmosphere. Ultimate examples have already been suggested: the tight but transparent ensemble of piano, harmonica, vibes, solo winds, and a handful of strings in *A Patch of Blue* used there not for the sake of economy (as in those live TV days) but for intimacy's sake; the aggressively eccentric collection of percussion instruments and reverberation effects that disturbed the already sharp orchestral writing in *Planet of the Apes*. As an early and leading champion of incorporating synthesized sounds into the traditional orchestra, Goldsmith exploited a wide range of electronic voicings over the years that illustrate this category of sound-design: tone beds and singular sounds to give a film its own aural profile. Examples include the electronically reproduced Andean flutes and South American drums in *Under Fire*, the computer-sampled and altered African tribal chants that became part of the fabric of the score to *Ghost and the Darkness* (1996), and the synthesized moans and creaks and shrieks and knocks mixed in with Goldsmith's vivid paraphrase of Liszt in *The Mephisto Waltz* (1971) later exaggerated to comic proportions in *Gremlins* (1984). The sound-world of *Warlock* (1991), if not as memorable in its synthesized snarling as was *The Omen*, was still the more interesting aspect of its score than the composition itself. This gift for sound design must be an instinctual, highly personal, probably unteachable talent. I still cannot quite fathom the creative mindset from which Goldsmith once said that, on seeing the film *Chinatown* for the first time and considering a sound-world for its score, he immediately "heard a solo trumpet, strings, four pianos, four harps, and a chime" (Prendergast 159–61). Of course, that's a score that proved inseparable from its film—one of the best of its decade. But where does such intuition come from?

A third overall trait of Goldsmith scoring is the least concrete but the most important, and it's not a quantifiable procedure like using mottos or settling on a sound-design—it is a qualitative style of Goldsmith the composer: that the narrative body of his best scores, the functional descriptive music, is equally committed to both its prosaic storytelling function *and* to sheer musicmaking. It is musical prose, a kind of instrumental recitative impulsively following the action onscreen, yet it sustains its own kind of internal logic. It is instinctual but sounds intentional. Thus, for instance, the orchestral seascapes heard in films like *Islands in the Stream* (1977) or *Papillion* (1973), while not shaped or paced in any formal or symmetrical way, play out as interesting, purposeful impressionistic sketches, blessedly free of clichés, musically satisfying and yet always in service of the cinema. Internal architecture and external musicmaking likewise characterized Goldsmith scores to TV's *The Red Pony* (1973), adventure films like *The Great Train Robbery* (1979), or *First Knight* (1995). For a classroom demonstration of such functional music that is also compositionally legit and satisfying, try the "Trip to the County Fair" from *Raggedy Man* (1981), the "Restless Hours" sequence from *Seconds* (1966), the tennis match in *The Reincarnation of Peter Proud* (1975), that frantic Raisuli attack music in *Wind and the Lion*, or the suddenly emotional scoring behind a bleak phone call being placed from frozen outer space to a warm home planet in *Outland* (1981). Goldsmith's sad, lyrical scoring there is light-years away from the rest of that cold mechanical score. Half prose, half poetry.

For Jerry Goldsmith laboring, as it were, in isolation over these bits of film trying to match them with music, gut-wrenching over thematic inventions and sound-designs, stringing together longish descriptive passages that also make music, probably never to be noticed, film scoring could indeed seem to be a thankless job, a transient career at best. He said he went out on the road as a guest conductor, late in life, mainly to beat the isolation of composing and to overcome that old feeling of anonymity—to replace the professional resentment with some public applause. Sure enough of his own talents, he did not become bitter in the end or reclusive. Indeed, he softened in his old age; his scores still offered one main theme but he less often labored over motive variations and counterpoints: his later orchestrations rested on simple long-lined tunes, simply harmonized with whole sections of the orchestra replaced by synth pads. Still, it was not for laziness that his final scores slackened in scope and style: after all, only a composer of personal integrity could find such fun and color in a film score called *Mom and Dad Save the World* (1991) or new spook-sounds in *The Haunting* (1999) or *The Hollow Man* (2000). And, now and then, there were still sincere themes that occurred to him like the song in *Not without My Daughter* (1991). Meanwhile, the generation of directors who sought his services and the audiences who begged him to concertize grew younger and broader every year. Now there's even a commemorative star on the pavement of his Hollywood hometown.

I still worry somewhat, though, that his support is shallow and that his main fame still rests only with those brassy action movies rather than with the rich and varied catalogue I have spotlighted here. I could only hope that the next generation of students/listeners might take the time to test out these three Goldsmithian characteristics described above and follow them through to some kind of appreciation, thereby debunking his own apparent pessimism about posterity. It's still a thankless field; he was right about that, though. I think back to one impeccable little Goldsmith score to a 1972 occult film by Robert Mulligan, *The Other*. It was a period piece set on a Depression era farm asking us to decide which of two twin brothers was the naïvely Good one and which murderously Evil. At the time of its release, the critic for *Films in Review* gave the score such a high level of detailed attention and lasting appreciation as I am hoping our generation (and the next) might aspire to in support of a talent like Goldsmith:

> *The Other*, 1972's most beautiful film music to date, adds a guileless and moving voice to the film. . . . From the opening credits we hear the main theme briefly whistled as introduction to an ensuing, superbly orchestrated setting. The melody itself is a fragile one, sad and winsome Americana discreetly harmonized and later turned into a veritable ballet as Grandma Ada urges one boy to play a game of soul-transference scored by a rather thrilling waltz. . . . Goldsmith's tendency to dissolve more complex harmonies into the simplest tonal combinations is one of his hallmarks and his theme for the boys' damaged mother is some of his most poignant music: a strings and piano duet to bring realization to her inner torture and loneliness. This is music of contour, proportion and a direction that is individual but with the advantage of flexibility and restraint. Goldsmith's extraordinary score . . . may be the year's stunner. (*Films in Review* 23, no. 6 [1972])

They don't bother with detailed reviews like that anymore. But that was just one of many fairly functional, easily missed Goldsmith accomplishments in his fifty-year career. And it turns out that his early pessimism was often justified: in this case, it so happened that the producers of *The Other* somehow found fault with the perfect twenty minutes of music Goldsmith provided for their film—and so only about half of his score was ever heard in the final film. If the film industry treats even its masters like that while they're alive, what hope have we that posterity (that is, current and future fans and critics) will make amends? I'd say Goldsmith was right to be guarded and skeptical way back when. Even the Walk of Fame can be fickle.

Part IV

A Successor Generation

13

David Shire (b. 1937)

Setting the Stage

Figure 17. David Shire. *Source*: Courtesy of the composer.

Most other screen composers came over to the field of movie music from classical careers or from big band pop music or from contributing a few music cues to someone's documentary production. So, the arrival of David Shire from the Yale Drama School and then the Broadway musical stage into mainstream movie scoring was already unique. By the time he had reached the status of major Oscar-winning film composer through association with hit movies like *All the President's Men* (1976), *Farewell My Lovely* (1975), and *Saturday Night Fever* (1977),[1] two singular qualities stood out, setting any Shire film score apart as unique: a sharp sense of drama and a singing sense of melody.

Actually, Shire had entered Yale as an English major but, since his father was an orchestra leader and teacher in Buffalo, New York, music was already on David's mind. He took all of his elective classes in music and dabbled in student musicals throughout each semester. One polished stage show became his senior thesis. After Yale, he went to Brandeis University for graduate work, also in music, and followed what seemed a logical next step, setting the stage for a musical career somehow tied to drama: at first a showbiz life in Manhattan, working as a rehearsal pianist for other people's shows around town, creating one off-Broadway musical, *The Sap of Life*, with collaborator Richard Maltby Jr. and writing a series of impeccable songs that were soon picked up by the young ingénue Barbra Streisand, circa 1965. The success of that threesome—Shire, Maltby, Streisand—shot Shire out to California by 1969 to produce another musical with the support and mentoring of Broadway's Stephen Sondheim who respected Shire's songwriting. It was not long, then, before TV and the movies were hearing about "this Yale composer," and major screen directors like Robert Wise and Francis Ford Coppola (by then, Shire was married to Coppola's sister, Talia; he married actress Didi Conn in 1982) gave him the breaks he needed, beyond songwriting, to display his formidable orchestral skills. A Shire movie career was launched.

He has succeed in both directions: writing pertinent and poignant melodies that encapsulate each film (the world-weary trombone theme from *Farewell, My Lovely*; the restless rhapsodic solo violin in *Bed and Breakfast* [1992]; the Oscar-winning song "It Goes Like It Goes" from *Norma Rae* [1979]) and writing dramatically effective orchestral scores for films that also reflect his compositional sophistication and daring (a wordless vocalese invoking German WWI history for *The*

Hindenburg (1975); a chromatic piano étude to represent postmodern angst in *The Conversation* (1974); satiric exaggeration for the comedy *Big Bus* (1976); a foray into twelve-tone serial jazz for the terrorist thriller *The Taking of Pelham 1-2-3* (1974).

It's all experience that has served Shire well—growing up around the tuneful background of his father's dance band, the range of compositional techniques and devices he learned through university, the stage management aspects of writing for a Broadway show, which must help the future film scorer to write music that unifies a story onscreen. In that sense, maybe the unique training-ground of stage music is the perfect school for a film composer after all.

Meanwhile, apart from film scoring, Shire musicals live on in new productions around the country: *Starting Here, Starting Now*; *Closer than Ever*; *Baby*; *Big*; *Take Flight*. The year 2008 saw the premiere of Shire's one-act children's opera, *A Stream of Voices*, while 2022 saw him traveling to the United Arab Emirates for the nineteenth Abu Dhabi Festival to collaborate with fellow composers Ihab Darwish and John Debney in the creation of a "unity cantata" among Christians, Jews, and Muslims called *Symphony of Three: Peace, Love, Tolerance* of which the twenty-five-minute second movement, "Peace," for chorus and orchestra conducted by Diego Navarro was Shire's. Finally, as if to emphasize the free-flowing nature of all the composer conversations in this book, one of my talks with Shire, as reproduced below, is certainly the only time I've been interrupted in the middle of an interview by the intrusion of a helicopter. Read on. (Happily, Shire took it in stride.)

Interview with David Shire

JOHN CAPS: Maybe the first thing people note about any David Shire music is its thoughtful, even intellectual, foundation—the solid framework of your songs for Broadway and some pretty adventurous ideas in your film writing—but one thing I've noticed over the years is a strong sense of yearning in much of this music—an emotional tug that is, of course, a good quality to bring to a film score, wanting to draw the audience into a screen story and sympathize with the characters. There's a leaning harmonic in many of your early scores. I hear it in the first Shire music I ever heard, which were the TV scores for an Americana play, *Appalachian Autumn* (1969), and the feminist melodrama *Tell Me Where It Hurts* (1974)—but it's also all through the violin scoring of *Bed and Breakfast*, the viola theme in *Old Boyfriends* (1979), and the guitar music in *Paris Trout* (1991), and indeed, it seems to be the subject of your most expansive score, *Return to Oz* (1985). That brings up the question: Are you, as a composer, instinctively looking for the emotional POV of each of those main characters—the emotional center of each film—even before you address the story's setting or period or action?

DAVID SHIRE: I certainly am. That's the process that is the starting point for my work on almost all my scores, as it is, I think, for most film composers. Underlying or enhancing that emotional center is arguably Job One. Getting on the same wave length, whether instinctually or not, is what gets the music going. But, interestingly enough, trying to duplicate a film's emotion is not as ideal a scoring solution as a director might think. In fact, it can be problem. I was hired to do the score to (the very emotional divorce drama by Robert Benton) *Kramer vs. Kramer* (1979), and I was crying when I came out of the screening room after first seeing it. I told the producer, Stanley Jaffe, that I thought a score was not only unnecessary but could actually diminish the performances of Meryl Streep and Dustin Hoffman. Jaffe was grateful that I was so moved but he insisted that I, at least, give it more thought and try to write a score. So, I wrote about thirty minutes of music, which was duly mixed into the soundtrack. Then, after the first preview, Stanley said he thought we didn't need about ten minutes of what I had written. After the second preview, he said we should lose another third of the score. At that point I asked that he make a mercy killing of the last ten minutes of music since he was surely going to want to lose that as well. And so, the only music that did end up in the picture was some Vivaldi and Bach source-scoring. I was sorry to lose my connection with such a great picture but, in the end, my original instinct about it (that the emotional center of the story was already there onscreen, and any music underline would have only been redundant) was correct.

JC: An honest self-sacrifice on your part.

DS: Well, at least I got paid for my attempt.

JC: When music *is* wanted to represent a main character or enhance that emotional center of a film story, you often seem to assign a specifically chosen solo instrument to carry the task. Solo violin and cello play a major role in *Return to Oz*, the bluesy trombone in *Farewell, My Lovely*, and of course, the loner piano solos in *The Conversation*. But is there any danger in highlighting a solo instrumentalist throughout a score? I mean, couldn't it draw attention away from the film toward the player, the score, or even the composer?

DS: I don't think there's danger if it's the right approach for that film. I mean, for example, the solo zither playing incessantly through (the classic 1949 film) *The Third Man* or, say, the solo piano, being the heart of my score for *The Conversation*, were hardly hinderances. Any instrumentation goes, as long as it's the correct choice for the film. Also, the sound of a certain solo instrument often is the first aural correlative that I think of to get started on a score. In my score for *Return to Oz*, the solo violin representing Dorothy and the solo cello representing her alter ego, Ozma, even helped to dramatize the unification of those two characters when their individual themes came together in counterpoint in the penultimate mirror scene when Dorothy reconnects with the part of her soul that was left behind in Oz and she can move on with her life. By the way, it was director Walter Murch's idea that the Ozma theme should be written to work in perfect counterpoint to the Dorothy theme for that specific purpose.

JC: What about scoring for specific settings—locales or periods of history? What's your experience adjusting to those? I'm thinking of the quaint Americana in *Appalachian Autumn*, the 1930s style for the TV movie *Amelia Earhart* (1976), and of course, the 1940s film noir style necessary to *Farewell, My Lovely*. But also, the black gospel tone in *The Women of Brewster Place* (1989), the Middle Eastern influences in *The Defection of Simas Kudirka* (1978) and *Raid on Entebbe* (1976) . . .

DS: Yes, I certainly do research on the music and instruments of the specific setting for a film, especially if it's an exotic music I'm not familiar with. My first big scoring job for a CBS Playhouse TV drama, for instance, *The Final War of Olly Winter* (1967), was set in Vietnam and when I was hired way back in sixty-something, I didn't know bupkes about their indigenous music.

JC: Your score starts with a light finger-bell in tempo, then harp and a flute theme in a certain mode—maybe pentatonic?

DS: Well, reading and visiting an ethnic percussion expert's warehouse helped prepare me for that gig. Now, thankfully, with the advent of the internet and Wikipedia, research like that is instantly and copiously available without leaving my studio.

JC: Over the years, I've questioned film composers about the supposedly happy, but actually tricky, task of scoring comedy films. What are the dangers that you see? In some cases, you play for laughs through exaggeration: *The Big Bus* was a satire on Hollywood's recent penchant for disaster films where you scored with mock-catastrophe music; *Harry and Walter Go to New York* (1976) was scored with purposely wrong notes and bad singing; *The Skin Game* (1971) just had fun chase music all through it. In all cases, I assume you want to support but not duplicate the humor onscreen because that would "step on the laugh."

DS: It's important not to be musically funny. No slide trombone or Spike Jones[2] percussion these days! For *The*

Big Bus, I tried to write a slightly tongue-in-cheek Michel Legrand or John Williams disaster movie score to blend with the comedic tone of the film. In the beginning, it wasn't at all clear to me how to begin because there is nothing going on for the first two and a half minutes that explains what this movie is going to be about, or even that it's going to be a big farce. So, I was asking the director, "What do you want the Main Title music to do?" and he said he just wanted you to feel that this is going to be a big, marvelous, exciting movie.[3] Well, so, I thought, what if we purposely play this tremendous cataclysmic piece of music against the fact that nothing is happening onscreen and I'll have these big builds and modulations that lead to nothing but a bus door opening and somebody getting off who you don't even know! So, I just wrote it as big and loud and melodramatic as I could and then continued the whole score like that—including a bigger than necessary love theme and all. The movie was about the first nuclear-powered passenger bus making a nonstop ride from New York to Denver and somebody is trying to blow it up from the gasoline industry: a parody of the disaster-film craze of the 1970s. For me, it was just a nice excuse to write all those kinds of clichéd music cues that you usually can't write because you've got to be in better taste! For *The Skin Game*, I just tried to write a modern western score for a comedy western film.

JC: Over your career, there are scores that don't fit categories and, therefore, resulted in one-of-a-kind music from you. For instance, what could music possibly do for *All the President's Men* (about the Nixon-era political scandal)? You wouldn't think it needed music because it's such a straight, crime investigation story; it's like a news documentary; and yet the music you provided seems to have an emotional quality in that it serves to humanize the story onscreen . . . the story of manipulated government . . .

DS: How very perceptive of you because when I first saw the movie, I told them it shouldn't have music at all and I really tried to argue myself out of a job, there. I had some talks with the director, Alan Pakula, who said, "Look, you may be right but if you want to take a chance, I feel that the right kind of music could . . . what you just said, 'humanize' the story." He said he had a fear the movie was too cold and that people had to be reminded that it really was the story of two reporters, two people, hearts beating fast, trying to get the story of the century. So that's precisely what the score tried to do. He just wanted some musical signposts and so that's what you hear in the sort of slow-pulsing brass music cues that are spaced throughout the film. Actually, I wrote twice as much music as was in the movie, just to see where it would "stick," where it seemed to be needed, and getting rid of it where it seemed superfluous or just distracting.

JC: And have you found that people noticed the tense music cues that finally made it into the film?

DS: No, not really. So, except for aesthetically speaking, it was a thankless task. In fact, the Motion Picture Academy disqualified it for nomination from the Oscar awards on the grounds that there wasn't enough of it. Anyway, it's in there, if you see the movie, doing its job. That's what matters.

JC: A couple of other uncategorizable scores you've done would certainly be *The Taking of Pelham 1-2-3* about the hijacking of a New York subway train, and *The Hindenburg* about the 1937 airship disaster of the German dirigible. The latter film gets into a whole speculative soap opera plot about how maybe the explosion was not due to the flammable helium fuel in the zeppelin and a lightning strike, but some sort of sabotage instead. And in your score, there is, first, the sort of floating, soaring main theme for the zeppelin heard on a solo trumpet; then a Wagner-like theme for the pre-Nazi element and a Brahms-like theme for the romantic characters . . .

DS: Yeah, well, it may sound kind of artsy but, you know, we invent these structures for ourselves to keep us interested.

For that main theme, I had in mind the last songs of Richard Strauss—'cause Strauss had that same . . . big, overblown—beautiful but overblown—kind of light-but-heavy, big-but-floating musical style . . . all of the things that the zeppelin was to me. And he was writing in that style, certainly in 1937 when this story is set, but actually all the way up until 1948 when the *Four Last Songs* were done. So, it just seemed like a nice way to tie that in and get the German element as well. Really, the *Hindenburg* was like a dinosaur—a little bit bigger than it should have been. And that kind of orchestral style, I thought, ultimately toppled of its own weight, because you had to either fall into atonality or adopt the serial style of Webern and Schoenberg. You just couldn't go any farther harmonically. So, it just had little parallels to me. Also, the connection between Wagner and Hitler via Nietzsche. And that led to when I had to come up with a love theme for the Countess and the George C. Scott characters: they were anti-Nazi so I made them Brahms because, as you probably know, Brahms was very anti-Wagner.

JC: Wow, that *is* artsy.

DS: There's even more! Originally, the Main Title theme, the zeppelin theme, was written as a vocalese, a wordless aria for soprano and orchestra. And the director, Robert Wise, was thrilled with the idea. But I did a demo tape first with trumpet and piano—actually a trio including the soprano intertwining in this strange nostalgic way. We recorded it that way and Bob Wise was in tears, it was so affecting; we really thought it was a winner. But after he took the film out on the road for first previews, he came back to me very apologetically saying that the executives had a nervous reaction to it because some woman in the preview audience had written, on her preview card where they give reactions to the movie, that she "couldn't understand the words"—couldn't understand the "lyrics."

JC: . . . lyrics to a wordless vocalese.

DS: So, these are the kinds of things we have to put up with in this business. A movie is a business product, after all, and if a consumer, someone in an audience, expresses disapproval or even confusion, the executives in the tower would rather not take a chance. And so, we changed the soprano to that solo trumpet that you hear.

JC: Still a tremendously effective opening.

DS: Well, I hope so. Even there, it was very laborious for me to orchestrate in that style because I usually go for transparency in orchestration whereas Wagner and Strauss went for doublings and thickness, the antithesis of what my philosophy is . . . Can you hold on a moment, John. [Leaving the phone; returning after a few moments:] I'm hearing, like, helicopters buzzing outside. Let me see what in the world . . . [A brief, tense period of silence:] Listen, it looks like there's a brush fire happening out there in the lot just adjacent to my house! I don't know if . . . let me see if there's anything we're going to have to . . . hang on. [A few more minutes of suspension and muffled sounds; then, returning to the phone:] Well, okay, I think those helicopters have gone away so at least my house is not going to burn down after all! I'm sorry about that. At least people will know we're not scripted!

JC: Well, it's all part of the exciting Hollywood experience, right?

DS: Life interrupts Art. But back on track, here. Where were we?

JC: Okay, another outlier score is *The Taking of Pelham 1-2-3*, a modern urban thriller about that highjacked subway train. The score contains not only a jazz-funk combination but, thematically, a serial or twelve-tone avant-garde take on jazz.

DS: So, it's a brass-led orchestra pitted against some rather harsh blocks of winds and, as you say, a kind of funk bass driving it all. But structurally, the right hand, so to speak, is strict twelve-tone or serial style and the left hand is an ostinato beat, which is related, interval-wise, to what's going on in the serial row. And that row is made up of two basic intervals—minor thirds and major sevenths, which are kind of the basic jazz intervals to me; or minor seconds and major sixths. I fell into it by ear and then saw what was happening and completed it as a row, so it would have certain properties—so that, no matter what form of it I used—retrograde or inversion or whatever—it always sounded like demented jazz because it had those two intervals. In other words, if I designed the row to have the properties that my ear was groping for, I could manipulate it any way I wanted and have a quick way to get a nice dissonant New York jazz sound that didn't sound like every television police story episode. So, once I had the row, then I just fooled around with it and it started to work over that ostinato. The ostinato is a minor third, a minor second away from the tonality of the tone row. So, it's related to the intervals that are within the tone row and it all kind of fell into place. This kind of writing I got from the composer Paul Glass who coached me into exploring these kinds of rows and relationships—a wonderful fellow and composer. I just informally had studied with him and he was trying to get me to write twelve-tone but I had said the style usually bored me and I felt it's so arbitrary and I didn't naturally tend toward that kind of extreme dissonance. And he said, "Well, you can design rows to give you any sound you want."

JC: And so, you were able, in the functional parts of the score, to exploit that dissonance by writing the harshest kind of dark funky jazz to represent the violent underground of Manhattan. But then, surprise, as the film is coming to a close and the tensions are being resolved, suddenly in the music score you bring that serial avant-garde theme into what would be called a "release" if this were a pop song—the middle section of a song before it returns to the main melody. In this case, you take the familiar harsh serial theme and harmonize it sympathetically, tonally—that is, making it sing an actual blues melody.

DS: That happened at the end, yes. The day before I was supposed to record the End Title music, I was all set to just recapitulate the main serial theme, but we were finding that the end credits-roll was running about thirty seconds longer than expected. And I didn't know what to do with the extra time in the music because I had really said everything I had wanted to say. And I was complaining to my wife at dinner that I had to think of something that evening. Big deadline. And she asked, "Can atonal music, can serial music, ever sound tonal or conventionally melodic?" I said, "Well, yes, it's just a question of how you harmonize the row." She said, "Well, why don't you make it, like, really, beautiful so that it will sound like what New York was like before there were muggers and hijacked subway trains and all of these awful things. A little bit of nostalgia." So, I did exactly that; I took the row and just transplanted the octaves and changed it rhythmically so there are two more versions of the row that form a kind of cocktail melody with "Mancini chords." And that's how the film ends, now—the tough beat of the serial theme, somewhat capitulated by that melodic release, before returning to a harsh climax.

JC: Well, it's an exciting score all along and then that last "knowing" manipulation gives quite a thrill, albeit a private one.

DS: Well, I owe it to my wife.

JC: Maybe the ultimate of your outlier scores would be *The Conversation*. A solo piano score (with some electronic manipulation of the piano sound as the film proceeds) for a film about a professional surveillance wiretapping expert who starts to lose his balance between the real and the virtual worlds—starts to obsess, internalizing the life of a spy. And for the opening music, you've written a kind of revolving, very chromatic, and obsessive piano prelude, a broken waltz—mysterious, a bit sinister, but even more sad and lonely.

DS: It's a collection of things. There was a late-night jazz station I used to listen to in college where a kind of cultish beatnik character would be delivering a running commentary over the microphone ("Hi there, kids and kiddies; this is Wolfman Jack talkin' at you . . ." It wasn't really him, but like that character) while there was this loop of a piano player just noodling around in the background. And it just stuck in my mind as a sort of lonely sound. A real midnight sound. And, also, the Gene Hackman character of Harry in the movie is a closet fifties jazz freak . . . and so I went with the whole thing of dated jazz. And there's a little Chopin in there too; I don't know where it came from. But it was mainly that fifties jazz sound and that kind of lonely midnight San Francisco sound, trying to get inside of Harry's head.

JC: The use of influences and memories and past genres raises questions about your own background, your biography. Your father was a pianist and had a sort of dance band during the war years and, I imagine, influenced your awareness of, and attraction toward, music growing up. You wrote most movingly about his influence in a much-later song called "If I Sing" ("My father's pride was in his hands; the piano was his soul . . . what he loved he taught me . . ."), I mean, there's a Father's Day tribute if there ever was one![4]

DS: Actually, Richard Maltby and I cowrote the lyric to "If I Sing." His father was also a musician—the trumpet-playing leader of the famous Richard Maltby [Sr.] Orchestra who inspired his son's work. We both wanted to write a song that paid tribute to our fathers.

JC: You had originally met Richard Maltby Jr. at Yale and together you guys started writing off-Broadway musical revues and songs. This would have been in the mid-1950s—right around the time that there was a huge revolution happening on Broadway, namely the first appearance of the innovative show by Leonard Bernstein and a young Stephen Sondheim, *West Side Story*. Were you in New York around that time?

DS: I was in my freshman year and I remember being awestruck and smitten with that score. We listened to it in the drama club and in our rooms and practically wore out the record album. So, naturally the first musical that Dick and I wrote at Yale was very *WSS*-influenced. It was a show that produced maybe one good song that didn't sound like Leonard Bernstein, called "Autumn" [later put into a revue of Shire-Maltby songs called *Starting Here, Starting Now*].

JC: That is a song that doesn't really remind of any other pop composer. Sometimes your songs can have a French influence, either directly or indirectly through someone like Ned Rorem.

DS: More like Ravel. It's all music that I love and that I know I'm influenced by. I try to keep it an influence and not a plagiarism. I don't know, sometimes it might get out of hand. I like to think of it as homage rather than stealing. It depends on the style of the thing I'm working on; it's a very grateful style.

JC: What does that mean?

DS: Just that it's easy to fall into a particular style if you already have an affinity for it—in terms of melody and transparency of texture and harmonic things. Steve Sondheim does that a great deal too . . . the very strong influences of Ravel and Poulenc in his shows like *A Little Night Music* or *Sunday in the Park*. I guess you know, Steve has been a very influential mentor to me for a number of years now.

JC: How in the world did you get from stage musicals to Hollywood orchestral movie scores, which can seem to be a very different career altogether?

DS: Via a Broadway tryout, actually. In New York, I was earning some cash being a rehearsal pianist for some of the Broadway people while Dick Maltby and I were peddling our musicals; I was playing piano in the pit band for the run of Barbra Streisand's show *Funny Girl*[5] and I was doing a little television work, writing some minor background scores for "live" or taped TV dramas. My main goal was still to get a show on stage. Dick and I had worked together for ten years at that point. But we finally got involved with a show called *Love Match* in 1969, which told the Queen Victoria and Albert story in a confused way. Someone else had started the show and we were called in just to write a few songs, to doctor the score, but ended up rewriting the whole thing. We believed we could fix all the problems that the show had, which, it turned out, we couldn't, but anyway, it was supposed to be a full-fledged Broadway thing with an out-of-town tryout in Los Angeles and so we traveled out there for the first time. By then, I was a bit discouraged with the career prospects in New York and I had a friend who was working in LA at Universal Studios, the film composer Billy Goldenberg. And he said to come over and meet the head of the music department at Universal and, because I had some tapes of the television things I'd done in New York, they gave me a chance. So, there I was, in town because of *Love Match*, which died quickly, but on the scene to try my hand at scoring some weekly television series like *The Virginian* and *McCloud*. That led to better television and then to features. So, the turning point was that failed show that brought me out here.

JC: Those early-stage efforts tended to be packaged as stage revues—medleys of separate songs. Was it your idea that the revue format—given the naturally independent quality of your individual songs—was the best way to critique modern life . . . which was the general subject matter of those shows and certainly of Maltby's lyrics?

DS: Actually, Richard and I never really wanted to write revues. The so-called book musical—a full theatrical play acted out on stage supported by a song score—was our much-preferred form and the first things we wrote were those two musicals produced by the Yale Drama School when we were undergraduates. When the Manhattan Theater Club invited us later to put together an evening of some of our songs, we had a good deal of material already in our trunk from previous unfinished or unproduced projects, which we put together with ones we wrote specifically for this new opportunity, and what came out was a so-called revue. What finally resulted after several cabaret tryouts was an evening of twenty-five songs that seemed to have an underlying unifying thread and not a collection of unrelated things. Maltby later perfected this approach in his Tony Award–winning smash *Ain't Misbehavin'*[6] and in our second revue, *Closer than Ever*. We did eventually develop to the full-fledged music, although we've never written a fully through-composed score á la, say, Sondheim's *Sweeney Todd*, although our scores tend to tell the whole story arc in the music and lyrics alone. Our more recent show, *Take Flight*, has, in fact, now been rewritten to be virtually all sung while another one, a musical adaptation of *The Country Wife*, has so elaborate a score that it has more the texture of an operetta than a typical book musical.[7]

JC: Wow; wish I could hear that. Anyway, it's certainly gratifying that you learned the songwriter's art so early and since then have been working in the direction of more and more complex theatrics. But I'm equally glad that you've been able to groom a simultaneous career of film scoring. Can I assume that you value both jobs, both disciplines, equally?

DS: Oh, I'd love to keep doing both. Why, with the film music I've been able to write in styles and types of music that I never thought I would write or could write. So, it's been a very good experience but at different times I also like to put some of that technique back in the service of a vision of my own, so to speak, on stage. The bottom line is, I wouldn't want to give up either kind of work, either coast, as it were. Each art stretches different muscles and the two help each other technically. Sure, sometimes in the middle of a really tough problem on a film score, it suddenly seems very rosy in the musical Broadway garden: if only I had some songs to write instead of this four-minute cinema chase. But then, when I'm sitting, trying to come up with a fresh way to write a tonal melody, I think, Gee, if only I were writing a movie chase. That's how things keep refreshing one another.

JC: Speaking of how close your work in dramatic scoring is to your work in songwriting, I'm thinking of several of your film scores that rely on strong melodies as their foundation. In your really charismatic score for *Farewell, My Lovely*—that throwback film from the 1970s that's so effective at recreating the 1940s Philip Marlowe film noir atmosphere of private detectives and femme fatales—you caught the whole weary private-eye, back-alley world in the kind of scoring that runs throughout the film, but it's immediately captured in the slow, bluesy trombone theme that opens the film and then recurs.

DS: Yes, that was useful for establishing and then reinforcing the film noir atmosphere and tradition that they wanted to emphasize. If you notice, the theme has fairly weary lines to it—heavy, tired steps at first, only barely rising and then heading back down a long scale to the chord where it started. So, yes, it was a very useful theme for both atmosphere and character profiling.

JC: And a second strong theme in that film for Mrs. Grayle, shot through with irony and mystery (and possibly deception) and yet harmonically part of the same *Farewell* world.

DS: Yes, it was a thematically anchored score while trying to keep a heavy load of atmosphere going at the same time—and consciously applying what I thought of as a 1940s orchestral sound. Except in the drug sequence—do you remember?—where the music was enhanced electronically to distort things.

JC: Sure. Meanwhile, I'm glad no one tried to put lyrics to your *Farewell* theme that would cheapen it, but it really is in song form. Same with a clarinet theme I'm thinking of—do *you* remember?—for a television film called *Tell Me Where It Hurts* about a middle-aged woman taking stock of her life and deciding that she needs some self-affirmation . . .

DS: Oh, yes, a sort of blue-collar women's liberation story.

JC: It's another songlike theme that stands out as representative of the whole drama.

DS: Yeah, it begins sadly in the Main Title and it's under Maureen Stapleton kind of looking very sad in her house . . . and then going out and walking alone before her husband comes home . . . it's all very low key. You can tell something's wrong; something's bothering her. And I just heard that clarinet and piano sound. The lone woman trying to cope, trying to figure out "where it hurts," because she can't quite locate the source of her dissatisfaction . . .

JC: Unless she looks to herself.

DS: Again, it's kind of a Poulenc theme, do you think?

JC: Sure, but pure enough to have been a simple Copland Americana theme.

DS: Well, yes, okay. Elements of both.

JC: And yet, even when you have a strictly dramatic score that needs action music, functional music, as opposed to any kind of singable theme, you often proceed by thematic lines. I'm thinking of another TV movie, *Raid on Entebbe*—the particular sequence you sent me of the military preparations for war. It has the Hebraic pulse of a Hora dance, a little klezmer-like clarinet figure, against two minor key orchestral lines—so that's about four or five separate lines all twining into counterpoint, but if I follow any one of them, it's a theme-of-sorts.

DS: Well, yes, that was sort of the structure there, working under a lot of pressure because of the production schedule to get the thing done. For the actual writing of that score, from when we spotted the film, I had nine days, which was, by far, the shortest amount of time to do a major thing with a lot of music in it that I've ever had. I had seen some of the shooting of it and I had read the script and started to think about it at least a month before because I knew it was going to be a rush like that. They had warned me. So, I got as much of the thematic lines done ahead of time as I could (though nothing songlike; just themes and motifs) so that when they were ready to go, I could plow ahead. So, yes, the way you describe that one sequence, where the various thematic elements all intertwine and sort of charge ahead altogether was probably due to the big rush—because they had to.

JC: To me, one of the best clues of a genuine composer in films, that is a fully literate composer, is how he/she does with so-called functional music—nonthematic music behind action scenes (what Andre Previn called "busy music") for transitional cues that hold attention between scenes while also, perhaps, facilitating a mood change. These require a composer to have real orchestral skills beyond just theme writing: how to move vertical scoring forward so that it keeps up with the movie scene or sequence. I guess my question is about your narrative/functional scoring, which is not primarily thematic but prosaic, framing action scenes. Of current composers in film, I have already mentioned a couple of interesting part-time minimalists—Thomas Newman, Alexandre Desplat—who don't really do functional or descriptive music cues anymore. They set a tone, pick a recognizable motif that becomes the flag for the film, and then offer ambient support throughout.[8] There are exceptions, of course.

DS: There are so many different styles and techniques for film scoring now—even different technologies—compared to when I started out! I haven't noticed any clear trends but, naturally, as the methods and means of producing a soundtrack evolve, it can alter the *kind* of music being written. And young composers are definitely moving in to do that. As for my own approach to functional music, I have always tried to relate it in some way to the thematic material I've composed for the movie, basing it on some melodic, harmonic, or rhythmic elements of my primary material. In fact, it's always been relatively difficult for me to do otherwise. In creating the main thematic material, I always am aware of (the main theme's) developmental possibilities for creating functional cues. It's very important for me that the main melodic material naturally provides these subsidiary possibilities.

JC: That must be the stage composer in you coming out to join the film guy.

DS: You might be right!

14

Rachel Portman (b. 1960)

The Storyteller

Figure 18. Rachel Portman. *Source*: Photo by Ben Ealovega. Used with permission.

Straightaway while studying music at Worcester College, Oxford, future screen composer Rachel Portman was drawn to dramatic/theatrical composing rather than to the pure forms of concert and recital music. Her imagination seized on the prospect of storytelling through music—at least on the power of music to support and enhance a story. Her first public scores were for college theater productions and backgrounds for classmates' student films. Born in Surrey, her inclinations toward music date from the age of fourteen when she began to practice piano, imagining elementary plots, or at least scenes, in her head to accompany her own keyboard improvisations. It is not a huge leap, then, to scoring the characters and scenarios of other people's stories. Among her first commercial music jobs were dramatic "specials" for the BBC and a syndicated TV series for producer Jim Henson, *The Storyteller* (1987–1989). There, she had the inspiring chore of illustrating in music an anthology of folk stories and fairy tales with a medieval tone using a quirky ensemble of instruments from various electronic keyboards to strange percussion, from soprano sax to bass clarinet. The series gained an appropriately quirky reputation, as much for its sounds as for its storytelling. But it was Portman's lively music for the 1994 film *War of the Buttons* (1994), which was Portman's first big budget movie contribution, and from there she was off and running.

But could a female composer, even in the rapidly encroaching New Millennium, expect to be welcomed into the business on a par with male contemporaries? If she wanted to try film scoring, she'd probably face the same gender gap that had persisted in the world of classical concert music, curtailing women composers and conductors.[1] And yet, there were a number of pioneering figures to take note of: in fact, there had been quite a vigorous international roster of successful female composers throughout the twentieth century if one only did a little research. For instance, after composer Amy Beach's famous concert tour of 1911, doors were opened for both female performers and writers, and her reputation has only grown since her death in 1944. In the decades that followed, Britain's Elisabeth Lutyens (b. 1906), Russia's Sofia Gubaidulina (b. 1911), Finland's Kaija Saariaho (b. 1952), Australia's Anne Boyd (b. 1946), Scotland's Judith Weir (b. 1954), and lately the young American Augusta Reed Thomas (b. 1964) are all either established or rising examples of women whose original music is both vital and personal. One can find these women's music being programmed by major orchestras around the world these days.

Augusta "Gusty" Thomas's *Astral Canticle* was nominated for the 2007 Pulitzer Prize.

Although film music has lagged behind such progressive ways, there have been notable female figures over the years in movieland. Shirley Walker, Anne Dudley, Jocelyn Pook come to mind as composers who refused to be sidelined by the gender traditions of their day. But Rachel Portman has stood out as perhaps the most successful and versatile. Initially, it was the leanness and naturalness of her music that succeeded in distracting people from the important historical fact of her gender, but it was not long before she would rise to the very top of the game, gender aside, through talent alone: in 1996 she would become the first woman to win the Best Scoring Academy Award—for the Jane Austin comedy of manners *Emma*.

Her relatively formal compositional style, often aided by a collaborative orchestrator, typically has her layering a polite classical theme-line over a traditional rolling ostinato; therefore, period films are heavily represented in her résumé: *Nicholas Nickleby* (2002), *Beloved* (1998), Roman Polanski's version of *Oliver Twist* (2005). But she has also provided effective storytelling behind an assortment of more modern, quirky literary adaptations: *The Cider House Rules*, *Chocolat*, *The Joy Luck Club*, *Snow Flower and the Secret Fan*, and a couple of the near-improvisational films by Mike Leigh (*Four Days in July*, *Life Is Sweet*).[2] And hear how her sly score for *Benny and Joon* (1993) works to, at once, accompany a cast of whimsical misfit characters and evoke something of the silent film era with which one of the characters is obsessed. To her, these films were theatrical pieces in need of music that was equally evocative and narrative in nature. But Portman is a subtle storyteller, more often supporting than directly illustrating what's happening onscreen: you seldom find a film where her music actually drives the action; she is more of a backseat driver. And yet the story is being told. Sometimes, if the milieu of the story is already theatrical (as in the opening narration of *Nicholas Nickleby* where Nathan Lane's character speaks directly to the camera about "the story you'll be seeing" or in a screenplay about backstage Hollywood such as *Their Finest*, 2016), her score will start with that typical turning ostinato that rolls along beside the action—a context, a host; again, the storyteller rather than the story.

Theatrical music, performance music more often has the advantage, in fact the responsibility, of being direct, not just supportive or evocative like a screen score can be. It was natural, then, that as soon as she graduated from the 1990s, Rachel Portman's New Millennium career would be attracted to at least as many stage and concert projects as film scoring opportunities. One of the first of those nonfilm commissions resulted in her dramatic choral symphony called *The Water Diviner's Tale*, followed soon after by her representational tone poem for the BBC Symphony on the theme of global warming and environmental warning, *Endangered*. By 2003, she was ready to premiere a true stage-set vocal work together with the Houston Grand Opera, her own original opera based on the famous Saint-Exupéry children's fable, *The Little Prince*. I found her willing to talk about what had led her to such a daring, transformative experience as tackling modern opera—and then some conversation about the relative pleasures of both stage and screen music.

Interview with Rachel Portman

RACHEL PORTMAN: Well, as you've already chronicled, my earliest real composing for money was for the screen and I learned really fast that it's not so far removed from the music behind a stage play—a screen story plays off on its own stage. The first film I did was only a year after I left Oxford. It was a Channel 4 TV film. Then I started getting commissions but still only periodically. That was in 1982 or '83 and I was twenty-one or twenty-two, but I knew fairly quickly that's what I wanted to do. In those days, it still involved a lot of waiting (between jobs)—so I worked as a cook; I worked stuffing envelopes. But I had a huge faith that that was the right thing to do; I was completely fixated on writing music for drama and, therefore, waiting around for those opportunities. I look back now and sometimes think, "Gosh. I wasted it. Why wasn't I writing other (pure) music; why wasn't I developing?" But I couldn't see beyond it. I just knew that I had to learn the craft, learn to write music for the screen. There was a composer back then who influenced me a lot: Benedict Mason, a close family friend, and he helped me when I was in my teens and couldn't write out the pieces I was composing. He wrote them out for me and, later, helped me get into a better school, which helped me get into Oxford. He was my mentor and, in time, in exchange, I would help him copy some of his scores. So that was the best school in the world—to have somebody like that. And it was through him that I had these grand career desires.

JOHN CAPS: I guess the obvious question that comes up here is, Are there ways in which the scoring of a theatrical production compares to the scoring of a film? First, though, what are your thoughts on what music can do for a film? What can a background score contribute to a storytelling movie?

RP: Well, all sorts of things: it can be an equal partner to the actors; it can be like another actor in the film; also, if it's used wisely, it can inform and affect the scene just as much as dialogue can. And that is what you should be thinking about when you do the score to a movie. A movie score plays a supporting role like that but it's an important one. If you take it all away, there's no color in the film. It can feel like that. Of course, when it's used badly, it's the most annoying and irritating thing, especially if it's music that you find repellent! It's certainly overused in films these days and I'm always fighting that. But you know how it is: there's a fear coming from filmmakers and studios, a fear of having scenes without music at all, a fear of silence. And if you think about this life we lead, how everyone walking down the street these days has music plugged into their ears—constant, constant music on demand—we live our lives to a soundtrack. And so, some movie people insist that we cover their movie with music like that. That, of course, completely works against the effectiveness of music onscreen. It's not that "less is more"; it's that "enough is enough." But intelligent film music can add a separate element, a new perspective all its own—and the whole film can be so much more interesting if you're allowed to do that as a composer. There's one film I did a few years ago called *The Human Stain* (2003), a wonderful film by Robert Benton, and he let me put in music that stood up with the film without interfering. Music added a force there that you can't really tell where it's coming from; music was like another character. And the director let me go ahead and do it that way. He didn't discuss why or what it should be or anything, but he let music make its own contribution. That's how it should be.³

Oliver Twist was another really interesting collaboration for me. Roman Polanski was so knowledgeable about music. It takes someone with a lot of confidence in music to be able to leave you alone if you're composing for him. In a way, music can be very threatening to a director because he or she usually can't hear what it is you're doing and then you're in the studio recording and it's too late to alter anything. But he had the confidence to talk in emotional terms about what each scene was doing, and not what music should be but rather what he wanted *from* music. And actually, now that you've got me thinking, music is used in a very operatic way in Polanski's *Oliver Twist*. For instance, when a villain arrives like Bill Sykes, his theme arrives with him, playing up the scene. It was really a fun project.

JC: So, is that direct use of music, where it really supports the story, what attracted you trying an opera—along with your fondness for vocal and lyrical music?

RP: Exactly. I was searching for a subject to make a children's opera, since there are so few operas you can take a child to. And, as you've hinted, I was also looking to expand my own activities beyond the cinema; like vocal writing, which can be so much more assertive, per se, than film composing can be—that is, film music can't be too melodic or it turns into song, and it can't be too insistent or it starts to distract. So, anyway, I was thinking in terms of lyric opera as a genre. I have four children myself and I just decided to write my own opera for them and their kind. I was working with a producer, Jim Keller, who also works with Philip Glass and he's the one who originally suggested *The Little Prince* idea to me. But I thought it would be too hard to dramatize. Sometime later, the same thing was suggested as an idea for Philip to compose but he had said, "This is not really interesting to me but what about Rachel?" So, I reconsidered it and it all grew out of that.

JC: By then you already had a solid history in film composing, but had you written vocal music before?

RP: A little. Of course, there's not really any chance to use voice in film. Some people do use wordless chorus but it's very difficult—it's very attention-seeking. But I've always loved writing for the voice and wanted to understand it more, and as we've already hinted, I've always been passionately interested in storytelling with music. So, it's natural that I want to tell stories through singing. And it turns out *The Little Prince* is a fantastic subject for an opera.

JC: As I started to ask before, are there similarities between scoring a film and writing an opera? Both are dramatic situations; both give the composer extramusical absolutes to adhere to.

RP: I found it was a very natural transition. In particular in dramaturgy and in pacing, they are alike—because a lot of what I do on a film has to do with pacing. It really helps to have that experience. I think I realized very young that as a composer if I had a gift at all it was for laying behind stories, providing an ambiance and a disposition that underlies the whole thing. Even as I was writing *The Little Prince*, I had the book open beside me and I was thinking, "Do I feel the same inside this music as I did when I read the book?" That was my test. Is it ringing completely true all the time? In the opera, there's a lot of the Prince asking questions of the Pilot and, so, one of the thoughts I really wanted to get across in the kind of music I wrote was that the Little Prince is a child and he just says things—so, a lot of it is very matter-of-fact and his music needs to have that simplicity and practicality—except where the story turns serious in the end, and except when he's talking about missing his favorite rose or missing his home planet. Those are little moments where you feel his pain and loneliness. But the rest of the time he's a child and it's very important not to put our perceptions onto him but to let him be himself. And there's also been another interesting thing: the whole learning curve of writing for him. At the beginning, I was developing it with the director Francesca Zambello, whom Philip Glass introduced me to, and Nicholas Wright, the fantastic librettist—and we had a discussion about how could a small child as the lead singer of the whole opera take such a big role? Should it rather be done by a young female soprano playing the child? But I always thought that would be such a big turnoff for any child that you take to see the opera. If we did that, they wouldn't be connected to the story anymore. We also had to think about ways to take the pressure off him (the boy soprano in the lead role). So, one of the things we did was to bring the Pilot more into the parts-writing (and, thinking it through, that was a good musical idea anyway). As a result, the boys who have performed the opera so far have had no problems and they're just as professional as the adults that they're playing with—and no strain in learning the piece, either. Also, I had to keep it simple—not to have too much of a vocal strain, not to keep their lines too long. In fact, there are hardly any places where the boy has an extended line to sing. Although he's on all the time, they're quite quick, his little songs. He might sing about how he likes to look at the sunset but it's a brief arioso and well within his comfortable range.

JC: What about other operas with major child roles? Did you consciously try to avoid those examples? Menotti's *Amahl and the Night Visitors* or Ravel's *L'Enfant et les Sortileges*? Or even Richard Rodney Bennett's *All the King's Men*?

RP: I love those first two; don't know the Bennett. But, no, I wasn't avoiding . . . I just was following my own path with regard to the book.

JC: Your personal sound in film scores has so often been in the very-British tradition.

RP: I think all the music I write is very similar. Although, if you take a film like *The Manchurian Candidate* (2004 version), I was trying to write literally very frightening music. That was fun to do because it was out of my normal. And I don't know—I would say that I approach each project freshly. I don't have a conscious sense of self in what I'm writing—I guess I'm always servicing the material.

JC: Would your personal music for an adult opera tend to be more astringent?

RP: Yes, I think it would; I think it certainly would. But at the same time, I'm always going to want to write with clarity and I'm always distilling and wanting to write things that are simple and clear. It's a tough question to answer. I think it will be . . . the music I write will always be . . . hopefully communicative and not hard for people to understand. I realize I'm writing in a world where the musical establishment expects very intellectual types of music from people who're doing new operas. But I know I'm not part of that.

JC: So, what's been the critical reaction to your *Prince*?

RP: Very good. Incredibly positive. Occasionally there'll be a comment about "Well, Rachel Portman is a film composer so there's a lot of sweeping film melody here . . ." as though I'm borrowing a lot of techniques from film composing. I mean, maybe I am to somebody else, but I don't know where they're hearing that or where it comes from. It's certainly not conscious and, goodness knows, that's an old cliché that ought to be gone by now—the idea that film composers are anything less than real composers. I hope to be able to pop back and forth between screen music and the stage. It's all, in its own way, storytelling. And it's certainly all real music.

15

Jermaine Stegall (b. 1977)

For a Digital Age

Figure 19. Jermaine Stegall. *Source*: Courtesy of the composer / The Gorfaine/Schwartz Agency, Inc.

It was David Shire who observed previously in these pages, "There are so many different styles and techniques for film scoring now—even different technologies—compared to when I started out! I haven't noticed any clear trends but, naturally, as the methods and means of producing a soundtrack evolve, it can alter the *kind* of music being written. And young composers are definitely moving in to do that."

One smart example of this successor generation is Jermaine Stegall, who was actually born in the 1970s and now is heir to a whole range of New Millennial digital tools for composing and editing soundtracks that even pros like Shire never dreamed of. Besides his own individual voice, which, of course, is unique to each and any composer, there are two aspects of Stegall's career that make him a "successor": (a) the much wider range, these days, of sources and sponsors for his screen-scoring assignments—commissions coming from traditional movie studios like Disney and Paramount but just as often from newborn online streaming services, indie filmmakers, and multimedia consortiums, and (b) the new generation's access to and facility with all the latest and constantly changing digital software packages for composing, manipulating, and mastering music, then applying it to film.

Technological innovation in the craft of film scoring would seem to involve only procedural changes but, as Stegall's description of working in futuristic state-of-the-art sound labs with the newest online music apps and processors has helped me understand, the very act of composing is being altered by this digital age. More about that shortly, but at the same time I have been encouraged to note that, alongside his tech know-how, Jermaine Stegall is equally a musician who has remained an advocate for traditional acoustic performance on soundtracks. Once his chosen software has rendered a mock-up of how the planned score will sound, he can most often be found standing in front of a standard orchestra or pop combo or jazz jam translating those synth files for real (that is, acoustic) players, and producing what are traditional functional music cues in a classic tone of voice that any veteran screen composer would easily recognize. He has done a few wholly synthesized scores too, of course, and oftentimes his live acoustic players will record separate tracks in studios miles apart that will be blended later. But through younger figures like him, we can begin to see a future for film scoring that includes, indeed merges, the two worlds: virtual and actual sound. In either case and no matter how many shortcuts these digital aids may offer, the musical ideas are still what give a film score life—the composer's mind-space is the true creative lab, and as Stegall's example shows, it takes the combination of a legitimate musical training and this acquired computer-savvy to produce the most promising talents in each successor generation.

Certainly, the scope and style of film projects coming down the line to Jermaine Stegall have been more diverse than his predecessors experienced. Still, the practical and aesthetic challenges of film music have remained the same: What does music need to do for this film, this TV series, this opening theme tune? What kind of music? Should it lay back to create a mood or stand up and sing? It goes without saying that a serious composer is needed to deal with such questions, not just a "hummer" who improvises tunes in his head and not just a computer jockey clicking icons on a screen, opening a drone base and a beat box. For Stegall, as ever before, real composing was needed if he would ever be able to propose solutions to the divergent musical needs of screen productions ranging from the Lucasfilm digital documentary series *Our Star Wars Stories* (profiles of ordinary people who have been impacted by the whole ethos of the *Star Wars* movies) to a tense dramatic indie film like *Proximity* by Eric Demeusy (which needed orchestral density and a certain dark edge to its central musical line). A Disney film of *Peter Pan and Wendy* in 2023 saw Stegall at his most ingratiating. That combination of versatility and literacy is the mark of a composer with a good future in film. And so, to me, Jermaine Stegall seemed a curious and capable enough fellow to approach with some of the questions I had about the interface (a favorite digital word) between newfangled media and old-fashioned musicmaking. After all, the future of film scoring would be in hands like his.

Interview with Jermaine Stegall

JOHN CAPS: One of my favorite Stegall scores is the sometimes dissonant, sometimes sympathetic music in *Proximity* (2020). It's participatory scoring that rather closely follows the action onscreen and yet is careful with it. It sets a question mark over the film about alien invaders and how humans react to them, but then other times it becomes more directly threatening with that *Le Sacre*–like stomping meter in the orchestra and a buzzing sound from the strings that is genuinely creepy. For one scene of direct conflict, you have horns harmonized in thirds over vigorously active strings in a configuration that composer John Williams, whom you've praised as a model, has done a lot. Can you describe the central line of the score for this film—what you were scoring to?

Jermaine Stegall: I'm so glad that you enjoyed that one. It's one of my favorites and that style is one of my favorites to ride in. The central line or theme is definitely all about mystery and a sense of adventure, being the story of a NASA Jet Propulsion Lab technician who's apparently abducted by extraterrestrials but scoffed at when he tries to report it. Naturally, he gets kind of obsessive in his search to find some proof of the whole encounter. The musical sonorities you mention definitely remind me of all that and, so, I scored it with fairly large and dramatic forces.

JC: And fairly classic melodramatic descriptive orchestration.

JS: Well, sure; I actually had the opportunity to record live brass at the mind-blowing Lucasfilm Skywalker Ranch studios in Marin County for that, even though it was an independent film. I went in under the auspices of some Lucasfilm folks I had met while attending one of the workshops of the Sundance Composers and Sound Design Lab. We students who were there were encouraged to return anytime with our own projects and use the facility if we ever wanted to record our own stuff or do any postproduction audio editing or mixing on it. So, I've been able to use the postproduction stages several times there. Also, the BMI conducting workshop has been very helpful in developing my tool kit and confidence as a working film composer. I agree with your general point that the central line or main theme of a film in terms of storytelling needs to be stated in every score. It also needs to be reiterated throughout a score, and it ought to be quite clear each time. Plus, there should be unity between the music cues of the film you're working on. We are always looking to find puzzle pieces within a score that will unify the entire thing.

In a remarkably short period of time, Stegall had managed the passage from promising student to scoring some A-list films and one cutting-edge TV series. The film *Proximity* was more or less a traditional thriller film that needed a narrative score, which is what it got most effectively. But the influential digital series that Stegall worked on from 2018 to 2020, *Our Star Wars Stories*, was not a narrative—not even about the *Star Wars* films per se, but about the fans: a quirky assignment. Still, his stated admiration for the original film and the Williams score—not to mention the career-building prestige of a young composer being able to work within the Lucasfilm empire—made it a personally desirable project for him. The series' general idea was for each episode to profile one specific ordinary moviegoer who had been personally inspired by the *Star Wars* universe: the films, the marketing, connections to ancient mythology, and all. Of course, these had to be fans who were articulate enough, interesting enough, and natural enough on camera to be followed around in their home settings and interviewed about their penchant for the *SW* franchise. For Stegall, the trick was to base his music scoring, somehow, in a familiar *Star Wars* tonal galaxy but then have some kind of a musical logo for the personality of each interviewee.

> JS: Yes, for this one, the idea was to have an original score that underlies the drama of what each participant is talking about and, harmonically and melodically as well as sometimes rhythmically, to represent the particular *Star Wars* film or scenes they are talking about—all without quoting any actual *Star Wars* music, which I wasn't allowed to do, but creating a kind of nostalgia for the original films, indirectly, while representing each fan's story of how the movies have impacted them. Being made in the middle of a worldwide flu pandemic (2018–2020), these programs, while trying to keep to schedule, tried to adapt to new public health protocols by using medically masked video crews and remote

interviews. And so, me too: I had to adapt. We recorded the orchestral portions piecemeal. The symphonic parts were laid down at a nearby studio, while some of the featured vocal sections and the solo instrumental parts (bass, drums, guitar, harp, organ, winds) were recorded separately through remote flu-safe hookups, sometimes in the players' own homes! Then mixed down later for a final assembly. So, this score was done even more modularly than the common contemporary method of stacking elements to create a whole ensemble. The only reason things worked out well in the end was that the individual score cues for such a talk-heavy docuseries tended to be fragmentary anyway, heard in bursts and bits and, so, didn't have to establish a flow. And, anyway, the whole practice of modular assembly of different score elements onto separate digital tracks isn't unique to those pandemic times: it's common practice—just to a lesser degree.

And it is true: Stegall did not really need these special pandemic circumstances to urge the industry's embrace of the new modular means of recording and mixing music. Most working film composers in recent times, at least those since the most-elder names interviewed herein, have produced their initial score demos through some sort of DAW (Digital Audio Workstation). Music sequencing software such as Digital Performer designed to work through Apple Mac and Microsoft Windows platforms was one of the first systems to gain acceptance among composers in Hollywood. With it, the musician/creator could install a comprehensive sound library including synthesized versions of most acoustic instruments, command which notes to play, at what volume and duration; record and manipulate those lines of music, then edit them onto a timeline and move the tracks around, stack them to create new harmonies or counterpoints, and record the whole construction so that it could be rehearsed against the movie scene that was being scored. In addition, each instrumental simulation itself could be altered to feature any number of dynamics such as a legato tone, reverberation, tremolo, and so forth. Any such synthesized module of music could also be mixed with any live microphone input. For the New Millennium version of Digital Performer, pitch-correction capability and EQ plug-ins were added, and a vastly more detailed readout of the composition could be displayed onscreen.[1]

> JS: Yes, I've been working on Digital Performer myself for nineteen years now—tools that help me keep up with the needs of ever-changing technology as well as facilitating the music that's in my imagination. But it's funny you should bring this up now, because I've spent the last two and a half months learning a new program, Cubase. I've only been scoring with it for a month or so, but it's much improved and streamlined over Digital Performer. Basically, Cubase is just another software package used to edit and sequence audio signals coming from either an external sound source like a live mic or sounds created within the system. But the amazing features for me are that it can actually keep track of a composition's chordal changes, default to suggested harmonies (if you program it that way), even trigger chords and arpeggiations based on the rest of the composition. It can suggest changes to a line of music to bring it in synch with material elsewhere in the piece, and understand manual orders like playing legato or pizzicato, whether for a single note or a whole line or section being edited. It's like a music coach, in a way but, again, only if you ask it for that much input. You can also tell it to butt out, of course, bypass it and carry on with your own composing.[2]

Stegall's generation of film composers is certainly the first to be so well versed in such technical assistance as Cubase. Still, one of the reasons Stegall stands out is that he is just as literate in scoring (and conducting) traditional symphonic and jazz instruments as he is designing and layering and balancing all those digital tracks. After all, once mastered and properly used as a helpmate rather than as a crutch, a system like Cubase can serve the successor generation as a kind of mental shorthand allowing the composer to concentrate on the content of the lines, the meaning of the scoring, and leave the grammar of the music, the surface, to a later stage of planning when more detailed advice may be helpful. And so, rather than limiting

Stegall to a handful of packaged responses, as one might fear from a pushy robot limited to a set cafeteria menu, his experience scoring through such supplements seems to have left him freer to evolve his own voice, and more confident to accept an ever-wider variety of film, television, and online projects.

JC: Before I pick out some really diverse titles from your résumé and ask about their "central line scoring," I'm curious about your musical upbringing. You were born the same year that *Star Wars* came out! So, no doubt that film and maybe that score were important to your youth and you *have* expressed an admiration for some of the John Williams ways of scoring things. But did you notice music in films from a young age? I mean music behind films? Was yours a musical family? And, then, what was your formal music training?

JS: Well, *The Wizard of Oz* is my favorite film of all time, but not because I noticed any background scoring. It was the experience of the film. I always remember hauling out the giant screen TV on wheels to watch that film once a year when it was broadcast. Growing up in Joliet, Illinois, in the 1980s, we went to the outdoor drive-in theaters over the summers, as well as watched movies in theaters about once a week from my childhood through high school. So, that's where the love of movies began and I guess I was already noticing some of the music behind them. I certainly didn't think about it as a career until super, super late. In 1995, I saw the movie *Apollo 13* (Oscar-nominated score by James Horner), and when the rocket ship took off, that was a moment when I realized that the music that occurs behind that scene was on purpose: it had been written to make us feel that launch experience! That was also my freshman year of college that fall, studying music at Northern Illinois University. I got a saxophone performance degree from there (I had been playing sax since grade school), then went to University of North Texas (2000–2003) for a master's in composition before going off to USC to complete their Scoring for Motion Pictures and Television program. After that is when I got the chance to apprentice with, or sometimes just sit in with, a few working film composers—for instance, interning with Marco Beltrami as he scored the film *I, Robot* (2004). (Other established film composers whom Stegall shadowed include Danny Elfman and Harry Gregson-Williams.)

JC: So, now, thinking of a few individual film projects, can you characterize your music in them, whether comedies or dramas? You did *Oracle* (2021) for Universal Studios, and a short film called *Dome* (2017), and that Pixar-related cartoon *Canvas* (2020). There's also a TV series for 2021–2022, *We Will Be Monsters*. And what about that comedy, *Senior Year* (2022), or the sequel you scored of Eddie Murphy's *Coming to America* (1988) called *Coming 2 America* (2021)? How to approach them . . .

JS: I just react to each film as a whole. *Oracle* as a score had to do with my experimentation in dissonant textures. That was the central idea in my head. I spent three months creating a certain sound-design for that one before I even started scoring it. These days, contriving a sound-design is often as important for a film scorer as the music part. The animated film, *Canvas*, was directed by a filmmaker who worked at Pixar Studios, though it's actually a Netflix film. It's a short film that was a personal project for the director and super exciting for me as well. We recorded that score at Skywalker Ranch and it received an NAACP award and was nominated for Best Sound at the Golden Reel awards that year. *Dome* was scored with a sixty-eight-piece orchestra and was one of the favorite experiences that I've had because I had almost complete freedom to write the way I most enjoy. It never got a national release, though.

JC: *Senior Year* isn't really narrative music at all: it's a bouncy guitar-led score with sax and bass and keys. More of an accompaniment score, would you say? The different cues behave more like punctuation throughout the film than like any kind of developmental scoring?

JS: I guess so. It was a different approach and with a comedy like this that had so many songs in it, we actually didn't weight too heavily on a score to drive the musical tone of the film. The director really relied on songs to dictate the main story. Any narrative scoring was there to pull out the heart of the film and the characters.

JC: Any thoughts or warnings about scoring for comedy, per se? Like, is it considered bad form to have a score that hits each joke on the head?

JS: I actually have not developed an overall philosophy about the scoring of comedy. I think in those situations, the music has to feel as good as possible. Sometimes we are actually *asked* to hit things on the head. Ultimately, it's a matter of taste and it's always subjective. There's a fine line between being cheesy and I try to stay far away from it!

JC: To me, your scoring of the Eddie Murphy comedy *Coming 2 America* for Paramount, which is a sequel to the hit film, accomplished both narrative storytelling following the action and attention to locale. You had all sorts of ethnic percussion and a huge bass flute contraption in there, plus the pure sound of an eight-voice chorus doing a sort of African chant. There were specific character themes that appear in different places. And it's a score that uses big forces not only for the African landscape but, in the opening celebratory music, a rather joyous sense of arrival, coming to America. But this time, as opposed to the prohibition on using *Star Wars* music in your Lucasfilm work, you were encouraged to reference a little of the Nile Rodgers music that had been important to the original film.

JS: Encouraged, yes. I tried to do it subtly, incorporating it into scenes that recalled the strongest characters from the first film and trying to vary what instrument played it—sometimes trumpet, sometimes kalimba, sometimes strings. So there are those few references to the original film. But I tried to stay away from actual quotes because we were doing something new and original and I wanted to be as fresh as possible.

JC: Do directors often work with you to decide what music should do for their film or is there such a wide range that you can't generalize? Some directors consider music to just be decorative, like set decoration; others avoid it because they think it's intrusive; others actually want to collaborate with a composer. Some scorers who aren't trained composers just hook up a drone machine and hum over it—and they get away with it. Some directors will accept that.

JS: I honestly feel that each director is different to work with and different approaches are always challenging but absolutely welcome. Because, often when you begin to think of scoring, a composer can tend to fall back on ideas that are familiar already or that you've done before or that are being done all the time. So, whatever advice a director might give can be a benefit, can suggest a new idea. It's helpful. Here's where the multitracking technology can be helpful: you're able to move tracks around and try different music against a scene to show the director . . . or change the orchestration right there in the mock-up, again to audition it for the director. All sorts of digital manipulations right there available on scene that the system and the software can suggest. But then, of course, left completely alone, it's also exciting to just use my imagination and run with it. And do you know what? I have found so far that, depending on who you're working with, just about all approaches are welcome—at least they'll listen to you—and that includes hooking up a digital drone and humming over it. That can work in some places. See? It's all subjective. And the digital hookups encourage experimentation.

JC: Certainly, all kinds of scoring can be considered. There's thematic scoring where different defined themes can represent each character; there's atmospheric scoring, which just lays behind the scene to influence the mood; or narrative scoring, which rises and falls with the action onscreen.

JS: Absolutely. Thematic scoring comes from a more traditional approach, especially where traditional orchestras are used. That atmospheric approach you mention can become very conventional, though, where the composer just seems to be "finger painting" with sound. Too easy. My favorite and what I believe to be the most challenging approach is using melodies and harmonies to score an entire film with instruments being played by musicians. The possibilities of combinations, dramatically speaking and storytelling-wise, are endless with the use of traditional instrumentation. But every film is different and every director may want different things.

JC: If the aesthetic landscape is so open these days in the business, what about the cultural landscape? Elsewhere, you've noted in other interviews that "there don't seem to be a lot of opportunities for black people in film scoring," at least at one time. Henry Mancini tells the story of how, in the 1960s, some big producer called him up wondering if he thought that Quincy Jones, being an African American jazz guy, could possibly handle a standard dramatic movie score. Mancini set him straight on that score but, being a representative of black culture, have you experienced that kind of clichéd attitude, at least before you got the chance to prove yourself before big players like Lucasfilm, Disney, and Lionsgate? And here you came with your jazz sax degree, which could actually encourage the cliché. It seems to be loosening up now with awards to folks like Terence Blanchard and regular features being scored by Kathryn Bostic, Chanda Dancy, Michael Abels, Dara Taylor . . .

JS: Most of the composers you mentioned like Kathryn and Chanda are friends of mine. Chanda and I actually went to USC together, studying film scores from 2003 and 2004. There are countless successful and working black film composers, male and female these days. There's even an organization, Diversity Collective, where composers who are underrepresented can go to meet each other or be found by producers who are looking for new talent. In terms of a future for minorities in the business, it hasn't honestly ever been brighter!

JC: For the future: you've interned with successful screen composers like Beltrami and William Ross and watched what's happening in the business. So, naturally, the craft of film scoring can be learned, but can it actually be *taught*?

JS: I suppose it can. But maybe the craft of film scoring should be studied more than taught, if you know what I mean. If one can be under a mentor like the ones you mentioned, you can gain experience by watching what they do, listening to how they respond to the director's notes—and perhaps have them critique your own dramatic approach if you have the opportunity. All of that, you can study, whether or not you're actually formally being taught. The lesson's in the listening.

16

Interlude

A Pair of Glasses—Philip Glass versus Paul Glass

"SILENT SNOW, SECRET SNOW" was a celebrated short story (1934) by Conrad Aiken whose poetic prose describes the last stages of a twelve-year-old boy's descent into madness and withdrawal from the world—stoic at school, silent before the family physician, distracted and defiant even in front of his increasingly alarmed parents. Young Paul can only explain that he is thinking about the snow. "There outside were the bare streets," Aiken confides, "and here inside was the snow . . . a secret screen between himself and the world." Twice, the indie director Gene Kearney sought to bring this story to the screen: once in a shaky black-and-white version from 1964 meant for the college art-film circuit and then, definitively, in 1971 meant for national broadcast during *Rod Serling's Night Gallery* TV series. It is in this latter incarnation that we notice how the short music score by Swiss-American composer Paul Glass[1] so deeply burrows inside the boy's head relying on an apprehensive A-minor waltz, every bit as haunted and fixated as the snowbound boy in the story.

Paul Glass's score shares the soundtrack with the charismatic narration of Orson Welles that urges the boy, at one point, on behalf of the snow, to "go upstairs to your room now. I will be waiting for you. I will tell you something new, something cold, something of cease and peace and the long bright curve of space! I will surround your bed, pile a deep drift against the door so that none will ever be able to enter." Here, in eleven short music cues for a handful of strings and two flutes, Paul Glass spins his waltz among cue titles like "Delectable Secret," "His Very Secrecy," and finally, "Snowed In." It is a score of variations and digressions from that obsessive waltz—some curiously joyful like a child playing in the snow; some contemplative; some distressed and searching with swirling figures in the strings. It is this music, together with the musical prose, that is drawing us into the world of this troubled boy. And whether you interpret this story as a metaphor for a magic world of the senses that exists just under the surface of ordinary life, or as a stark clinical description of childhood autism, it is at least a memorable showcase for film music.

"Even now," Welles intones, "it must be snowing hard; the white ragged lines drifting and sifting, whispering and hushing, seething and getting deeper and deeper; silenter and silenter . . ." And here violins play a double-time counterpoint in keeping with the blizzard inside the boy's room, inside his head; a kind of baroque allegro behind the solo flute theme, and all within that ongoing waltz.

This is quite sophisticated scoring for a mere TV episode. It certainly draws attention to the composer himself whose name, let's face it, is most often confused with the better-known minimalist composer Philip Glass,[2] late of several successful experimental operas (*Einstein on the Beach, Satyagraha*) and a growing list of film scores. One could say that the main difference between the soundtrack scoring of these two composers (who are not related, as far as I can tell) is that the rolling repetitive figures that make up a Philip Glass minimalist score when applied to a film subject most often hang back behind any action onscreen, merely observing, and providing a kind of flowing pulse—whereas any Paul Glass score seems to start from a definite point of view and then takes great pains and specific means to declare it; if not always interactive with the material onscreen, always interpretive. For the Paul Glass score to a film called *George Groszi's Interregnum*, a 1964 documentary about Germany between the world wars, he evocatively uses a low-register clarinet behind the concentration camp scenes. But then he steps off into interpretive territory, bringing in a 1920s-styled cabaret dance band to lay against dissonant musical representations of Germany's growing fascism. This trivial dance music acts as overt commentary on the nation's increasing distraction with trivial tween-war entertainments and decadence, which eventually allowed the Nazis to insinuate themselves into power. A seductive tenor sax doubling flute insinuates itself, too, behind the dance band and, thus, is Paul G's score having its own personal say.

With similar interpretive intentions is his 1964 score to the American film, *Lady in a Cage*, where director Walter Grauman locks star Olivia de Havilland in her mansion's stalled cage-like elevator for the duration of the film, imprisoned and taunted by a trio of home invaders who are apparently less interested in robbery than in just tormenting the lady of the house, once they see how luxurious that house is and how, having the upper hand for once, they can indulge all the household luxuries—a spacious bedroom, a warm bath. For this tense and sexually charged standoff, Paul Glass composed a twelve-tone serial score using a small ensemble of players: volatile music full of sudden dissonant interjections, surprising percussive blasts, broken rhythms—"restless music," as one critic put it, "with more than a touch of hysteria" (Bazelon 101). This is the composer entering into the scene and situation; not exactly an interpretation but an interaction with the characters, identifying as much with the deviant trio as with the innocent victim. In fact, its atonal pointillistic style is much in keeping with Paul Glass's personal composing voice in concert works like his cello concerto (1961) or the eight sinfonias he composed between 1959 and 2019. Only as the camera cuts to a few shots outside the house, showing de Havilland's more-than-comfortable neighborhood, does Paul Glass introduce a faintly tonal lyrical line evocative of "life before the fall" adding an additional interpretation—that is, that the real conflict between these characters, the real home invasion, is the space between the privileged matron locked in her absurd cage and these envious resentful intruders. So, this is participatory and interpretive film scoring in the way it chaperones the story and explores the whole situation onscreen.

On the other side, we can certainly call Philip Glass's minimalist score to the Godfrey Reggio film *Koyaanisqatsi* (1983) participatory, too, as it not only accompanies but shapes its film. On screen for ninety minutes is a continuous series of documentary shots—landscapes, cityscapes, construction sites, often filmed in slow motion or time lapse—soon narrowing the focus down to feature virginal nature scenes juxtaposed with scenes of how Mankind is gradually devouring and denuding the whole natural world of our planet in favor of the crass machine-made city life. The film's title is a Hopi word meaning "life out of balance" and it is not long before the relentless forward roll of Philip Glass's repetitive, ostinato-driven music begins to sound like a steam-rolling, life-destroying machine itself, and as the astonishing visuals parade past onscreen, some have called the scoring "mesmerizing" while others consider it a tonal test of patience. And it's true that the very redundancy and insistence of this kind of music can exhaust the alert listener waiting for variety and modulations of any kind. But wasn't this the appropriate voice for the type of films that Reggio was making? Indeed, when strings enter the Glass orchestra at one point, suggesting a sense of warmth, it seems somehow ill-advised, intrusive, because it's an anachronism in such an apocalyptic scenario. The Glass minimalist agenda seems right for *Koyaanisqatsi* and it was even more participatory in Reggio's sequel film, *Powaqqatsi* (1988), because there it proved to be even more interactive, incorporating ethnic themes and rhythms since the subject this time was international: "out of balance" Third World locations scored with African, Chinese, Indian, and Middle Eastern music forms.

But what can minimalist music do for a narrative story onscreen? No more abstract essaying about the environment or the clash of cultures, but flesh and blood stories that require a direct musical storyteller? Is there a change in Philip Glass's minimalist style when he approaches fiction films or does he feel no need to adapt? A narrative film like 1985's *Mishima* about Japan's controversial writer/actor/militarist Yukio Mishima is perhaps not the best example to answer those questions, though it is an interesting showcase, scored for string quartet and sounding a bit like Bach. This is a score that spins around a minor-key core, Glass alternating between a kind of fast Bach toccata (which feels like a dance, though an obsessive one referencing the tightly wound Mishima character) and an elegiac Bach aria, perhaps commemorating Mishima's bold but tragic ritual suicide. It is not only the repetitiveness but the stoic mood of the score that one remembers most once the film is over. Nothing is directly commented on, but the unblinking minimalist gaze (detractors call it a "stare") *is* commentary. It's certainly not a narrative score but it has semi-narrative similarities with Glass's string music for the 1997 film *Bent*. This was the equally disturbing story about a brash, ambitious German trying to work his way up through the layers of

Hitler's hierarchy, but who, because he is gay, is eventually betrayed and sent to Dachau. Under the usual rotor-effect in the foundation scoring, the deepest strings suggest a more direct sense of drama than the stylized cinema of *Mishima* could have used. While evoking minor-key Bach throughout, there are chorale-like sections where all the strings form block chords and proceed through a series of formal modulations; there is a dramatic passage for pizzicato strings suggesting the main character's ambitiousness and enterprise although even this active piece keeps falling back to the same chord as though stuck in a groove: the main character may be manipulative but, like a minimalist score, he's confined to the same circular treadmill—and in this Nazi era, being "bent" rather than straight, he's punished for it. There are other gestures in the score that seem to want to personalize and particularize the relationship between music and the characters onscreen—certain sliding slurring phrases, for instance, suggesting the sinister national climate and the main character's vulnerability. The point here is that Philip Glass's musical language seems to be evolving to accommodate a story onscreen, not quite to the point of narrative music such as Paul Glass would be eager to do, but something more than ambient minimalism.

Philip Glass's most famous film score to date may be for Martin Scorsese's *Kundun* (1997) and it is notable that this tends to be a more linear and even semi-melodic score than usual for a minimalist. Maybe it was the watchful eye of Scorsese that encouraged him to a more expressive tone of voice or maybe it was the fact that Philip Glass himself was already well steeped in the Eastern Buddhist mindset and culture that was the setting for the film and that made him more conversant with this story of the early life of the Dali Lama. Indeed, Glass's score contains and compares East-West elements in its key centers and harmonies, in the instrumentation (using both long Tibetan horns and regular trombones, for instance), and in the philosophy (Eastern ambient drones coupling with Western linear thinking). Added to the mix are voices of the Gyuto monks and monks of the Drukpa Order. This is Philip Glass determined (or being told by the influential Scorsese) to interact more with the story, the setting, the cultural specifics of the film at hand. Reportedly, in the spirit of collaboration, Scorsese was even willing to recut some of his film sequences to match some of Glass's provided music cues. All he asked was an equal homage in the music to the Tibetan milieu and a neoromantic sensibility. *Kundun* resulted in Philip Glass's first Oscar nomination for Best Score. Even so, critics of the day observed about Glass (and I have heard the same from American symphony players faced with a Glass concert commission to perform) that the "composer's repetitive idioms work best, in fact exceptionally well, when they can pursue their own autonomous course set against vivid or contemplative visual images that do not require linear logic. But the essentially static nature of (his) music . . . can hinder the pacing of more conventional narrative strictures" (Cooke, *History* 481–82). Such critics then go on to prefer the "more flexible" minimalist film works of Thomas Newman (*The Horse Whisperer*, 1998)—and I would add Alexandre Desplat (*Birth*, 2005).

With *Notes on a Scandal* (2006), it sounds as though Philip Glass has indeed actually learned several lessons from Scorsese, for here we have very nearly narrative, illustrative scoring, though still rotating and minimalist in nature. This film told the true story of an American teacher who began an affair with one teenage student and then struggled through the lust, then guilt, then public humiliation once the news was splashed throughout the media. Here, Glass's orchestration is broader, looser, more colorful—a string ensemble sparked with solos from oboe, flute, bassoon, clarinet, harp, piano, horn. There are actual melodic motifs here, too, and some chromatic phrases that take the ear far away from Bach toward almost a romantic Italian dialect. This is still minor-key obsessive minimalist music-at-heart, emphasizing the errant teacher's sin rather than any sentimental acceptance of a teacher-adolescent love fest. But there is a conventional melodramatic opening to the score—a single dark line in the basses till the rest of the string orchestra fills in and those solo woodwinds each have a thematic say. Still, a rolling minimalist meter lies behind it all, but there are more thematic details that become the subject here. Solo horn rises from the mix to warn this teacher of the peril she is about to face once society finds out what homework she has been assigning to this one boy. So, here is the music score participating with the plot and here is Philip Glass developing a more interactive, descriptive movie score self. One sequence stuns us with unexpected percussive aggression while another darkens in the basses until it almost sounds like an execution scene; then the meter becomes a heartbeat pounding and the strings crescendo into a kind of ecstatic swoon. Again, this is far more expressive music than this particular Glass is usually known for and the new, more humanistic, perspective is welcome.

The fairly interactive scoring in Philip Glass's *Notes on a Scandal* has its counterpoint in Paul Glass's rather famous 1965 score for Otto Preminger's *Bunny Lake Is Missing*. There, the two incompatible extremes of innocent melody and demonic pointillistic atonal scoring are key features. Like *Silent Snow, Secret Snow*, *Bunny Lake* opens with a simple childlike melody—major key, this time played on a grade-school recorder. This introduces the story of a young woman who claims (to police chief Laurence Olivier) that her infant daughter has been kidnapped. Gradually, however, it becomes doubtful that there ever was such a crime or even that there ever was a child called Bunny Lake. Paul G's likeable nursery theme is effective both in setting up the family portrait and, then through a series of impressive variations, suggesting the twists and conundrums of this psychological/mystery plot: there is a simple lilting arrangement of the tune, a more forthright version with a pizzicato counterpoint, even a richly scored grand waltz arrangement à la Tchaikovsky/*Nutcracker*. A cast of eccentric side characters eventually comes to light during the missing-persons investigation. But it is becoming clearer as we go along that darker truths and motives lie at the heart of this case. And for those, Paul Glass's score bursts out into complex atonal fortissimo passages of considerable violence—tonal percussion, barking brass, dissonant strings slurring up and down the scale, woodwind combos in broken interjections as though sections of the orchestra were dueling one another. We are in uncharted fictional territory here: is this a heinous crime or a crackpot scam—or is there something darker that Paul Glass is trying to tell us? Is this not a mystery film at all but a horror film? In the end, only the music score ever goes that deep and a charming rendition of the nursery theme appears at the end to confuse us further, ending with an unsettling suspended chord. Detailed orchestration this virtuosic would seem to be more narrative, more revealing, and more valuable in support of a story onscreen than some generic revolving minimal approach.

So, what about these two composers: Paul versus Philip? The former was born in LA in 1934, studied at USC and Princeton and under Ingolf Dahl, Witold Lutoslawski, and Goffredo Petrassi in Rome; moonlighted from a concert composing career to multimedia composing but retired from media work to become a Swiss citizen and then to write his own music; composer of more than seventy works including 2021's Trio no. 2. And the latter was born in Baltimore in 1937 (the great-nephew of Al Jolson!); studied with Nadia Boulanger and with Ravi Shankar, having noticed the similarities between revolving, minimalism, and circular Indian ragas; already the composer of seventy works before he took up classes at Juilliard; he has experienced both great success and scorn for the "sameness" of his output. So, again, what about them: Paul versus Philip? In consideration of this pair of Glasses, we can't say that any one method, any one POV, is best for films. Where Philip has clearly grown in the sense that his vocabulary has expanded with his cinematic experience, Paul remains an individualist, but increasingly capable of applying different aspects of his training. For a TV movie called *Sandcastles* (1972) he composed in a simulation of a Schumann impromptu. For another TV film about a military jet downed in a desert landscape, *Sole Survivor* (1970), he scored for a brass choir that had to negotiate his severe pointillistic avant-garde style, a military fanfare, and in one hallucinogenic scene, take up the strains of "Take Me Out to the Ball Game." For a late 1970s project, *To the Devil, a Daughter*, there were choral passages and one intentionally off-key soprano. *Overlord*, from 1975, was an elegy for strings. He has even composed conventionally for a TV episode of *Columbo* and counts among his admirers mainstream TV and media composers like David Shire and Irwin Bazelon. And Philip? The 2000s have seen a sharp increase in his devotion to film music—and a concerted effort to broaden his style—to expand the tonal and structural resources available within his established minimalism. His music for a film version of *The Hours*, from the prize-winning novel about three women living decades apart, including novelist Virginia Woolf, received a BAFTA award (2002). He could have relied on period clichés for such a score but instead clung to a steady ticking meter with the intention of tying all the characters and their separate eras together. In that sense, still within minimalism, he was interacting with the film in a new way. In 2007, director Woody Allen abandoned his usual soundtrack penchant for using old records as his scoring and hired Philip Glass to provide a more narrative orchestral score for *Cassandra's Dream* about two British working-class brothers—one in too deep with debts, the other too deep in love. Glass sounds like he is listening to Scorsese-advice in the more thematically inclined score he provided. And he thought he was going to be further encouraged in this new descriptive direction of film scoring when the prize-winning Russian director Andrey Zvyagintsev called him (2011) to help with his new film, *Elena* . . . but what Zvyagintsev really wanted was the right to use portions of the Glass Symphony no. 3. So, it remains to be seen how deeply or laterally Philip Glass may develop within or away from his minimalist roots and how many more films may or may not value his revolving, repeating pinwheels.

Paul Glass, at eighty-seven, left the movies long ago but remains active in Magadino, Switzerland, having composed seven major works, just since 2020. Sampling some of that latter music reveals an interesting irony: that the voice of Paul Glass over the years has softened somewhat, allowing for tonal and ambient compromise more often now than when those strict narrative lines were so important to him, while Philip can seem to be hardening in terms of more detailed and quasi-thematic writing, at least in his film work, showing signs of impatience with the limits of sheer minimalism, the featureless backdrop of revolving arpeggios while the story onscreen wants a real collaboration from its soundtrack.

It's not likely that this pair of Glasses will ever be mistaken for one another, but it has been interesting to hear how, from opposite directions, they have been inching toward a center, and they seem to have the film medium to thank for that.

17

Interlude

The New Millennium—Enter Ex-Rockers

What follows is all speculation about what film scoring may sound like, what sort of music films may require, and where future film composers might be coming from, as what's called the New Millennium transitions into postmillennial arts and entertainment. For representatives of the subject, I can choose two striking films from the 2020s whose scores stand at opposite poles, yet each accompanies its film in the same episodic scene-setting way, rejecting a traditional narrative style—and each is by a composer bussed in from a musical world far from Hollywood: in this case, two refugees from rock bands. Indeed, there have been several of the more ambitious band members from the hyperactive world of rock music who have imagined, as it were backstage between shows, the prospect of doing more with their musicianship than backing up the lead singer but, instead, writing some dramatic music of their own to back up some cutting-edge indie film. And some of them have actually proven resourceful. Jonny Greenwood from the pop-rock band Radiohead, Anne Dudley from The Art of Noise, Hans Zimmer from various new wave bands like Krakatoa and Buggles, Danny Elfman from Oingo Boingo are prime examples who have transitioned into successful movie scoring careers. Even Robert Diggs, known as RZA with the rap group Wu Tang Clan, took to movie scoring in a tone far removed from that other career. But what sorts of film music do these crossovers produce? With what compositional styles and, just as important, what kind of support does such music offer to any given film? Is it just beat-based antinarrative music, mood-setting rather than scene-setting? Is it juxtaposed to the scenes onscreen rather than interactive—standoffish and ironic in intent like playing a rock song against a dramatic moment? Two films from the United States and United Kingdom are interesting test cases by two former band members, Rich Vreeland who called his rocking onstage act Disasterpeace, and Jocelyn Pook who spent the 1980s, and beyond, playing with two bands and assisting two pop stars, are the focus here as represented in two particular films from the New Millennium. These are certainly radical films I have chosen but the soundtrack question applies beyond them—is this postmillennial scoring? Is this what film music will be like as the next successor generation of screen composers takes over?

Of initial focus here is the audacious neo-noir fantasy/mystery film by David Robert Mitchell, *Under the Silver Lake* (2018). The sheer flamboyance of its cryptic dreamlike plot (it follows a twenty-something slacker dude rushing, stumbling across a contemporary LA/Hollywood landscape of pools and bedrooms, boutiques and offices and parking lots) had young audiences fascinated and Cannes Film Festival panels confused. And there was further puzzlement over the fact that, although this seemed to be an anarchical postmodern film, it was scored with a sober, didactic, apparently traditional orchestral music score for forty strings, a dozen winds, a dozen horns, a synth keyboard and a formal conductor controlling it all, Neal Desby. So, what's the idea here—a schizoid whodunit that races headlong like a video game but relies on a semi-symphonic sound in the background while applying it in ways that seem to advocate anarchy? Explain.

Credits assign the scoring only to Disasterpeace,[1] but a little research shows there were two minds at work here: Rich Vreeland (who came up through video game music and sound design) and Kyle Newmaster, who is listed as Vreeland's orchestrator but, one could imagine, had at least a hand in those new classroom courses that stand halfway between tradition and divergence with titles like Composition for Contemporary Media. But, according to Vreeland, the music itself in concept and composing is fully his own (Vreeland correspondence, 7 January 2024). And it carries a serious sound all the way through; this is not just arcade music (although video game scoring has occasionally proven itself to be a satisfying and accomplished cousin to film music). Vreeland takes on both the dreamscape atmosphere of *Silver Lake* . . . and the forward motion of the film in his music. What seems to make it all postmodern is the eventual realization that, although dramatically it holds our attention, it doesn't actually go anywhere or make a statement—characteristics said to be true of any slacker dude . . . and of postmillennial mentality.

What is the plot that so confounded them at Cannes? Young Sam is the dude. Most of the time he lies around present-day LA more interested in daydreaming about conspiracy theories (What secrets are stashed deep within the pop culture around us? Are there conspiratorial messages hidden in cereal box ads and Nintendo maps? Are all things connected somehow, leading to mind control?) than in paying his overdue rent. A tangle of bizarre coincidences (conspiracies?) begins to engulf Sam once his sexy neighbor disappears and he is drawn into the search for her. He follows clues that he believes were meant for him—seeing messages in random graffiti, in passing commercials and newscasts; his obsession leads him into local prostitution rings and political campaigns, posh parties and neighborhood gossip. He encounters crazy homeless performance artists, gets involved with the author of an underground comics series, even questions a rich old man holed up in a secret bunker awaiting direct access to the Afterlife. One wacky thing leads to another. So, is it all connected somehow? Before long, Sam is losing his bearings. He's not even sure anymore that he isn't guilty of the girl's disappearance himself.

It's all a wicked satire of the scattered, self-absorbed postmillennial culture, not neglecting commentary on today's stereotypical younger generation mesmerized by games, distracted by shortcuts, hidden treasures, and anything that moves—ambitious only for more stimulation. What the Cannes panel didn't get was *Silver Lake*'s purposeful portrait of the dude, looking for meaning in all the wrong places. But what the film's most serious critics complained about was that it was too random, flashy, and shallow to actually support the issues it seemed to want to raise.

To what extent, then, did the Vreeland-Newmaster scoring support or even address this film-phantasm? This is not, as I've said, narrative or even sequential music. The individual cues, which are all of one piece compositionally, are used as scene markers and fillers as the game plays out. Consistent features of the score are its dark sophisticated blends of wind instruments, often with solo clarinet figures above, and brass blends as more drama is happening: deep trombones when clues lead Sam further underground into the suburban nightmare; and there is a heroic horn motif once clues appear to comport at last. But it is the string writing that carries the weight of the score, most often dark and prescient brooding but also occasionally rhythmic and dynamic; some sectional counterpoint and some attention to performance details that show a solid composer behind it all. But who is really responsible?

Rich Vreeland's past multimedia scoring and incidental theater music had been smart but had never risen to this level of literacy. What about orchestrator Newmaster, then? (and there are three other orchestrators credited, too). When I raised the question, Vreeland explained, "Kyle (that's Newmaster) orchestrated the score—that is, he took my fully arranged compositions, prepared parts for the players, (and was a) sounding board for questions about what works/doesn't work in regard to the ranges and techniques for various instruments. But he didn't have a large role in the composition itself or the arrangement of the final score. As someone who had only dabbled in orchestra-ish music before, this was really a huge undertaking and easily the most challenging project I've ever had. I am very proud of the work we did" (Vreeland correspondence, 7 January 2024). Director Mitchell claims to have asked for "a forties-like Herrmann sound," but the tonal language here, once all these fragments are heard together, is more akin to the golden age world of Miklós Rózsa's noir crime dramas, without the inner intricacies. There is an impressive dancelike cue for strings that moves among time signatures. There's a moment of fifties-style academic jazz, then a kind of thirties promenade piece, then a few bars of lyricism leading to a grand waltz. These are sounds and voicings we can begin to recognize as they repeat but they soon dissolve back into the ongoing mystery and melancholy of the score as a whole. So, is this a fascinating score, successfully evoking the modern miasma of postmillennial life through pure music, or is it, like Sam's aborted journey, a hoax, a pantomime? Whatever the truth, *Silver Lake* is a compelling White Rabbit Wonderland journey such as Alice endured, and if the script never quite makes its case to blend fantasy and philosophy and fan culture, the music score comes closer, while still remaining murky. That may be another characteristic of postmillennial art, intriguing but frustrating enough to make slackers of us all.

It is easier to trace the origins and effects of Jocelyn Pook's screen music for the second striking film in this inquiry: the powerful play/screenplay by Mike Bartlett, *King Charles III* (2017).[2] When directed for the screen by Rupert Goold (more famous for his film bio of Judy Garland: *Judy*, 2020), it drew some additional power and prestige (the British BAFTA award for Best Original Score) from Pook's apparently formal, properly regal, and yet secretly expressive music score. As composer, Pook seems to be a traditional figure, formally trained in both viola and composition (Guildhall School of Music and Drama), yet she has proven herself to be conversant with multimedia and especially with the outlier world of rock music, spending the 1980s playing with the bands Massive Attack and The Communards, then assisting pop acts like P. J. Harvey and Peter Gabriel. Onscreen, her personal sound is frequently classical, even baroque—clean consonant beds of harmony, often with a vocal obbligato over it (she also has extensive choral credentials away from films leading the Jocelyn Pook Ensemble choir as well as an instrumental group she calls Electra Strings).

Certainly, the milieu of the play *King Charles III* fits well with her existing courtly style but the film version had some specific needs beyond that. There are two striking things about Bartlett's script: its rather daring fictional premise about Britain's real-life royal family, *and* the fact that, although the dialogue sounds naturally conversational for its present-day setting, it is actually written in blank verse! The plot (predating actual events only a couple of years later) presents Prince Charles, who has been waiting all his life on the sidelines while his mother Queen Elizabeth II reigned, as succeeding to the throne on her death. He determines to make his mark early, refusing to support a Parliamentary bill introduced by his conservative prime minister, which would rescind freedom of the press in order to protect the powers that be. As in a Shakespeare tragedy, the members of his own family rally against him in this debate, in favor of the ambitious PM.

The character who stands in for the real Prince William remains sheepishly aloof from the controversy, but his American wife schemes with the PM to gain power: thus, she is presented as a kind of evil, manipulative Lady Macbeth. Meanwhile, the Prince Harry-ish character wants no part of the royal life (again, unknowingly predating real life) being half in love with a commoner (note how even their youthful dialogue is rendered in Bartlett's clever hip version of blank verse). Still keeping the Shakespearean allusions alive, Bartlett has even staged several mystical Hamlet-like scenes in which the new king in his crisis of conscience is visited by a ghostly apparition of the late Princess Diana, who counsels him, reassures him from the grave with words like: "An indecisive man, and oft' so sad, will be the greatest king we ever had."

Jocelyn Pook's scoring for all of this has obviously to relate to the regal setting, accompanying at least a couple of royal ceremonies with some soaring liturgical music, but it also has to stay out of the way of the precisely nuanced language of the script. This she does handily. The opening scene of the queen's funeral is formally scored with a noble requiem chorus moving between D minor and D sharp with a countertenor voice singing the words of the mass. In the midst of that ceremony, the king character steps away from the formalities and, not for the last time, turns to us, the camera, to confess: "My life has been a lingering for the throne." Pook uses a small ensemble of strings, still with that liturgical tone, to let us know that the story to come will not be regal but personal—the conscience of the king, which in his story, wants to stand with the people. An early conference between king and PM shows the first signs of conflict—and as the sinister workings of politics begin to turn, the score lays out the arpeggio notes of a revolving bass line for bassoon. Then accompanying strings begin to harmonize; then another layer stirs in: a minor key andante is taking shape that will become a motif of sorts.

Shortly, the drama switches to a London pub where Harry has fled to be with his unroyal mates—there's a pumping club tune playing and a hot female vocalist singing a Pook original: "I know it's hard; I know we want something that money can't buy . . ." Here Harry meets Jessica the commoner who understands his torn loyalties right off. Somehow behind their pub-talk, Pook's scoring melds from that club music down into a tentatively tender string quartet (Harry loves Jessica?). The scene ends with a suspended chord.

Thoughtful comments and more suspended harmonies from that same string quartet frame and advance the subsequent intrigues as the new king tries to argue his position and Lady Macbeth plots behind the throne. Official pressure even falls against Harry to stop his seeing Jessica and Pook unpacks that same baroque andante bass line from before—on cello this time, then bassoon, with winds for counterpoint, building by layers, quickening, doubling the meter nearly toward the establishment of a theme; but it never actually materializes. As a scoring device, though, that slowly intensifying andante piece is used to mimic the accumulation of inexorable events. Lady Macbeth seems a very modern character to us, urging authoritarian over humanitarian rule while the PM claims to be preserving democracy.

Like *Silver Lake*, Bartlett and Goold's *KC3* seems to aspire toward being a present-day protest as, at least in America, real-life leaders are indeed calling the free press an "enemy of the people" whenever it criticizes them and authoritarian regimes are on the increase around the world. Pook's scoring never becomes histrionic with all these provocations but holds to its own minor key gravitas—her warnings are private, literally behind the scenes. Her music for those mystical appearances of the ghostly Diana (countertenor singing a "Lachrymose") is likewise only subtly, privately sympathetic to the king while, at the same time, being half-magical, is also open to reinterpretation.

The other fiercely scored scene in *KC3* comes at the center of the film: Parliament has convened to consider the censorship bill when there comes a thunderous pounding on the chamber door to which all heads turn. There is a deep ground note in the strings; then higher strings in minor thirds over it: the king enters, dressed in full regalia, and strides up to the Speaker of the House to deliver his edict on the current state crisis. A male chorus and the lower half of the string orchestra remind us of the film's opening processional music, but now it's weighty with the king's defiant spirit and a dash of Shakespearean tragedy. Together, writing, staging, and performance have stopped the drama cold and the scoring, while supposedly just representing the court, has been equally significant in raising our conscience.

Jocelyn Pook's most famous score to date for Stanley Kubrick's *Eyes Wide Shut* (1999) took a similar noncommittal yet influential stance using string interjections between film scenes rather than narrative music cues to carry the soundtrack—in that case, they were sounds from her Electra Strings ensemble juxtaposed with imported music tracks from other composers (as Kubrick always chose to do) like the stark solo piano tones near the end of the film from Gyorgy Ligeti and others. And there is more noncommittal string music in her score to the Al Pacino version of *Merchant of Venice* (2004)—again used as scene-dividers and backdrops.

But back to the subject: these two films, *Under the Silver Lake* and *King Charles III*, divergent in style and setting, do seem somewhat related in the ways they take on contemporary issues and in the manner of their objective-but-resonant functional scoring. And in the end, each score taken as a whole does represent and advocate for the main message of its screen story; each seems as striking as its film even though neither admits themes or forward development or even a point of view. We are wondering, Is this what postmillennial film scoring will always be like? More likely, screen music will just carry on with its one constant: always in transition.

Part V

A New Exemplar

18

John Williams (b. 1932)

Another Birthday Toast

Figure 20. John Williams. *Source*: Courtesy of the Film Music Society.

It used to be said, back in the Hollywood days when Alfred Newman was head of music at the Fox studios, that Newman was the king of music award nominations—by my count, 45 Oscar nominations for 255 films. But now comes John Williams—54 nominations as of 2024. In twelve of those years, he had double nominations, his own scores competing against one another; in one year, 1995, he had three nominations all at once. This is unprecedented for any artist in any category of the motion picture awards. Not only in the music category, then, John Williams is alone at the top. He's been invited to write for many of the classical virtuosos of his time: Itzhak Perlman, Yo-Yo Ma, Anne-Sophie Mutter, Luciano Pavarotti, not to mention jazz greats like Stan Kenton and Toots Thielman. This kind of dominance would seem to indicate that there is simply no serious competition around him these days in film scoring. Among the current crop are talented music people who have been successful at applying various appropriate sounds to various films, but precious few produce music of compositional complexity or narrative energy. This is speaking from the perspective of the 2020s, well past the prime of most of the composers in this book. And so, year after year, there is the Williams name on the awards nominations list, not even for his best work but just because it so often outshines its surroundings. Of course, he *did* have the advantage of being trained right in the heart of the studio system, sometimes as the session pianist at the right hand of the aforementioned Alfred Newman. So, his dominance now is not just by comparison. A lot of his secret has been a story of hard work, keen observation, and sheer productivity.

John Williams as an elder statesman presides over recording sessions that are closed to press and patrons to preserve his energy, spending more and more time on personal concert composing now. But where did such a conqueror come from? It's not enough to say that he worked his way up through the Hollywood studio ranks, although that apprenticeship explains part of the story. I propose to review the record here, like some defense attorney; gather evidence, consult witnesses, and even have the defendant testify on his own behalf, drawn from phone chat and correspondence.

Opening the File

John Williams's preparatory years don't seem like a major composer's story. Born in Queens, New York, in 1932, the son of a percussionist, he learned to read music and practice piano at home. "I used to sit in the basement of our house in Flushing, Long Island, and pore over orchestration books. I'd apply the principles of Rimsky-Korsakov to the pop tunes of 1940 and 1941." By the time he was sixteen, his father took them all out to California, determining to find steadier work as a percussionist in one of the movie studio music departments. By then, music was becoming a greater interest for the teen Johnny and, so, he decided to commit to a music major at LA City College and, later, UCLA. The renowned Robert Van Epps was teaching him orchestration in those early years but he had begun to consider a pianist's career, either as a jazzman or even a classical soloist.

A stint in the US Air Force hijacked his late teens but, on returning to civilian life, he auditioned at Manhattan's Juilliard School and trained there with the great piano impresario Rosina Lhévinne. She was encouraging but she was a reality check too. As he told me once, "I don't think I ever believed I was extrovert enough or good enough to have a career as a pianist." He described hearing, in one of the adjacent practice rooms, the rehearsal sounds of the young keyboard virtuoso John Browning "and thought perhaps I should consider another profession! Plus, I was always lured by the orchestra" (*Ovation* [June 1983], 12–15, 42–43).

After a year at Juilliard with extra music theory classes, Williams hit the road as a band manager/arranger for touring pop crooners like Vic Damone or even the gospel-great Mahalia Jackson for whom he arranged seven record albums. One singer he met at this time in the mid-1950s would become his future wife, Barbara Ruick, and they would settle in Hollywood. (Barbara can be seen in the role of Carrie in the film musical *Carousel*.) Like his father, he would find work in some of the movie studio music departments helping soundtrack composers with their music for TV shows and supplementing that work with gigs as a pianist around town for jazz guys like Shorty Rogers, Art Pepper, and Bud Shank. In the studios, he would play the piano parts in scores by veteran composers like Alfred Newman ("Who always wrote beautifully, I thought, for films") or Bernard Herrmann ("Benny was encouraging; he never flattered but he encouraged me").[1] Even more than encouraging—in fact, downright championing of Johnny—was another classically trained jazz pianist and rising film composer, André Previn, roughly his contemporary (three years older), whose eventual influence on him was, I will be suggesting here, considerable.[2] Certainly, Previn was more extrovert, to use Williams's word. He had a broader European education, a passive-aggressive personality, an active career as a recording pop pianist—and he was scoring dramatic films under his own name—goals that Johnny, so far, coveted only as a spectator.

Active Apprentice

The late 1950s is where the Williams evidence begins to spill out of that introductory file and becomes its own story. I first became aware of Williams as the session pianist on Henry Mancini's innovative jazz-based scores for *Peter Gunn* and on three of Mancini's subsequent jazz-pop record albums. What Mancini appreciated in Williams's playing was his combination of sparse-but-sophisticated improvisation and, somewhere in the midst of his solos, a composer's know-how of what chords to employ in support of the tune under consideration there. On Mancini's impeccable album from 1960 called *Combo*, you can hear Williams winging it on jazz harpsichord. I always found his piano playing on those dates to be satisfying in conjunction with the other experienced soloists; he was aware of how to fit into the arrangements without taking over—perhaps a bit hesitant and simple as a soloist, but ultimately effective. As the 1960s took off, Mancini switched to the more stylish, subtle, and jazz-savvy pianist Jimmy Rowles and a series of ever more ambitious records ensued. But that was not because Johnny Williams was being overruled as a Mancini regular—it was just that Williams was starting to get offers to write some screen scores of his own. And, by my hearing, his apprentice soundtrack work shows the influence of the two mentors already mentioned here: Henry Mancini and, soon, André Previn.

The Mancini model can be heard, first, when Williams began to score a 1959 TV mystery series, *Checkmate*, lifting the jazz-pop style from *Peter Gunn*, though sounding a bit more formal, more in the tradition of a studio orchestra than of a big band or combo. His blends were smooth and his orchestral settings showed a broad academic education, even if his melodies were not as natural, and his interaction with the screen not as original, as Mancini's. At the same time, though, he was learning how to score fifties TV westerns like *Wagon Train*, police shows like *M Squad*, and sixties comedies like *Gilligan's Island* and *The Tammy Grimes Show*, each genre having its own musical needs and its own clichés to memorize (then, later, to avoid). "I had to write about twenty to twenty-five minutes of music a week," Williams remembered, "then score it and record it. A tremendous learning opportunity, though" (author correspondence, 5 December 1975).

Before too long, a few small-budget theatrical films were willing to take him on as composer—teen-oriented movies like *Because They're Young* (teen hipster music with bongos, etc.) or *Gidget Goes to Rome* (with lots of accordions in the score); suburban comedies like *Bachelor Flat*; or urban dramas like *Nightmare in Chicago* (suspense music in gray tones). He was glad to get the work and to see how the visual medium of film absorbed the medium of music. What he wanted, though, was to try his hand at a higher calling: scoring A-list motion pictures like his other mentor and pal Previn.

Although I set his true emancipation as a major film composer some six years after this period, I trace his first efforts in that direction to his Previn-inspired score for the 1963 melodrama *Diamond Head*. A brace of French horns attempts to set an epic tone at the beginning of the Hawaii-based film and there are two main motifs that will appear throughout the score, hoping to tie it all together: one is a wafting, tropical island song (not by Williams but by Hugo Winterhalter) and the other is a more serious, modal, and rather Previn-like "problem" motif. These themes and motives are not varied, but the narrative music throughout the film draws on them, giving at least an impression of integration, though Williams has not quite come to that level of mature scoring, not quite up to Previn's experience yet. Previn, in his best film scores, had used a motif approach, too, but he had also been as careful with his narrative music—the merely illustrative background music—as with his themes. This made his scores like *Elmer Gantry* (1960) or *Irma la Douce* (1963) exciting and orchestrally alive, all the way through—not just when they were pushing a tune. Previn was also willing to go further and explore dissonance and modal themes, if the film allowed it, such as in his complex score to *Four Horsemen of the Apocalypse* (1962), where the faint awareness of Shostakovich can be heard as different keys jostle and resolve at will. Johnny Williams's *Diamond Head* was certainly not up to that level, but it aspired to be.

I take all these examples and comparisons as evidence that, right from his beginnings in Hollywood, Williams was ambitious beyond the easy-listening love themes and conventional tension-music he had been hearing during other guys' scoring sessions. Ambitious like Previn, but as he had once said, he just had a more introverted, long-term way of pursuing it.

I hear nothing special in the rest of his TV work from those sixties days—episodes in series like *Alcoa Presents*, *The Virginian*, *The Wide Country*—although there *is* a spark in one of his title themes for the 1965 kids series *Lost in Space* with its dotted-note fanfare: half-heroic (leaps of major fourths and minor ninths) and half-amused (playful tumbling lines and a mock-robot sound). As an orchestral setting and a curtain-raiser, it recommended its composer. And so, when he finally *was* chosen to score a major film, the caper-comedy with Audrey Hepburn and Peter O'Toole, *How to Steal a Million* (1966), you can hear his enthusiasm and confidence in how he has chosen to emulate his mentors: you hear Mancini's way with a glamorous, opening melody assigned to a distinctive solo instrument (in this case, some splashy and difficult solo piano decoration), and you hear some Previn-approved counterpoint along the way. Mostly, it is a pop score with rich fashion-show harmonies and glitz—but appropriate for its film and noticeable for itself.

As Williams's *Checkmate* music had drawn on the *Peter Gunn* model, two of his mid-1960s comedy scores were copying a page from the wider Mancini catalogue: multi-tuneful, clean, and carefully balanced big band scores, unique only when, for instance, Williams would layer in strings over the samba in a sunny poolside scene or put his own spin on a sixties rock 'n' roll song for the femme fatale comedy *Penelope* (1966). Better yet was his cool, big band song, written with Johnny Mercer, called "Big Beautiful Ball" from the farce *Not with My Wife, You Don't!*, also 1966. Once, I asked him about songwriting per se and about comedy scoring in general: "Certainly, I think of myself as an orchestral writer first," he said, "and a composer who writes songs, when asked, second. As far as comedy scores that I admire, I remember one in particular that I worked on years ago as a pianist for a man whom I admired very much in those days, Adolph Deutsch, and the picture was *Some Like It Hot* (1959). Deutsch always used to say that music shouldn't try too hard to be funny itself, otherwise one would have something on the level of Tom-and-Jerry. I think I believe this: If a scene in a film is funny, I would almost prefer to leave it unscored unless, of course, it is some kind of slapstick or burlesque where music can provide, in a balletic sense, tempo." With that much know-how in his bag of tricks, to me it all seemed to prove that, by this time in his history, Williams was ready with any kind of writing, whether for the traditional full orchestra or studio jazz-pop players. He would release a pop album of his own in 1961, *Rhythm in Motion*, and arrange/conduct another with André Previn at the piano, circa 1965, called *Music of the Young Hollywood Composers*, offering film themes from Previn, Mancini, Elmer Bernstein, Michel Legrand, among others, in clean, conservative, easy-listening versions.

But Previn was even more restless than Williams, looking for ways to legitimize himself in the concert world, negotiating with a series of symphony orchestras for conducting gigs. He urged Williams to do the same—at least to devote himself more seriously to writing concert music. (Previn conducted Williams's first symphony in Houston in the sixties and again in London in the seventies.) Williams has commented on his own relationship to classical composing: "I've always felt that my efforts in that area were, more than anything, exercises in self-instruction and self-development, presenting myself with opportunities that I wouldn't have in the restricted field of composing film music. I certainly value both fields, though; concert and screen music" (author correspondence, 5 December 1975 and 3 July 1976; *BBC Music* [December 2012]; *Gramophone* [May 2006]). But, unlike Previn, his concert work didn't have to be limited to the classical realm. I'm thinking of his ten-minute piece of progressive big band jazz, *Prelude and Fugue*, composed for Stan Kenton's Neophonic Orchestra. It opens with free-form atonal comments by various solo winds, like dots around a canvas. Those sounds consolidate gradually as brass build to a screaming climax; a slow walking bass line moves in, then, behind a chromatic motif, as near to a theme as this work will get. There's a development section, a second brass climax, and an eventual return to the free-form winds in retreat, leaving a kind of medieval air because of the narrow harmonic of the whole piece.

Even though he never left film scoring behind for very long, upon returning from such concert work, Williams always approached the next film project with the same spirit of creativity as he had conjured for the concert hall. His 1967 score for the trivial comic film *Fitzwilly* surprised even the film's producers by amounting to, of all things, a formidable baroque orchestral suite—not funny music, as Deutsch had warned about, but ironically classical and elitist music—that's the joke: part Scarlatti and Handel, part opera buffa, but in any case, way more energetic, focused, and participatory than the film (featuring Dick Van Dyke as a butler who has to commit robberies to save his boss) had ever asked for. Consequently, the music lifted the whole film a couple of quality-notches and, as a happy by-product, made people wonder about the composer: could such a formal and concert-worthy piece of scoring come from a guy called Johnny?

The year 1967 also gave Williams a chance to connect with André and (then wife) Dory Previn on one of the Previns' last Hollywood contracts, the box-office bomb *Valley of the Dolls* (1967). Williams would orchestrate and conduct what ended up being an attractively sensitive score with a hit theme song recorded by Dionne Warwick and others. If nothing else, the project brought the two fast friends together one last time, then sent them off in their own separate directions for good—Previn to become the principal conductor of the London Symphony Orchestra and Williams, at last, off to tackle big-time TV and a big-budget film where, as it turned out, fate awaited him.

Johnny into John

As a special TV movie event, Delbert Mann's 1968 production of the children's novel *Heidi* had attracted international investment for its rebroadcast potential and its global cast. The only evidence I can find as to why the still-unsung, still-known-as-Johnny Williams got the commission to score this major project is that it was a coproduction between Europe's Omnibus Films and the American CBS network, which had also owned *Lost in Space*. Although Williams was not allowed to conduct *Heidi*'s soundtrack (Eberhardt Soblick conducted a Hamburg orchestra), the lavish and pictorial music he provided gave the broadcast the necessary scope and class, as though it were a theatrical feature film, and earned its own Emmy Award that year. He kept his themes kid-simple and in a romantic style emphasizing winds and strings but giving the six French horn players the major task of representing Heidi's noble Alpine setting. Any angular harmonies may have derived from such past concert classics as Richard Strauss's *Alpine Symphony* or a few leftover influences of André Previn.

A second Omnibus TV film aimed at the same international network came two years later and would earn Williams his second

Emmy Award for Best Score, *Jane Eyre*. His music, this time, in an absolutely legit nineteenth-century English milieu, incorporated a compelling minor-key misterioso for harpsichord and strings, a plush romantic piano love theme, a polite string quartet playing a piece of parlor music, and a riveting scherzo that took the studio orchestra several "takes" (with Williams allowed to conduct, this time) to get its tricky time signatures right. Eventually, Williams would mention this score as one of his own personal favorites and I have Previn on tape enthusing about it.

But this is also the time, 1969–1970, of what I hold to be the composer's breakout score and the one film for which his own onscreen credit finally reads "John Williams" as though announcing his graduation from resourceful apprentice to composer-in-charge. This is the film adaptation of William Faulkner's Pulitzer Prize–winning novel *The Reivers*—directed by the young former-actor Mark Rydell (*Crime in the Streets*, 1955)—the Americana story of a charismatic rascal in the Old South, circa 1905, who borrows the family's new motor car to joyride to the big city. His eleven-year-old cousin tags along. A conventional Americana music score—some Copland, some dialect instruments like banjo and harmonica and slide guitar—was all that was required for such a film. Indeed, that's what the original composer, Lalo Schifrin (*Cool Hand Luke*, 1967), had given them. But, when the producers saw how Rydell's film projected so much "heart" and a rich feeling for its Alabama/Mississippi settings, they felt it needed something more from its music track. Schifrin was fully capable of supplying a rewrite, but he was already off, working on concert commissions for a jazz quintet and a choral madrigal piece. Williams, with his *Heidi* award in hand, was called instead.

Those localized sounds of banjo, harmonica, and slide guitar *are* key elements in Williams's score for *The Reivers*, but they are just condiments to what is actually a large-scale symphonic portrait of the American south, laced with bayou tunes and a whole lot of joyous orchestral energy that one critic described as "so fresh, it sounds like it was conducted with a fishing rod in country air!" (Charles Burr, soundtrack album liner notes for *The Reivers* [Columbia Records 0066130]). Its elements: a large, bright and breezy string section sometimes scored in unison lines, sometimes in open harmonics as if for a country hoedown—raucous stomping rhythms for backwoods chase scenes featuring a crazy double-time figure on an old-time tin piano—a pumping brass/strings gallop for a horse race scene—a grand waltz for the unveiling of that brand-new automobile, the fabulous Wynton Flyer—and some genuinely lovely pastoral music from the massed strings. Without such a fully symphonic score, the film would have missed the narrative sweep and rich atmosphere of the Faulkner original: it would have just been a picaresque period comedy with a soft center—and a novelty vehicle for the star, Steve McQueen. So, it was *The Reivers* that officially turned the studio pianist Johnny Williams into John, the major film composer we take for granted today. It also garnered his first motion picture Academy Award nomination for Best Original Music Score. "The banjo parts, by the way, were both composed and improvised," Williams wanted to be sure I reported; "about 50 percent each, since the banjo player was not an expert reader. With regard to the inspiration that one may detect in *The Reivers* score, I think it must have had to do with the film itself, since I worked to a final print and not a graphic storyboard. Also, I find all of Rydell's pictures especially musical and, since Rydell himself is something of an amateur musician, the question of what *kind* of music was arrived at mutually. We have always collaborated very comfortably. Lastly, the fact that the little boy in the film looked exactly like my youngest son at the time of the creation of the movie may have had something to do with the affinity I felt for the film!"

Naturally, award nominations and the publicity that goes with them bring a whole new level of attention to an artist, and job offers start coming in from unexpected places. A case in point, one year later: when they adapted the iconic Broadway musical *Fiddler on the Roof* (1971) for the screen, the studio quickly recommended Williams. To supervise orchestral settings for those all-too-familiar songs would seem to be a thankless task, but Williams dug into the assignment with the energy of a newcomer, creating a vigorous and virtuosic rendition of the big opening number "Tradition," and yet elsewhere, distilling the Hebraic elements down to a gentle few for the plaintive paternal lullaby "Little Bird" and scoring it to feature the pure violin sound of Isaac Stern. The whole experience would bring Williams his second Academy Award nomination (for scoring adaptation) and his first win.

After another film job for Mark Rydell (*The Cowboys*, with its rollicking Coplandesque score), the years 1972–1974 would present two separate and opposing career opportunities. One tract brought Williams's avant-garde side up for air, thanks to one abstract film and one progressive concert commission. The film was Robert Altman's bizarre tale *Images* (1972), about a contemporary woman lost in memories and hallucinations, mixing up images of herself as a child, her husband, and two lovers. Altman hoped to disturb the viewer by replicating the woman's disoriented mind. It's all like a bad trip. In response, Williams's score rotated three elements that never blend but stand apart: (a) an obsessive piano-and-strings children's tune as Susannah York recites a nursery rhyme to herself; (b) a kind of avant-garde essay for strings that seems to include every manipulation possible of a stringed instrument: plucked, tapped, muted, tremolo, jeté . . . by turns, sinister and violent and brooding; and (c) a cauldron of tonal percussive sounds produced by a setup of stainless steel rods, prisms, gongs, and glass tubes that are part of a standing sculpture by the artist Baschet, here being manipulated, being "played," by percussionist Stomu Yamashta. It's not right to say that those three streams—the sculpture sounds, the nursery tune in various arrangements, and the atonal string passages—mingle with one another. It is their very contrast that exemplifies the main character's mental imbalance. Williams would always refer to this score as a highlight of his career, but another Academy Award nomination for Best Score was its only public recognition.

Considering *Images* and string writing in general, Williams says, "You talk about the *Images* score as being almost a kind of extension of my concert piece, *Essay for Strings*. I have often thought that I might make a second essay out of that material used in *Images*. I think, to my mind, strings make the purest music—strings vibrating on a violin or a vocal cord vibrating or the string of a keyboard instrument vibrating. I don't play a stringed instrument but I love them, and I suppose this would explain whatever affinity I may have for them. From the piano I do play chamber music with violinist and cellist friends whenever possible."

The other aggressively progressive music of this period, sans strings this time, was his concert piece, *Sinfonia for Wind Ensemble*, recorded on the prestigious classical label Deutsche Gramophone. This seventeen-minute, three-movement music relies on the precise placement of juxtaposed chords, solo wind entrances, and surprising combinations of winds, rather than on theme lines or performance to declare itself. Williams introduces high winds playing in clots of atonal harmony with a slow stepping meter underneath, then midrange winds play the same clots with muted brass adding to the mix. At about the two-minute mark, the color darkens and brass add more tension, building in complexity and volume to about the six-minute mark where the work's "problem motif" comes out, and the first movement (*lento assai*) ends. Three solo oboes twine around one another for the second movement's introduction; then atonal brass play cluster chords and that stepping meter returns, modified. Jangling sounds of glockenspiel and vibes introduce the third movement with timpani and some aggressive brass writing until an unexpected waltz figure intrudes from a piccolo against those jangling sounds. But not for long. The climax comes with brass and winds blotting thick chords; French horn calling out and winds adding in, beginning to reassert the central "problem" of the piece before cresting to a crash.

Neither Williams's *Sinfonietta* nor his *Essay for Strings* stand out from the rest of midcentury progressive music, but in their command of ensemble forces and careful design, they demand respect today and deserve to be heard, preferable to the other academic fad music of its time—that is, the bankrupt collage style or the elementary ideals of minimalism. Williams had cause to be proud.

The other career tract of this period was unintentional and both a blessing as a big source of income and a curse as it got to be a kind of joke about him—that, for a while, he became the King of the Disaster Films—those star-studded apocalyptic melodramas, all made in a row during the 1970s, that purported to portray ordinary people under dire circumstances—a flood, a fire: Who will survive? How dire will it get? The whole fad had begun in 1970, without John Williams, with an old-fashioned thriller about a bomb aboard an airplane: Ross Hunter's *Airport*. That film had Alfred Newman's music; in fact, it was his final score as that Golden Age generation gave way to the Williamses of the future. Disaster films, then, suddenly became a genre all their own, and a craze. The second disaster film went to Williams: 1972's *The Poseidon Adventure* about an ocean liner smacked sideways by a tidal wave and now floating helplessly upside down in the middle of the sea. Its hundreds of passengers would have to work their way through the ship's innards, up toward the hull, hoping to cut their way out of what used to be the bottom of the ship, to find the sky. The compelling score wisely stays away from the passengers' personal stories or any direct depiction of the disaster, rendering instead the suspense and the ominous natural forces around everyone—that is, the encroaching sea. Meanwhile, the inverted ship lists and bobs and is gradually sinking.

To mimic the push and pull of the tide, Williams composed an undulating, surging figure for low strings and brass that laps at regular tidal intervals. And for the overall seascape, he borrowed (or independently discovered the value of) a particular modulation device heard in another film score about a fateful sea journey: Ralph Vaughan Williams's music for *Scott of the Antarctic* (1948) that had so effectively evoked the boundless and bottomless fathoms of ocean below the ice. Most of Williams's functional score for *The Poseidon Adventure* was not the violent stuff we would come to associate with disaster scenes but the more suspenseful, weighty sounds of the bottom half of the orchestra, underlining a sense of constant peril rather than of explosive action. (Williams: "Your assessments, relative to my motives in *Poseidon*, are certainly correct. As far as any connection between my score and Vaughan Williams's *Antarctica*, I would say two things. First, my admiration and affinity for his music is great. Fortunately, disasters have a universal significance, in that all humankind is subject to their affects and, therefore, the subject of a disaster is, in that sense, larger than melodrama. *Poseidon* and *Antarctica* also share in common the vastness of the sea, tidal waves, continental ice cracks, etc. This connection that you make between the two Williamses flatters me greatly!")

And lest it be thought I am critical of the notion of film composers borrowing from well-known classical works, or just referencing them in the process of fashioning an expressive soundtrack, I should mention several places in Williams's oeuvre where he has done this with very positive results, exploiting the legitimate and effective affinities (to use his other favorite word) between existing pieces: the heraldic "Throne Room" music from *Star Wars*, which is an obvious paraphrase of William Walton's processional anthem in *The First of the Few* (1942); his love theme from *Superman* (1978), which is straight out of Richard Strauss's "Death and Transfiguration." Meanwhile, a whole college class could be taught on the matchups between the bike-chase music or the farewell crescendos at the end of *E.T. the Extra-Terrestrial* (1982) and the last movement of Howard Hanson's emotional Symphony no. 2 from 1930. These references and borrowings are not dodges or cheap hand-me-downs; they are valid and, for those who recognize the repertoire, exciting examples of the interconnectedness of all music.

For a third disaster film, 1974's *Earthquake*, Williams wrote modestly with the same subtle, hands-off philosophy as for *Poseidon*. The main selling point of this film had been the idea that the audience could experience low rumblings from some specially installed Dolby Surround Sound speakers in each movie theater to simulate an earthquake during the show (while, onscreen, a shaky camera, computer-generated images of crumbling buildings, and actors with panicked expressions were supposed to complete the illusion). Again, Williams stayed away from the havoc onscreen, addressing only a few quiet concepts: a rather sad, reflective piano theme for the human element and a rather more hopeful city theme for Los Angeles recovering from the quake and looking toward the dawn.

The most active disaster film score, then, comes as Williams's next entry in this unintended series, *The Towering Inferno* (1974)—another star-studded thriller in which a proud corporate high-rise building goes up in flames. I note two features of this inferno scoring that make it a positive example of the high rise of John Williams: (a) its exciting and well-shaped opening title cue, introducing us to the fitful urban landscape—concert-worthy music that pulses with all the urgency and bravado of a big city newscast, and (b) the strength and solidity of the film's functional scoring, which, although it's just there to keep the action going and keep the tension up, also makes musical sense here and has its own logic: it's not just a series of transitions and setups and climaxes.

Disasters, Indeed

But even in Hollywood, the land of make-believe, Reality is never quite replaced by fiction and fantasy. Here, in the mid-1970s, John Williams would find Real Life about to interpose itself on all his newfound success: it had disasters of its own to impart, now. For 1974 would especially be remembered for the unexpected death of his wife, Barbara. As a measured and modest personality, Williams made no public acknowledgment of his loss. Instead, he packed up those feelings, personal and private, and put them into some especially intimate music—true disaster music: a genuinely heartfelt violin concerto, dedicated to Barbara; music eventually premiered by Leonard Slatkin and the St. Louis Symphony with Gil Shaham as soloist. Intensely posed questions of love and loss focus this concerto somewhere between atonality and romanticism, though its ultimate effect is one of neoclassicism. His orchestral textures are clear, and the voice of the soloist is lyrical, while an elegiac mood pervades, especially in the middle movement marked "in peaceful contemplation." Solo French horn repeats the violin's main motif, with flute and viola comments; then the full orchestra takes up the tragedy, and the violin pursues the same emotion from many sides. Whether under Slatkin's or the composer's baton, public performances by Shaham and, later, by Mark Peskanov, navigated the piece with consistently warm results. It is a work that holds up as affecting music to this day, deserving to be programmed again by other orchestras, other soloists, even though it's "only by a film composer."

One more disaster would come during this same period—a career misstep to aggravate the personal trial Williams had just been through: I am thinking of his failed foray into the world of the Broadway musical. The production, which never made it past a London tryout performance, was supposed to be a smart, tuneful (seventeen songs) period piece about Thomas à Becket, Britain's twelfth-century martyr-priest with a script by Edward Anhalt, lyrics by James Harbert, and a score by Williams: *Thomas and the King* (1975). It's unfair to call the whole project a disaster but, for those involved, it was certainly a downer. Audiences came to the London theater out of curiosity; but critics only stayed out of courtesy: its dramaturgy, they said "lacks a definable style"; choreography "is lackluster"; musical score "doesn't rise above the serviceable" (*Variety*, 29 October 1975). One fellow composer who respected Williams's career as a whole told me, diagnosing the problem, that "he just can't write a memorable tune." I didn't bother to quote back to him the number of Williams tunes that I could easily remember, nor how much trouble that critic-composer always had, trying to write his *own* memorable melodies. Certainly, in writing *Thomas and the King*, Williams had been trying for more than just tunes—still, as a creative project, it failed, putting a final seal on a bad time. But right around the corner was 1975.

Rise to the Top

Just as no one can predict disaster, no one could have foreseen the number of massive successes that were waiting around the corner for John Williams from 1975 on. First, would be his association with the breakout hit movie by Steven Spielberg, *Jaws*, the tale of a great white shark terrorizing vacationers at an East Coast beach resort—a modern version of a Grand Guignol nightmare with its own mindless, remorseless villain. Spielberg's forte as director was audience manipulation—to confine, then surprise, then appall and gross out, then excite, and finally release his viewers, very much like an amusement park ride. *Jaws* turned out to be his perfect vehicle for such antics. As for scoring options, a composer could have either supported the adventure as Korngold or Rózsa would have done, or somehow tried to get inside the panic and inflate it. Williams, of course, chose the latter.

Mass audiences who had never noticed film music before here found themselves able to recognize Williams's vivid shark motif on the soundtrack and to anticipate it: double basses repeating just two notes—E to F—then, an ominous silence; then E/F/E; then again, with the pauses becoming more worrisome, the motif hardening into accented strokes; the E/F sawing back and forth and coming on faster, soon baited by a hollow drum and sharp brass hits; then a three-note warning from a tuba in a foreign key. Once the rest of the orchestra comes in, we understand the dimensions of the threat—that it isn't so mindless after all: in fact, this shark has an agenda. By now, Williams has single-handedly taught the nervous viewer to beware of each return of that E/F motif because it's linked to the presence of the shark. And, of course, now he can manipulate us at will, both by presenting the motif as a false alert to trick us when no threat is near, and by withholding it, only to have the shark spring out of nowhere and scare us to death.

But the invention of that motif, what Berlioz used to call an *idée fixe*—a repeated motif used as a narrative gimmick—is really only an ingenious conceit of this soundtrack. The real accomplishment is the virtuosity and precision of the functional score, the orchestral writing that encompasses some downright primitive Stravinskian siege-music, a seafaring fugue of some complexity, and a heroic chase taken by the orchestra at a thrilling sixty knots. This is film scoring that not only narrates but takes over its film, while also maintaining its own compositional integrity and interest. The addition of a magical impressionistic underwater nocturne and a buoyant sea shanty to satirize the blissfully naïve tourist population are yet more scoring features that signify this *Jaws* score as one of the fifty best screen soundtracks ever.

(Further proof of Williams's integrity is that, when they produced an unnecessary sequel in 1978, *Jaws II*, while the shark motif returned, the rest of his scoring was thoroughly new: two delightful new sea shanties, and so forth.)

As an A-level film composer now, he got the chance to score what turned out to be Alfred Hitchcock's final film, the mystery-comedy *Family Plot* (1976) about a phony psychic who becomes involved tracking a real murderer. For the mysticism aspect of the script, the score has a dreamy, floating theme for female voices while, for the conventional detective angle, a crisp harpsichord sound conjures the feeling of a nineteenth-century parlor game. It was clear that *Family Plot* was never going to challenge the serious history of Hitchcock and the score seemed to know that—in fact, it had the same transient glamor as the music for *How to Steal a Masterpiece* ten years earlier. It didn't bother to invest more.

The year 1977, however, would prove to be the biggest emancipation for Williams yet—his introduction to director-producer George Lucas and his megahit *Star Wars*. Called "elaborate; imaginative" by critics in its day, this was Lucas's homage to the sci-fi space adventures of his youth—all the matinee flicks in which a young idealistic generation took on the imagined villains of the universe. In this case, virtue would triumph with the help of a sage, a couple of robots, an alien, and a kind of cowboy character who knows no fear. What was wanted for the soundtrack was rousing adventure music and what Williams proposed was a fully traditional symphonic score, descriptive and melodic, heroic, romantic, colorful, and yet knowingly sophisticated—like Korngold had done for *The Sea Hawk*; like Rózsa had done for *Thief of Bagdad*. Thus, besides the blatant fanfare that became its opening theme, *Star Wars* got an intentional pastiche score with those past soundtrack examples in mind. More subtly, the score also rang with echoes of classic composers like Holst (*The Planets*) and Prokofiev (*Juliet*, *Alexander Nevsky*) and, as I've already said, William Walton. More references can be found all the time: notice how the Princess Leia theme fairly purrs with likeness to *Scheherazade*. Intentionally and cleverly on Williams's part, no one was safe from such a grab bag of musical tributes and tributaries. But that was part of the matinee fun everyone was having.

Since *Star Wars* is so well known, it's unnecessary to rehearse its features here, except to note that its themes were plain, its orchestrations vast and facile (Lucas paid the London Symphony to record them), and it treated outer space as some exotic land while treating combat as the ultimate test of courage and manhood. With the enormous success of this style of scoring (the soundtrack record album sold four million copies), Williams had initiated, without meaning to, a whole renaissance of full-scale symphonic music in motion pictures—a rebirth, it was said, of the Golden Age that has now lasted well into the New Millennium and has spawned a whole generation of, alas, Williams imitators.

That same year, André Previn, who had long since moved on from the London Symphony to conduct the Pittsburgh Symphony (later the Oslo Philharmonic; then, somewhat contentiously, the LA Philharmonic), in 1977 helmed a televised concert of film music excerpts and invited Williams onto the broadcast for a personal interview and to conduct the Pittsburghers in a *Star Wars* suite. And so, of course, from now on Williams became the chief epic adventure film composer (*Superman, Dracula, Far and Away, Raiders of the Lost Ark, War Horse, The Fury, Munich, War of the Worlds*) and it began to seem as though all the big-budget scoring jobs were offered to him first. And even when others took his place, they were asked to write like him. Some critics began to grumble about what they considered the clichéd Williams themes—big blustery pronouncements based on the interval of the so-called heroic fifth and all that busy music. So many of his scores for comic book fantasies or boyish adventure films could be accused of resorting to the same unadventurous C-major scales harmonized in simple thirds, and all those ubiquitous fanfare intros. Likewise, his pious or nationalistic music (*Monsignor, The Patriot, Born on the Fourth of July*)[3] seemed forced to some, culminating in the controversy over his Pops concert piece *America: The Dream Goes On*, which, one orchestra member complained, was full of clichés—a rebellion that nearly led to Williams resigning.[4] *High Fidelity* magazine's writer "P. A. S." worried that Williams's film music had all become "slickly synthetic symphonic Muzak"—"more of the same stylistic sleight-of-hand." And yet, at the same time, another writer, summarizing film music history, concluded that the most important composers Hollywood had ever known were Korngold, Rózsa, Herrmann, Waxman, and Williams. Even after his skepticism in that *High Fidelity* article, P. A. S. concluded, "In truth, Williams has manipulated his malleable talents with enormous care, skill, taste, and ingenuity and he has successfully resisted a resort to self-plagiarism" (*High Fidelity* [September 1980], 104). That's another way of saying that, although Williams does compose within a fairly conservative range of styles and grammar and of narrative/illustrative response, he usually well matches the demeanor of each score to its film, music that's fitting and empathetic. By the same token, then, when he finds himself working on a disappointing film, the quality of his scoring instinctively retreats and weakens: titles like *Empire of the Sun*, *Always*, *Heartbeeps*, *Story of a Woman* come to mind.[5] But it also means that if a film aspires to some higher vision, Williams seems to encourage the effort with more inspired music, wanting to pull everyone up: thus, you have the magical scores to the *Harry Potter* series, the moving patriotic anthem at the heart of *Saving Private Ryan* (1998), or the abstract choral cluster-chords and washes of impressionism coming from Spielberg's *Close Encounters*. Indeed, the whole insightful score to *Close Encounters* only missed copping the Academy Award that year because Williams was already winning for *Star Wars*. Now, not only were colleagues competing for attention against him; he was competing, as it were, against himself, alone at the top.

An issue of the industry journal *The Cue Sheet* quoted the veteran Hollywood orchestrator Herbert Spencer, who had often worked on Williams scores, acknowledging the composer's dominance and detailing his admiration for Williams's knowledge and ability. There, he pinpointed a lot of technical details that I find crucial in differentiating Williams from so many of the other wanna-be film composers who may come up with themes but then have no idea how to actually score them. "I'd known him since he was younger," Spencer was saying, "since he was known as 'Johnny,' but right away I noticed the quality of his writing. Very up-town. And when he finally did get his act together, he had it all. It was wonderful to see. You see a good mind working there . . . a full-grown, real composer (who knows how to write for the orchestra) . . . So many times, with other guys, you listen to a score and it sounds like the instruments have been transposed—written in an incorrect or an uncomfortable key because the guy doesn't do his homework—doesn't know where the strings sound best, how to blend the instruments and so forth. So, he scores in the wrong key where the strings don't sing there; they're playing on the middle strings with the wrong fingerings—all the flats—whereas John is very conscious of where things lay on the string and how to write effectively for each instrument; he's tremendously conscious of all that. He knows the classical repertoire, too, so players respect him and I, as an orchestrator, respect him. John generally makes a very good (compositional) sketch. If you look at it carefully, all the information is there . . . I must say, my last years with John Williams have been the most enjoyable of all. Truly" (*The Cue Sheet* 7, no. 3, interview with Herbert Spencer).

And the whole story I've been outlining here is only the first half of John Williams's career. Two major occurrences, which bring this case file to its halftime climax, come from the early 1980s. One is his decision to sign a contract—a non-Hollywood contract, perhaps after the example of André Previn—to become the permanent conductor of a major concert orchestra, the Boston Pops, of whose thorny history more at another time or from some other listener. The other occurrence, returning to the spaced-out world of Spielberg movies, is Williams's composing the most sensational example of what music can do for a film, 1982's *E.T. the Extra-Terrestrial*. So crucial was this music to both supporting and humanizing this film that even the staid and self-important audience at the Cannes Film Festival premiere of the film found themselves cheering like kids at one point in the movie's climactic bicycle-chase sequence. Music did that.

The story of *E.T.* takes a ten-year-old boy as its hero and combines several genres into one tale: thriller, sci-fi serial, space opera, Wild West yarn, and treasure-map mystery where only the kid knows the secret of the plot. Here, the boy Elliott becomes the trusted liaison of a friendly, inquisitive alien from "somewhere out there in space," an extraterrestrial who lands—where else would Spielberg's generation have it?—in suburbia USA, and the story then cleverly and sensitively compares the otherworldly visitor (who's lost on Earth and trying to communicate with his own mother ship) to Elliott. Though pampered in an upper-middle-class household with more toys and siblings and prospects than most kids in the world will ever have, Elliott misses his divorced father and feels lost. Spielberg knows exactly how to exploit the sweetness of that childhood scenario and the magic of the space milieu, even as he once exploited our fear of sharks—and so does John Williams. *E.T.* has all the classic B-movie suspense but with a breathless 1980s pace, some occasional humor, and a not-too-scary villain: in this case, the government authorities who want to confiscate E.T. first and understand him later.

So now it's boyhood innocence against another mindless antagonist, the power of the Feds. All of that, Williams understands, and there is not a single aspect that I have just described that's not represented in his score. It is not what you'd call advanced composition. It relies on all the soundtrack clichés that P. A. S. was worrying about in his *High Fidelity* article—busy music when E.T. is on the run, the usual blatant main theme whose first two notes span the heroic fifth again; there's anachronistic piano music to accompany the sight of Elliott and E.T. magically airborne on a bicycle. But there are darker hues, too, as it begins to look like E.T. will become the victim of human xenophobia; and there is a humorously bitonal cue as E.T. steps out into the suburban neighborhood to experience Halloween. Above all, there is the bighearted, eventually soaring music that fills and warms the theater at the film's emotional goodbye scenes once E.T. has found his ride home. It is the only time I've ever been to the cinema where, as the lights went up following the gushing music at the end, there actually were children weeping in the aisles for the sentiment of it all, and parents trying to comfort them. This is Spielberg's talent for benign manipulation, of course, but let it be said that it is also the power of film scoring and the wisdom of Williams. The two major characteristics of great film music are there: the master craftsmanship of composition and the personal sincerity and commitment of the composer to the story onscreen.

Williams's desire to communicate, whether through sentimental family-friendly music, a very personal violin concerto, atonal concert experiments, or heroic anthems and fanfares, has sustained something like seventy years of screen music. For the second half of his career beyond this present summary, he would set himself new goals—including that stint as a Pops conductor presenting music directly to the public for a change. But he wouldn't let up on movies, either, scoring a series of presidential film biographies (JFK, Nixon, Lincoln); more sci-fi epics like *War of the Worlds* (2005) and all those *Star Wars* sequels; and more serious moral tales like *Schindler's List* (1993). Distinctive films would still inspire unexpected gestures from him: the choral chanting of *Amistad*; the quiet piano-and-winds ballade of *Angela's Ashes* (1999); the wicked romping humor of *The Witches of Eastwick* (1987); the close-harmony third-stream jazz score for *Catch Me If You Can* (2002). Apparently, the desire to reach out and reach in is not exhausted. But it would take a part 2 of this profile to unpack all that.

For now, suffice it to say that none of his successors has yet such a record of productivity and dominance, and even though new means and methods of creating screen music are being invented by young composers every year, none can completely avoid his influence.

Notes to the Future

WITH THE NEW MILLENNIUM, although the movie industry had changed in every possible way (venues, values, production, distribution, and display methods—and a new cadre of music soundtrack suppliers), a few quality composers from the previous generation held on to remain influential—names like Dave Grusin, Lalo Schifrin, Ennio Morricone, Philippe Sarde, John Barry. Young fans got to know their earlier contributions and their late submissions. Then a younger crowd, born in the 1950s, stepped up to the podium: Thomas and Randy Newman (sons of Alfred Newman), Alan Silvestri, Anne Dudley, Patrick Doyle, James Horner, James Newton Howard, Bruce Broughton. It was surprising how much of the technique, habits, and ideas from the composers interviewed in this book carried over into the film scores of that next generation.

But another generation rapidly supplanted them, and these were from the widest spectrum of backgrounds yet in the history of film scoring: apprentice composers, intrigued by the film scores they had been hearing all their lives. And they were coming from extremely diverse backgrounds: some, as we have seen, from rock bands; some from the strange realm of video games (John Powell, Michael Giacchino); and a few holdouts from classical careers who no longer felt the stigma against film composing, wanting to mix refined concert styles with electronic effects with old-fashioned Hollywood hype (resourceful folks like Elliot Goldenthal, John Corigliano).

The byword for most of these composers and most of this music has been pluralism. As is true of the rest of musical society at this writing, film scoring now boasts (or confesses) influences from all over the musical universe and the new generation of films seems to welcome them. Yet the standards for film music must remain the same: narrow and elite—those same few principles that Aaron Copland outlined so many years ago and that the composers interviewed herein have championed: Does music help set the pace and the place of the story (or documentary agenda) onscreen; does it help tell the tale; and, finally, is it in some way interesting music? If, in addition, it can also express something personal of the composer and catch something universal in the audience, why, then there will be successor generations of worthy screen composers to be interviewed long into the future.

Notes

Introduction

1. Composer-author Bazelon is more interested in aesthetic questions of music's relation to dramatic cinema than in chronicling the careers of composers who have passed through the field. His chapters on scoring technique and "What does music actually do?" are key in this discussion of music versus image.

The earliest of excuses for soundtrack music (i.e., to "normalize" the initially alarming experience of illuminated moving pictures on a screen) are analyzed in Kracauer, in Adorno and in Eisler. The improvisatory style of this fledgling film music is described in Cooke, *History* 7–21; in Bazelon 13–19; and in Limbacher 15–24.

2. Bazelon asks his several interviewees, "Does one have to be a composer to write film music?" Their answers range from "Of course, you need to be a composer to write any music" to "Not really. A couple of chords can compel a film score." See Bazelon 11, 186, and so on.

3. In what ways can a score effectively interact with drama onscreen? See Brown 92–147; Cooke, *Reader* 209–22; Copland, *What* 202–10; Lumet 170–85; Smith 358–64; Waxman 132–37.

4. The question is, Are film composers developing a more refined aesthetic as they evolve alongside the movie industry itself? See Thomas Newman in Schelle 269–92; Jerry Goldsmith in *Film Music Notebook* 3, no. 2; see also Morgan; MacDonald; Karlin and Wright; Hubbert.

5. On Eisenstein, see Brown 134, 145; Cooke, *History* 347–53; on Gance, see Caps, *Crisis Music* 102–5; Cooke, *History* 309–12; multiple Gance references in Halbreich and in Brown 20, 54.

6. Interview with cinema organist Gaylord Carter in McCarty 22–28, 38–39, 42–43, 48–51.

7. Passacaglia—a musical and dance form that is basically a set of variations over a regular or ground bass in triple time like 3/4 or 3/8.

8. Fugal—a form of musical counterpoint in which two, three, or more voice parts sound and repeat a melody or part of a melody perhaps with slight variations, the theme line or fragments of the theme proceeding and intertwining by strict rules and in strict relationship to one another.

9. Leitmotif—a short musical theme or motif used to stand for a person, object, place, or idea that reappears throughout a composition or an opera.

10. Serial or twelve-tone composition—a method of composition where the composer takes the twelve tones of the chromatic scale in any order and uses that series of tones as one would a traditional tonal scale. That particular sequence of notes becomes "the key of the piece" and one composes in relation to that "tone row."

11. Among the American-based film composers who took advantage of more sophisticated compositional techniques in Hollywood in the 1940s and 1950s besides Rosenman were Hugo Friedhofer (*The Best Years of Our Lives*, 1946; *Above and Beyond*, 1952) and Alex North (*Spartacus*, 1960; *A Streetcar Named Desire*, 1951). By "sophisticated" we mean fluid use of both melody and dissonance, both classical and jazz styles.

12. "The next new tone" after the acceptance of jazz into film scoring was the subtle blending of jazz with pop musicmaking song structures and easy-flow melody the basis of many a modern soundtrack. Several popular scores of this type were produced by Henry Mancini in the early 1960s for films like *Charade*, *Breakfast at Tiffany's*, and *Me Natalie*, making movie music listenable and attractive to the unsuspecting audience and hoping to draw the home listening music sales market, perhaps after they had seen the film and wanted to hear the music again. Record sales of movie soundtracks became a viable subgenre to everyone's surprise.

13. On Mancini's lead, a host of other pop/jazz-oriented composers began to arrive on the movie scoring stages all over Hollywood—at first only visitors, but soon setting up shop for the same sorts of modern films that Mancini had been scoring: composers like Quincy Jones (*In the Heat of the Night*), Dave Grusin (*The Heart Is a Lonely Hunter*), John Barry (the *James Bond* franchise), Michel Legrand (*Thomas Crown Affair*), and Lalo Schifrin (*Mission: Impossible*).

14. Steven Spielberg (*Jaws*, *E.T.*), George Lucas (*Star Wars*), Martin Scorsese (*Mean Streets*, *Raging Bull*), Francis Ford Coppola (*The Godfather Trilogy*).

15. Minimalism—compositional style characterized by a relentlessly pulsing beat over which a simple repeating motif is placed that varies only slightly if at all, giving the impression of rotation more than progression, although some small forward movement can occur and the recognition of

that movement represents the drama of the piece. This is a style of music begun by La Monte Young in the early 1960s, taken up and made famous by such composers as Philip Glass, Terry Riley, and Steve Reich.

1. Elmer Bernstein

1. Arising out of the Great Depression, such folk singers as Woody Guthrie traveled around the country performing a repertoire of songs about the hardscrabble life of the hobo, the field-worker, the sharecropper, and freight-hopper. In time, as their music got better known, more established singers took over the "folk music" catalogue and moved into the mainstream of recording artists: singers like Pete Seeger and Joan Baez and Harry Belafonte made folk music an accepted genre in the recording industry, though it retained some level of the protest message with which it had begun, and when the civil rights movement spread across the United States in the 1960s, for a time folk music artists and their songs of discontent resurfaced into the national consciousness.

2. Composers and artists of all kinds across the spectrum of American music received summons from the House Un-American Activities Committee spearheaded by Senator Joseph McCarthy commanding appearances before the Senate to answer certain inquiries about their political activities and beliefs. The dreaded telegram read, "You are hereby directed to appear before this committee at 2:30 in Senate Room 357" and the mere rumor of questioning was enough to finish a composer, an actor, an agent in the business—at least, future work was hard to come by once the committee had identified you as a person of interest. In the end, McCarthy overplayed his hand and was censured by the Senate; the HUAC hearings ceased. But not before a number of careers were disrupted, curtailed, or ruined.

3. Ondes martenot—electronic keyboard instrument invented in 1928 using a single oscillator to produce pitches of about seven octaves, one at a time; its sound being a kind of swooping whistle with an ethereal feel to it—some say a ghostly distant sound. Composers like Messiaen and Jolivet made use of it in their mid-twentieth-century music. Film composers such as Elmer Bernstein and Richard Rodney Bennett have exploited it, both for its otherworldly connotations and the way it seems to imply memory recaptured.

4. Robert Mulligan, director *To Kill a Mockingbird, Summer of '42, The Other*.

5. Martha Coolidge, director *Ramblin' Rose, Lost in Yonkers, Tribute*.

6. Bazelon asks nearly all his fourteen interviewees how they feel as dramatic composers about what he called circa 1975 the "title song mania" of film producers—the penchant for demanding that a pop song lead off each

film and each score: a tune that could be exploited for record sales ahead of the movie—a tune that would then have to be reminded throughout whatever dramatic score the film might have. All narrative composers were against the practice. Nevertheless, a number of successful and valuable songs did result from certain films and did help the narratives onscreen: in the 1940s David Raksin's yearning melody in *Laura*, Dimitri Tiomkin's cowboy ballad "Do Not Forsake Me" in *High Noon* in the 1950s, and Henry Mancini's "Moon River" in *Breakfast at Tiffany's* in the 1960s. For a while, then, executives seeing the huge promotional value of a hit song attached to their film naturally sought to hire songwriters for their next picture and then to cram that song into their soundtrack wherever they could. This is the behavior that Bazelon begrudges here. Fortunately, the practice was mostly a passing fad, though there are still abuses. A well-wrought, well-placed song can also be a genuine help to a film and provide a good anchor for an otherwise dramatic narrative music score.

7. Politics and folk music.
8. Shorty Rogers (1924–1994), West Coast jazz musician, arranger, orchestrator.
9. *The Great Santini* (1979), directed by Lewis John Carlino.
10. Roy Harris (1898–1979), William Schuman (1910–1992).

2. Miklós Rózsa: Orthodoxy

1. Autobiography by Miklós Rózsa (1982).
2. Jacques Feyder, director *Knights without Armor* and *Le Grand Jeu*.
3. Alexander Korda, director *The Jungle Book* and *Thief of Bagdad*.
4. Selar Shaik Sabu (1924–1963).
5. Karlheinz Stockhausen (1928–2007).
6. *Madame Bovary*, directed by Vincente Minnelli (1949).
7. *Gesamtkunstwerk* = supposedly the ideal work of art embracing all forms at once—for instance, in a staged opera where a storyline is acted out through vocal and instrumental music, dance, visual art, and set design. It used to make people think of Wagner's cycle of *Ring* operas; then the cinema was supposed to be the fulfillment of the ideal: where story, music, visual backdrops, even dancelike movement were on display. Today it makes people think of Wagner's aesthetic, but what it really recalls is ancient Greek theater as the model for the blending of all the arts.
8. Salvador Dalí, surrealist artist whose images and dreamscapes were used as backdrops in the fantasy sequences of Hitchcock's *Spellbound* film to represent the Gregory Peck character's unbalanced mental state.

9. The first released movie music recording was the Miklós Rózsa score to the 1942 film *The Jungle Book*, a rerecording of the film score conducted by the composer with the film's star, Sabu, narrating the tale of the jungle boy Mowgli and his animal friends, each creature represented by a different orchestral motif in the score, somewhat like Prokofiev's previous 1936 symphonic work *Peter and the Wolf*. Rózsa's score, turned into a narrated suite and recorded in 3/42, was released as the first record album of a film score: Victor CS 073223/8 and CS 8206/8 in set DM 906.

3. David Raksin: The Provocateur

1. Charles Chaplin, director (1889–1977).
2. Alfred Newman, studio music director and composer (1900–1970).
3. Second Viennese School—the collective name given to that trio of composers (Schoenberg, Berg, Webern) from the turn of the twentieth century who composed in a style apart from traditional tonal centers using some form of Schoenberg's serial of twelve-tone method. Though they are often considered together, they wrote quiet differently: Schoenberg's serialism was strict but searching; Berg's was introverted and sensual; Webern's intellectual and often harsh. The two controversies that came out of this school of composition were the serial insistence on declaring no traditional key or tonal basis for each musical work and, conversely, the seeming desire and tendency (especially in Berg) to refer to, at least to recall, tonal relationships and melodic influences.
4. Johnny Mercer (1909–1976), lyricist and early radio performer; writer of hits with Harold Arlen (b. 1905), Duke Ellington (b. 1899), Henry Mancini (b. 1924), Jerome Kern (b. 1885), and Hoagy Carmichael (1899–1981).
5. Alex North, composer for *Spartacus* and *A Streetcar Named Desire* (1910–1991).
6. Plainchant—As Raksin has said about the unusual-looking procession of seven time signatures in this example, "I had been aiming for the kind of free melodic flow found in music arising from plainsong (a kind of rhythmically unmeasured melody that tries to meter out in specific beats the natural breaths and pauses and thrusts of a person's voice when speaking or singing; they are not always precise in duration; there is give and take to accommodate normal breathing and those variations can be figured into a carefully measured line of music" (as quoted in liner notes of RCA CD *David Raksin Conducts His Great Film Scores* 88697 81268 2).
7. On the limitations of film music (prejudice, skepticism), see Gorbman; Kalinak; Cooke, *Reader*.

8. Leonard Rosenman (1924–2008), *Rebel without a Cause, Cobweb, East of Eden, Fantastic Voyage*.

9. *Ben Casey*—prime time TV medical series starring Vince Edwards and Sam Jaffe; ran for five seasons from 1961 on American TV. Raksin's opening theme for the series written in a tense 5/4 time signature was recorded apart from the broadcast as a pop disc by pianist Roger Williams.

4. Jerome Moross: Americana to the Fore

1. *Wildflowers: Songs of Jerome Moross* CD produced by Susanna Moross Tarjan and Tommy Krasker featured five singers and seven-instrument ensemble in songs from Moross shows and revues, *Underworld, Golden Apple, Ballet Ballads, Gentlemen Be Seated*—PS Classics 2001.

2. The practice of reediting, basically rethinking, a film after it has been put together, thereby cutting into the music score track that has already been recorded had happened a lot to such composers as this book features: Raksin's story about movie stars toying with the recorded volume of his music even once it had been attached to the film; Elmer Bernstein having his music for *The Grifters* fragmented and tracked into different places in the film where it was not meant to go; Henry Mancini's experience having his symphonic score for *Lifeforce* sliced and altered as the unprepared filmmakers realized that their whole film was too slow and that maybe if they rushed Mancini's music cues around within the film it might create energy. The resulting chaos, of course, dealt a deathblow to the Mancini score—the one potential lifeforce in the whole film project. Other composers cited in this text experiencing score rejections after they had submitted their best efforts include Jerry Goldsmith (*Legend*), Richard Rodney Bennett (*The Go-Between*), Bernstein again (*Gangs of New York*), Michel Legrand (*Robin and Marian*), David Shire (*Kramer vs. Kramer*, though this time abandonment of the scoring was voluntary in that he believed the film was already as emotionally honest and intimate as it could be and any kind of commentary music would only be redundant).

3. *Wagon Train* began as a TV series on NBC in 1957 starring Ward Bond and lasting eight seasons, finishing over on ABC as a top-rated western.

4. George Rochberg (1918–2005). Former serial composer who switched to tonal composing after the death of his twenty-year-old son, seeming to appreciate the muse of melody in the Cold War world around him.

5. Collage style—compositional practice and then movement mimicking the graphic arts where newspaper clippings or bits of colored paper were pasted on canvas to create patterns and designs—in music, the wholesale borrowing of chunks of existing music combined with original composing to create a kind of quiltlike work that may begin with a composer's own

statement, then pass by a quote from Mozart or a crescendo from Copland, a lift from an old folk song, only to rejoin the original statement by the end. It is the plain inclusion of those musical quotes—not just references to existing music but actual excerpts incorporated, often without transition, that make the collage style almost more of a dramatic/theatrical gesture than an authentic musical one.

5. Interlude: Black Composers for Film—A Mini-History

1. Edward Kennedy (Duke) Ellington (1899–1974).
2. Will Vodery (1885–1951).
3. Black pianists/orchestrators Phil Moore (b. 1917) and Sy Oliver (b. 1910).
4. Ulysses Kay (1917–1995).
5. Composers who benefited from some of the US government employment aid programs through the Federal Music Project directed by Dr. Nikolai Sokoloff between 1933 and 1939—musicians such as Norman Dello Joio, Virgil Thomson, Marion Bauer, Paul Bowles, Henry Brant, Otto Luening, Darius Milhaud, the Kronos Quartet, and William Schuman.
6. Miles Davis (1926–1991), iconic jazz trumpeter known for free-form jazz solos and blending his improvisations with other ensembles like chamber players, rock musicians, and avant-garde elements.
7. John Lewis (1920–2001).
8. Quincy Jones (1933–present).
9. Sidney Lumet, director (1924–2011).
10. Terence Blanchard (1962–present).
11. Camara Kambon (1973–present).
12. Chanda Dancy (1978–present).

6. Interlude: Choral Music in Films—A Mini-History

1. The rules of diegetic music onscreen almost apply here in that formal choral music is almost expected to be associated with warmaking, marching armies, nationalistic causes, and one's final survey of a field of the dead after battle. In other words, although choral scoring can only be very gingerly done in most films for fear of drawing attention to itself, for war films there is an understanding that allows more leeway: the universe of battle onscreen seems to hold a place for the chorus of voices.
2. Michel Legrand to Stéphane Lerouge on CD Universal France 830/530 8464.

7. Henry Mancini: The Populist Movement

1. Chapters and musical examples: "The Essentials," "Saxophones," "Woodwinds," "Brass," "Show and Act Music," "The Rhythm Section," "Latin Instruments and Rhythms," "The Combo," "The String Section," "Conclusion."

2. More examples of Mancini instrumental miniatures: "Joanna" from *Peter Gunn*, "Theme for Losers" from *Me Natalie*, "Piano and Strings" from *Pink Panther*, "Elegant" from *The Party*, "Blue Mantilla" from *Mr. Lucky*, "Royal Waltz" from *The Great Race*, "Blackie's Tune" from *The Man Who Loved Women*, "Harry's Theme" from *Harry and Son*.

3. Some concert works: *Beaver Valley '37* (1969, three movements) and *Piece for Jazz Bassoon and Orchestra* (1981, in sonata form).

4. In each international style, Mancini takes the basic mode and scale of that culture—Japan in the first, a sort of pan-European in the second with an Italian indulgence, and only the most clichéd Arab theme line in the third—but personalizes them all so that while they seem convincing as representatives of the setting of their film, they seem, more importantly, sincere, memorable, respectable.

5. Leslie Bricusse (1931–2021).

6. Alan (b. 1925) and Marilyn (b. 1928) Bergman.

7. The famous memo from Welles about the fact that he wanted from a music score in *Touch of Evil* was often mentioned by Mancini in later years, probably because the ideas expressed in it were what he had wished to do all along. He had not seen it since those days but it says, in part, "It is very important that the usual rancheros and mariachi numbers should be avoided and the emphasis should go on Afro-Cuban rhythm numbers. Those few places where traditional Mexican music is wanted will be indicated by special notes. Also, a great deal of rock n' roll is called for. Because these numbers invariably back dialogue scenes, there should never be any time for vocals. This rock n' roll comes from radio loudspeakers, juke boxes and, in particular, the radio in the motel" (Brady 502).

8. Diegetic music—music on the soundtrack of a film whose source apparently comes from some element within the film story—a juke box that is visible, a street band, a symphony orchestra on stage, a singer or a combo in a club. In some special scenes where the scoring has been granted a particular task, that music which serves a routine function in the story can begin to become subtly entangled with the drama onscreen and can begin to intensify beyond the simple dance band it started out to be, becoming more and more excited by the action of the scene right along with the viewer. In that case, the reality of the diegetic scoring takes on a little unreality, the implications of the drama underway gradually taking over the setting and circumstance.

9. Glenn Miller—pop band leader traveling/performing overseas during World War II, lost at sea on a flight to move his orchestra to France for a

series of concerts in December 1944. On his disappearance, the organization was taken over by his right-hand man, Tex Beneke, who carried the band over into peace time in the United States, retaining many of the same players, including pianist/arranger Henry Mancini as the 1950s began.

10. Universal Studios Music Department. "Stocking" a movie soundtrack referred to the practice of scoring the film with a combination of original music composed within the studio music department and pulling existing music cues from the studio's library of past score examples, usually filed by type of scene: that is, romantic music, royal music, music for tension scenes, chase scenes, mysterioso cues, humorous cues, and so on. The assigned composer would then assemble a full score from these music cues so that the final product somewhat resembled a patchwork quilt and the studio orchestra would be assembled to record this amalgam as though it were a continuous piece. Usually the music credit onscreen would be assigned to the music department supervisor, though many hands were in the creation.

11. The film *Lifeforce* was a production of Cannon Films, one of the smaller companies, known for releasing limited-market film titles meant for matinee showings or for release directly to the home video markets rather than out into public theaters across the country. They tended to be genre titles aimed at very specific demographics: kung fu movies for that subgenre audience, salsa films for Spanish markets, copycat horror film titles, exploitation comedies, and derivative sci-fi films like *Lifeforce*.

12. The *Lifeforce* director, Tobe Hooper, had been in trouble, not knowing how to finish his earlier film, *Poltergeist*, and so Cannon was one of the few production houses open to him. Again, his indecision and Cannon's unsubtle method of trying to produce films quickly (and if there are any difficulties, retreat, recut, rerelease) gave *Lifeforce* a shaky premiere. The one to suffer the most was probably Mancini, who had joined the project because he saw a chance to write some broad descriptive music for an adventure film. But in the end, he would see his carefully crafted symphonic score slashed into pieces to accommodate various new versions of the movie. In fairness to Golan and Globus, the men behind Cannon, their company had started out as a legitimate producer of first-rate films in Israel, including two Oscar-nominated dramas, *I Love You Rosa* and *The House on Chelouche Street* released in Hebrew in the early 1970s. The later subgenre productions were the result of a subsequent production/marketing plan aimed at shipping out a higher quantity of cheaper product, realizing a fast return, and plowing the profits back into a revolving catalogue of titles at Cannon.

13. Even as Mancini puzzled what to do with the opening title music for *The White Dawn* and the director Philip Kaufman cut into the musical sequence he had provided, the question remained as to what sorts of indigenous music might be scored for the various scenes depicting Eskimo village life. He admitted, "I was concerned what to do with Inuit Eskimo music.

I found that about all they had in the way of music was the human voice (which is, of course, the first instrument) and some strange drums made of hoops stretched with walrus or seal bladders." And yet, Mancini seized on a chant voiced by an elderly tribeswoman in the film and recreated the vocal line as a theme of migration throughout the film's score. "Surprisingly, she was right on pitch with our European tempered scale," Mancini observed later. "So much so that I could take the woman's voice and put orchestra behind it. She was perfectly in tune with our system and with herself" (CD Booklet notes by John Takis, Intrada Label SC 253).

14. Had the filmmakers left Mancini's original concept for the opening of *The White Dawn*, their film would have enjoyed a ten-to-twelve-minute musical overture consisting of the adventurous whale hunt allegro, then the mysterious lost-in-the-ice-world music written for high, thin pipes answered by deep brass passages and sustained by a tremulous pulse as the three shipwrecked sailors trek out into the unknown. Instead, the filmmakers decided they wanted the soundtrack to be more directly threatening there—to be scary in itself. Mancini's compromise, right then and there in the dubbing studio, was to substitute a series of weird percussive sounds, a scraped gong, a rubber ball tapping against piano strings, and a bevy of electronic sounds. The director pronounced himself satisfied: the assembled weirdness was just unsettling enough to worry the viewer and underline the sailors' plight. What I wish is that, if they insisted on "fixing" the track there, they would have left Mancini's music where it was and perhaps put those otherworldly sounds over it. Then they would have had their threatening atmosphere and their narrative music score intact.

15. As an experienced director of musical films from way back (*The Band Wagon*, *Seven Brides for Seven Brothers*), Stanley Donen had highly sensitive antennae against any kind of indulgent emotion onscreen or in music. Mancini's first instinct in scoring this tale of a rocky marriage, *Two for the Road*, and trying to empathize with the character played by Audrey Hepburn, was to write a slow, saddening theme for her—something that knows this young couple is their own worst enemy as they bicker and cheat, accuse and regret while making the Grand Tour of Europe and reminiscing about their younger days. Donen objected and Mancini, properly chastened, came back with a more complex song structure in F-sharp minor, freer-roaming over two long lines and harmonically more interesting than the dour tune that had first occurred to him. He gave it a rolling meter, too, for the road.

16. Stéphane Grappelli (1908–1997).

8. Laurence Rosenthal: More than Respect

1. Nadia Boulanger (1887–1979).

2. *The Miracle Worker*, a 1956 play by William Gibson and 1962 film by Arthur Penn set in 1880s Alabama about the deaf-blind student Helen Keller and her teacher, Annie Sullivan.

3. Douglas Allanbrook (1921–2003) and Paul Des Marais (1920–2011).

4. "Papa Doc" Duvalier, self-proclaimed president of Haiti and leader of a personality cult from 1957 to 1971. Subject of the play *The Comedians* by Graham Greene about European ex-patriots living there during his reign.

5. Thomas de Hartmann, Ukrainian composer (1884–1956) and disciple of mystic teacher of Armenian and Greek descent Gurdjieff (1866–1949).

6. The question is controversial when a composer repeatedly produces similar sounds and familiar modulations in his or her work whether that is a legitimate reflection of a personal language such as everyone has to oneself or the limitation of a small vocabulary. Certainly Mozart and Beethoven had familiar gestures in their music to which they referred on occasion; Ravel and Copland and Schubert all turned to familiar phrases and reconciliations sometimes in completing a musical line. But when a sameness across one's own repertoire starts to be noticed, the question of originality, of versatility, begins to be asked.

7. Although the formidable composer Leonard Rosenman had scored the first film of this duo, *A Man Called Horse*, with authentic songs and dance motifs of the Plains Indians, it was Laurence Rosenthal's desire to chart his own original research for the similar sequel film, *Return of a Man Called Horse*. To writer John Takis, he has explained, "Director Irvin Kershner was . . . voluble, articulate, dynamic . . . [and] the influence of the extraordinary recordings I was given to work with, actual performances by Lakota chiefs of their traditional chants, was a huge factor in my work on the score. I often literally blended these recordings with my own music, enveloping them in an orchestral texture in which neither would have been complete without the other" (Intrada CD 314).

9. Richard Rodney Bennett: The Complete Musician

1. The experience of concert composers like Aaron Copland hoping to break into Hollywood to score a motion picture or two is chronicled in Pollack 336–51. At the same time, up-and-coming concert composers like the young Leonard Rosenman who had been receiving critical acclaim and promising prospects for his avant-garde music reported that, as soon as it was known that he also spent some of his time writing movie music, invitations to perform his concert works and commissions to create new ones virtually dried up. It was as though he had betrayed some trust and gone over into some enemy camp.

2. Pierre Boulez (1925–2016), composer, conductor, teacher.

3. One good summary of Bennett's serial days comes from Peter G. Davis, who remarked about RRB's Symphony no. 2, "Bennett had supplied only the briefest analysis of the symphony in the program notes, but even with this sketch as a guide, one could easily follow his line of thought as one structural event succeeded another with admirable inevitability. Such a readily comprehensible, closely reasoned, articulate score is a rarity among latter-day serialists—especially, it seems, among those with such strong cravings for tonality as Bennett" (*Musical America* [April 1968], 19).

4. On the revival of Bennett's serial opera *The Mines of Sulphur* but his own drift, over the years, toward more tonal music, even including a repertoire of popular songs, see *New York Times* (21 October 2005), B1–4.

5. *The Nanny*, 1965 film by Seth Holt in which Bette Davis plays a domestic suspected of murder and Bennett's polite harpsichord-led score refuses to take sides.

10. Interlude: The Exasperating Michel Legrand

1. This was written on the occasion of Legrand's typically rash announcement that he wanted to tour eighty-five cities in his eighty-fifth year. After all, he would probably be up and playing at the piano anyway if he were home so, after such a long life of public concertizing, why not share the same music with a few hundred guests?

2. Ross defines Boulanger's influence, whether on Legrand or Copland or whomever, as "the aesthetic of the twenties: the revolt against Germanic grandiosity, the yen for lucidity and grace, the cultivation of Baroque and Classical forms" (Ross 291). See also Rosenstiel for a general Boulanger biography.

3. French New Wave (Nouvelle Vague) critic/filmmaker Alexandre Astruc's call for a "new wave" in cinema expression—a visual language that might be just as rich and personal as an essay or a novel—was answered in 1959 with a number of French directors turning out their first films in especially original styles. Men like Godard, Truffaut, Demy released films like *The 400 Blows* and *Breathless*, creating a whole new market for "art house" cinema—films that were as much about their own visual style as about the story onscreen. Legrand has said of the New Wave movement, "The Nouvelle Vague was a well-defined area in my life. It was an age of youth, freedom, invention. . . . We had the feeling we were starting from scratch, working without any commercial or logistic sense, art for art's sake, imagination was in charge . . . [for instance] Godard rolled up to my house saying 'Here, I've got a script,' and pulled this screwed-up ball of paper out of his pants

pocket, saying already 'I think I want a musical theme with eleven variations. Can you do that?'" (SACEM 983-9579).

13. David Shire: Setting the Stage

1. *Saturday Night Fever* (1977) was one of the best-selling soundtrack albums of its day featuring the several hits songs of the Bee Gees, but the film told a story of a Brooklyn youth whose life only seemed to come alive when he could get out on the dance floor of the local disco. Some of that broader scene-setting instrumental music was written by Shire, including a four-minute pop miniature called "Manhattan Skyline."

2. Spike Jones (b. 1911) was the leader of a so-called spoof band that was active on radio and recordings taking advantage of wacky instrumentations and comic songs.

3. Since the film of *The Big Bus* was, from the start, one big parody—in this case a knowing tease of the then-craze of melodramatic "disaster films"—the most important question a composer should ask the director at the beginning of the assignment is the same question that ought to be asked every time any soundtrack is discussed: What do you want music to do for this scene, for this film? In this case, the idea was to tease the disaster genre itself: big crescendos and dramatic suspensions in the music as though something big is about to happen, but then no fulfillment. That was the ongoing joke of the scoring here (and it included an overly romantic love theme that played ridiculously behind the laughably awkward love dialogue).

4. As Shire's father was a popular dance band leader in their native Buffalo, New York, David was seriously influenced by him to follow a musical career and penned both music and lyrics to the song "If I Sing" in tribute to him. It appears in the Shire-Maltby show *Closer than Ever* and, written for piano, a trained tenor voice, and solo French horn, it says, "My father's pride was in his hands; the piano was his soul. I watched in wonder as he played show tunes, miles off from rock 'n roll. What he loved he taught me; now music's what I do. And often when I'm writing, in my hands Dad's there too. If I sing, you are the music; if I fly you're why I'm good; if my hands can find some magic, you're the one who said they could."

5. The show *Funny Girl* is the 1964 stage musical written around the life of entertainer Fanny Brice with music by Jule Styne and lyrics by Bob Merrill. Singer Barbra Streisand rode to fame as star of the show and film.

6. The show *Ain't Misbehavin'* is the 1930s stage musical (mentioned in Shire's lifetime as a 1978 revival) with music and lyrics by café pianist Fats Waller.

7. The several kinds of Broadway shows developed across the twentieth century were the book musical that told a single story decorated by stand-alone songs (in the more sophisticated shows, those songs were not just entertainments but helped tell the story or expressed the characters on stage), the revue that was generally just a collection of songs performed by an ensemble cast not attempting to develop a storyline, and eventually the sung-through show whose roots go back to operetta. The chief difference between a traditional Broadway musical and a sung-through show is that, in the former, the stage play (called "the book") is acted out in dialogue and any songs are performed separately after a pause and applause, while in the latter form of show even most of the dialogue that tells the story is delivered in music—sung narrative that spans between set songs. This narrative vocal line, which may refer to but isn't directly part of the show's main songs, is called "recitative" and is a practice from opera through operetta. Late twentieth-century Broadway musicals by Stephen Sondheim often ventured into this more sophisticated level of composing, and Sondheim was always encouraging when any Shire-Maltby show dared to go there, even a little.

8. This is a difficult topic. I was not urging a return to the hyperdescriptive kinds of scoring done in the 1940s where every movement of the villain or every thought of the heroine is underlined in the music score, nor even the visually descriptive scoring of the 1960s where the gunshot or the starburst is sounded by the orchestra. Nor do I mean to denigrate a music score that just lays an ambient atmosphere behind the whole film, so long as that atmosphere is saying something continuous about the people or plot we are watching. There are different ways that music can help a film. The practice of creating a single motto—a theme or a tonal phrase—and then bringing it back in variations throughout a film can be most effective as a narrative device—variations matching the mood changes onscreen. All these styles of musicmaking, as Shire says, remain legitimate scoring methods to this day . . . and that includes the fully descriptive, orchestrally detailed composition that could stand apart from the film as a concert piece, if anyone cares to write such a thing these days—provided, of course, it truly does serve its film first.

14. Rachel Portman: The Storyteller

1. Where are the prominent women composers for film or the concert hall? Successful concert composers include Judith Weir, Kaija Saariaho, Elizabeth Maconchy, Sofia Gubaidulina, Augusta Reed Thomas. In films, women such as Anne Dudley, Wendy Carlos, the aforementioned Rachel Portman, Dara Taylor, Kathryn Bostic, Tamar-kali, Amanda Jones, have made their presences known.

2. *The Cider House Rules* (1999), *Chocolat* (2000), *The Joy Luck Club* (1993), *Snow Flower* (2019), *Four Days in July* (TV-84), *Life Is Sweet* (1990).

3. Whether it is courageous or foolish for a film director to let the music score "make its own contribution" to the film, contributing its own personality and perhaps taking it in some private direction, it is certainly risky. Music can be tremendously influential with an audience. Music that overplays the emotion of a scene can kill the feeling; nostalgic music takes the audience one way while modernist tones give the whole film an analytical interpretation. Many directors maintain absolute control over what kind of music goes with every scene; those are usually the films that end up with very little music at all. And yet, when a filmmaker can meet with a creative composer and take the film both seriously and personally, some impressive screen results (and some first-class music) can emerge.

15. Jermaine Stegall: For a Digital Age

1. About Digital Performer—a DAW (digital audio workstation) and music sequencer software package originally from 1985 for Apple and Microsoft Windows platforms. By 2000, it allowed recording, mixing, and mastering of audio, and every few years thereafter, new capabilities were added so that by version 10 in 2019 there was a fifteen-gig instrument sound-bank, a time/pitch audio stretching feature, and signal triggering functions—all of this to aid the home-based music producer, basic enough to be within a layperson's reach but refined enough for commercial purposes.

2. About Cubase—a more advanced DAW (digital audio workstation) developed for music and MIDI arranging, editing, and recording released first in 1989. It can be used to edit and sequence audio signals coming from any external sound source whether synthetically (electronic generator) or acoustically (instrumental or vocal sounds coming from a microphone) produced. Some of the subtleties that composers like are that it can keep track of chord changes, automatically harmonize audio, create changes to an instrument's articulation and dynamics, plus alter volume and filtering to selected tracks of the recording while leaving others alone. By 2020, so-called Cubasis 3 was made adaptable to Android tablets and a range of smartphones.

16. Interlude: A Pair of Glasses— Philip Glass versus Paul Glass

1. Paul Glass (1934–).
2. Philip Glass (1937–).

17. Interlude: The New Millennium—Enter Ex-Rockers

1. Disasterpeace is all but left behind as he tackles dramatic film music. His history producing video game music and sound design for theater presentations was of use in approaching screen storytelling and atmospheres but I was wondering to what extent that other name that kept coming up next to his credit as orchestrator, Kyle Newmaster, was influencing the scoring. Having seen my question, Vreeland answered, "Thx for the review. Kyle did play a large role in the score. He led orchestration and I relied on his experience for logistics, team assembly, and as a resource/sounding board, but I wrote and arranged all the music myself. Being new to it, it was not without great difficulty!"

2. *King Charles III* as a stage play by Mike Bartlett premiered in 2014 and, by 2022, it was oddly mirroring reality as, indeed, Queen Elizabeth II did pass away as in the play, leaving Charles to be king of a rather fractious kingdom, including some of the same controversies that are fictionalized on stage about a not-so-free press and about the abdication, as it were—really, the resignation under protest—of Prince Harry from the royal family to go off with his nonroyal woman. Bartlett was never trying to predict or even reflect history, but he did sharply place the grindings of national politics and public society, as did Shakespeare, whom this play references, into the frame of All Time. So did the stately-but-anxious music score of Jocelyn Pook.

18. John Williams: Another Birthday Toast

1. John Williams on "Previn and the Pittsburgh," PBS-TV Network, October 1977.
2. André Previn (1929–2019).
3. *Monsignor* (1982), *The Patriot* (2000), *Born on the Fourth of July* (1989).
4. Williams had signed on as the nineteenth conductor of the Boston Pops Orchestra, succeeding the famous Arthur Fiedler, in 1980. The relationship was one of mutual respect through most of his tenure there, although there did develop a period within the orchestra after a few years where discipline was breaking down, where they weren't taking Williams's leadership as seriously as before. Indeed, it would get to the point where, during a June 12, 1980, rehearsal of a short patriotic anthem that Williams had written for a holiday concert, one player was heard disparaging the piece, and the usually mild-mannered Williams walked off in exasperation to resign the next day. The *Boston Globe* reported the orchestra's principal clarinetist Pasquale Cardillo as saying, "We did not drive Williams away . . . [but the

rehearsal] was close to intermission. He stopped the orchestra because there was talking going on. There was inattentiveness. People were supposed to be playing. I knew it was noisy." The orchestra returned from the twenty-minute break and took up Williams's own composition, *America, the Dream Goes On*. When it was concluded, there was hissing from some unidentified orchestra member. Cardillo explained, "That happens not only in the Pops but in the Symphony. There are things that I play that I detest." Symphony players sometimes disparage the sorts of "pops" material they are asked to play in these less-than-classical concerts and such prejudice can sometimes spill over as complaint. In truth, Williams's tenure with the Pops encompassed a lot more respectable concert material than the thin arrangements and accompaniments they had often had to play under Fiedler's baton. Still, the personal nature of the orchestra's rebuke stung. Williams's resignation letter came the next day. But the coming season was going to be the one hundredth anniversary of the Pops Orchestra and management very much wanted Williams to be in place for all the celebration events to come. There are those who claim that the whole incident was really just a backstage ploy to earn new contracts but, in any case, apologies were offered, fences were mended, Williams agreed to stay on at least through the centennial events. Instead, he ended up staying through 1993 when he officially retired from the organization—on good terms.

5. *Empire of the Sun* (1987), *Always* (1989), *Heartbeeps* (1981), *Story of a Woman* (1969).

Works Cited or Recommended

Books

Abel, Richard, and Rick Altman, eds. *The Sounds of Early Cinema*. Bloomington: University of Indiana Press, 2001.

Adorno, Theodor, and Hans Eisler. *Composing for the Films*. London: Athlone Press, 1947, 1994.

Antheil, George. *Bad Boy of Music*. New York: Da Capo Press, 1981.

Bazelon, Irwin. *Knowing the Score: Notes on Film Music*. New York: Van Nostrand Reinhold, 1975.

Bellis, Richard. *Emerging Film Composers: Introduction to the People, Problems, and Psychology of the Film Music Business*. Self-published, 2007.

Bernstein, Elmer. *Film Music Notebook: A Complete Collection of the Quarterly Journal*. Sherman Oaks, CA: Film Music Society, 2004.

Bernstein, Leonard. *The Unanswered Question: Six Talks at Harvard*. Cambridge, MA: Harvard University Press, 1976.

Bick, Sally. *Unsettled Scores: Politics, History, and Film Music of Copland and Eisler*. Urbana: University of Illinois Press, 2019.

Brady, Frank. *Citizen Welles*. New York: Charles Scribner's Son, 1989.

Brown, Royal S. *Overtones and Undertones: Reading Film Music*. Berkeley: University of California Press, 1994.

Buhler, James, and David Neumeyer. *Hearing the Movies: Music and Sound in Film History*. Oxford: Oxford University Press, 2015.

Buhler, James, and Hannah Lewis. *Voicing the Cinema: Film Music and the Integrated Soundtrack*. Urbana: University of Illinois Press, 2020.

Burlingame, Jon. *Mancini Music for TV's Peter Gunn*. New York: Bear Manor Media, 2024.

———. *Music of James Bond*. Oxford: University of Oxford Press, 2012.

———. *Music for Prime Time: A History of American Television Themes and Scoring* [update of *TV's Biggest Hits*]. Oxford: University of Oxford Press, 2023.

———. *Sound and Vision: Sixty Years of Motion Picture Soundtracks.* New York: Billboard Books, 2000.
———. *TV's Biggest Hits.* New York: Schirmer Books, 1996.
Burt, George. *The Art of Film Music.* Boston, MA: Northeastern University Press, 1994.
Cameron, Evan William. *Sound and the Cinema* [chapter on Herrmann]. Pleasantville, NY: Redgrave, 1980.
Caps, John. *Crisis Music: The Life-and-Times of Six Twentieth-Century Composers* [includes mention of film music of Honegger, Takemitsu, Pärt]. Brighton, UK: Sussex Academic Press, 2022; reprint, Liverpool University Press, 2023.
———. *Henry Mancini: Reinventing Film Music.* Urbana: University of Illinois Press, 2012.
Cooke, Mervyn. *A History of Film Music.* Cambridge: Cambridge University Press, 2008.
———. *The Hollywood Film Music Reader.* Oxford: University of Oxford Press, 2010.
Copland, Aaron. *Our New Music.* New York: McGraw Hill, 1941.
———. *What to Listen for in Music.* New York: Penguin Putnam, 1939, 1999.
Darby, William, Jack Du Bois. *American Film Music.* Jefferson, NC: McFarland, 1990.
Davis, Richard. *Complete Guide to Film Scoring, Second Edition.* Boston, MA: Berklee Press, 2010.
DesJardins, Christian. *Inside Film Music: Composers Speak.* Beverly Hills, CA: Silman-James Press, 2003.
Dickinson, Kay. *Moving Music: A Film Reader.* London: Routledge, 2003.
Doherty, Thomas Patrick. *Cold War, Cool Medium: Television, McCarthyism, and American Culture.* New York: Columbia University Press, 2005.
Evans, Mark. *Soundtrack: Music of the Movies.* New York: Hopkinson and Blake, 1975.
Gorbman, Claudia. *Unheard Melodies: Narrative Film Music.* Bloomington: Indiana University Press, 1987.
Hagen, Earle. *Advanced Techniques of Film Scoring.* Winona, MN: Alfred Music, 1990.
Halberstam, David. *The Fifties.* New York: Villard Books, 1993.
Hill, Andy. *Scoring the Screen: The Secret Language of Film Music.* Winona, MN: Hal Leonard Music, 2017.
Hoover, Tom. *Keeping Score: Interviews with Top Film, Television, and Game Music Composers.* Boston: Cengage Learning, 2009.
Hubbert, Julie. *Celluloid Symphonies: Texts and Contexts in Film Music History.* Berkeley: University of California Press, 2011.
Kalinak, Kathryn. *Settling the Score: Music and the Classical Hollywood Film.* Madison: University of Wisconsin Press, 1992.

Karlin, Fred, and Rayburn Wright. *On the Track: A Guide to Contemporary Film Scoring*. New York: Schirmer Trade Books, 1990, 2004.

Kompanek, Sonny. *From Score to Screen: Sequences, Scores, and Second Thoughts—The New Film Scoring Process*. New York: Schirmer Trade Books, 2004.

Kracauer, Siegfried. *Theory of Film*. New York: Oxford University Press, 1960; reprint Princeton University Press, 1997.

LaFave, Kenneth. *Experiencing Film Music: A Listener's Companion*. Lanham, MD: Rowman & Littlefield, 2017.

Larson, Randall. *Musique Fantastique*. Metuchen, NJ: Scarecrow Press, 1985.

Limbacher, James L. *Film Music: From Violins to Video*. Metuchen, NJ: Scarecrow Press, 1974.

Lumet, Sidney. *Making Movies*. London: Bloomsbury, 1995.

MacDonald, Lawrence E. *The Invisible Art of Film Music*. Lanham, MD: Rowman & Littlefield, 2013.

McCarty, Clifford. *Film Composers in America*. New York: Oxford University Press, 2000.

Mancini, Henry. *Sounds and Scores: A Practical Guide to Orchestration*. Northridge, CA: Northridge Press, 1962, 1967.

Mancini, Henry, with Gene Lees. *Did They Mention the Music?* Chicago: Contemporary Books, 1989.

Meredith, Anthony. *Richard Rodney Bennett: The Complete Musician*. New York: Omnibus Press, 2010.

Morgan, David. *Knowing the Score: Composers Talk*. New York: Harper Collins, 2000.

Navasky, Victor S. *Naming Names: McCarthyism in the Fifties*. New York: Penguin, 1980.

Palmer, Christopher. *The Composer in Hollywood*. London: Marion Boyars, 1990.

Pollack, Howard. *Aaron Copland: The Life and Work of an Uncommon Man*. Urbana: University of Illinois Press, 1999, 2000.

Prendergast, Roy M. *Film Music: A Neglected Art*. New York: W. W. Norton, 1977, 1992.

Previn, André. *No Minor Chords: My Days in Hollywood*. New York: Doubleday, 1991.

Rapee, Erno. *Motion Picture Moods for Pianists and Organists*. New York: Schirmer, 1924.

Rosenstiel, Léonie. *Nadia Boulanger: A Life in Music*. New York: W. W. Norton, 1982.

Ross, Alex. *The Rest Is Noise: Listening to the Twentieth Century*. New York: Picador 2007.

Rózsa, Miklós. *Double Life: The Autobiography of Miklós Rózsa*. New York: Hippocrene Books, 1982.

Schelle, Michael. *The Score: Interviews with Film Composers*. Beverly Hills, CA: Silman-James Press, 1999.
Schifrin, Lalo. *Music Composition for Film and Television*. Boston, MA: Berklee Press, 2011.
Smith, Steven C. *A Heart at Fire's Center: The Life and Music of Bernard Herrmann*. Berkeley: University of California Press, 1991.
Thomas, Tony. *The Film Score: The Art and Craft of Movie Music*. Burbank, CA: Riverwood Press, 1991.
———. *Music for the Movies*. South Brunswick, NJ: A. S. Barnes, 1973.
Tiomkin, Dimitri, with Prosper Buranelli. *Please Don't Hate Me!* New York: Doubleday, 1959.
Wegele, Peter. *Max Steiner*. Oxford: Oxford University Press, 2015.
Wescott, Steven D. *A Comprehensive Bibliography of Music for Film and Television*. Detroit: Information Coordinators, 1985.
Wierzbicki, James. *Music in the Age of Anxiety: American Music in the Fifties*. Urbana: University of Illinois Press, 2016.

Related Articles

Alwyn, William. "How Not to Write Film Music." *British Film Academy Journal* (Autumn 1954).
Antheil, George. "Hollywood Composer." *Atlantic Monthly* 165 (February 1940).
Bernstein, Elmer. "Whatever Happened to Great Movie Music?" *High Fidelity/Musical America* (July 1972): 55–58.
Bradley, Scott. "Personality on the Soundtrack." *Music Educator's Journal* 33, no. 3 (January 1947): 28–29.
Caps, John. "Crossing the Line: Why Serious Opera Composers Write Film Music." *New York City Opera: Opera Notes* (October 2005).
———. "Running Track: Fifty Scores from World Cinema." *Film International* (January 2011): 21–29.
———. "Soundtracks 101: Essential Movie Music, a Listener's Guide." *Film Comment* (November/December 2003): 31–49.
———. "The Surprising Breakthrough of Everyone's Third Symphony." *Music-Web International: The Boston Intelligencer* (March 2018).
Dahl, Ingolf. "Igor Stravinsky on Film Music." *Musical Digest* (1946). Archive copyright through Reichhold.
———. "Notes on Cartoon Music." *Film Music Notes* 8, no. 5 (May–June 1949): 3–13.
Dyer, Richard. "Making 'Star Wars' Sing Again." *Film Score Monthly* 4, no. 5 (June 1999): 18–21.

Farach-Colton, Andrew. "Special Music for the Silver Screen." *Gramophone Presents Film Music* 5 (January 2024): 30–33. gramophone.co.uk.

Frith, Simon. "Mood Music: Inquiry into Narrative Film Music." *Screen* 25, no. 3 (1984): 78–87.

Gorbman, Claudia. "The State of Film Music Criticism." *Cinéaste* 21, nos. 1 and 2 (1995): 72–75.

Handzo, Stephen. "The Golden Age of Film Music." *Cinéaste* 21, nos. 1 and 2 (1995): 46–55.

Hasan, Mark Richard. "King of Hip: A Quincy Jones Retrospective." *Film Score Monthly* 6, no. 8 (September 2001): 16–23.

Phillips, James. "A Touch of Elegance: Film Music of RR Bennett." *Film Score Monthly* 7, no. 2 (February 2002): 24–28.

Sternfeld, Frederick W. "On Friedhofer's *The Best Years of Our Lives*." *Musical Quarterly* 33 (1947): 517–32.

Stravinsky, Igor. *Musical Digest* 28 (September 1946): 4–5, 35–36.

Tobias, James. "Cinema, Scored: Toward a Comparative Methodology." *Film Quarterly* 57, no. 2 (2003): 26–36.

Winkler, Max. "The Origin of Film Music." *Films in Review* 2, no. 10 (December 1951): 34–42.

Private Music Society Journals

The Cue Sheet (Journal of the Society for the Preservation of Film Music):
5, no. 3—"It Started with Saint-Saëns," by Tony Thomas.
6, no. 2—"Where Are the Women Composers?," by Liz Shropshire.
7, no. 3—"Interview with (Orchestrator) Herbert Spencer," by Carl Johnson.

Film Music Notebook (Journal of "Elmer Bernstein's Film Music Collection"):
Autumn 1974—"Whatever Became of Movie Music?," by David Raksin.
Summer 1975—"Bernard Herrmann: Unauthorized Bio-Sketch," by Fred Steiner.
Winter 1978—"Aesthetics of Film Scoring," by Elmer Bernstein.

Log of Composer/Author Contacts and Correspondence

Conducted over a period of decades, these interviews and contacts have fallen into periods that somewhat follow the chronology of this collection: **part 2** "golden age" composers were interviewed in the 1970s about their earlier careers; **part 3** composers by this book's outline were approached somewhat later into the 1980s and 1990s; **part 4** "successor generation" figures conversed and corresponded with the author well into the 2000s—all in all, a nearly fifty-year span of movie history and composer encounters.

Elmer Bernstein: ongoing correspondence through 2000; formal interviews from July 1979 and February 1984.

Miklós Rózsa: correspondence 24 December 1976, 10 July 1976, 11 September 1975, 21 May 1975, and phone introduction from April 1975.

David Raksin: from 10 July 1979 interview.

Jerome Moross: from 31 August 1979 interview and ongoing correspondence.

Camara Kambon: correspondence/contacts March 2023.

Henry Mancini: interviews from 5 May 1992, 1, 3, 8, 21 April 1992, 15 October 1976, 18 August 1976, and ongoing correspondence through 1992.

Laurence Rosenthal: from correspondence April, September, and October 2023 and scattered through 2016 and 2018; interviews September 1986, March 1985, September and October 1981.

Steven Bramson: correspondence April and May 2023.

Richard Rodney Bennett: from interviews September 2005, May 1976, and ongoing correspondence from 1977 to 1981.

David Shire: from correspondence March and April 2023; June and August 2022; September, October, and December 2021; February and April 1990; March and April 1986; and 1978–1984. Interviews 17 February 1990 and 19 July 1977.

Rachel Portman: from interview 5 October 2005.

Jermaine Stegall: from correspondence through November and December 2022.

Rich Vreeland: from correspondence 7 January 2024.

John Williams: from correspondence through 1990s and interview January and March 1976.

Index

10 (Mancini), 135, 157–58
100 Rifles (Goldsmith), 248
114 Songs (concert work-Ives), 93
2001-A Space Odyssey (film), 229
Abels, Michael, 296
Abyss, The (Silvestri), 125
Adventures of Don Quixote (Legrand-TV), 218
Adventures of Huckleberry Finn (Moross), 89, 100
Adventures of Mark Twain (Steiner), 10
Adventures of Robin Hood (Korngold), 5, 11
Age of Innocence, The (Bernstein), 27
Aiken, Conrad, 299–300
Ain't Misbehavin' (stage musical-Domino), 270
Airplane (Bernstein), 27, 44
Airport (Newman), 330
Albright, Lola, 155
Alcoa Presents (Williams-TV), 324
Alexander Nevsky (Prokofiev), 8, 9, 58, 124, 335
Alien (Goldsmith), 150
Alliance for Women Composers, 231, 234

All That Money Can Buy {aka Devil and Daniel Webster} (Herrmann), 14
All the King's Men (children's opera-Bennett), 282
All the President's Men (Shire), 256, 261–62
Allen, Dede (film editor), 106
Allen, Woody, 306
Allanbrook, Douglas, 170, 353n3
Alpine Symphony (concert work-Strauss), 326
Altman, Robert (director), 329
Always (Williams), 337, 359n6
Alwyn, William, 8, 226
Amahl and the Night Visitors (opera-Menotti), 282
Amants du Tage, Les (Legrand), 217
Amazing Howard Hughes, The (Rosenthal-TV), 163–64
Amelia Earhart (Shire-TV), 260
America: The Dream Goes On (concert work-Williams), 336
American Fiction (Karpman), 231
American History X (Dudley), 231
Amérique Insolite, L' (Legrand), 218, 220

Amistad (Williams), 128–29, 339
Amour (stage musical-Legrand), 220
Anastasia (Rosenthal-TV), 163, 189
Anatomy of a Murder (Ellington), 100, 109–10
Andrews, Julie, 158–59
Angela's Ashes (Williams), 15, 339
Anthony Adverse (Korngold), 11
Any Given Sunday (Kambon), 118
Apollo 13 (Horner), 292
Appalachian Autumn (Shire-TV), 258, 260
Arabesque (Mancini), 136
Arlen, Harold, 137, 192, 196, 347n4
Asphalt Jungle, The (Rozsa), 54
Astaire, Fred, 156
Auric, Georges, 8
avant garde music influences, 2, 13, 33, 47, 55, 67, 78, 100, 113, 160, 193, 200, 209, 222, 225, 264–65, 306, 328, 329, 349n6, 353n1

Baby (stage musical-Shire), 257
Bach, J. S., 7, 62, 113, 162, 209, 216, 228, 258, 302–304
Bacharach, Burt, 125
Bachelor Flat (Williams), 323
Bachelor in Paradise (Mancini), 141
Bad and the Beautiful, The (Raksin), 13, 68, 79, 80
Bakshi, Ralph (director), 129
Ballad of Baby Doe (opera-Douglas Moore), 96
Ballard, Carroll (director), 231
Ballet Ballads (stage show-Moross), 89, 92, 95, 348n
Barry, John, 15, 124, 126, 341, 344n
Bartlett, Mike, 313–15, 358n
Bartók, Bela, 52–53, 56, 144, 171, 229, 243, 246
Basic Instinct (Goldsmith), 248
Batman (Elfman), 230

Batman animated (Walker), 230
Bay of Angels [*La Baie des Anges*] (Legrand), 210
Bazelon, Irwin, 3, 240, 301, 306, 343n1, 2, 345n6
Beau Fixe (Legrand), 217
Beaver Valley '37 (concert work-Mancini), 136, 350n3
Because They're Young (Williams), 323
Becket (Rosenthal), 162, 176
Bed and Breakfast (Shire), 256, 258
Beethoven, Ludwig van, 168, 229, 353n6
Beloved (Portman), 277
Beltrami, Marco, 293, 297
Belushi, John, 44
Ben Casey (Raksin-TV), 84–85
Beneke, Tex, 144, 351n9
Ben-Hur (Rozsa), 13, 53, 57, 59, 60
Bennett, Richard Rodney, 80–81, 163, 191–213, 218, 222–23, 225, 237, 282, 345n3, 348n2, 354n3, 4, 5
Bennett, Robert Russell, 198
Benny & Joon (Portman), 277
Bent (Glass), 302
Benton, Robert (director), 258, 279
Berg, Alban, 67–68, 220, 347n
Bergman, Alan and Marilyn, 137, 350n6
Berklee College of Music, 117
Berlioz, Hector, 54–55, 334
Bernstein, Elmer, 14, 23–48, 69, 98, 100, 112, 126, 143, 198, 240, 243, 244, 325, 345n3, 348n2
Bernstein, Leonard, 52, 91, 202, 212, 268
Best Years of Our Lives (Friedhofer), 13, 344n11
Beyond the Forest (Steiner), 10
Big (stage musical-Shire), 257

Index 369

Big Bus, The (Shire), 257, 260–61, 355n3
Big Country, The (Moross), 14, 88–91, 98
Big Jake (Bernstein), 27, 46
Biguine (concert work-Moross), 93
Biker Boyz (Kambon), 119
Billion Dollar Brain (Bennett), 210
Billy Liar (Bennett), 192, 201
Birdman of Alcatraz (Bernstein), 28
Birth (Desplat), 304
Birth of a Nation (film), 7
Bishop's Wife, The (Friedhofer), 13
Bizet, Georges, 59
Black Nativity (Karpman), 231
Black Patch (Goldsmith), 242
Black Stallion (film), 231
BlacKkKlansman (Blanchard), 117
Blake, Eubie, 117
Blanchard, Terence, 117, 119, 296, 349n10
Blige, Mary J., 118
Bliss, Arthur, 8, 223
Blitzstein, Marc, 111
Blue Max, The (Goldsmith), 245
BMI Conducting Workshop, 288
Bolt, Robert, 197–98
Boots Malone (Bernstein), 25
Born on the Fourth of July (Williams), 336
Bostic, Kathryn, 233–34, 296, 3561n1
Boulanger, Nadia, 162, 168–69, 171–72, 184, 188, 210, 217–18, 220, 306, 352n1, 354n2
Boulez, Pierre, 192, 194–95, 353n2
Boys in Brown (Carwithen), 226
Brahms, Johannes, 6, 27, 59, 262–63
Brainstorm (Horner), 125
Bramson, Steve, 188–90
Brant, Henry, 88

Brass Target (Rosenthal), 164
Breakfast at Tiffany's (Mancini), 14, 135, 137, 155, 158, 344n12, 346n6
Brick Lane (Pook), 232
Bricusse, Leslie, 137, 154, 350n5
Bride of Frankenstein (Waxman), 12
Britten, Benjamin, 8, 59, 200
Brooks, Richard (director), 115
Broughton, Bruce, 190, 341
Brown, Ray, 219
Browning, John, 321
Brubeck, Dave, 111
Buchman, Sidney, 25
Bunny Lake is Missing (Paul Glass), 100, 305
Burlingame, Jon, 230–31
Butch Cassidy and the Sundance Kid (Bacharach), 124–25

Cabin in the Sky (stage musical-Vernon Duke), 96
Cahill, U.S. Marshall (Bernstein), 27, 46
Candide (stage musical-L. Bernstein), 91
Cannes Film Festival, 310–11, 338
Canticum Sacrum (concert work-Stravinsky), 196
Canvas (Stegall), 293
Capra, Frank (director), 13, 57
Capricorn One (Goldsmith), 248
Captain Blood (Korngold), 11
Captains Courageous (Waxman), 12
Cardinal, The (Moross), 90, 99–102
Carlos, Wendy, 228–30, 235, 356n1
Carmen Jones (film), 35
Carmichael, Hoagy, 158, 347n4
Carnival of the Animals (concert work-Saint-Saens), 61
Carrie (Raksin), 68, 83

Carter, Elliot, 88
Cartoons (scoring for animation), 4, 43, 83, 96, 129, 135, 190, 227–28, 230, 237, 293
Carwithen, Doreen, 226–27
Casablanca (Steiner), 11
Cassandra's Dream (Philip Glass), 306
Cassavetes, John (director), 83–84, 112
Castelnuevo-Tedesco, Mario, 144, 240
Cat Women of the Moon (Bernstein), 25, 34, 48
Catch Me If You Can (Williams), 15, 339
Centrifuge: the Powers That Separate Us (concert work-Dancy), 121
Champion (opera-Blanchard), 117
Chaplin, Charles (director), 8, 65–67, 347n1
Charade (Mancini), 135, 156, 159, 344n12
Charge of the Light Brigade (Steiner), 10
Checkmate (Williams-TV), 322, 324
Cherry, Don, 209
Chinatown (Goldsmith), 298–99
Chinese influences, 47, 302
Chocolat (Portman), 277
Chopin, Frédéric, 32, 120, 187, 267
Cider House Rules, The (Portman), 277, 357n2
Citizen King (doc-Kambon), 118
Citkowitz, Israel, 24
City of Fear (Goldsmith), 242
Clarembard (Cosma), 126–27
Clash of the Titans (Rosenthal), 163
Cléo from 5 to 7 (Legrand), 218
Climax! (Goldsmith-TV), 240

Clockers (Blanchard), 117
Clockwork Orange, A (Morley), 229
Close Encounters (Williams), 125, 337
Closer Than Ever (stage musical-Shire), 257, 270, 355n4
Close-up (Moross), 89
Cobweb (Rosenman), 13, 198, 348n8
Colombo (Paul Glass-TV), 306
Comancheros, The (Bernstein), 24, 46
Comedians, The (Rosenthal), 78, 184, 353n4
comedy, scoring for, 24, 35–36, 100, 101, 179, 202, 215
Coming 2 America (Stegall), 294
Coming to America (Rodgers), 294
Computer generated/electronic music, 4, 16, 27–28, 34, 62, 120, 135, 163, 165, 209, 225, 228–31, 233, 249–50, 266, 272, 276, 286, 290, 310, 341
Conan the Barbarian (Poledouris), 124
Concerto for Cello (concert work-Paul Glass), 301
Concerto for Cello (concert work-Korngold), 11
Concerto for Cello (concert work-Legrand), 220
Concerto for Piano (concert work-Legrand), 220
Concerto for Violin (concert work-Rozsa), 52
Concerto for Violin (concert work-Williams), 332
Conn, Didi, 256
Conti, Bill, 69
Conversation, The (Shire), 15, 257, 259, 266
Cool Hand Luke (Schifrin), 327
Coolidge, Martha (director), 31, 345n5

Index

Copland, Aaron, 2–4, 14, 24–25, 28–29, 39, 59, 78, 88, 93, 95, 98, 111, 170, 200, 243, 245, 272, 327–28, 342, 343n3, 349n5, 353–54n1, 2, 6
Coppola, Francis Ford (director), 15, 256, 344n14
Corigliano, John, 341
Corona, La (Kambon), 118
Cosma, Vladimir, 126–27
Cotton Club Encore (Karpman), 231
Country Wife, The (proposed stage musical-Shire), 270
Cowboys, The (Williams), 328
Cowell, Henry, 93–94
Crawford, Joan, 25, 135, 138
Crime in the Streets (Waxman), 13, 327
Crying Game, The (Dudley), 231
Cubase [digital processing software program], 291, 357n2

Dahl, Ingolf, 111, 305, 364
Dali, Salvador, 58, 346n
Dancy, Chanda, 120–21, 296, 349n12
Darby, Ken, 125
Dark City (Steiner), 10
Darling Lili (Mancini), 159
Darwish, Ihab, 257
Davis, Bette, 10, 197, 201, 354n5
Davis, Miles, 112, 218, 349n6
Davis Jr., Sammy, 155
DAW [Digital Audio Workstation] 290, 357n1
Day of the Dog (Zimmer), 230
Days of Wine and Roses (Mancini), 15, 154, 156–57
Dear White People (Bostic), 233
De Hartmann, Thomas, 179–82, 353n5

De Mille, Agnes, 164
De Mille, Cecil B. (director), 24, 26, 31, 34–36
Death and Transfiguration (concert work-Strauss), 331
Death of a Salesman (North), 13
Death Watch [aka La Mort en Direct] (Duhamel), 128
Debney, John, 124, 257
Debussy, Claude, 32, 157, 222
Defection of Simas Kudirka, The (Shire-TV), 260
Delius, Frederick, 222
Demeusy, Eric (director), 287
Demy, Jacques (director), 217, 220
Deray, Jacques, 127–28
DeRosa, Vincent, 154
Des Marais, Paul, 170, 353n3
Desplat, Alexandre, 16, 126, 273, 304
Deutsch, Adolph, 324–25
Devil Doll (Waxman), 12
Diamond Head (Williams), 323
Diane (Rozsa), 55
Dickens's Christmas Carol (stage musical-Legrand), 220
Die Tote Stadt (opera-Korngold), 11
Digital Performer (editing/processing software program), 290–91, 357n1
Dingo (Legrand), 218
Diversity Collective, 296
Doctor Zhivago (Jarre), 14
Doll's House, A (Legrand), 210
Dome (Stegall), 293
Dominion (Bramson), 188
Donen, Stanley (director), 153, 155, 352n15
Double Indemnity (film-Rozsa), 13, 52, 62
Double Life, (autobiography-Rozsa), 52, 54, 59

Double Life, A (film-Rozsa), 52
Douglas, Gordon, 33
Downpayment on Murder (Rosenthal-TV), 163
Doyle, Patrick, 124
Dracula (Williams), 336
Drango (Bernstein), 27
Dr. Jekyll and Mr. Hyde (Waxman), 12
Dr. Terror's House of Horrors (Lutyens), 225
Drums Along the Mohawk (Newman), 14
Duchin, Eddie, 204
Dudley, Anne, 231, 277, 309, 341, 356n1
Duhamel, Antoine, 128
Duke, Vernon, 96

E.T. the Extra-Terrestrial (Williams), 331, 338–39, 344n14
Earth Dies Screaming (Lutyens), 225
Earthquake (Williams), 332
East of Eden (Rosenman), 199, 348n8
Eastman School of Music, 162, 188
Easy Money (Rosenthal), 174
Echo of Thunder (Rosenthal-TV), 164
Edward Scissorhands (Elfman), 125, 230
Einstein on the Beach (opera-Glass), 300
Eisenstein, Sergei (director), 6–8, 343n52
El Cid (Rozsa), 53, 60
Elena (film), 307
Elfman, Danny, 125, 230, 293, 309
Elkind, Rachel, 229
Ellington, Duke (Edward), 100, 109, 110, 112, 347n4, 349n1

Elmer Gantry (Previn), 323
Emma (Portman), 233
Empire of the Sun (Williams), 124, 337, 359n6
Endangered (concert work-Portman), 278
Enfant et les Sortiléges, L (opera-Ravel), 282
Engel, Lehman, 88
Evénement le plus important, L' (Legrand), 219
Everything Before Us (Dancy-TV), 120
Everything But the Truth (Mancini), 146
Exodus (Gold), 14, 100
Eyes Wide Shut (Pook), 232, 315

F for Fake (Legrand), 220
Fallen Idol (Alwyn), 226
Family Plot (Williams), 335
Far and Away (Williams), 336
Far from Heaven (Bernstein), 28
Far from the Madding Crowd (Bennett), 192, 197, 201, 205
Farewell My Lovely (Shire), 256, 259, 260, 271–72
Feliciano, José, 116
Femme est une Femme, Une, (Legrand), 220
Feyder, Jacques, 52, 56, 346n2
Fiddler on the Roof (film musical orch. by Williams), 183, 328
Field, Todd (director), 236
Figures in a Landscape (Bennett), 192, 205–206
Final War of Olly Winter, The (Shire-TV), 260
Fine, Vivian, 88
Fire Shut Up in My Bones (opera-Blanchard), 117
First Knight (Goldsmith), 250

First of the Few (Walton), 331
Fitzwilly (Williams), 325–26
Five Finger Exercise (Moross), 99
Five Graves to Cairo (Rozsa), 52
Flash, The (animation-Walker), 231
Fletcher, Lucille, 96
Folk music influences, 24–26, 34, 38–39, 56, 98, 205, 345–46n1
Force of Evil (Raksin), 67–68, 70, 76
Ford, John (director), 9
Forever Amber (Raksin), 67, 74–76
For Love of Ivy (Jones), 116
Fountainhead, The (Steiner), 10
Four Days in July (Portman), 277
Four Feathers, The (Rozsa), 52, 57
Four Horsemen of the Apocalypse (Previn), 323
Four Last Songs (concert work-Strauss), 263
Four Weddings and a Funeral (Bennett), 192
Francis the Talking Mule (film series), 145
Franck, Cesar, 216
Franco, Germaine, 234
Frankenstein (film), 12, 145
Frankie and Johnny (concert/ballet work-Moross), 89, 90, 93
Frantic (film), 112
French New Wave (50s/60s cinema style movement), 217, 220, 354n3
Freud (Goldsmith), 243, 246
Friedhofer, Hugo, 13, 74, 344n11
Full Monty, The, (Dudley), 231
Funny Face (film), 156
Funny Girl (stage musical-Styne), 355n5
Fury, The (Williams), 336

Gance, Abel (director), 6, 7, 343n5
Gathering of Eagles, A (Goldsmith), 243

Gentlemen, Be Seated (Moross-stage operetta), 92, 348n1
George Washington (Rosenthal), 189
German Requiem (concert work-Brahms), 59
Gershensen, Joseph, 144–45, 147
Gershwin, George, 14, 89, 93, 137, 156, 192, 196
Getz, Stan, 219
Ghost and Mrs. Muir, The (Herrmann), 40–41
Ghost and the Darkness, The (Goldsmith), 249
Ghost of Flight 401 (Raksin-TV), 84
Ghostbusters (Bernstein), 24, 27, 45
Giacchino, Michael, 341
Giddyap (cartoon-Raksin), 83
Gidget Goes to Rome (Williams), 323
Gillespie, Dizzy, 117
Gilligan's Island (Williams-TV), 322
Glass Menagerie (Mancini), 147–48, 159
Glass, Paul, 100, 265, 299–307, 357n1
Glass, Philip, 16, 280, 282, 299–307, 345n15, 357n2
Glazunov, Alexander, 180
Go-Between, The (film), 208–209
God's Little Acre (Bernstein), 27, 38–39
Goddard, Jean-Luc (director), 220, 354
Gold, Ernest, 100
Golden Apple (stage musical-Moross), 89–90, 92, 95–96, 348n1
Goldenberg, Billy, 200, 269
Goldenthal, Elliot, 341
Goldsmith, Jerry, 54, 126, 128, 143, 149, 200, 202, 239–52, 343n4, 348n2

Goldwyn Jr., Sam (producer), 99
Gone with the Wind (Steiner), 10
Goodman, Benny, 67
Good, the Bad and the Ugly, The (Morricone), 126
Goold, Rupert (director), 313, 315
Gordon, Dexter, 112
Gore Vidal's Billy the Kid (TV-Rosenthal), 164
Gormenghast (Bennett-TV), 212
Grabner, Hermann, 52
Grand Budapest Hotel, The (Desplat), 126
Grappelli, Stephane, 154, 219, 352n16
Grauman, Walter (director), 301
Great Santini, The (Bernstein), 38, 346n9
Great Train Robbery, The (Goldsmith), 250
Greenwood, Jonny, 309
Gregson-Williams, Harry, 293
Gremlins (Goldsmith), 249
Grieg, Edvard, 59
Gries, Tom (director), 73
Griffith, D. W. (director), 7, 8
Grifters, The (Bernstein), 27–28, 348n2
Grusin, Dave, 15, 341, 344n
Guild Hall School of Music, 313
Gunfight, A (Rosenthal), 165
Gunfighter (Newman), 14
Guðnadóttir, Hildur, 234–36

Hail Hero (Moross), 104
Hallelujah Trail, The (Bernstein), 27, 126
Hampton, Lionel, 117
Hangover Square (Herrmann), 82
Hans Christian Anderson (film), 102
Hanson, Howard, 331
Harbert, James, 333
Harrington, Curtis (director), 79
Harris, Roy, 39, 111, 346n10
Harry and Son (Mancini), 149, 350n2
Harry and Walter Go to New York (Shire), 260
Harryhausen, Ray (stop-motion animation director), 97
Harry Potter (film series-Williams), 337
Haunting, The (Goldsmith), 250
Hawaii (Bernstein), 27, 47
Hawaiians, The (Mancini), 136
Hayes, Isaac, 116
Heartbeeps (Williams), 337, 359n6
Hearts of the World (film), 6
Heidi (Williams-TV), 326–27
Heiress, The (Copland), 4
Henry V (Doyle-1989 version), 124
Henson, Jim, 276
Hepburn, Audrey, 137, 152, 156, 159, 324, 352n15
Herrmann, Bernard, 13, 14, 40, 41, 77, 82, 88, 93–95, 97, 126, 240, 244, 312, 321, 336
Heston, Charlton, 26, 60, 71–73, 88
High Noon (Tiomkin), 14, 346n6
Hindemith, Paul, 111, 200
Hindenberg, The (Shire), 257, 262–64
Histoire du Soldat, L' (Stravinsky-concert work), 243
Hitchcock, Alfred (director), 14, 52, 58, 335, 346n8
Hollander, Frederick, 11–12
Hollow Man, The (Goldsmith), 250
Holst, Gustav, 194, 335
Honegger, Arthur, 7, 200
Horner, James, 125, 292, 341
Horse Whisperer, The (T. Newman), 304
Hot Rock, The (Jones), 116
Hotel Paradiso (Rosenthal), 162, 174, 184

Hours, The (Philip Glass), 306
Hovey, Tim, 146
How the West Was Won (Newman), 125
How to Steal a Million (Williams), 324
Howard, James Newton, 341
Human Stain, The (Portman), 279
Hungaria (concert work-Rozsa), 52
Hungarian Twilight (concert work-Rozsa), 56
Hupfeld, Herman, 11

I, Robot (Beltrami), 293
Ice Station Zebra (Legrand), 218
Images (Williams), 329
Improvisation (concert work-Stockhausen), 55
In Cold Blood (Jones), 115
Indiscreet (Bennett), 192
In Enemy Hands (Bramson), 188
Informer, The (Steiner), 9
Inherit the Wind (Rosenthal-TV), 165
Interpol (Bennett), 192
Interregnum (concert work aka *George Groszi's Interregnum-Paul Glass)*, 300
Intolerance (film), 6
Invisible Ray, The (Waxman), 12
Irma la Duce (Previn), 323
Island of Dr. Moreau (Rosenthal), 163, 176–78, 183
Islands in the Stream (Goldsmith), 250
Ives, Burl, 34
Ives, Charles, 88, 92–93

Jackson, Mahalia, 321
Jackson, Michael, 114, 116
Jaffe, Stanley (producer), 258, 348n9

JAG (TV-Bramson), 188
Jane Eyre (Williams-TV), 327
Janssen, Werner, 82
Japanese influences, 35, 47, 136, 140
Jaubert, Maurice, 8
Jaws (Williams), 15, 334, 344n14
Jaws II (Williams), 335
Jayhawkers, The (Moross), 89, 103
jazz influences in film music, 5, 13–15, 24, 26–27, 33, 36–37, 79, 111–13, 117, 134, 144, 198, 209, 218, 233, 257, 267, 291
Jezebel (Steiner), 10
John, Calvin, 109
Johnny Belinda (Steiner), 10
Johnson, Plas, 154
Joker (Guònadóttir), 235–36
Jones, Jack, 219
Jones, Quincy, 15, 113–16, 217, 296, 344n13, 349n8
Joy Luck Club, The (Portman), 277
Judy (Garland-film), 313
Juilliard School, 24, 94, 134, 144, 195, 306, 321
Julius Caesar (Rozsa), 13, 54
Jungle Book, The (Rozsa), 13, 52–54, 57, 61, 346–47n3, 9
Jungle Fever (Blanchard), 117
Jurassic Park (Williams), 15

Kambon, Camara, 117–20, 349n11
Kaper, Bronislau, 13
Karpman, Laura, 231
Kay, Ulysses, 110–11, 349n4
Kaye, Danny, 102
Kearney, Gene (director), 299
Kenton, Stan, 320, 325
Kentuckian, The (Herrmann), 14
Killer Cove (Dancy), 120
Killers, The (Rozsa), 13, 62
King Charles III (Pook), 232, 313, 316, 358n2

King Kong (Steiner), 5, 10
King of Kings (Rozsa), 53, 60, 124, 126
King's Row (Korngold), 11
Knight Without Armor (Rozsa), 52
Knights of the Round Table (Rozsa), 53
Kodály, Zoltán, 52, 56
Korda, Alexander (producer/director), 52, 61, 346n3
Korngold, Erich Wolfgang, 11, 75, 245, 334–36
Kosma, Joseph, 8
Koyaanisqatsi (Philip Glass), 301–302
Kramer versus Kramer (film), 258, 348
Krenek, Ernst, 144
Kubrick, Stanley (director), 229, 232, 315
Kundun (Glass), 303–304

L'Arlesienne (concert suite-Bizet), 59
L'Assassinat du Duc de Guise (Saint-Saens), 6
Lady Caroline Lamb (Bennett), 197–98, 207–208, 210–11
Lady in a Cage (Paul Glass), 301
Laine, Cleo, 192
Lampell, Millard, 24
Lancer (Moross-TV), 104
Landis, John (director), 44
Last Call (TV-Bramson), 188
Last Judgment, The (concert ballet work-Moross), 89–90
Last Valley, The (Barry), 124
Latouche, John, 90, 96
Laura (Raksin), 13, 14, 35, 67, 68, 77, 80–82, 346n6
Lava, William, 146
Learning Tree, The (Parks), 116
Lee, Spike (director), 117

Legend (Goldsmith-rejected score), 128, 348n2
Legrand, Cristiane, 127, 217
Legrand, Michel, 127–28, 170, 209–11, 215–20, 261, 344n13, 348n2, 349n2, 354n1, 2
Leigh, Mike (director), 277
Leigh, Mitch, 131
Letter, The (Steiner), 10
Levitt, Helen, 111
Lewis, John (MJQ), 113
Lhevinne, Rosina, 321
Lieutenant Kije (Prokofiev), 8, 9
Life is Sweet (Portman), 277, 357n2
Life of Emile Zola, The (Steiner), 10
Lifeforce (Mancini), 149, 150, 348n2, 351n11
Lift to Hell (Dancy), 120
Ligeti, Gyorgy, 229, 232, 315
Lion in Winter, The (Barry), 124, 126
List of Adrian Messenger, The (Goldsmith), 244
Liszt, Franz, 56, 102, 249
Little Night Music, A (stage musical-Sondheim), 96, 268
Little Prince, The (children's opera-Portman), 278, 280–81
Little Prince, The (film-Morley), 227
Lonely Are the Brave (Goldsmith), 243, 248
Lord of the Rings (Rosenman), 129
Lord of the Rings (Shore), 125, 129
Loren, Sophia, 60, 183–84
Losey, Joseph (director), 206, 208
Lost Horizon (film), 58
Lost in Space (Williams-TV), 326
Lost Weekend, The (Rozsa), 52, 61

Love Match (stage musical-Shire), 269
Lucas, George (director/producer), 15, 162, 287–89, 294, 296, 335, 344n
Lumet, Sidney (director), 115, 202, 343n3, 349n9
Lure of the Wilderness (Waxman), 12
Lust for Life (Rozsa), 13, 52
Lutoslawski, Withold, 305
Lutyens, Elizabeth, 221–26, 236–37, 276
Lydia (Rozsa), 55

M Squad (Williams-TV), 322
Ma and Pa Kettle (film series), 145
MacKenna's Gold (Jones), 116
Madame Bovary (Rozsa), 52–53, 55, 61, 346n6
Madeline (Legrand), 219
Madigan (Jones), 116
Magnificent Seven, The (Bernstein), 24, 27, 46
Mahler, Gustav, 106–107, 170, 196, 245
Malcolm X (Blanchard), 117
Malcolm X: Make It Plain (Kambon-TV), 117–19
Malle, Louis (director), 112
Maltby, Jr., Richard, 256, 267–70, 355–56n4, 7
Man Afraid (Mancini), 147
Man of La Mancha, The (film musical orch. by Rosenthal), 182–83
Man Who Could Cheat Death, The (Bennett), 192
Man Who Loved Women, The (Mancini), 159, 350n2
Man with the Golden Arm (Bernstein), 14, 26, 36, 37, 100, 198

Manchurian Candidate, The (Portman), 283
Mancini, Ginny O'Connor, 144, 154
Mancini, Henry, 14, 15, 43, 48, 112, 114, 116, 126, 133–60, 201, 217, 218, 244, 266, 296, 322, 324–25, 344n12, 13, 346–48n6, 350n2
Mancini music albums, 134
Mandel, Johnny, 112
Mann, Delbert (director), 326
Manne, Shelly, 219
Mannix (Schifrin-TV), 15
Mantrap (Carwithen), 226
Marguerite (stage musical-Legrand), 220
Marinsky Ballet Company, 180
Marnie (Herrmann), 244
Martel, Philip, 225
Martin, Claire, 192
Mason, Benedict, 278
McCarthyism-1950s Senate HUAC history, 24–26, 33–34, 68–69, 345n2
McCloud (Shire-TV), 269
Me, Natalie (Mancini), 126, 157
Meatballs (Bernstein), 27, 44
Meetings with Remarkable Men (Rosenthal), 163, 179
Meisel, Edmund, 7
Mendelssohn, Felix, 193
Menotti, Gian Carlo, 282
Mephisto Waltz (concert work-Liszt), 102
Mephisto Waltz, The (Goldsmith), 249
Mercer, Johnny, 67, 137, 155–56, 159, 324, 347n4
Merchant of Venice (2004 version), 316
Messiaen, Olivier, 114, 345n355

Meteor (Rosenthal), 162, 184
Metropolitan Opera of New York, 117
Meyers, Sidney (director), 111
Michelson, Henriette, 24
Michener, James, 47
Milhaud, Darius, 200, 349n5
Miller, Glenn, 144, 350n9
Mines of Sulphur, The (opera-Bennett), 193, 195, 354n4
minimalism, 16, 232, 273, 300–307, 330, 344n15
Miracle Worker, The (Rosenthal), 162, 164, 167–68, 175, 186, 353n2
Mishima (Philip Glass), 302–303
Mission, The (Morricone), 124
Mission: Impossible (Schifrin-TV), 15, 344n13
Miss Robin Crusoe (Bernstein), 25
Mitchell, David Robert, 310, 312
Modern Jazz Quartet, 113
Modern Times (Raksin), 66
Mom and Dad Save the World (Goldsmith), 250
Mommie Dearest (Mancini), 135, 138–39
Monk, Thelonious, 117
Monsignor (Williams), 336
Moon is Blue, The (film), 35
Moore, Douglas, 96
Moore, Dudley, 157
Moore, Phil, 109, 349n3
Morley, Angela, 226–28, 237
Morley, Robert, 141
Moross, Jerome, 14, 87–108, 348n1
Morricone, Ennio, 124, 126, 341
Morton, Arthur (orchestrator), 78, 240, 245
Morton, Jelly Roll, 111
Mozart, Wolfgang, 106, 171, 349n5, 353n6

Mr. Hobbs Takes a Vacation (Mancini), 141
Mr. Lucky (Mancini-TV), 134, 144, 350n2
Mulligan, Robert (director), 31, 251, 345n4
Mummy, The (film), 12
Munich (Williams), 336
Murch, Walter (director), 259
Murder on the Orient Express (Bennett), 192, 203–204, 211
Music for Strings, Piano and Celeste (concert work-Bartok), 246
Music for the Flicks (concert suite-Moross), 99, 102
Music Lovers, The (film), 181
Mussolini (Rosenthal-TV), 163
My Friend Flicka (Newman), 14
My Left Foot (Bernstein), 28
My Teacher, My Obsession (Dancy), 120
Mysterious Island (Herrmann), 97

Nanny, The (Bennett), 201, 354n5
Napoleon (Honegger), 7
National Lampoon's Animal House (Bernstein), 27, 44
Navarro, Diego, 257
Never Wave at a WAC (Bernstein), 25
New York City Opera, 92, 193
Newman, Alfred, 14, 66–67, 125, 320–21, 330, 341, 347n2
Newman, Paul (director), 105–106, 112, 147
Newman, Randy, 341
Newman, Thomas, 16, 273, 304, 343n4
Newmaster, Kyle, 310–12, 358n1
Nicholas and Alexandra (Bennett), 202, 208, 210, 211
Nicholas Nickleby (Portman), 277

Night and the City (Waxman), 12
Night Chase (Rosenthal-TV), 162
Nightmare in Chicago (Williams), 323
Noiret, Philippe, 127
No Sun in Venice (Lewis), 113
Norma Rae (Shire), 256
North, Alex, 13, 14, 71, 143, 198, 241, 248, 344n11, 347n5
Not with My Wife, You Don't (Williams), 324
Not Without My Daughter (Goldsmith), 250
Notes on a Scandal (Glass), 304–305
Now, Voyager (Steiner), 10

O'Brien, Willis, 10
O'Toole, Peter, 183, 324
Objective Burma (Waxman), 12
Obsession (Herrmann), 126
Odd Man Out (Alwyn), 226
Odds Against Tomorrow (Lewis), 113
Of Mice and Men (Copland), 4
Offenbach, Jacques, 7, 62
Oktober (film), 7
Old Boyfriends (Shire), 258
Oliver Twist (Portman), 277, 280
Oliver, Sy, 109, 349n
Omen, The (Goldsmith), 126, 249
On the Waterfront (L. Bernstein), 212
ondes Martenot (electronic instrument), 28, 45, 345n3
Opera Theater of St. Louis, 117
Oracle (Stegall), 293
Orphan Train (Rosenthal-TV), 164, 185–86
O Saisons, O Chateaux (concert work-Lutyens), 222
Other Side of the Wind The (Legrand), 220

Other, The (Goldsmith), 251–52
Our 'Star Wars' Stories (Stegall-TV), 287, 289
Our Town (Copland), 95
Outland (Goldsmith), 250
Overlord (Paul Glass), 306

Pacific 231 (concert work-Honegger), 7
Paeans (concert work-Moross), 94
Page, Ruth, 93
Pakula, Alan, 262
Papillon (Goldsmith), 250
Parade: A Musical Revue (concert work-Moross), 89, 94
Paris Blues (Ellington), 112
Paris Can Wait (Karpman), 231
Paris Conservatoire, 188, 210, 217, 220, 223
Paris Trout (Shire), 258
Parker Jr., Ray, 45
Parking (Legrand), 218
Parks, Gordon (director), 116
Parsons, Estelle, 106
Partita (concert work-Bennett), 193
Passion of the Christ (Debney), 124
Pat and Mike (Raksin), 68
Patch of Blue, A (Goldsmith), 202, 244, 247–49
Pather Panchali (Shankar), 115
Patricia Neal Story, The (Rosenthal-TV), 164
Patriot, The (Williams), 336
Paul Bunyan (opera-Moross), 89
Pawnbroker, The (Jones), 115
Peabody Conservatory of Johns Hopkins Univ, 209
Peck, Gregory, 88, 346n8
Peer Gynt (concert suite-Grieg), 59
Penderecki, Krzysztof, 62, 229
Penelope (Williams), 324
Penn, Arthur (director), 167, 353n2

Penny and the Pownall Case (Lutyens), 224
People v. Leo Frank, The (Pook), 232
Pepper, Art, 321
Perry Mason (Goldsmith-TV), 242
Peskanov, Mark, 333
Peter and the Wolf (concert work-Prokofiev), 58, 347n9
Peter Gunn (Mancini-TV), 14, 134, 136, 144, 155, 159, 322, 324, 350n2
Peter Pan and Wendy (Stegall), 287
Peter the Great (Rosenthal-TV), 163, 189
Petrassi, Goffredo, 305
Peyton Place (Waxman), 13
Philadelphia Story (Waxman), 12
Piano Quintet, Op. 2 (concert work-Rozsa), 56
Piece for Jazz Bassoon (concert work-Mancini), 136, 350n3
Pierce, Billy (sax), 119
Pigeon Kings (Dancy), 120
Pink Panther, The (Mancini), 15, 135–36, 154, 159, 350n2
Piscine, La (Legrand), 127, 218
Place in the Sun, A (Waxman), 12
Planet of the Apes (Goldsmith), 202, 245–47, 249
Planets, The (concert work-Holst), 335
Polanski, Roman (director), 277, 280
Poledouris, Basil, 124
Polly Magoo [aka *Qui êtes-vous Polly Magoo?*] (Legrand), 218
Pook, Jocelyn, 232, 236, 277, 310, 313–15, 358n2
Porgy and Bess (film), 100
Porter, Cole, 196
Portman, Rachel, 233, 236–37, 275–83, 356n1

Poseidon Adventure, The (Williams), 330–32
Potemkin (film), 7
Poulenc, Francis, 185, 200, 268, 272
Powaqqatsi (Philip Glass), 302
Powell, Edward (orchestrator), 66
Powell, John, 341
Power and the Glory, The (TV-Rosenthal), 163, 166, 168
Prelude and Fugue for Big Band (Williams), 325
Preminger, Otto (director), 26, 35–36, 67, 75, 100–102, 109, 305
Previn, Andre, 273, 321–27, 336, 338, 358n1, 2
Prince and the Pauper, The (Korngold), 11
Prokofiev, Sergei, 8, 9, 29, 58, 124, 200, 245, 335, 347n9
Proud Rebel, The (Moross), 14, 89, 99, 100
Providence (Rozsa), 53, 62
Proximity (Stegall), 287–89
Psycho (Herrmann), 14
Purcell, Henry, 113, 229

Questioning Faith, A (Kambon), 117
Quiet One, The (Kay), 111
Quo Vadis (Rozsa), 13, 53, 124

Rachel, Rachel (Moross), 105–106
Rachmaninoff, Serge, 62, 180
Raggedy Man (Goldsmith), 250
Raid on Entebbe (Shire-TV), 260, 272–73
Raiders of the Lost Ark (Williams), 336
Rain Man (Zimmer), 230
Raisin in the Sun, A (Rosenthal), 164, 166
Raksin, David, 13, 14, 65–85, 346n6, 347n6, 348n9, 2

Index

Rambling Rose (Bernstein), 28, 345n5
Rap music influence, 45, 114, 118, 309
Raphael, Frederic, 153
Rashomon (stage show-Rosenthal), 162, 166
Rat Race, The (Bernstein), 27, 37
Ravel, Maurice, 108, 157, 160, 185, 268, 282, 353n6
Ray, Satyajit (director), 115
Rebel Without a Cause (Rosenman), 2, 199, 348n8
Red Pony, The (Goldsmith-TV), 250
Red Pony, The (Copland), 14
Reflections on a Scottish Folk Tune (concert work-Bennett), 193
Reggio, Godfrey (director), 301
Reich, Steve, 16, 345n15
Reincarnation of Peter Proud, The (Goldsmith), 250
Reivers, The (Williams), 15, 327–28
rejected scores, 123, 218–19
Requiem for a Heavyweight (Rosenthal-TV), 162, 166
Resnais, Alain (director), 53, 62
Return of a Man Called 'Horse' (Rosenthal), 162–63, 186–87, 353n7
Return of the Seven (Bernstein), 27
Return of the Soldier (Bennett), 192
Return to Oz (Shire), 258–59
Richards, Emil, 152
Rimsky-Korsakov, Nikolai, 180, 229, 321
Rite of Spring, The [Le Sacre du Printemps] (concert work-Stravinsky), 196, 288
Ritt, Martin (director), 112
River, The (Williams), 15

Robin and Marion (Legrand-rejected score), 219, 348n2
Robot Monster (Bernstein), 25, 34
Rochberg, George, 106, 348n4
rock music performers in film music, 309–16
Rock Pretty Baby (Mancini), 146
Rod Serling's Night Gallery (Glass-TV), 299
Rodgers, Nile, 294
Rodgers, Richard, 137, 192
Rogers, Shorty, 37, 321, 346n8
Roman Carnival Overture (concert work-Berlioz), 55
Romeo and Juliet (concert work-Berlioz), 55
Romeo and Juliet (concert work-Prokofiev), 335
Rosamunde (concert work-Schubert), 59
Rosenman, Leonard, 2, 3, 13, 80, 129, 198, 202, 344n11, 348n8, 353n7
Rosenthal, Laurence, 18, 161–90, 193, 353n7
Ross, William, 297
Rossini, Gioachino, 6, 106, 229
Roue, La (Honegger), 7
Rowles, Jimmy, 322
Royal Academy of Music, London, 194, 199, 223
Rozsa, Miklos, 13, 51–63, 77, 124, 126, 240, 312, 334–36, 346n1, 347n9
Ruick, Barbara, 321
Rumi; Brecht; Rilke concert songs (Rosenthal), 164, 169
Russell, Ken (director), 181
Russell, Rosalind, 99
Russia House, The (Goldsmith), 248
Rydell, Mark (director), 327–28

RZA (aka Robert Diggs) rap soundtrack performer, 309

Sabu, Selar Shaik, 52, 53, 61, 346n4
Sahara (Rozsa), 52
Saint-Saëns, Camille, 6, 7, 61
Sandcastles (Paul Glass-TV), 306
Sap of Life (stage musical-Shire), 256
Sarde, Philippe, 341
Saturday Night Fever (Shire), 256, 355n1
Saturday's Hero (Bernstein), 25, 32
Saturn 3 (Bernstein), 24, 47
Satyagraha (concert work-Glass), 300
Saving Private Ryan (Williams), 16, 124, 337
Schaffner, Franklin (director), 202
Scheherazade (concert work-Rimsky-Korsakov), 107, 335
Schifrin, Lalo, 15, 327, 341, 344n13
Schindler's List (Williams), 339
Schlesinger, John (director), 192, 201
Schöenberg, Arnold, 15, 67, 88, 94, 107, 196, 220, 263, 347n3
Schubert, Franz, 59, 108, 353n6
Schuman, William, 39, 346n10
Scorsese, Martin (director), 15, 31, 303–304, 306, 344n14
Scott of the Antarctic (Vaughan-Williams), 126, 331
Scriabin, Alexander, 130
Sea Hawk, The (Korngold), 11, 335
Seconds (Goldsmith), 250
Secret Ceremony (Bennett), 206–207
See No Evil (Bernstein), 24
Seeger, Pete, 25, 34, 345n1
Sellers, Peter, 43
Sendry, Alfred, 144
Senior Year (Stegall), 293
Separate Tables (Raksin), 68

serial (12-tone) composing system, 13, 15, 62, 67, 192, 194, 196, 198, 222–25, 242, 245, 247, 257, 263–66, 301, 338, 344n10, 347n3, 354n3
Sessions, Roger, 29
Shadow Box, The (Mancini), 149
Shadows (film), 112
Shaft (Hayes), 116
Shaham, Gil, 332–33
Shank, Bud, 321
Shankar, Ravi, 115, 306
Sharkfighters (Moross), 90
Sherlock Holmes in New York (Bennett-TV), 198, 202–203
Shining, The, (Carlos), 229
Shining Hour, The (Waxman), 12
Shire, Talia, 256
Shire, David, 15, 200, 203, 255–74, 286, 306, 348n2, 355n3
Shootist, The (Bernstein), 27, 46
Shore, Howard, 125, 129
Shostakovich, Dimitri, 200, 232, 323
silent films, music accompaniment, 4, 6, 7, 8, 16, 66, 69, 277
Silent Snow, Secret Snow (Glass-TV), 299–300
Silvestri, Alan, 125, 149, 341
Simone, Nina, 112
Sinatra, Frank, 36–37, 114
Since You Went Away (Steiner), 10
Sinfonia for Wind Ensemble (concert work-Williams), 329
Skin Game, The (Shire), 260–61
Skull, The (Lutyens), 224
Slatkin, Leonard, 332
Slipper and the Rose, The (Morley), 227
Snow Flower and the Secret Fan (Portman), 277, 357n2
Soblick, Eberhardt, 326
Sodom and Gomorrah (Rozsa), 53

Index

Sole Survivor (Paul Glass), 306
Some Like it Hot (Deutsch), 324
Sometimes a Great Notion (Mancini), 149
Sonata for Two Pianos and Percussion (concert work-Bartok), 171
Sonatinas for Diverse Instruments (concert work-Moross), 90, 92
Sondheim, Stephen, 88, 96, 203, 256, 268, 270, 356n7
Song of Bernadette (Newman), 125
Songs Before Sleep (concert work-Bennett), 193
Sonny Liston: Mysterious Life & Death of a Champion (Kambon), 117
Sons of Katie elder, The (Bernstein), 27, 46
Sorry, Wrong Number (Waxman), 12
Sorry, Wrong Number (Moross-stage musical), 96
sound design engineering, 166, 169, 172–73, 198, 201, 206
Sounds and Scores (textbook-Mancini), 134, 350n11
Spellbound (Rozsa), 52, 54, 58, 346n8
Spencer, Herbert (orchestrator), 337–38
Spencer's Mountain (Steiner), 11
Spiegel, Sam (producer), 201, 202, 208
Spielberg presidential films (Lincoln, JFK, Nixon), 16
Spielberg, Steven (director), 15, 128, 190, 334, 337–39, 344n14
Spiral Road, The (Goldsmith), 243
Stalling, Carl, 190
Star is Born, A (Steiner), 10
Star Trek, the Motion Picture (Goldsmith), 248

Star Wars (Williams), 15, 54, 69, 287, 289, 292, 294, 331, 335–37, 339, 344n14
Starting Here, Starting Now (stage musical-Shire), 257, 268
Stealing America Vote by Vote (Rosenthal), 165
Stegall, Jermaine, 285–97
Stein, Herman, 146
Steiner, Max, 9–11, 171, 200
Stern, Isaac, 328
Stockhausen, Karlheintz, 55, 62, 346n5
Stone, Oliver (director), 118
Story of a Woman (Williams), 337, 359n6
Storyteller, The (aka *Jim Henson's Storyteller*-Portman-TV), 276
Strauss, Richard, 245, 263, 264, 326, 331
Stravinsky, Igor, 2, 12, 59, 88, 108, 126, 162, 196–97, 243, 246
Strayhorn, Billy, 109
Stream of Voices (children's opera-Shire), 257
Street Scene (Newman), 14
Streetcar Named Desire, A (North), 13, 14, 344n11, 347n5
Streisand, Barbra, 90, 219, 256, 269, 355
Stripes (Bernstein), 27
Studio One (Goldsmith-TV), 240
Studs Lonigan (Goldsmith), 243–44
Sudden Fear (Bernstein), 25, 33
Summer and Smoke (Bernstein), 24, 27, 39–41
Summer Love (Mancini), 146
Summer of '42, The (Legrand), 210, 217–18, 345n4
Summer Place, A (Steiner), 11
Sundance sound design labs, 288

Sunday in the Park with George (stage musical-Sondheim), 268
Sunflower (Mancini), 136
Sunset (Mancini), 135
Sunset Boulevard (Waxman), 12
Superman (Williams), 336
Susskind, David, 166
Sweeney Todd (stage musical-Sondheim), 96, 270
Sweet Smell of Success, The (Bernstein), 27, 37
Switch (Mancini), 154
Sylvia (Raksin), 83
Symphony No. 2 (concert work-Bennett), 193, 354n3
Symphony No. 3 (concert work-Bennett), 193
Symphony No. 3 (concert work-Philip Glass), 307
Symphony No. 2 (concert work-Hanson), 331
Symphony No. 4 (concert work-Ives), 93
Symphony No. 1 (concert work-Moross), 89–90
Symphony No. 1 (concert work-Williams), 325
Symphony of Three (Shire/Debney/Darwish concert work), 257

Take Flight (stage musical-Shire), 257, 270
Taking of Pelham 123, The (Shire), 15, 257, 262, 264–66
Tall Story (concert work-Moross), 93
Tammy Grimes Show, The (Williams-TV), 322
Tangerine Dream (pop group), 128
Tar (Guðnadóttir), 236
Taras Bulba (Waxman), 13
Tarjan, Susanna Moross, 90, 348n1
Tavernier, Bernard (director), 128

Taylor, Dara, 296
Tchaikowsky, Petr, 6, 181, 305
Te Kanawa, Kiri, 219
Tell Me Where It Hurts (Shire-TV), 258, 272
Temple, Shirley, 78, 146
Ten Commandments, The (Bernstein), 24, 26, 34–35
Theater of Death (Lutyens), 225
Their Finest (Portman), 277
Theme, Variations and Finale (concert work-Rozsa), 52
Thief of Bagdad (Rozsa), 13, 52, 54, 57, 335, 346n3
Things to Come (Bliss), 8
Third Man, The (film), 259
This is Russia (Rosenthal), 165
Thomas and the King (stage musical-Williams), 333
Thomas Crown Affair, The (Legrand), 210, 217–18, 344n13
Thoroughly Modern Millie (Bernstein), 28
Thrasher Road (Dancy), 120
Three Musketeers, The (Legrand), 218
Three Worlds of Gulliver (Herrmann), 97
Threni (concert work-Stravinsky), 196
Thriller, Boris Karloff's (Goldsmith-TV), 243
Time After Time (Rozsa), 53
Time for Loving A (Legrand), 218
Tin Star, The (Bernstein), 46
Tiny Toon Adventures (Bramson), 190
Tiomkin, Dimitri, 13, 14, 346n6
To Kill a Mockingbird (Bernstein), 24, 28, 41, 345n4
Toni Morrison: The Pieces I Am (Bostic), 234

Too Late Blues (Raksin), 83–84
Toprak, Pinar, 234
To the Devil, a Daughter (Paul Glass), 306
Touch of Evil (Mancini), 135, 142–43, 147–48, 350n7
Towering Inferno, The (Williams), 332
Toy Tiger (Mancini), 146
Trading Places (Bernstein), 44
Tristan und Isolde (opera-Wagner), 103
Trojans, The (opera-Berlioz), 55
Tron (Carlos), 228–30
True Grit (Bernstein), 27, 46
Turnage, Mark-Anthony, 193
Twilight Zone, The (Goldsmith-TV), 242–43
Two Brothers (Newman), 14
Two for the Road (Mancini), 152–59, 352n15

Umbrellas of Cherbourg, The (Legrand), 217, 220
Under Fire (Goldsmith), 248–49
Under the Silver Lake (Vreeland), 310–12, 315–16
Underworld (unproduced stage musical-Moross), 90, 348n1
Unmarried Woman, An (film), 69

Valley of Gwangi (Moross), 97
Valley of the Dolls (Previn; arr. by Williams), 326
Van Epps, Robert, 321
Varda, Agnes (director), 218
Vaughan-Williams, Ralph, 8, 126, 192, 200, 222, 331
Victor/Victoria (Mancini), 135
Victor/Victoria (Mancini-stage musical), 136
Virginian, The (TV), 269, 324

Vivaldi, Antonio, 258
Vodery, Will, 109, 349n2
Von Suppé, Franz, 6
Vreeland, Rich (aka Disasterpeace), 310–12, 358n1

W. C. Fields and Me (Mancini), 141
Wagner, Richard, 57, 59, 102, 177, 196, 262–64, 346n7
Wagon Train (Moross-TV), 103–104, 348n3
Wagon Train (Williams-TV), 322
Wait Until Dark (Mancini), 135, 139–41
Walk on the Wild Side (Bernstein), 27, 37
Walker, Shirley, 230–32, 277
Walter, Bruno (conductor), 11
Walton, William, 8, 29, 192, 200, 223, 331, 335
War Horse (Williams), 336
War Lord, The (Moross), 90
War of the Buttons (Portman), 276
War of the Worlds (Williams), 336
Warlock (Goldsmith), 249
War Requiem (concert work-Britten), 59
Water Diviner's Tale, The (choral symphony-Portman), 278
Watership Down (Morley), 227–28, 230
Waxman, Franz, 9, 11–13, 77, 336, 343n3
Wayne, John, 27, 46
Weavers, The (folk music group), 34
Welles, Orson, 135, 142, 143, 147, 220, 299, 300, 350n7
Wells, H. G., 53, 176
Wells, Robert, 73
West Side Story (stage musical-L. Bernstein), 268

We Will Be Monsters (Stegall), 293
Whale, James (director), 12
What's the Matter with Helen? (Raksin), 78
Where's Jack? (Bernstein), 27
White Dawn, The (Mancini), 150–52, 159, 351–52n13, 14
Who Is Killing the Great Chefs of Europe? (Mancini), 141
Who'll Stop the Rain (Rosenthal), 162
Wide Country, The (Williams-TV), 324
Wife, The (Pook), 232
Wilder, Billy (director), 12–13, 52
Wildflowers (Moross-song recital CD), 90, 348n1
Will Penny (Raksin), 71–74
Williams, John, 8, 15, 16, 18, 33, 48, 54, 69, 120, 124–25, 128, 143, 149, 163, 183, 200, 261, 288–89, 292, 319–39, 358n5
Williams, Tennessee, 38–40, 147
Wilson, David, 154
Wind and the Lion, The (Goldsmith), 248, 250
Winterhalter, Hugo, 323
Wise, Robert (director), 113, 256, 263
Witches of Eastwick (Williams), 339
Without a Clue (Mancini), 135
Wizard of Oz, The (film), 292
Women composers in concert (Beach, Lutyens, Gubaidulina, Saariaho, Boyd, Weir, Thomas), 276–77
Women composers in film (Walker, Dudley, Portman, Pook), 221–37
Woman's Vengeance, A (Rozsa), 55
Women of Brewster Place, The (Shire-TV), 260

Woodward, Joanne, 105–106
Word, The (North-TV), 71
World of Henry Orient (Bernstein), 27, 43–44
Wright, Nicholas, 282
Wyler, William (director), 88

Yamashta, Stomu, 329
Yentl (Legrand), 217–18
Young Bess (Rozsa), 55
Young Composers Group (Copland), 88, 95
Young Indiana Jones Chronicles (TV-Rosenthal), 164, 188
Young, Victor, 26

Zambello, Francesca, 282
Ziegfeld Follies, 109
Zimmer, Hans, 230, 309
Zvyagintsev, Andre (director), 307

A Few Songs By
Featured Composers

"As Time Goes By" (song-Hupfeld), 11
"Autumn" (song-Shire), 268
"Big Beautiful Ball" (song-Williams), 324
"Charade" (song-Mancini), 156, 159
"China Doll" (song-Legrand), 216
"Come All Ye Fair and Tender Maidens" (song-trad.), 39
"Crazy World" (song-Mancini), 158
"Days of Wine and Roses" (song-Mancini), 15, 156–57
"Dear Heart" (song-Mancini), 157
"Dis-Moi" {aka Tell Me}(song-Legrand), 216
"Do Not Forsake Me" (song-Tiomkin), 14, 346n6

"Dreamsville" (song-Mancini), 136, 155
"Dry Your Tears, Africa" (song-Williams), 128–29
"Good Friend" (the Meatballs song-Bernstein), 27
"I've Even Been in Love" (song-Moross), 90
"If I Sing" (song-Shire), 267
"Impossible Dream, The" (song-Mitch Leigh), 182
"It Goes Like It Goes" (song-Shire), 256
"It's Almost Time Now" (song-Moross), 90
"It's Easy to Say" (song-Mancini), 157
"Laura" (song-Raksin), 14, 67, 80, 346n6
"Lazy Afternoon" (song-Moross), 90
"Le Jazz Hot" (song-Mancini), 135
"Life in the Looking Glass" (song-Mancini), 159
"Little Boys" (song from The Man Who Loved Women-Mancini), 159
"The Lonely Rider" (song-Raksin), 73
"Martina" (song-Legrand), 219
"Moods of a Wanderer" (instrumental-Legrand), 219

"Moon River" (song-Mancini), 15, 135–37, 155–56, 158, 346n6
"Paris By Night" (song-Mancini), 136
"Peach Tree Valley Waltz" (instrumental-Bernstein), 39
"Pieces of Dreams" (song-Legrand), 216
"Pink Panther" (instrumental-Mancini), 15, 135
"Soldier in the Rain" (song-Mancini), 159
"Slow Hot Wind" {aka Lujon} (song-Mancini), 159
"Summer Knows, The" (song-Legrand), 216
"Two for the Road" (song-Mancini), 153–57, 159
"What Are You Doing the Rest of Your Life?" (song-Legrand), 216
"Where Grows the Learning Tree?" (song-Parks), 116
"Whistling Away the Dark" (song-Mancini), 136, 159
"Windmills of Your Mind, The" (song-Legrand), 210, 216
"Years of My Youth" (song-Legrand), 219